MISSISSIPPI RIFLES

A Muster Listing of All Known Mississippi Soldiers, Sailors and Marines Who Served in the Mexican War, 1846-1848

I0094178

H. Grady Howell, Jr.

Please Direct All Correspondence and Book Orders to:

SOUTHERN HISTORICAL PRESS, Inc.
1071 Park West Blvd.
Greenville, S.C.   29611
southernhistoricalpress@gmail.com

ISBN # 0-89308-801-3

Library of Congress Catalog Number: 2002103898

Printed in the United States of America

In Memory of
Fr. **Patricio Quinn**
1931-1997
Padre
Nuestra Señora del Perpetuo Socorro
Saltillo, Mexico

"Your life was one of kindly deeds,
A helping hand for others needs,
Sincere and true in heart and mind,
Beautiful memories left behind."

This work is dedicated to the above and especially to the memory of every
Mexican War Soldier from Mississippi, Known and Unknown.

❧ NOTICE ❧

The compiler of this work is actively researching, for publication, a narrative history of Mississippi's role in the Mexican War, 1846-1848. A portion of his research includes completing a character profile on each Mexican War veteran from the State. This information includes: full name, birth/death dates, occupation, Mexican and Civil War service and burial site. Anyone possessing information and/or photographs regarding any of these soldiers (or materials pertaining to Mississippi in the Mexican War) is urged to contact:

H. Grady Howell, Jr.
103 Trace Harbor Rd.
Madison, MS 39110

Table of Contents

CAMP INDEPENDENCE.

NEAR VICKSBURG.

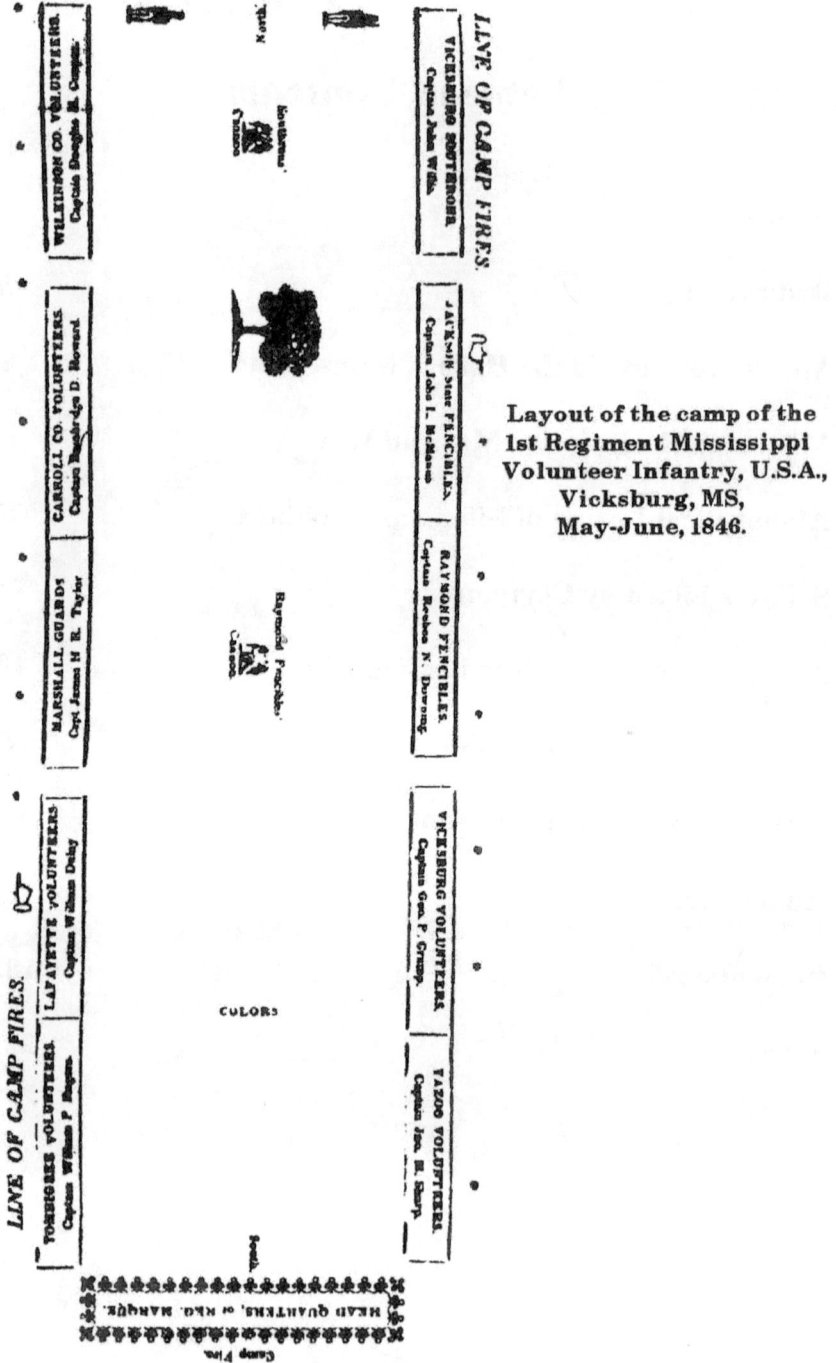

LINE OF CAMP FIRES.

LINE OF CAMP FIRES.

North

South

WILKINSON CO. VOLUNTEERS.
Captain Douglas H. Cooper

VICKSBURG SOUTHRONS.
Captain John Willis

CARROLL CO. VOLUNTEERS.
Captain Benjamin D. Howard

JACKSON State FENCIBLES.
Captain John L. McManus

MARSHALL GUARDS.
Capt James M. R. Taylor

RAYMOND FENCIBLES.
Captain Reuben N. Downing

LAFAYETTE VOLUNTEERS.
Captain William Delay

VICKSBURG VOLUNTEERS.
Captain Geo. P. Crump.

TOMBIGBEE VOLUNTEERS.
Captain William P. Rogers.

YAZOO VOLUNTEERS.
Captain Jas. H. Sharp.

Raymond Fencibles.
Camp

COLORS

HEAD QUARTERS, or MKQ. MARQUE.

Camp Fire.

vi

Mississippi Boys in the Halls of Montezuma

The 1840's was truly one of the most colorful, significant and turbulent decades in the history of our country. The nation was growing and stretching like a youngster and was finding that it needed more *cloth* for its suit of boundaries. Indeed, the worn fabric of the fifty-nine year old Republic was beginning to rip and tear in the form of snarls, threats, outrages and even duels between otherwise rational men. The reason was no secret. The national power structure heretofore controlled in large measure by the slaveocratic system of the South was understandably, grudgingly giving way to the oft-times offensively self-righteous, abrasively hypocritical, growing dominance of the northeast. "The times they were a-changin." Expansion and Slavery were central themes of the '40's and the whiff of gunpowder was in the air.

Men were quoted as uttering such treasonous outbursts as:

> "Any people anywhere, being inclined and having the power, have the right to rise up, and shake off the existing government, and form a new one that suits them better. This is a most valuable,--a most sacred right--a right, which we hope and believe, is to liberate the world. Nor is this right confined to cases in which the whole people of an existing government, may choose to exercise it. Any portion of such people that can, may revolutionize, and make their own, of so much of the teritory as they inhabit. More than this, a majority of any portion of such people may revolutionize, putting down a minority, intermingled with, or near about them, who may oppose their movement."

So said "Honest Abe" Lincoln on the floor of the U. S. House of Representatives on January 12, 1848. Another Representative, Jefferson Davis, had uttered his strong nationalist views earlier on February 6, 1846 in the same chambers:

> "Sir, it is true that republics have often been cradled in war, but more often they have met with a grave in that cradle. Peace is the interest, the policy, the nature of a popular Government. War may bring benefits to a few, but privation and loss are the lot of the many. An appeal to arms should be the last resort, and only by national rights or national honor can it be justified."

Fourteen years later their attitudes would be completely reversed.

After more than a decade of growing border friction, the talons of the eagles of Mexico and the United States ripped at each other over the latter's annexation of the Republic of Texas in 1845. The resulting *Mexican War* was fought between both powers during the years 1846-1848. It was a war that saw the first military usage of the term "doughboy;" it was the first war in the history of the world to be covered by both correspondents and photographers; and it was the first major foreign war of the United States fought almost entirely on foreign soil. At its termination the political boundaries of America stretched "from sea to shining sea," creating the nation's largest growth spurt since the Louisiana Purchase of 1803.

Remarkably, the Mexican War has received relatively light treatment from national historians over the years for a number of purely sectional reasons. These begin with President James Knox Polk, a slave-owning, Democratic Tennessean, who, even though the country expanded and reached its near-final political borders during his progressive term of office, was chastised by a growing abolitionist movement, and by a sectionally-oriented northeastern press. Consequently, there was much apathy by the northeast toward the war which was reflected in that section's unwillingness to wholeheartedly support it. Massachusetts balked at sending troops and threatened secession and Henry David Thoreau popularized civil disobedience by going to jail for refusing to pay taxes to support the war. The war would be fought and won largely by men from the South and Mid-West.

Current prevailing impressions of the Mexican War have been derived from the writings of those who viewed the westward push of population north of 36 degrees 30 minutes of North latitude (the Missouri Compromise Line of 1850) as "Manifest Destiny" to civilize a heathen land, while viewing the similar advance westward south of this line as being strictly in the interests of the "slaveocracy" of the South. Regretfully, there have been many misconceptions concerning this war perpetuated over the years, most of which revolve around the false thesis of a stronger power, the United States, taking advantage of a weaker one. Nothing could be further from the truth!

At the outbreak of hostilities the Mexican army consisted of approximately 30,000 veterans while the U.S. army was composed of roughly eight regiments, numbering about 5,300 men spread around numerous frontier posts. Many of these soldiers were new Irish-Catholic immigrants to the U.S. who had taken the quick way to citizenship by joining the army. A goodly number of these men, under inducements of free land, would later defect from the American army and join their fellow Roman Catholic brethren in Mexico's *San Patricio Battalion.* The Mexican army, even with great weaknesses of class difference in the ranks, was a force to be reckoned with. Its ranks consisted of everything from Indian conscripts to crack infantry and cavalry. It had been fighting to either create or put down revolutions and minor rebellions for over 25 years leading up to 1846 and was considered one of the finest military organizations in the world even though Mexico had bankrupted its own economy for each of the twenty years leading into the war in order to cover enormous graft and corruption within its ranks.

On a side note, perhaps Mexico's greatest weakness in fighting the U.S. was the difference in artillery. Basically the Mexicans would rely on cumbersome, oxen-drawn, heavy artillery that fired solid shot. The more experimental U.S., however, relied on swift, horse-drawn "flying artillery" using explosive shells.

When called upon to supply volunteers for the war, Mississippi responded in typical patriotic style. The *Magnolia State* was ready to provide 17,000 men, but only 1,000 were initially called into service. A storm of controversy arose over which companies were to be selected. The state was divided politically between Whigs and Democrats, financially between old planter money and new, and socially between the older-settled southern half of the State versus the newer Choctaw and Chickasaw Treaty counties to the north. By war's end the State would send at least 2,500 of her sons into Mexico. Most of these would serve in either of the two regiments, one battalion and several companies of infantry provided to the national army by the state. Additionally, individuals such as Lieut. Earl Van Dorn of Port Gibson served as soldiers in the regular army.

Due to time constraints and the exasperating beauroracy of having each state's legislative, executive and judicial branches come together to agree in order for militia companies to be fielded outside of their particular state's boundaries, volunteer organizations were called upon to serve from each state.

Hinds County, as an example, fielded at least ten companies for the war with such names as: the "Brown Guards," "Utica Guards," "Brownsville Volunteers," "Jackson Dragoons" and "Oregon Guards." Two companies from the county made the cut for the new regiment being organized, they were the "Raymond Fencibles," which had been organized as state militia in 1836, and the "State Fencibles," which had been organized in 1845 and reorganized in 1846.

The United States was in an expansionist mode and Mississippians, like everyone else caught up in the *land fever*, looked to better their positions in life. Each man enlisted for his own personal reason, or reasons. Some farmers joined because they were simply tired of looking a mule square in the butt from daylight until dark. Most men, however, rationalized the war in the broader more complex view of national self-determination and the national honor being at stake. Honor counted much more in those days, particularly to Southern men.

The most famous unit fielded by Mississippi in the Mexican War was the First Regiment Volunteers, commanded by Col. Jefferson Davis. Davis was an 1828 graduate of West Point Military Academy. After serving in the regular army he resigned his commission in 1835 and married Sarah Knox Taylor, the daughter of his ex-commanding officer, Zachary Taylor. Taylor would not agree for his daughter to marry a soldier and be forced to suffer the fate of an army wife. Within weeks of their marriage Sarah died and Davis became a reclusive, book-reading planter. He later entered politics, gained control over his grief and married Varina Howell. At the outbreak of the war he was serving a well-respected stint in the U.S. House of Representatives. He played an instrumental role in resolving the "Oregon Question" prior to leaving Washington, D.C. to "take command of a regiment of Mississippians" for Mexico. While in Mexico he left his trusted black overseer, James Pemberton, with the responsibility of managing his plantation, *Brierfield*.

For Davis' service in Washington he was assured by the President that his regiment would be universally armed with the model 1841 Whitney Rifle, even over the objections of the army's commander-in-chief, Gen. Winfield Scott. During this period most regiments were armed with smoothbore "Brown Bess" muskets. Only certain regiments were allowed two rifle companies and these companies normally served on each flank of the regiment when in combat. No regiment before the First Mississippi had ever been fully equipped with rifles.

The .54 caliber Whitney Rifle was the most advanced up to that date. Developed by the inventor of the cotton gin, Eli Whitney, it had a percussion nipple and could be loaded and fired more rapidly than the antiquated smoothbore, flintlock musket. Also, its accuracy was much greater and it was the first firearm issued with interchangeable parts. In the hands of good men like Davis' Mississippians this weapon was at its full lethal *best*. By war's end it would forever after be known as the "Mississippi Rifle." The only weakness of the Whitney was that there was no attachment point for a bayonet. Consequently, the Mississippians carried artillery-style swords and Bowie Knives to compensate the lack of bayonets on the end of their rifles.

In the beginning Davis and his principal staff members, Lieut. Col. Alexander Keith McClung, an infamous duelist dubbed "The Black Knight of the South," and Maj. Alexander Blackburn Bradford, a Seminole War veteran, had their hands full. In a relatively short period of time they had to mold 991 souls of Mississippi clay into an effective fighting force. But they did it!

Under Davis' ever-vigilant eye and strict discipline the fat began to melt from the First Mississippi until it gained its fighting prime. The regiment consisted of the normal quota of ten companies. The companies selected were: (A) "Yazoo Volunteers," (B) "Wilkinson Volunteers," (C)"Vicksburg Southrons," (D) "Carroll County Volunteers," (E)"State Fencibles," (F) "Lafayette Volunteers," (G) "Raymond Fencibles," (H) "Vicksburg Volunteers," (I) "Marshall Guards" and (K) "Tombigbee Volunteers." The men largely represented the middle-class fabric of the State with a good sprinkling of the "well-to-do." The occupations of Mississippians serving in this war ranged from a Lowndes County "hog drover" to a Warren County member of the U.S. House of Representatives.

The morals of the men were just as varied. One company from Lowndes County, on its march across the State to the Vicksburg point of rendezvous, stole chickens, geese, turkeys and turnips along the way. Drank gallons of whiskey, had one member shot in a *donnybrook* in Kosciusko and were pronounced by Gov. Brown in Jackson to be "the finest looking volunteers he had ever seen." This, despite the fact that at one point a frustrated officer had angrily exclaimed, "I thought we had a company of gentlemen, but you are turning out to be a parcel of thieves."

In the extreme heat of coastal Mexico disease immediately began to take its toll. Camargo, Mexico, in the Rio Grande River Valley, was referred to as a "Yawning Grave." Other pestilence plagued the men and is evidenced by the remark of one soldier writing home from Mexico's coastal fever zone. "For every one mosquito in Mississippi," he wrote, "there are 100 here! And bigger!" Casualties to disease declined measurably when the men moved into the higher elevations of the Sierra Madre Oriental Mountain Range. On reaching Mexico the First Mississippi was assigned to Gen. Zachary Taylor, Davis' ex-father-in-law. It was a joyful reunion and the regiment became Taylor's personal guard and referred to as "Taylor's Own." He, himself, called them his "Mississippi Tigers" in reference to the uniforms many wore.

Though a few of the companies had been uniformed in the pattern of local militia before leaving home, at Vicksburg each man had been issued an annual stipend of $42.50 to purchase his own uniform. The resulting varied dress in the regiment, especially after raw recruits dealt with price-gouging sutlers, bartenders, gamblers and prostitutes, ranged from a mild form of uniform to no uniform at all. Consequently, the dress of the regiment reflected the individual state of mind of the soldier wearing it. For after all, even under Davis' stern countenance the men still considered themselves as volunteers and not completely subject to the rigid discipline of the regulars. Somewhere between Vicksburg and New Orleans, however, the men were issued "stripped uniforms". The shirts were cut in the local "cock of the walk"

Mississippi river man style. The officers, however, wore the standard regulation U.S. uniform.

The first major engagement of the regiment was in the taking of Monterey, Mexico on September 19-24, 1846. Lieut. Col. McClung was the first soldier to enter "La Teneria," a fortified tannery in the eastern defenses of the city. He was closely followed by Capt. William P. Rogers, who would lose his life in a later war leading a heroic Confederate assault against Union-held Corinth, Mississippi. Out of the corner of his eye at Monterey, McClung saw the "variegated uniforms" of his "Tombigbee Volunteers" and other companies of the First Mississippi. The Mississippians captured the fort, its cannon and many of the garrison's troops. They did not have their flag, however, and to their chagrin had to watch the blue regimental standard of the First Tennessee hoisted over the gutted tannery.

After Monterey was secured following bitter house-to-house street fighting, correspondents from both states wrote home claiming the victory. All solid evidence supports the Mississippians' claim, but much rivalry existed, and Davis, with his typically strong ego, was personally stung by the claims of the Tennesseans. A number of duels between principals were nearly fought over the issue. Fortunately the continuation of the war diverted everyone's attention. Reflecting upon the confusion caused by this incident, and realizing that the lack of a standard uniform had helped to create it, sometime between November, 1846 and February, 1847, Davis saw to it that all of his men were clothed in the same style of dress. This new uniform consisted of "a red shirt worn outside of their white duck pants, and black slouch hat."

Col. Davis, at Taylor's direction, negotiated the controversial capitulation terms of the city which allowed the defeated Mexican Army to vacate the city with their arms and proclaimed an eight-week respite in fighting. Shortly after the Battle of Monterey, Pvt. James M. Miller of Company B, First Mississippi, wrote his wife:

> "William is still in the hospital in town and getting well fast altho he will have a stiff knee. Two of our wounded men have since died of their wounds - R. N. Chance & John H. Jackson - Jackson had his leg cut off and died the same evening We have no idea how things will turn out and we will hardly know until the 60 days truce turns out and we receive orders from Washington. There is nothing going on here only the soldiers robbing corn patches, sugar fields, pigs and poultry, etc. with shooting a Mexican once in a while when he says anything which the Mexicans pay back when they catch a stragler out by himself. The men never leave camp without their arms for it is dangerous. The regulars have quiet possession of the town which we ought to have as we done the most in taking the place. It is the strongest fortified place I ever dreamed of seeing, [each] house is a fort and every street is filled up by batteries & cannon...we have pretty hard living, some flour, beef & coffee with the roasting ears we can hook is our living. The days are pretty hot but the nights are colder than they are in Woodville...I want to get home and see my wife and

children and be at peace. War is not the thing it is cracked up to
be. It may look well to those at home in security but not to those
in camp or in action."

Miller was seriously wounded four months later in the most decisive battle of the war.

The First Mississippi won fame at Monterey, but it achieved immortality on a mountainous plateau near a hacienda (ranch) named Buena Vista on February 21-23, 1847. Buena Vista was a battle fought largely by volunteers as most of the regulars had been previously detached from Taylor's army into Scott's which was forming at Vera Cruz.

In this signal battle, Taylor's army of 4,800 was outnumbered by Gen. Antonio Lopez de Santa Anna's force of roughly 19,000. Control of northern Mexico, hence the campaign, hung in the balance. After much vicious fighting and a last day's action which witnessed a famous 'V' formation composed of the First Mississippi and Third Indiana, supported by Thomas W. Sherman's and Braxton Bragg's Artillery, these units saved Taylor's army from anniliation, gave him his greatest battlefield victory and put him in the White House within two years. Taylor stated later, with a smile, that Davis' Mississippians were beaten three times during the battle and didn't have the sense to know they were licked. "If they had been regulars," he said, "They would have retreated!"

On the second day of battle a veteran in the "Raymond Fencibles" observed: "by weight of numbers [the enemy] were driving our troops before them when we approached. The enemy were so eager in pursuit that they did not notice our advance until we were within good rifle range of them. Although they did not see us, the Mississippi rifles soon told them of our whereabouts, and at the second fire they ingloriously fled." On the battlefield during the fight and in their last assault with Bowie knives on a strong column of enemy lancers, whose saddles their "Mississippi Rifles" had emptied, the Mexicans were heard to exclaim, "Diablos-Camisa colorados!" (Devils-Red shirts!).

The Second Mississippi Infantry arrived in Mexico in February, 1847. Whereas the First Mississippi had the good fortune to have Jefferson Davis with political clout who could get his regiment shipped to Mexico aboard a steamer. The Second Mississippi had Reuben Davis as its commander. He had no military experience of note and little influence. Reuben's regiment was shipped to Mexico slowly, painfully aboard schooners. The skeletons of many of this unit lay at the bottom of the Gulf of Mexico.

When the Second Regiment arrived at Gen. Taylor's Headquarters, a minor incident occurred that reflected how the volunteers viewed their new commander. Dr. Thomas Neely Love, the regimental surgeon wrote:

"Our regiment passed the old hero, and perhaps not one of them
recognized him; for he was more ordinarily dressed than any one
among them. Here, I am reminded of a joke upon Dr. [David A.]
Kinchloe, who seemed to be uninterested and careless of the
Company we were in. At night he remarked that he wished to go
up, the next day and see Genl. Taylor. 'Why, said I, you saw

Genl. Taylor to-day - shook hands with him, & talked to him.'
'No, I did not,' replied the Dr. 'But you did,' said I. 'I did not' he
protested. 'I tell you that you did.' 'Well, which was he? That
large red-faced man?' No; He is a large rather low, fleshy, dutch-
like looking man with an old brown surtout coat on?' 'Well, by
God, you dont say that old squint-eyed devil with the ragged
checked shirt on was Genl. Taylor?' 'Yes' 'Major Genl Taylor?'
continued the astounded Dr. 'Well, well, that gets me.'"

The Second would not win glory in battle. It would be relegated to serve in the Army
of Occupation and its rapidly mounting casualty lists were due to disease and an
occasional murder by Mexican Guerillas and Comanche Indians. On April 3rd,
Surgeon Love logged in his journal, "Here in the wagon poor [Francis M.] Greenlee
breathed his last - If he had been discharged at Matamoros he might have been saved
- though it is hard to tell the destiny that awaits us here - we are but frail mortals, and
life sometimes clings to us with a slender thread. He is gone - he was a good
innocent boy - he has, poor fellow, found an early grave in a distant country. He
sleeps in a lovely spot in the enemy's country - no companion will perhaps ever find
his grave, over which to strew the flowers, in kindness, in tenderness, and fond
remembrance of his youthful virtues." In another entry he relates the death of a
young soldier named Shockley, who, in his final hours said, "I left a young wife at
home - She is perhaps a mother now - and will soon be a widow ...I left home with
no wicked designs - My object was to serve my country - to improve myself, and be
useful to others - I want what money I have loaned to the boys collected. I have a
white shirt in my knapsack; put that on me when I am dead...Now is there no one
here to help me get religion?"

Mississippi's Brigadier General John Anthony Quitman was the highest ranking
officer to serve from the State in this war. Commanding brigades in both Zachary
Taylor and Winfield Scott's armies, he became a hero in the Battle for Belen Gate on
the outskirts of Mexico City. After the fight had been won he was appointed
America's first, and only, civil and military governor of Mexico City.

Only 376 of the original 991 "First Mississippi Rifles" returned to Mississippi
under arms after their part in the Mexican War had been concluded. They, and other
of their fellow statesmen who went to Mexico, would become the officer's corps for
Mississippi in the American Civil War, 1861-1865.

Lineage companies of state units that served in Mexico also served in the Civil War.
There were only a few. The "Raymond Fencibles" was one. It became Company C,
12th Regiment Mississippi Volunteer Infantry, Confederate States of America. The
namesake "Mississippi Rifles," Company A, 10th Mississippi, C.S.A., initially
consisted of several Mexican War veterans. This unit was presented the banner of
the old First Mississippi's "State Fencibles" company on their departure to the "Seat
of War" in 1861.

Jefferson Davis, hero of the Battle of *Buena Vista* (Spanish for Beautiful View)
became President of the Confederacy. Years later, after his nation lay in ruins, he
would retire to a home on the Mississippi Gulf Coast appropriately named *Beauvoir*
(French for Beautiful View) to spend his last days. On his death in 1889, Davis'

8

coffin was draped with the flag of his beloved and immortal First Mississippi.

Today, it is appropriate that we should remember those men who served our State and country in a war that most of the nation has apparently either forgotten, or chooses to ignore.

Mississippi Counties
1846-1848

Mississippi Militia Districts
1836-1846

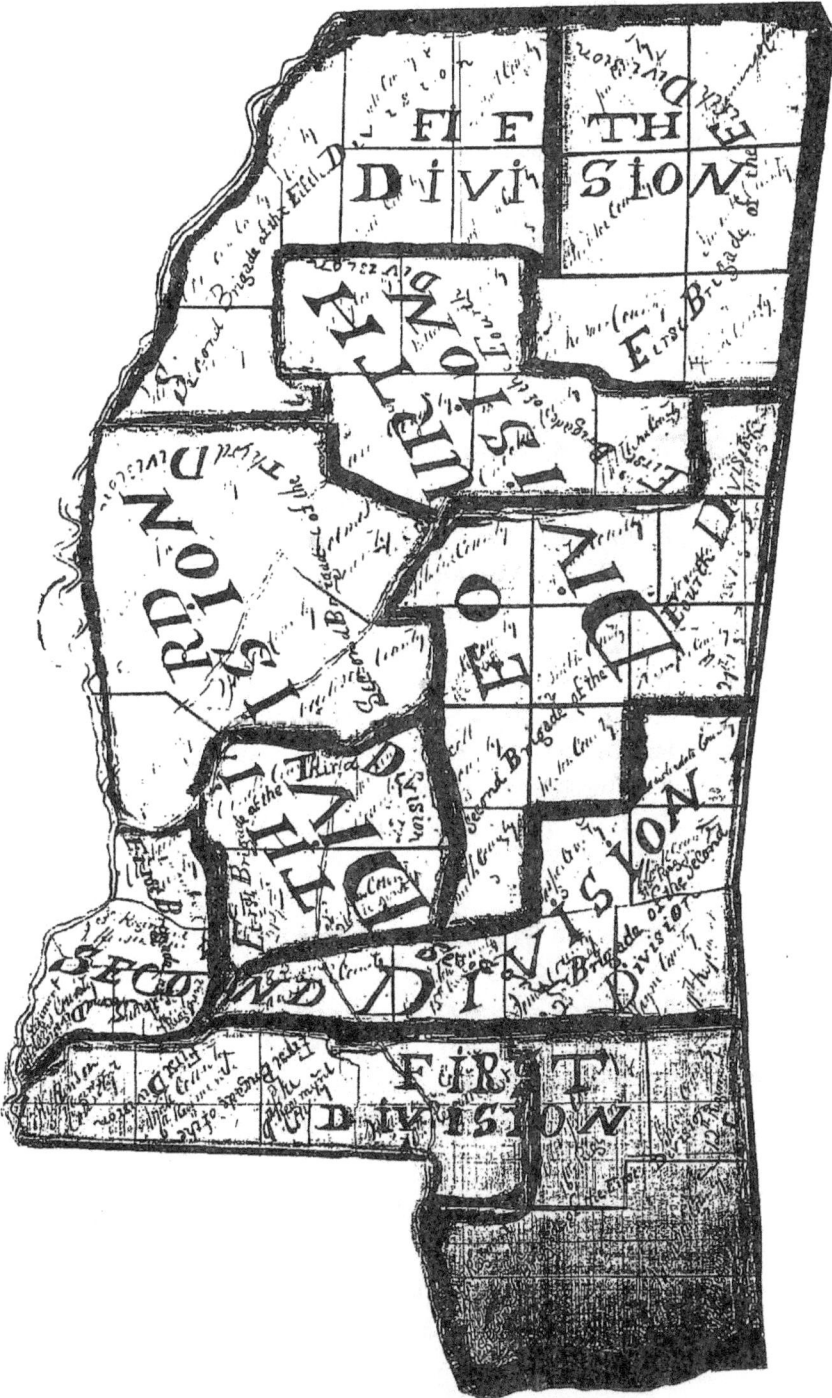

Mississippi Units in the Mexican War

1st Regiment Mississippi Volunteers
A Yazoo Volunteers (Yazoo)
B Wilkinson Volunteers (Wilkinson)
C Vicksburg Southrons (Warren)
D Carroll County Volunteers (Carroll)
E State Fencibles (Hinds)
F Lafayette Volunteers (Lafayette)
G Raymond Fencibles (Hinds)
H Vicksburg Volunteers (Warren)
I Marshall Guards (Marshall)
K Tombigbee Volunteers (Lowndes)

2nd Regiment Mississippi Volunteers
A Lowndes Guards (Lowndes)
B Marshall Relief Guards (Marshall)
C Choctaw Volunteers (Choctaw)
D Monroe Volunteers (Monroe)
E Tippah Guards (Tippah)
F Lauderdale Volunteers (Lauderdale)
G Thomas Hinds Guards (Hinds)
H Union Grays (Attala)
I Panola Boys (Panola)
K Capt. Buckley's Co. (Lawrence)

1st Battalion Mississippi Volunteers
A Capt. Keyes' Co. (Chickasaw)
B Capt. Crowson's Co. (Copiah)
C Capt. Anderson's Co. (DeSoto)
D Pontotoc Avengers (Pontotoc)
E Capt. Stewart's Co. (Monroe)

1st Regiment Texas Foot
Company I (Jefferson)

4th Regiment Louisiana Volunteers
Company E Sparrow Volunteers (Adams)

Alphabetical Listing
of
Mississippi Soldiers
Who Served
in the
Mexican War

(1846-1848)

"Mississippi Rifle" carried by Sgt. Joseph Schmaling, Co. H, "Vicksburg Volunteers," 1st Regiment Mississippi Volunteers during the war. These rifles were presented to the men who carried them through the war by the Mississippi Legislature upon their return home.

Cartridge pouch carried by Pvt. Charles Hanson Gibbs, Co. G, "Raymond Fencibles, 1st Regiment Mississippi Volunteers. This was the style issued to the Mississippians. This pouch saved the life of its owner on the battlefield (See page 202).

Soldiers

Abbott, Richard H.; pvt.; **C**; 1st Regt. Infan.
Abbott, William H.; pvt.; **D**; 2nd Regt. Infan.
Abrams, Emanuel; pvt.; **I**; 2nd Regt. Infan.
Abrams, Washington H.; mus., pvt.; **K**; 1st Regt. TX Foot Vols.
Abston, Albert L.; pvt.; **I**; 1st Regt. Infan.
Acee, William B.; pvt.; **C**; 2nd Regt. Infan.
Acker, Joel M.; Capt.; **D**; 2nd Regt. Infan.
Acklin, Morris; **Q.M. Dept.**; U.S.A.
Adair, Francis Marion; pvt.; **D**; 1st Regt. Infan.
Adair, Isaac Granger; pvt., cpl., 2nd Sgt.; **D**; 1st Regt. Infan.
Adams, Jackson; pvt.; **F**; 2nd Regt. Infan.
Adams, James; pvt.; **G**; 2nd Regt. Infan.
Adams, John; pvt.; **F**; 2nd Regt. Infan.
Adams, John; pvt.; **Unknown**; 2nd Regt. Infan.
Adams, John G.; pvt.; **A**; 1st Battalion Infan.
Adams, John L. C.; pvt.; **B**; 2nd Regt. Infan.
Adams, John R.; pvt.; **A**; 2nd Regt. Infan.
Adkinson, J. G.; pvt.; **D**; 1st Regt. Infan.
Adkinson, Pinkney G.; pvt.; **D**; 1st Regt. Infan.
Agee, David G.; pvt.; **C**; 1st Battalion Infan.
Aiken, John; pvt.; **A**; 1st Regt. Infan.
Ainsworth, William D.; pvt.; **G**; 1st Regt. Infan.
Akin, R. T.; 2nd cpl.; **B**; 2nd Regt. Infan.
Albertus, Bruno; pvt.; **D**; 2nd Regt. Infan.
Aldridge, Jasper N.; cpl.; **C**; 2nd Regt. Infan.
Alexander, Barton W.; 3rd, 2nd Sgt.; **E**; 2nd Regt. Infan.
Alexander, J. M.; pvt., 4th cpl.; **G**; 1st Regt. Infan.
Alexander, Jeremiah; pvt., 2nd Lieut.; **D**; 2nd Regt. Infan.
Allen, Edward C.; pvt., cpl.; **H**; 1st Regt. Infan.
Allen, James W.; pvt.; **B**; 2nd Regt. Infan.
Allen, John A.; pvt.; **B**; 2nd Regt. Infan.
Allen, Robert J.; pvt.; **K**; 1st Regt. Infan.
Allen, Samuel M.; pvt., hospital steward; **I**; 1st Regt. Infan.
Allen, William; pvt.; **I**; 2nd Regt. Infan.
Allen, William R.; pvt.; **I**; 2nd Regt. Infan.
Alverson, Elias; pvt.; **C/D**; 2nd Regt. Infan.
Ambrose, John; 3rd, 1st Sgt.; **H**; 2nd Regt. Infan.
Ames, Thomas G.; mus.; **K**; 1st Regt. Infan.
Amyx, Flemming; 1st Lieut., Capt.; **H**; 2nd Regt. Infan.

Anderson, Garland; pvt., 3rd Sgt.; **I**; 1st Regt. Infan.

Anderson, Hartley; pvt.; **F**; 2nd Regt. Infan.

Anderson, James Patton; Capt., Lieut.-Col.;**C/F&S**; 1st Battalion Infan.

Anderson, Jesse; pvt.; **C**; 1st Battalion Infan.

Anderson, John A.; Adjut.; **C/F&S**; 1st Battalion Infan.

Anderson, John L.; pvt.; **B**; 1st Regt. Infan.

Anderson, Joseph M.; pvt.; **E**; 2nd Regt. Infan.

Anderson, Thomas Jefferson; pvt.; **G**; 1st Regt. Infan.

Anderson, Thomas S.; lst Sgt.; **C**; 1st Battalion Infan.

Anderson, William; pvt.; **C**; 1st Battalion Infan.

Andrews, James D.; pvt.; **I**; 2nd Regt. Infan.

Andrews, Lemuel J.; pvt., 4th cpl.; **I**; 2nd Regt. Infan.

Andrews, O. H.; pvt.; **B**; 2nd Regt. Infan.

Andrews, William; pvt.; **D**; 1st Battalion Infan.

Anglin, Jasper; mus., pvt.; **A/B**; 1st Battalion Infan.

Anglin, William C.; pvt.; **D**; 2nd Regt. Infan.

Applegate, Richard; pvt.; **D**; 1st Regt. Infan.

Appling, Edward R.; 3rd Sgt.; **A**; 1st Battalion Infan.

Archer, Joseph; pvt.; **A**; 2nd Regt. Infan.

Arandes (aka Allinder, Armanders and Oranders), John; pvt.; **K**;
        2nd Regt. Infan.

Armour, Henry L.; mus.; **C**; 1st Regt. Infan.

Arnold, Solomon A.; pvt.; **H**; 2nd Regt. Infan.

Arnold, William; lst mus.; **D**; 1st Battalion Infan.

Arthur, Rufus K.; 1st Sgt., 2nd Lieut.; **C**; 1st Regt. Infan.

Ashley, Thomas; pvt.; **B**; 1st Battalion Infan.

Askew, James; pvt.; **E**; 2nd Regt. Infan.

Astin, Samuel C.; pvt., 1st Lieut.; **K**; 1st Regt. Infan. and **E**; 1st Battalion
        Infan.

Ater, H. C.; pvt.; **F**; 1st Regt. Infan.

Atkins, Robert M.; pvt.; **D**; 2nd Regt. Infan.

Atkinson, Asa B.; pvt.; 3rd, lst cpl.; **G**; 1st Regt. Infan.

Austin, James M.; pvt.; **Unknown**; 2nd Regt. Infan.

Austin, John; pvt.; **D**; 2nd Regt. Infan.

Austin, William; pvt.; **A**; 1st Battalion Infan.

Ayes (Ayers), Charles; pvt.; **Unknown**; 2nd Regt. Infan.

Babb, James D.; pvt.; **G**; 2nd Regt. Infan.

Bagby, Charles H.; lst Sgt., Act. Sgt.-Maj.; **A/F&S**; 2nd Regt. Infan.

Bailey, David F.; pvt.; **A**; 1st Regt. Infan.

Bailey, Thomas; pvt.; **B**; 2nd Regt. Infan.

Baird, James B.; pvt.; **B**; 1st Regt. Infan.

Baker, Thomas; pvt.; **D**; 2nd Regt. Infan.

Baldridge, William F.; pvt.; **G**; 2nd Regt. Infan.

Banks, Paul C.; pvt.; **I**; 2nd Regt. Infan.

Banks, Robert B.; pvt.; **C**; 1st Regt. Infan.

Banks, Winston; pvt.; **A**; 1st Regt. Infan.
Bankston, Thomas I. (J.?); pvt.; **F**; 2nd Regt. Infan.
Bankston, William M.; 4th Sgt.; **B**; 1st Battalion Infan.
Barclay, Joseph C.; pvt., cpl.; **G**; 2nd Regt. Infan.
Barden, John; pvt.; **B**; 2nd Regt. Infan.
Barefield, Elias; pvt.; **F**; 2nd Regt. Infan.
Barefield, Ervin; pvt.; **H**; 1st Regt. Infan.
Barfield, W. M.; pvt.; **C**; 2nd Regt. Infan.
Barfield, William F.; pvt.; **C**; 2nd Regt. Infan.
Barker, James; pvt.; **B**; 1st Battalion Infan.
Barker, William A.; pvt.; **B**; 1st Battalion Infan.
Barksdale, William; A.C.S.; **F&S**; 2nd Regt. Infan.
Barnes, Charles; pvt.; **C**; 1st Regt. Infan.
Barnes, John M.; pvt.; **C**; 1st Regt. Infan.
Barnes, Jasper N.; pvt.; **F**; 2nd Regt. Infan.
Barnes, John P.; pvt.; **C**; 1st Battalion Infan.
Barnett, John A.; pvt.; **D**; 1st Battalion Infan.
Barnett, William; pvt.; **C**; 2nd Regt. Infan.
Barnett, William; pvt.; **C**; 2nd Regt. Infan.
Barron, Ezekiel; pvt.; **C**; 2nd Regt. Infan.
Barrows, George; pvt., 2nd Lieut.; **K**; 2nd Regt. Infan.
Bartee, James L.; pvt., cpl.; **K**; 1st Regt. Infan.
Bartle, John G.; pvt.; **Unknown**; 2nd Regt. Infan.
Barton, Benjamin F.; pvt.; **E**; 1st Battalion Infan.
Bass, Benjamin; pvt.; **C**; 1st Regt. Infan.
Bass, James N.; pvt.; **D/G**; 2nd Regt. Infan.
Bass, John E.; pvt.; **I**; 1st Regt. Infan.
Bates, Marshall P.; 1st cpl.; **B**; 1st Battalion Infan.
Batton, Daniel H.; pvt., cpl.; **A**; 1st Regt. Infan.
Batts, Theodore D.; pvt.; **C**; 1st Regt. Infan.
Baughn, William P.; cpl., 1st Sgt., Sgt.-Maj.; **D/F&S**; 2nd Regt. Infan.
Bays, Henry; pvt., 4th, 3rd Sgt.; **C**; 2nd Regt. Infan.
Bays, James M.; pvt.; **C**; 2nd Regt. Infan.
Beale, Thomas I.; 2nd Sgt.; **B**; 1st Battalion Infan.
Beall, Egbert F.; pvt., 4th Sgt.; **D**; 1st Regt. Infan.
Beall, John M.; pvt., cpl.; **H**; 2nd Regt. Infan.
Beard, Harrison B.; pvt.; **D**; 1st Regt. Infan.
Beckham, Caswell D.; pvt.; **A**; 2nd Regt. Infan.
Bee, James; pvt.; **C**; 1st Battalion Infan.
Bekeart, Julius Francis; pvt.; **A**; 2nd Regt. Infan.
Bell, James A.; pvt.; **Unknown**; 2nd Regt. Infan.
Bell, James H.; pvt., 2nd cpl.; **A**; 1st Regt. Infan.
Bell, Richard; pvt.; **K**; 1st Regt. Infan.
Bell, Richard D.; pvt.; **H**; 2nd Regt. Infan.
Bell, William Henry; 1st Sgt.; **K**; 1st Regt. Infan.

Belt, David B.; pvt.; **E**; 1st Battalion Infan.
Benedict, Jacob; pvt.; **C**; 2nd Regt. Infan.
Bennett, Isaac M.; pvt.; **A**; 2nd Regt. Infan.
Bennett, John W.; pvt.; **A**; 1st Battalion Infan.
Bennett, Robert E.; pvt.; **E**; 1st Battalion Infan.
Bennett, Thomas; pvt.; **F**; 2nd Regt. Infan.
Benthall, John C.; pvt.; **D**; 1st Regt. Infan.
Benthall, Washington O.; pvt.; **C**; 1st Battalion Infan.
Best, Berry O.; pvt.; **I**; 1st Regt. Infan.
Best, Francis; 1st cpl., 3rd Sgt.; **B**; 1st Regt. Infan.
Beston, Patrick; pvt.; **D**; 2nd Regt. Infan.
Bethea, Thomas I.; pvt.; **G**; 2nd Regt. Infan.
Bettersworth, William A.; 1st Sgt.; **E**; 1st Battalion Infan.
Bibb, Benjamin F.; pvt.; **B/F**; 2nd Regt. Infan.
Bickerstaff, Marcas D.; pvt.; **I**; 2nd Regt. Infan.
Biddle, Marks J.; 1st Sgt., 2nd Lieut.; **G**; 2nd Regt. Infan.
Bigby (Bigbie), James N.; pvt.; **F**; 1st Regt. Infan.
Billings, Charles E.; pvt.; **D**; 1st Battalion Infan.
Binion, Ananias O.; pvt.; **C**; 2nd Regt. Infan.
Bird, Daniel A.; pvt.; **H**; 1st Regt. Infan.
Bird, George J. W.; pvt.; **G**; 1st Regt. Infan.
Bisbee, Noah; pvt.; **A**; 1st Regt. Infan.
Bixler, William; pvt.; **K**; 2nd Regt. Infan.
Black, Augustus H.; pvt.; **G**; 2nd Regt. Infan.
--Black, Martin; pvt.; **I**; 2nd Regt. Infan.
Black, Oliver H. P.; pvt.; **D**; 1st Battalion Infan.
Blair, George W.; pvt.; **A**; 2nd Regt. Infan.
Blake, J. W.; pvt., 4th cpl.; **D**; 1st Regt. Infan.
Blake, John H.; pvt.; **H**; 2nd Regt. Infan.
Blakely, James Witherspoon; pvt., 1st cpl.; **F**; 1st Regt. Infan.
Blount, Benjamin; pvt.; **K**; 2nd Regt. Infan.
Blum, George; pvt.; **F**; 2nd Regt. Infan.
Blythe, Andrew K.; Capt.; **A**; 2nd Regt. Infan.
Bobb, John Jr.; pvt., 2nd Lieut.; **H**; 1st Regt. Infan.
Boles, Samuel W.; pvt.; **H**; 2nd Regt. Infan.
Bolin, Jacob; pvt.; **Unknown**; 2nd Regt. Infan.
Bomar, John N. O.; pvt.; **B**; 2nd Regt. Infan.
Bond, Joseph S.; pvt.; **G**; 1st Regt. Infan.
Boone, Jordan R.; pvt.; **E**; 2nd Regt. Infan.
Boone, Joseph T.; pvt.; **E**; 2nd Regt. Infan.
Booth, George W. P.; pvt.; **C**; 1st Battalion Infan.
Bostick, Ferdinand; Sgt., 1st Lieut.; **A**; 1st Regt. Infan.
Bourk, Peter; pvt.; **D**; 1st Battalion Infan.
Boutwell, Chappel Spencer; pvt.; **F**; 2nd Regt. Infan.
Bowen, John; pvt.; **C**; 2nd Regt. Infan.

Bowen, Robert; pvt.; **G**; 1st Regt. Infan.
Bowen, William; pvt.; **K**; 2nd Regt. Infan.
Bowen, William B; pvt.; **K**; 2nd Regt. Infan.
Bowen, William H.; pvt., cpl.; **C**; 2nd Regt. Infan.
Bowman, Edward; 3rd cpl., Sgt.; **A**; 1st Regt. Infan.
Bowman, James; pvt.; **I**; 2nd Regt. Infan.
Bowman, John H.; pvt., 4th cpl., Sgt.; **E**; 1st Regt. Infan.
Box, Loving; pvt.; **B**; 2nd Regt. Infan.
Boyd, David W.; pvt.; **H**; 2nd Regt. Infan.
Boyd, J.; pvt.; **F**; 1st Regt. Infan.
Boyd, James; pvt.; **F**; 1st Regt. Infan.
Boyd, James; pvt.; **G**; 1st Regt. Infan.
Boyd, John; 2 cpl.; **B**; 2nd Regt. Infan.
Boyd, John L.; cpl.; **H**; 2nd Regt. Infan.
Boyd, Oliver H. P.; pvt.; **K**; 2nd Regt. Infan.
Boyett, Robert T.; pvt.; **H**; 2nd Regt. Infan.
Braden, John G.; pvt.; **B**; 1st Battalion Infan.
Bradford, Alexander Blackburn; Maj.; **F&S**; 1st Regt. Infan.
Bradford, Charles MacPherson; pvt., 2nd Lieut.; **E**; 1st Regt. Infan.
Bradford, Charles T.; pvt.; **C**; 1st Regt. Infan.
Bradford, Edmund; pvt.; **D**; 1st Battalion Infan.
Bradford, Ira Oscar; pvt.; **C**; 1st Regt. Infan.
Bradley, Jefferson C.; pvt.; **C**; 1st Battalion Infan.
Bradley, John; pvt.; **A**; 1st Regt. Infan.
Bradley, John Franklin; pvt.; **C**; 1st Battalion Infan.
Bradley, Joseph; pvt.; **F**; 2nd Regt. Infan.
Bradley, Thomas; pvt.; **G**; 1st Regt. Infan.
Bragg, Thomas Z.; pvt.; **B**; 1st Regt. Infan. and **F**; 2nd Regt. Infan.
Branch, John S.; pvt.; **I**; 1st Regt. Infan.
Branch, Michael; pvt.; **E**; 1st Battalion Infan.
Branch, William; pvt.; **A**; 2nd Regt. Infan.
Brand, John; pvt.; **K**; 1st Regt. Infan.
Braselton, James H.; pvt.; **G**; 2nd Regt. Infan.
Brazeale, Edward E.; pvt.; **K**; 1st Regt. Infan.
Brice, Presley; pvt.; **G**; 2nd Regt. Infan.
Briedlove, Isaac F.; pvt.; **Unknown**; 2nd Regt. Infan.
Bridges, Bird; 2nd Sgt.; **B**; 1st Battalion Infan.
Bridges, Joseph L.; pvt.; **I**; 1st Regt. Infan.
Bright, Alfred; pvt.; **D**; 2nd Regt. Infan.
Bright, William H.; pvt.; **C**; 1st Regt. Infan.
Brill, Philip; pvt.; **G**; 2nd Regt. Infan.
Britt, Joseph; pvt.; **B**; 1st Battalion Infan.
Brittain, D. A.; pvt.; **F**; 1st Regt. Infan.
Broach, William H.; pvt.; **F**; 1st Regt. Infan.
Brooke, George; pvt.; **A**; 1st Regt. Infan.

Brooks, William; pvt.; **F**; 2nd Regt. Infan.
Broom, George W.; pvt.; **K**; 1st Regt. Infan.
Broomley (Bromley), William C.; pvt.; **B**; 1st Battalion Infan.
Brosius, Daniel K.; Sgt.; **I**; 2nd Regt. Infan.
Brown, Alonzo L.; pvt.; **A**; 1st Regt. Infan.
Brown, Elijah; pvt.; **D**; 2nd Regt. Infan.
Brown, George W.; pvt.; **C**; 1st Regt. Infan.
Brown, Henry F.; pvt.; **B**; 1st Battalion Infan.
Brown, James S.; pvt.; **G**; 1st Regt. Infan.
Brown, Joseph E.; pvt.; **B**; 1st Battalion Infan.
Brown, Leonidas; pvt.; **B**; 2nd Regt. Infan.
Brown, Leonidas B.; pvt.; **I**; 1st Regt. Infan.
Brown, Samuel; pvt.; **D**; 2nd Regt. Infan.
Brown, Samuel W.; pvt.; **E**; 1st Battalion Infan.
Brown, Simeon; pvt.; **H**; 1st Regt. Infan.
Brown, Thomas; pvt.; **D**; 1st Regt. Infan.
Brown, William; pvt.; **A**; 1st Battalion Infan.
Brown, William G.; pvt.; **B**; 1st Battalion Infan.
Brown, William N.; 1st Lieut.; **F**; 1st Regt. Infan.
Browning, Alfred G.; pvt.; **F**; 1st Regt. Infan.
Browning, James C.; pvt.; **F**; 1st Regt. Infan.
Brownlee, Adam; pvt.; **C**; 1st Regt. Infan.
Brownley, Henry F.; 4th Sgt.; **E**; 1st Battalion Infan.
Bryan, Henry Herbert; pvt.; **E**; 1st Regt. Infan.
Bryant, William J.; pvt.; **B**; 1st Regt. Infan.
Buchanan, John H.; pvt.; **E**; 2nd Regt. Infan.
Buchanan, Perry J.; pvt., 3rd cpl., Sgt.; **I**; 2nd Regt. Infan.
Buchanan, Samuel T.; 2nd Sgt.; **E**; 2nd Regt. Infan.
Buckholts, John A.; pvt.; **D**; 1st Regt. Infan.
Buckley, Benjamin C.; Capt.; **K**; 2nd Regt. Infan.
Buie, Thomas J.; pvt.; **F**; 1st Regt. Infan.
Burge, Beverly; pvt.; **K**; 2nd Regt. Infan.
Burge, Beverly B.; pvt.; **A**; 2nd Regt. Infan.
Burgess, Thomas; pvt.; **D**; 2nd Regt. Infan.
Burks, A. T.; pvt.; **F**; 1st Regt. Infan.
Burland, Charles M.; pvt.; **G**; 1st Regt. Infan.
Burnett, Philip; pvt.; **G**; 1st Regt. Infan.
Burnett, V. S.; pvt.; **G**; 1st Regt. Infan.
Burnett, William; pvt.; **A**; 2nd Regt. Infan.
Burnett, Willis; 3rd Sgt.; **E**; 1st Battalion Infan.
Burney, Elonzo Pleasant; pvt.; **G**; 1st Regt. Infan.
Burney, Richard S.; pvt.; **H**; 1st Regt. Infan.
Burnham, A. P.; pvt.; **E**; 1st Regt. Infan.
Burrell, James H.; pvt.; **D**; 1st Regt. Infan.
Burriss, William H.; pvt.; **E**; 2nd Regt. Infan.

Burrus, Philip J.; lst Lieut.; **A**; 1st Regt. Infan.
Burton, Alexander S.; pvt.; **I**; 1st Regt. Infan.
Burton, Edmund; pvt.; **D**; 1st Battalion Infan.
Burton, Madison J.; pvt., cpl.; **I**; 2nd Regt. Infan.
Burwell, James; pvt.; **D**; 1st Regt. Infan.
Busby, George; pvt.; **F**; 2nd Regt. Infan.
Busby, James; pvt.; **Unknown**; 2nd Regt. Infan.
Buson, Samuel; pvt.; **Unknown**; 2nd Regt. Infan.
Bust, Luke S.; pvt., 3rd Sgt.; **G**; 2nd Regt. Infan.
Butler, Damascus L.; pvt., cpl.; **F**; 1st Regt. Infan.
Butler, James G.; pvt.; **B**; 1st Battalion Infan.
Butler, Joshua W.; pvt.; **D**; 2nd Regt. Infan.
Butler, William A.; pvt.; **E**; 1st Regt. Infan.
Byars, Wiley Thomas; 4th, lst Sgt.; **I**; 2nd Regt. Infan.
Byram, Jackson C.; pvt.; **H**; 2nd Regt. Infan.
Byrns, Calvin; pvt.; **E**; 1st Battalion Infan.
Cabler, Alexander; pvt.; **A**; 2nd Regt. Infan.
Cade, James; pvt.; **G**; 2nd Regt. Infan.
Cage, Albert G. Jr.; pvt.; **B**; 1st Regt. Infan.
Cage, Benjamin M.; pvt., 2nd cpl.; **B**; 1st Regt. Infan.
Cage, William L.; pvt.; **B**; 1st Regt. Infan.
Cain, William L.; pvt.; **B**; 1st Battalion Infan.
Caldwell, Samuel S.; mus.; **A**; 1st Regt. Infan.
Calhoun, James; 2nd Lieut.; **B**; 1st Regt. Infan.
Calhoun, Louchlin; pvt.; **F**; 2nd Regt. Infan.
Calhoun, Richmond N.; pvt., 5th, 3rd Sgt.; **F**; 2nd Regt. Infan.
Calvert, William; pvt.; **I**; 2nd Regt. Infan.
Calvit, Joseph; pvt.; **E**; 1st Battalion Infan.
Cameron, John; pvt.; **Unknown**; 2nd Regt. Infan.
Campbell, George W.; pvt.; **K**; 1st Regt. Infan.
Campbell, James; pvt.; **F**; 1st Regt. Infan.
Campbell, James B.; pvt.; **I**; 2nd Regt. Infan.
Campbell, John; pvt.; **E**; 1st Regt. Infan.
Campbell, Robert Bond; pvt.; **H**; 2nd Regt. Infan.
Campbell, Samuel; pvt.; **B**; 1st Battalion Infan.
Caperton, James S.; pvt.; **C**; 2nd Regt. Infan.
Caperton, William G.; pvt.; **C**; 2nd Regt. Infan.
Capshaw, A. C.; pvt.; **A**; 1st Regt. Infan.
Capshaw, Daniel C.; pvt.; **D**; 1st Regt. Infan.
Capshaw, William W.; pvt.; **A**; 1st Regt. Infan.
Caraway, Adam H.; pvt.; **G**; 2nd Regt. Infan.
Carey, Green B.; pvt.; **K**; 1st Regt. Infan.
Carger, J. H.; pvt., cpl.; **F**; 1st Regt. Infan.
Carithers, John M.; pvt.; **A**; 1st Battalion Infan.
Carlisle, Ellet; pvt.; **F**; 2nd Regt. Infan.

Carlisle, William; pvt.; **K**; 2nd Regt. Infan.
Carloss, M. D. C.; 1st Sgt.; **F**; 1st Regt. Infan.
Carloss, Robert; pvt.; **K**; 2nd Regt. Infan.
Carothers, Henry; pvt.; **Unknown**; 2nd Regt. Infan.
Carr, Madison H.; pvt.; **F**; 1st Regt. Infan.
Carr, William A. Jr.; pvt.; **F**; 1st Regt. Infan.
Carr, William S.; pvt.; **K**; 2nd Regt. Infan.
Carr, Young; pvt.; **D**; 1st Regt. Infan.
Carricer, Marton; pvt.; **D**; 1st Battalion Infan.
Carriger, Ido; pvt.; **B**; 1st Regt. Infan.
Carson, Eli B.; pvt.; **D**; 1st Battalion Infan.
Carson, James H.; pvt.; **K**; 2nd Regt. Infan.
Carson, Stephen D.; pvt.; **H**; 1st Regt. Infan.
Carson, William G.; pvt.; **D**; 1st Battalion Infan.
Carter, Edward B.; pvt.; **H**; 2nd Regt. Infan.
Carter, Green B.; pvt.; **B**; 2nd Regt. Infan.
Carter, Samuel K.; pvt.; **A**; 1st Regt. Infan.
Carter, Thomas T.; 1st Sgt., 2nd Lieut.; **G**; 2nd Regt. Infan.
Carter, William B.; mus. (Bugler), pvt.; **C**; 1st Battalion Infan.
Cartledge, Jesse; pvt.; **A**; 1st Battalion Infan.
Carvin, Arthur; pvt.; **K**; 2nd Regt. Infan.
Cary, Nathaniel Robert; 1st Lieut., Capt.; **D**; 1st Battalion Infan.
Cason, John A.; 3rd Sgt.; **A**; 1st Regt. Infan.
Cassel, Gardiner B.; pvt.; **E**; 1st Battalion Infan.
Caulfield, James Douglas; pvt.; **B**; 1st Regt. Infan.
Cayce, Joseph A.; pvt.; **A**; 2nd Regt. Infan.
Chaffin, William; pvt.; **H**; 1st Regt. Infan.
Chambers, James P.; pvt., cpl.; **F**; 2nd Regt. Infan.
Chambers, James R.; 3rd cpl.; **H**; 2nd Regt. Infan.
Champion, Sidney Smith; pvt.; **G**; 1st Regt. Infan.
Chance, Reuben W.; pvt.; **B**; 1st Regt. Infan.
Chaney, Archibald; 3rd, 2nd Lieut.; **F**; 2nd Regt. Infan.
Chapman, John A.; pvt.; **G**; 1st Regt. Infan.
Chapman, Theodore C.; pvt., 4th cpl.; **G**; 1st Regt. Infan.
Charleville, John; pvt.; **H**; 2nd Regt. Infan.
Charlton, Edward Francis; pvt.; **G**; 1st Regt. Infan.
Charlton, Edward S.; 2nd cpl., 1st Sgt.; **G**; 1st Regt. Infan.
Cheek, Isaiah V.; pvt.; **E**; 1st Battalion Infan.
Cheesman, Joseph H.; mus., pvt.; **F**; 2nd Regt. Infan.
Cheshire, Watson L.; pvt.; **D**; 2nd Regt. Infan.
Chester, Jacob R.; mus.; **F**; 1st Regt. Infan.
Childers, Alfred; pvt.; **B**; 2nd Regt. Infan.
Childers, David M.; pvt.; **B**; 2nd Regt. Infan.
Childers, James T.; pvt.; **C**; 2nd Regt. Infan.
Childers, Robert S.; pvt.; **C**; 2nd Regt. Infan.

Childres, James M.; pvt.; **F**; 1st Regt. Infan.
Chinn, Christopher C.; lst Lieut.; **B**; 2nd Regt. Infan.
Clamplett, Richard F.; pvt.; **B**; 1st Regt. Infan.
Clariday, Richard; pvt.; **E**; 1st Regt. Infan.
Clark, Charles; Capt., Col.; **G/F&S**; 2nd Regt. Infan.
Clark, Francis; pvt.; **C**; 1st Regt. Infan.
Clark, Henry D.; pvt.; **A**; 1st Regt. Infan.
Clark, John M.; pvt.; **I**; 2nd Regt. Infan.
Clark, Levi W.; pvt.; **G**; 2nd Regt. Infan.
Clark, Martin; pvt.; **B**; 2nd Regt. Infan.
Clark, Robert; pvt.; **D**; 1st Regt. Infan.
Clark, William H.; pvt., cpl.; **I**; 2nd Regt. Infan.
Clarke, Watson E.; pvt.; **G**; 1st Regt. Infan.
Clarke, Walton G.; pvt.; **B**; 2nd Regt. Infan.
Clarke, William G.; pvt.; **B**; 2nd Regt. Infan.
Clary, Newton; pvt.; **D**; 2nd Regt. Infan.
Clayton, Charles M.; pvt.; **D**; 2nd Regt. Infan.
Clelland, Robert; 2nd Lieut.; **I**; 2nd Regt. Infan.
Clements, William H.; pvt.; **C**; 1st Regt. Infan.
Clendenin, John S.; 2nd cpl., Bvt. 2nd Lieut., Capt.; **H**; 1st Regt. Infan.
Clinton, John H.; pvt., 2nd Sgt.; **G**; 2nd Regt. Infan.
Cloak, William G.; pvt.; **F**; 1st Regt. Infan.
Clough, Zebulon M. P.; pvt., 3rd cpl.; **C**; 1st Battalion Infan.
Coakley, John; pvt., cpl.; **D**; 1st Regt. Infan.
Coakley, William B.; pvt.; **A/E**; 2nd Regt. Infan.
Coatney, Thomas; pvt.; **F**; 1st Regt. Infan.
Cobb, Alpheus; pvt.; **D**; 1st Regt. Infan.
Cobb, Bayless E.; 4th cpl.; **C**; 1st Battalion Infan.
Cobb, George H.; lst Sgt.; **D**; 1st Battalion Infan.
Cobb, Josiah; pvt.; **C**; 1st Battalion Infan.
Cobb, William L.; pvt.; **I**; 2nd Regt. Infan.
Cochran, William F.; pvt.; **C**; 2nd Regt. Infan.
Cock, John Q. A.; pvt.; **B**; 2nd Regt. Infan.
Cocke, Daniel P.; pvt., 3rd, 2nd cpl.; **D**; 1st Regt. Infan.
Cocke, William T.; Bvt. 2nd Lieut.; **A**; 1st Battalion Infan.
Coe, Ezra; pvt.; **F**; 2nd Regt. Infan.
Coe, Milford G.; pvt.; **G**; 2nd Regt. Infan.
Coe, Thomas J.; pvt.; **H**; 1st Regt. Infan.
Coffey, Chesley Sheldon; 2nd Lieut., Capt.; **G**; 2nd Regt. Infan.
Cohea, Edward U.; pvt.; **E**; 1st Regt. Infan.
Coke, Addison; pvt.; **E**; 2nd Regt. Infan.
Colburn, Samuel G.; pvt.; **D**; 1st Regt. Infan.
Cole, Andrew J.; pvt.; **I**; 1st Regt. Infan.
Cole, John R.; pvt.; **H**; 2nd Regt. Infan.
Cole, Robert A.; pvt.; **H**; 2nd Regt. Infan.

Cole, Samuel M.; pvt.; **I**; 1st Regt. Infan.
Coleman, George A.; pvt.; **D**; 2nd Regt. Infan.
Coleman, James S.; pvt.; **E**; 2nd Regt. Infan.
Coleman, John; pvt.; **E**; 1st Regt. Infan.
Coleman, Reuben; pvt.; **E**; 1st Battalion Infan.
Coleman, William; pvt.; **E**; 1st Battalion Infan.
Collier, Jonathan Nichols; pvt., cpl.; **C**; 1st Regt. Infan.
Collingsworth, Addison; pvt.; **I**; 1st Regt. Infan.
Collins, Abraham; pvt.; **D**; 1st Battalion Infan.
Collins, Hiram W.; pvt.; **A**; 2nd Regt. Infan.
Collins, Joel; pvt.; **D**; 1st Battalion Infan.
Collins, Robert A.; 4th Sgt.; **D**; 1st Battalion Infan.
Collins, Samuel P.; pvt.; **C**; 1st Regt. Infan.
Collins, Thomas R.; pvt.; **D**; 2nd Regt. Infan.
Colton, Francis; pvt.; **A**; 1st Regt. Infan.
Conavey, Lawrence; pvt., cpl.; **B**; 2nd Regt. Infan.
Conger, Jephta; pvt.; **A/G**; 1st Regt. Infan.
Conley, Andrew; pvt.; **D**; 2nd Regt. Infan.
Conn, James W.; pvt.; **C**; 1st Regt. Infan.
Connell, John; pvt.; **F**; 2nd Regt. Infan.
Conner, Daniel; pvt.; **E**; 1st Regt. Infan.
Conner, John; pvt.; **F**; 1st Regt. Infan.
Conner, Thomas G.; pvt.; **B**; 1st Regt. Infan.
Connor, Benjamin G.; pvt.; **C**; 1st Regt. Infan.
Cook, Henry Felix; 1st Lieut.; **C**; 1st Regt. Infan.
Cook, Henry Mansfield; pvt.; **K**; 1st Regt. Infan.
Cook, James I.; pvt.; **F**; 2nd Regt. Infan.
Cook, Joseph B.; pvt.; **G**; 2nd Regt. Infan.
Cook, Robert W.; 2nd Lieut.; **B**; 2nd Regt. Infan.
Cook, Thomas E.; pvt.; **E**; 2nd Regt. Infan.
Cook, William; pvt.; **D**; 2nd Regt. Infan.
Cook, William M.; pvt.; **C**; 2nd Regt. Infan.
Cooper, Douglas Hancock; Capt.; **B**; 1st Regt. Infan.
Cooper, George W.; pvt.; **C**; 2nd Regt. Infan.
Cooper, Little I. B.; mus.; **E**; 1st Battalion Infan.
Cooper, Louis A.; pvt.; **G**; 1st Regt. Infan.
Cooper, Thomas C.; pvt.; **C**; 2nd Regt. Infan.
Cooper, William G. Jr.; pvt.; **G**; 1st Regt. Infan.
Coopwood, John; pvt.; **E**; 1st Battalion Infan.
Coopwood, Thomas B.; 4th, 3rd cpl.; **E**; 1st Battalion Infan.
Coor, Fleet M.; pvt.; **A**; 2nd Regt. Infan.
Coorpender, Lewis; pvt.; **G**; 1st Regt. Infan.
Coorpender, William F.; pvt.; **G**; 1st Regt. Infan.
Corbell, John R.; pvt.; **B**; 1st Battalion Infan.
Corbin, Vincent; pvt.; **H**; 2nd Regt. Infan.

Cornelius, James A.; pvt.; **D**; 1st Battalion Infan.
Corwine, Amos Breckinridge; pvt., 2nd, 1st. Lieut.; **A**; 1st Regt. Infan.
Cosby, James R.; pvt.; **I**; 2nd Regt. Infan.
Cosby, Morris; pvt.; **I**; 2nd Regt. Infan.
Cothran, William G.; 1st cpl.; **E**; 1st Battalion Infan.
Cotton, Charles F.; pvt.; **I**; 1st Regt. Infan.
Cotton, William A.; pvt.; **B**; 1st Regt. Infan.
Couch, William; pvt.; **C**; 1st Regt. Infan.
Coulter, Solomon M.; pvt.; **E**; 1st Regt. Infan.
Courtney, Thomas W.; pvt.; **B**; 1st Battalion Infan.
Covington, James B.; cpl., Sgt.; **A**; 2nd Regt. Infan.
Covington, Joseph L.; 3rd, 1st Sgt.; **K**; 1st Regt. Infan.
Cowan, J. C.; pvt.; **C**; 1st Regt. Infan.
Cowart, Andrew J.; pvt.; **A**; 1st Regt. Infan.
Cox, Allen; pvt.; **C**; 2nd Regt. Infan.
Cox, Edward; pvt.; **H**; 1st Regt. Infan.
Cox, Reuben T.; pvt.; **H**; 2nd Regt. Infan.
Cox, William R.; pvt.; **C**; 1 Battalion Infan.
Coyle, Peter; pvt.; **E**; 2nd Regt. Infan.
Cozart (Coyart?), George A.; pvt.; **Unknown**; 2nd Regt. Infan.
Craddock, William B.; pvt.; **B**; 2nd Regt. Infan.
Craft, John; pvt.; **H**; 2nd Regt. Infan.
Craft, John; pvt.; **C**; 1st Regt. Infan.
Craft, William H.; pvt.; **I**; 1st Regt. Infan.
Craig, Robert A.; pvt.; **Unknown**; 2nd Regt. Infan.
Cravens, John E.; pvt.; **K**; 1st Regt. Infan.
Crawford, A. G. H.; pvt.; **K**; 2nd Regt. Infan.
Crawford, John H.; pvt.; **I**; 1st Regt. Infan.
Crawford, Thomas F.; pvt.; **E**; 2nd Regt. Infan.
Creamer, Henry; pvt.; **D**; 1st Regt. Infan.
Creight, William; pvt.; **K**; 1st Regt. Infan.
Crenshaw, Cornelius M.; pvt.; **C**; 2nd Regt. Infan.
Crenshaw, Nathaniel M.; pvt.; **C**; 2nd Regt. Infan.
Crimm, James F.; pvt.; **A**; 1st Battalion Infan.
Cromer, Richard S.; Sgt., 2nd Lieut.; **C**; 2nd Regt. Infan.
Crook, Martin D.; pvt.; **Unknown**; 2nd Regt. Infan.
Crosland, Alexander; pvt.; **K**; 2nd Regt. Infan.
Cross, Franklin A.; pvt., 2nd cpl.; **F**; 2nd Regt. Infan.
Cross, William I.; pvt.; **F**; 2nd Regt. Infan.
Crossin, John; pvt., 1st cpl., 4th, 3rd Sgt.; **K**; 2nd Regt. Infan.
Crouch, Levi; pvt.; **I**; 2nd Regt. Infan.
Crowder, James C.; pvt.; **K**; 2nd Regt. Infan.
Crowson, Elisha; Capt.; **B**; 1st Battalion Infan.
Crumby, Absalom L.; pvt.; **C**; 1st Battalion Infan.
Crumby, Walter K.; pvt.; **C**; 1st Battalion Infan.

Crump, George P.; Capt.; **H**; 1st Regt. Infan.
Crumpton, William A.; 2nd Sgt.; **D**; 1st Battalion Infan.
Crunk, Joseph Wright; pvt.; **E**; 2nd Regt. Infan.
Culton, Samuel D.; pvt., cpl.; **D**; 2nd Regt. Infan.
Culverton, Robert; pvt.; **C**; 1st Regt. Infan.
Cumberland, Samuel; pvt.; **Unknown**; 2nd Regt. Infan.
Cummings, John W.; pvt.; **K**; 1st Regt. Infan.
Cummings, William; pvt.; **D**; 2nd Regt. Infan.
Curren, Robert; pvt.; **E**; 1st Battalion Infan.
Currie, Alexander M.; pvt.; **A**; 1st Battalion Infan.
Currie, Edward; pvt.; **C**; 1st Regt. Infan.
Currie, John H.; pvt., cpl.; **G**; 2nd Regt. Infan.
Curry, John B.; pvt., 3rd Sgt.; **A**; 2nd Regt. Infan.
Curtis, Cornelius; pvt.; **B**; 2nd Regt. Infan.
Curtis, Sanford; pvt.; **B**; 2nd Regt. Infan.
Dabney, John H.; pvt.; **G**; 2nd Regt. Infan.
Dalton, David L.; mus.; **C**; 1st Battalion Infan.
Dampier, William G.; pvt.; **B**; 1st Battalion Infan.
Daniel, James P.; pvt.; **H**; 2nd Regt. Infan.
Daniel, John; pvt.; **D**; 2nd Regt. Infan.
Daniels, William I.; Capt.; **F**; 2nd Regt. Infan.
Darden, Uriah M.; pvt.; **B**; 2nd Regt. Infan.
Dart, John Paul; pvt.; **H**; 1st Regt. Infan.
Daughtry, John M.; pvt.; **C**; 1st Regt. Infan.
Davanay, James; pvt.; **I**; 2nd Regt. Infan.
Davenport, Thomas; pvt., cpl.; **G**; 2nd Regt. Infan.
David, James; pvt.; **K**; 2nd Regt. Infan.
Davidson, George W.; pvt.; **G**; 2nd Regt. Infan.
Davidson, Thomas B.; pvt.; **D**; 1st Regt. Infan.
Davidson, Thomas Jefferson; pvt.; **H**; 1st Regt. Infan.
Davis, Anderson; pvt.; **B/F**; 2nd Regt. Infan.
Davis, Benjamin; mus., pvt.; **A**; 1st Battalion Infan.
Davis, Benjamin; pvt.; **E**; 1st Battalion Infan.
Davis, Benjamin E.; pvt.; **F**; 2nd Regt. Infan.
Davis, Benjamin F.; pvt.; **K**; 1st Regt. Infan.
Davis, C. David; pvt.; **D**; 2nd Regt. Infan.
Davis, Charles F.; pvt.; **K**; 1st Regt. Infan.
Davis, Edward A. C.; Sgt.; **B**; 2nd Regt. Infan.
Davis, Henry J.; pvt.; **G**; 2nd Regt. Infan.
Davis, James; pvt.; **K**; 2nd Regt. Infan.
Davis, James C.; pvt.; **H**; 1st Regt. Infan.
Davis, James M. A.; pvt.; **D**; 2nd Regt. Infan.
Davis, Jefferson; Col.; **F&S**; 1st Regt. Infan.
Davis, John A.; pvt.; **A**; 1st Battalion Infan.
Davis, John E.; pvt.; **G**; 2nd Regt. Infan.

Davis, John F.; pvt.; **B**; 2nd Regt. Infan.
Davis, John H.; pvt.; **F**; 2nd Regt. Infan.
Davis, John L. W.; pvt.; **E**; 2nd Regt. Infan.
Davis, John S.; pvt.; **E**; 2nd Regt. Infan.
Davis, Reuben; Col.; **F&S**; 2nd Regt. Infan.
Davis, Robert H.; pvt.; **C**; 1st Regt. Infan.
Davis, Spotswood H.; pvt.; **I**; 1st Regt. Infan.
Davis, Thomas A.; pvt.; **F**; 1st Regt. Infan.
Davis, Waller; pvt.; **F**; 1st Regt. Infan.
Davis, William; pvt.; **A**; 1st Battalion Infan.
Davis, William L.; pvt.; **B**; 2nd Regt. Infan.
Davis, Zachariah V.; pvt.; **H**; 2nd Regt. Infan.
Dawson, Joseph; pvt.; **K**; 2nd Regt. Infan.
Day, John E.; pvt.; **K**; 1st Regt. Infan.
Dearing, Joseph S.; pvt.; **H**; 2nd Regt. Infan.
Deason, John B.; 3rd, 2nd Lieut., Capt.; **K**; 2nd Regt. Infan.
Deason, Joseph L.; pvt.; **K**; 2nd Regt. Infan.
Deen, William D.; pvt.; **A**; 1st Battalion Infan.
Deheart, Lenbron; pvt.; **Unknown**; 2nd Regt. Infan.
Deigman (Degnan), Patrick; pvt.; **E**; 1st Regt. Infan.
Delaney, Joseph; pvt.; **D**; 1st Battalion Infan.
Delany, Edward; pvt.; **D**; 1st Battalion Infan.
Delap, Alford; pvt.; **B**; 2nd Regt. Infan.
Delap, Alfred; 1st mus. (Drummer); **I**; 1st Regt. Infan.
Delay, William Henry; Capt.; **F**; 1st Regt. Infan.
Dement, Thomas C.; pvt.; **E**; 1st Battalion Infan.
Dennehy, John; pvt.; **C**; 2nd Regt. Infan.
Denson, John S.; mus. (Fifer); **C**; 1st Regt. Infan.
Denton, Jerry W.; pvt.; **D**; 1st Battalion Infan.
Dhenny, John P.; pvt.; **Unknown**; 2nd Regt. Infan.
Dick, John W. N.; 1st Sgt.; **C**; 2nd Regt. Infan.
Dickens, Elijah; pvt.; **B**; 1st Battalion Infan.
Dickerson, Henry C.; pvt.; **I**; 2nd Regt. Infan.
Dickerson, Isaac D.; pvt.; **I**; 1st Regt. Infan.
Dickerson, Richard B.; pvt.; **E**; 1st Battalion Infan.
Dickinson, Joseph C.; pvt.; **A**; 1st Battalion Infan.
Dickson (Dixon), David H.; pvt., 1st Sgt.; **K**; 2nd Regt. Infan.
Dickson, Joseph P.; pvt., Q.M.S.; **C**; 1st Battalion Infan.
Dill, Samuel H.; 2nd Lieut.; **I**; 1st Regt. Infan.
Dillahunty, Henry I.; pvt.; **D**; 1st Battalion Infan.
Dillingham, William H.; Add'l. 2nd Lieut.; **E**; 1st Battalion Infan.
Dillon, John; pvt.; **A**; 1st Regt. Infan.
Dixon, A. L.; pvt.; **C**; 1st Regt. Infan.
Dixon, Almaron S.; 3rd Sgt.; **F**; 1st Regt. Infan.
Dixon, Elijah; pvt.; **A**; 1st Regt. Infan.

Dixon, Noland S.; pvt.; **B**; 1st Regt. Infan.

Dixon, Philip B.; pvt.; **Unknown**; 1st Regt. Infan.

Dixon, Robert C.; pvt.; **G**; 2nd Regt. Infan.

Dobbins, John W.; pvt.; **Unknown**; 2nd Regt. Infan.

Dobbs, Andrew J.; cpl., 2nd Sgt.; **D**; 2nd Regt. Infan.

Dockery, Tolbert; pvt.; **K**; 1st Regt. Infan.

Dodds, Stephen V.; pvt., Drum-Maj.; **C/F&S**; 1st Regt. Infan.

Dodge, Hamilton; pvt.; **D**; 2nd Regt. Infan.

Donald, James; pvt.; **E**; 1st Regt. Infan.

Donathan, James W.; 1st cpl.; **A**; 1st Battalion Infan.

Donnelly, James W.; pvt.; **B**; 1st Regt. Infan.

Dorman, Perry; pvt.; **I**; 1st Regt. Infan.

Dorsey, Hilliard; pvt., Capt.; **C**; 1st Battalion Infan.

Doss, Washington L.; pvt., cpl., Sgt.; **A**; 2nd Regt. Infan.

Dotson, W. M.; cabin boy; *U.S.S. Mississippi*

Douglass, Jeremiah M.; pvt.; **C**; 1st Battalion Infan.

Downing, Joseph A.; pvt.; **I**; 1st Regt. Infan.

Downing, Reuben Newman; Capt.; **G**; 1st Regt. Infan.

Downing, William R.; pvt.; **D**; 1st Battalion Infan.

Dowsing, Everard; 1st Lieut.; **A**; 2nd Regt. Infan.

Dowsing, Fielding L.; pvt.; **K**; 1st Regt. Infan.

Dowsing, Jeremiah; 2nd Sgt.; **A**; 2nd Regt. Infan.

Doyle, David R.; pvt.; **D**; 1st Regt. Infan.

Dozier, Edwin M.; pvt.; **F**; 2nd Regt. Infan.

Drake, Benjamin W.; pvt.; **A**; 2nd Regt. Infan.

Dubose, Daniel D.; pvt.; **H**; 1st Regt. Infan.

Duffield, John M.; State Adjt. Gen.

Dugan, John; pvt.; **C**; 1st Regt. Infan.

Dugan, Michael; pvt.; **E**; 2nd Regt. Infan.

Dunevant, Peter J.; pvt.; **F**; 1st Regt. Infan.

Dunlap, Elijah; pvt.; **G**; 1st Regt. Infan.

Dunlop, Daniel; pvt.; **H**; 1st Regt. Infan.

Dunn, Edward; pvt.; **H**; 1st Regt. Infan.

Dunn, George W.; pvt.; **C**; 1st Regt. Infan.

Dunn, John W.; pvt.; **K**; 1st Regt. Infan.

Dunn, Richard W.; pvt.; **C**; 2nd Regt. Infan.

Dunn, Thomas G.; pvt.; **C**; 2nd Regt. Infan.

Dupree, James H.; pvt.; **H**; 1st Regt. Infan.

Durden, Jonathan; 3rd cpl., 3rd Sgt.; **D**; 1st Regt. Infan.

Durham, James J.; pvt.; **H**; 2nd Regt. Infan.

Durham, W. T. S.; pvt.; **D**; 1st Regt. Infan.

Dyche, Samuel; pvt., cpl.; **A**; 2nd Regt. Infan.

Dyer, Alexander H.; 3rd Sgt.; **C**; 2nd Regt. Infan.

Dyer, Christopher C.; pvt.; **C**; 2nd Regt. Infan.

Eakin, John G.; pvt.; **H**; 2nd Regt. Infan.

Earp, Mason N.; pvt.; **I**; 2nd Regt. Infan.
Eason, Ashley D.; pvt.; **C**; 1st Battalion Infan.
East, Anderson; pvt.; **H**; 2nd Regt. Infan.
East, William I.; pvt.; **E**; 1st Battalion Infan.
Easterling, Simeon; pvt.; **F**; 2nd Regt. Infan.
Eastland, James; pvt., 1st Sgt.; **F**; 2nd Regt. Infan.
Eastland, William D.; 3rd, 2nd Lieut.; **F**; 2nd Regt. Infan.
Eaton, William W.; pvt.; **F**; 1st Regt. Infan.
Echols, Moses D.; pvt.; **K**; 1st Regt. Infan.
Eddins, Robert J.; pvt.; **I**; 1st Regt. Infan.
Edge, Julien O.; pvt.; **Unknown**; 2nd Regt. Infan.
Edmondson, Charles M.; pvt.; **I**; 1st Regt. Infan.
Edmonson, Archibald S.; pvt.; **C**; 1st Battalion Infan.
Edrington, George W.; pvt.; **H**; 2nd Regt. Infan.
Edwards, Benjamin F.; pvt.; **G**; 1st Regt. Infan.
Edwards, Benjamin Harrison; pvt.; **E**; 1st Regt. Infan.
Edwards, Samuel M.; pvt.; **H**; 1st Regt. Infan.
Edwards, Thomas; pvt.; **D**; 1st Battalion Infan.
Edwards, William; pvt.; **E**; 2nd Regt. Infan.
Eggleston, Dick H.; pvt.; **C**; 1st Regt. Infan.
Eilbott, Leon F.; pvt.; **G**; 1st Regt. Infan.
Elder, David M.; pvt.; **C**; 2nd Regt. Infan.
Elder, Enos; Capt.; **C**; 2nd Regt. Infan.
Elder, James I.; pvt.; **B**; 1st Battalion Infan.
Elder, William H.; pvt.; **C**; 2nd Regt. Infan.
Elliott, George W.; pvt., cpl.; **K**; 2nd Regt. Infan.
Elliott, John G.; pvt.; **D**; 1st Regt. Infan.
Ellis, Andrew I.; pvt.; **C**; 1st Battalion Infan.
Ellis, Benjamin T.; pvt.; **H**; 2nd Regt. Infan.
Ellis, Charles H.; pvt.; **C**; 1st Regt. Infan.
Ellis, John M.; pvt.; **A**; 2nd Regt. Infan.
Ellis, Thomas; pvt.; **Unknown**; 2nd Regt. Infan.
Ellis, Thomas J.; pvt.; **A**; 1st Regt. Infan.
Ellis, William L.; pvt.; **A**; 2nd Regt. Infan.
Ellison, John B.; pvt.; **E**; 1st Battalion Infan.
Eppes, William E.; pvt., Bvt. 2nd Lieut.; **I**; 1st Regt. Infan.
Erambert, Charles; 2nd cpl., 4th Sgt.; **B**; 1st Regt. Infan.
Erskins, John; pvt.; **I**; 2nd Regt. Infan.
Erwin, John W.; pvt.; **D**; 1st Regt. Infan.
Estelle, Preston; pvt.; **Unknown**; 2nd Regt. Infan.
Estelle, William M.; 1st Lieut., Capt.; **I**; 2nd Regt. Infan.
Estis, William E.; 4th cpl., 3rd Sgt.; **E**; 1st Regt. Infan.
Eubanks, James; 3rd cpl., 3rd Sgt.; **B**; 1st Battalion Infan.
Evans, Ezekiel W.; 1st Lieut.; **A**; 1st Battalion Infan.
Evans, James; pvt.; **I**; 1st Regt. Infan.

Evans, James A.; pvt., 4th cpl.; **K**; 1st Regt. Infan.
Evans, Joseph; pvt.; **I**; 1st Regt. Infan.
Evans, Joshua W.; pvt.; **I**; 2nd Regt. Infan.
Evans, Oliver C.; pvt.; **C**; 2nd Regt. Infan.
Evans, William; pvt.; **Unknown**; 2nd Regt. Infan.
Ewing, Andrew; pvt.; **D**; 1st Regt. Infan.
Ewing, William M.; 4th cpl.; **G**; 2nd Regt. Infan.
Fairchild, Joseph B.; pvt.; **G**; 1st Regt. Infan.
Falkner, Edmund G.; pvt.; **I**; 2nd Regt. Infan.
Falkner, Joseph; pvt.; **E**; 2nd Regt. Infan.
Falkner, Kelly; pvt.; **D**; 1st Battalion Infan.
Falkner, Thomas; pvt.; **E**; 2nd Regt. Infan.
Falkner, William C.; 1st Lieut.; **E**; 2nd Regt. Infan.
Fanning, William P.; pvt.; **A**; 2nd Regt. Infan.
Farish, Claiborne; 4th, 2nd Sgt.; **B**; 1st Regt. Infan.
Farrar, George Harding; pvt.; **E**; 1st Regt. Infan.
Fauntleroy, Frederick W.; pvt.; **E**; 1st Regt. Infan.
Feely, Daniel; pvt.; **B**; 2nd Regt. Infan.
Feltman, Jacob J.; pvt.; **K**; 1st Regt. Infan. and **E**; 1st Battalion Infan.
Felts, Robert; pvt.; **G**; 1st Regt. Infan.
Ferguson, Samuel T.; pvt.; **D**; 1st Regt. Infan.
Fields, Elias D.; pvt.; **A**; 2nd Regt. Infan.
Fields, John; pvt.; **A**; 2nd Regt. Infan.
Fields, Ripley; pvt.; **D**; 1st Regt. Infan.
Finch, John; pvt.; **H**; 1st Regt. Infan.
Finch, John; pvt.; **I**; 2nd Regt. Infan.
Finley, George P.; pvt.; **E**; 1st Regt. Infan.
Fisher, George; pvt., 2nd cpl.; **K**; 1st Regt. Infan.
Fisher, George S.; pvt.; **C**; 1st Battalion Infan.
Fisher, John; pvt.; **C**; 1st Battalion Infan.
Fisher, Robert; pvt., Sgt.; **A**; 1st Regt. Infan.
Flanagan, James; pvt.; **K**; 1st Regt. Infan.
Flanagan, William A.; pvt.; **K**; 1st Regt. Infan.
Fleming, William; pvt.; **G**; 2nd Regt. Infan.
Fleming, William H.; pvt.; **E**; 1st Regt. Infan.
Fletcher, Crawford; 1st Lieut.; **E**; 1st Regt. Infan.
Fletcher, Lorenzo Dow; pvt.; **H**; 2nd Regt. Infan.
Flippin, William; pvt.; **K**; 2nd Regt. Infan.
Flournoy, Jesse; pvt.; **E**; 2nd Regt. Infan.
Flowers, Ephraim A.; pvt.; **G/I**; 2nd Regt. Infan.
Flowers, Graham H.; pvt.; **G/I**; 2nd Regt. Infan.
Floyd, Elijah; pvt.; **A**; 1st Regt. Infan.
Floyd, George W.; pvt.; **I**; 1st Regt. Infan.
Floyd, Henry; pvt.; **A**; 1st Regt. Infan.
Flyn, Zachariah K.; pvt.; **D**; 2nd Regt. Infan.

Fogg, William; 2nd Sgt.; **B**; 2nd Regt. Infan.
Foil, David; pvt.; **K**; 2nd Regt. Infan.
Foil, John C.; pvt.; **K**; 2nd Regt. Infan.
Folly, Acy; pvt.; **F**; 2nd Regt. Infan.
Fondran, S. R.; pvt.; **G**; 1st Regt. Infan.
Forbes, Daniel; pvt.; **A**; 1st Regt. Infan.
Forbes, Joel; pvt.; **D**; 1st Regt. Infan.
Ford, Canaday; pvt.; **G**; 2nd Regt. Infan.
Ford, Henry F.; pvt.; **C**; 1st Regt. Infan.
Ford, John J.; pvt.; **A**; 2nd Regt. Infan.
Ford, William F.; cpl.; **F**; 2nd Regt. Infan.
Foreman, Andrew Jackson; pvt., 4th cpl.; **I**; 1st Regt. Infan.
Forkes, Benjamin; pvt.; **C**; 1st Regt. Infan.
Forkes, James L.; pvt.; **C**; 1st Regt. Infan.
Forrest, Hardeman C.; 2nd Lieut.; **C**; 1st Battalion Infan.
Forrest, John M.; pvt.; **C**; 1st Battalion Infan.
Forster, Charles A.; mus. (Bugler); **D**; 1st Regt. Infan.
Fort, Marcus L.; pvt.; **I**; 2nd Regt. Infan.
Fortenberry, James R.; pvt.; **E**; 1st Battalion Infan.
Fortner, George W.; pvt.; **K**; 2nd Regt. Infan.
Fortner, Joseph; pvt.; **Unknown**; 2nd Regt. Infan.
Foster, William; pvt.; **G**; 2nd Regt. Infan.
Foute, Marcellus A.; 4th, 2nd cpl.; **E**; 1st Regt. Infan.
Fowler, Adrian; pvt.; **F**; 2nd Regt. Infan.
Fox, Edwin; pvt.; **A**; 1st Regt. Infan.
Fox, Edwin; pvt.; **H**; 2nd Regt. Infan.
Fox, Isaac; pvt.; **C**; 2nd Regt. Infan.
Fox, Robert; pvt.; **E**; 1st Regt. Infan.
Fox, Thomas J.; pvt.; **C**; 2nd Regt. Infan.
Francis, James A.; pvt.; **F**; 2nd Regt. Infan.
Franklin, George W.; pvt.; **A**; 1st Battalion Infan.
Franks, Gabriel M.; pvt.; **D**; 2nd Regt. Infan.
Franks, James A.; pvt.; **D**; 2nd Regt. Infan.
Frazee, Carman; pvt.; **K**; 1st Regt. Infan. and **A/B**; 2nd Regt. Infan.
Frazier, David; pvt.; **E**; 1st Regt. Infan.
Frederick, Abraham C.; pvt.; **A**; 2nd Regt. Infan.
Fredericks, Jacob; pvt.; **E**; 1st Regt. Infan.
Freeland, James; pvt.; **A**; 1st Battalion Infan.
Freeman, William A.; cpl.; **A**; 2nd Regt. Infan.
Friar, William J.; pvt.; **C**; 1st Regt. Infan.
Fry, David B.; pvt.; **G**; 2nd Regt. Infan.
Fullerton, Elijah M.; pvt.; **D**; 1st Battalion Infan.
Fullerton, George W.; pvt.; **D**; 1st Battalion Infan.
Fuqua, Joseph S.; pvt.; **B**; 1st Regt. Infan.
Futch, Isham T.; 4th cpl.; **F**; 2nd Regt. Infan.

Gaff, Felix W.; cpl., 2nd Lieut.; **I**; 2nd Regt. Infan.
Gaffney, Edward; pvt.; **C**; 1st Regt. Infan.
Gage, James D. M.; pvt.; **D**; 1st Regt. Infan.
Gage, John J.; 2nd cpl., Sgt.; **H**; 2nd Regt. Infan.
Galbraith, James D.; Capt.; **E**; 4th Regt. LA Infan.
Gallaher, David L.; cpl.; **E**; 2nd Regt. Infan.
Gallman, William B.; pvt.; **G**; 1st Regt. Infan.
Galloway, George M.; pvt.; **D**; 2nd Regt. Infan.
Ganong, William L.; pvt.; **I**; 2nd Regt. Infan.
Gardner, D. Mc.; pvt.; **F**; 1st Regt. Infan.
Gardner, John; pvt.; **F**; 2nd Regt. Infan.
Gardner, Solomon; pvt.; **A**; 1st Regt. Infan.
Garland, Edward W.; pvt.; **C**; 2nd Regt. Infan.
Garner, George W.; pvt.; **K**; 2nd Regt. Infan.
Garner, Ransom; pvt.; **K**; 2nd Regt. Infan.
Garrett, Bartholomew; pvt.; **I**; 2nd Regt. Infan.
Garrett, John S.; pvt.; **C**; 1st Battalion Infan.
Garrett, Samuel; pvt.; **A**; 1st Battalion Infan.
Garrott, Enos; pvt.; **F**; 1st Regt. Infan.
Gayden, Iverson Greene; pvt.; **B**; 1st Regt. Infan.
Gee, William H.; pvt.; **F**; 1st Regt. Infan.
Gentry, Merenether T.; pvt.; **K**; 2nd Regt. Infan.
George, James H.; pvt.; **E**; 1st Battalion Infan.
George, James Zachariah; pvt.; **D**; 1st Regt. Infan.
Gerrald, Richard S.; pvt.; **A**; 1st Regt. Infan.
Gerrald, William G.; pvt.; **A**; 1st Regt. Infan.
Gibbons, George W.; pvt.; **E**; 1st Battalion Infan.
Gibbons, Seth; pvt.; **A**; 1st Battalion Infan.
Gibbs, Charles Hanson; pvt.; **G**; 1st Regt. Infan.
Gibson, Amos; pvt.; **F**; 2nd Regt. Infan.
Gibson, Ralph; pvt.; **K**; 2nd Regt. Infan.
Giddings, James D.; pvt.; **B**; 2nd Regt. Infan.
Giddins, Robert C.; pvt.; **B**; 2nd Regt. Infan.
Giffin, Robert; pvt.; **B**; 1st Battalion Infan.
Gill, William; pvt.; **B**; 2nd Regt. Infan.
Gill, William E.; pvt.; **A/B**; 2nd Regt. Infan.
Gilleland, Samuel M.; pvt.; **A**; 1st Battalion Infan.
Gillian, William P.; cpl.; **K**; 1st Regt. Infan.
Gilliland, John G.; pvt.; **H**; 2nd Regt. Infan.
Gillis, John M.; pvt.; **D/G**; 2nd Regt. Infan.
Glass, Thomas C.; pvt.; **A**; 2nd Regt. Infan.
Glaze, William; pvt.; **A**; 1st Battalion Infan.
Glenn, John W.; pvt.; **I**; 1st Regt. Infan.
Glenning, Patrick; pvt.; **B**; 2nd Regt. Infan.
Godwin, Josiah H.; cpl.; **C**; 1st Regt. Infan.

Goforth, James L.; pvt., 2nd Sgt.; **E**; 2nd Regt. Infan.
Goode, George B.; pvt.; **A**; 1st Battalion Infan.
Goode, Obadiah; pvt.; **A**; 1st Battalion Infan.
Goodman, James M.; pvt.; **A**; 2nd Regt. Infan.
Goodman, Joseph; 2nd Sgt.; **A**; 2nd Regt. Infan.
Goodwin, Crawford; pvt.; **F**; 1st Regt. Infan.
Goodwin, George W.; pvt.; **F**; 1st Regt. Infan.
Googer, Martin; pvt.; **D**; 1st Battalion Infan.
Goos, Frederick; pvt.; **E**; 1st Battalion Infan.
Gordon, Charles R.; pvt.; **A**; 1st Regt. Infan.
Gordon, James J.; pvt.; **B**; 2nd Regt. Infan.
Gore, Ashford; pvt.; **E**; 1st Battalion Infan.
Gore, Rufus; pvt.; **D**; 2nd Regt. Infan.
Gorman, John; pvt.; **B**; 2nd Regt. Infan.
Goss, George H.; pvt.; **B/D**; 1st Battalion Infan.
Gossett, Barnett; pvt.; **F**; 2nd Regt. Infan.
Gotsel (Godsil ?), Patrick; pvt.; **I**; 2nd Regt. Infan.
Goubeneaux, Charles; 2nd Lieut.; **K**; 2nd Regt. Infan.
Gourley, Hugh; pvt.; **E**; 1st Regt. Infan.
Gourley, Milton F.; pvt.; **E**; 1st Regt. Infan.
Graham, James W.; pvt.; **Unknown**; 2nd Regt. Infan.
Graham, John; pvt.; **B**; 2nd Regt. Infan.
Grant, Alhaney; pvt.; **K**; 2nd Regt. Infan.
Grant, James; pvt.; **E**; 1st Battalion Infan.
Graves, James H.; pvt.; **G**; 1st Regt. Infan.
Graves, John C.; pvt.; **Unknown**; 2nd Regt. Infan.
Graves, Thomas Arlander   U.S. Army
Gray, George H.; pvt.; **C**; 1st Regt. Infan.
Gray, James; pvt.; **F**; 2nd Regt. Infan.
Gray, James W.; 2nd Sgt.; **E**; 2nd Regt. Infan.
Gray, John; pvt.; **D**; 2nd Regt. Infan.
Gray, Robert; pvt.; **A**; 2nd Regt. Infan.
Gray, William P.; pvt.; **D**; 1st Regt. Infan.
Greaves, Stephen Arne Decatur; 1st Lieut.; **G**; 1st Regt. Infan.
Green, F. G.; pvt.; **E**; 1st Regt. Infan.
Green, Girault; pvt.; **E**; 1st Regt. Infan.
Green, Luther D.; pvt.; **Unknown**; 2nd Regt. Infan.
Green, Richard; pvt.; **A**; 1st Regt. Infan.
Green, William B.; pvt.; **A/H**; 2nd Regt. Infan.
Greenlee, Francis M.; pvt.; **A**; 2nd Regt. Infan.
Greer, Elkanah Brackin; pvt.; **I**; 1st Regt. Infan.
Gregg, Robert; pvt.; **H**; 1st Regt. Infan.
Gregory, Alston; pvt., 2nd Lieut.; **B**; 2nd Regt. Infan.
Gregory, Edward H.; pvt.; **K**; 1st Regt. Infan.
Grey, J. W.; pvt.; **C**; 1st Regt. Infan.

Griffin, James T.; pvt.; **E**; 1st Regt. Infan. and **C**; 1st Battalion Infan.
Griffin, Mack; pvt.; **Unknown**; 2nd Regt. Infan.
Griffin, Robert Henderson; pvt.; **A**; 1st Regt. Infan.
Griffin, Thomas R.; pvt., cpl.; **A**; 1st Regt. Infan.
Griffin, William N.; cpl., lst Sgt.; **E**; 2nd Regt. Infan.
Griffis, Pleasant A.; pvt.; **K**; 2nd Regt. Infan.
Griffith, Peter O. D.; pvt.; **I**; 1st Regt. Infan.
Griffith, Richard; 2nd Lieut., Adjut.; **C/F&S**; 1st Regt. Infan.
Grimes, Caleb; pvt.; **A**; 1st Regt. Infan.
Grisham, Vincent S.; pvt., 4th cpl.; **G**; 1st Regt. Infan.
Grisham, William H.; pvt., 3rd cpl.; **I**; 1st Regt. Infan.
Grizzle, Wilson P.; pvt.; **D**; 2nd Regt. Infan.
Grogan, George J.; pvt.; **I**; 2nd Regt. Infan.
Grove, William; pvt.; **E**; 1st Battalion Infan.
Groves, Benjamin L.; pvt.; **H**; 1st Regt. Infan.
Groves, William A.; pvt.; **G**; 2nd Regt. Infan.
Grugett, Benjamin F.; pvt., 4th Sgt.; **K**; 1st Regt. Infan.
Guess, Walker; pvt.; **E**; 1st Battalion Infan.
Guest, Isaac N.; pvt.; **F**; 2nd Regt. Infan.
Guffee, Benjamin W.; pvt.; **I**; 2nd Regt. Infan.
Gunn, John B.; pvt.; **E**; 2nd Regt. Infan.
Gunnells, Joseph W.; pvt., 1st cpl.; **E**; 2nd Regt. Infan.
Gunter, William M.; pvt.; **D**; 1st Regt. Infan.
Guy, J. M.; pvt.; **C**; 1st Regt. Infan.
Guynes, Bryant F.; pvt.; **B**; 1st Battalion Infan.
Guynes, John; pvt.; **B**; 1st Battalion Infan.
Gwaltney, Leonidas; pvt.; **C**; 1st Battalion Infan.
Gwinn, James; mus.; **C**; 1st Regt. Infan.
Gynn, Chisley R.; pvt.; **F**; 2nd Regt. Infan.
Hackler, George H.; pvt.; **H**; 1st Regt. Infan.
Hackler, James; pvt.; **H**; 1st Regt. Infan.
Hackworth, Francis M.; 2nd Lieut.; **B**; 2nd Regt. Infan.
Hague, Sydney F.; pvt.; **A**; 1st Battalion Infan.
Hale, James M.; pvt.; **K**; 1st Regt. Infan.
Haley, Isaac N.; pvt.; **H**; 2nd Regt. Infan.
Hall, Harmon Y.; pvt.; **D**; 1st Regt. Infan.
Hall, James; pvt.; **F**; 2nd Regt. Infan.
Hall, James T.; pvt.; **A**; 1st Battalion Infan.
Hall, John; pvt.; **I**; 2nd Regt. Infan.
Hall, John A.; pvt.; **K**; 2nd Regt. Infan.
Hall, Samuel S.; pvt.; **I**; 1st Regt. Infan.
Hall, William A.; pvt.; **E**; 1st Battalion Infan.
Hall, William C.; pvt.; **C**; 2nd Regt. Infan.
Halsey, Seymour; Surgeon; **F&S**; 1st Regt. Infan.
Hamilton, Alexander S.; pvt., 1st Sgt., 2nd Lieut.; **D**; 2nd Regt. Infan.

Hamilton, Archibald; pvt., cpl.; **A**; 2nd Regt. Infan.

Hamilton, Henry T.; pvt.; **A**; 2nd Regt. Infan.

Hamilton, Wiley; pvt.; **I**; 1st Regt. Infan.

Hamilton, William C.; pvt.; **K**; 2nd Regt. Infan.

Hammond, Job; pvt.; **G**; 1st Regt. Infan.

Hampton, Thomas H.; pvt.; **B**; 1st Regt. Infan.

Hampton, William Henry; 2nd Lieut.; **G**; 1st Regt. Infan.

Hancher, John; pvt.; **C**; 2nd Regt. Infan.

Hancock, George W.; pvt., 3rd cpl.; **C**; 1st Battalion Infan.

Hancock, John A. G.; pvt.; **F**; 1st Regt. Infan.

Hanks, Marion; pvt.; **D**; 1st Regt. Infan.

Hanks, Talliaferro; pvt.; **D**; 1st Regt. Infan.

Harden, Nicholas; pvt.; **D**; 2nd Regt. Infan.

Hardin, Green B.; pvt.; **E**; 1st Battalion Infan.

Hare, Martin; pvt.; **H**; 2nd Regt. Infan.

Harlan, Charles T.; 2nd Sgt., Sgt.-Maj.; **H/F&S**; 1st Regt. Infan.

Harlan, Columbus C.; pvt.; **E**; 2nd Regt. Infan.

Harlan, Dutton S.; pvt.; **E**; 2nd Regt. Infan.

Harley, Thomas; pvt.; **I/K**; 2nd Regt. Infan.

Harman, Theodore E.; pvt.; **A/G**; 2nd Regt. Infan.

Harper, John R.; pvt.; **D**; 1st Regt. Infan.

Harper, William B.; pvt.; **H**; 2nd Regt. Infan.

Harper, William E.; 3rd cpl.; **F**; 2nd Regt. Infan.

Harrell, Jesse M.; pvt., 2nd cpl.; **C**; 1st Battalion Infan.

Harrell, Wells C.; pvt., 1st Sgt.; **D**; 1st Regt. Infan.

Harris, Daniel C.; pvt.; **D**; 1st Battalion Infan.

Harris, David B.; pvt.; **B**; 1st Regt. Infan.

Harris, John A.; pvt.; **H**; 1st Regt. Infan.

Harris, Lewis B.; pvt., 3rd, 2nd, 1st cpl., Sgt.; **K**; 2nd Regt. Infan.

Harris, William E.; pvt.; **C**; 1st Regt. Infan.

Harris, William H.; 1st Sgt., 1st Lieut.; **E**; 2nd Regt. Infan.

Harrison, Aaron; pvt.; **A**; 2nd Regt. Infan.

Harrison, George W.; 3rd, 2nd cpl.; **G**; 1st Regt. Infan.

Harrison, Hilry; pvt.; **I**; 2nd Regt. Infan.

Harrison, John; pvt.; **E**; 1st Regt. Infan.

Harrison, Samuel R.; pvt., Bvt. 2nd Lieut.; **B**; 1st Regt. Infan.

Harrison, Thomas; pvt.; **K**; 1st Regt. Infan.

Harrison, William D. F.; pvt.; **H**; 1st Regt. Infan.

Harrison, William H.; pvt.; **E**; 1st Battalion Infan.

Harrison, William K.; pvt., 4th Sgt.; **D**; 2nd Regt. Infan.

Harrod, John; pvt.; **C**; 1st Regt. Infan.

Hart, Dominick; pvt.; **G**; 2nd Regt. Infan.

Hart, Jesse D.; pvt.; **C**; 2nd Regt. Infan.

Hart, Meredith; pvt.; **A**; 1st Regt. Infan.

Hartley, A.; pvt.; **C**; 1st Regt. Infan.

Hartman, John W.; mus.; **K**; 1st Regt. Infan.

Harvey, John W.; pvt.; **D**; 2nd Regt. Infan.

Harvey, William H.; pvt.; **H**; 1st Regt. Infan.

Hasty, William H.; pvt.; **E**; 1st Regt. Infan.

Hatton, Benjamin; pvt.; **H**; 1st Regt. Infan.

Hawkins, John L.; pvt.; **A**; 1st Battalion Infan.

Hayes, Garland H.; 2nd cpl.; **A**; 1st Battalion Infan.

Haynes, Granville O.; pvt., 2nd cpl.; **C**; 1st Battalion Infan.

Hays, A. J.; Lieut.; U.S.M.C.

Hays, Henry; pvt.; **B**; 2nd Regt. Infan.

Hays, James C.; 3rd Sgt.; **G**; 1st Regt. Infan.

Hays, James C.; 3rd, 2nd Sgt.; **K**; 2nd Regt. Infan.

Hays, Matthew; pvt.; **G**; 2nd Regt. Infan.

Hays, May; pvt.; **G**; 1st Regt. Infan.

Hazlewood, Calvin T.; pvt.; **A**; 1st Battalion Infan.

Hearn, Madison H.; pvt.; **A**; 1st Battalion Infan.

Hearn, William C.; pvt., 1st cpl., Sgt.; **C**; 2nd Regt. Infan.

Heath, J. B.; pvt.; **D**; 1st Regt. Infan.

Heaton, Joseph; pvt.; **I**; 1st Regt. Infan.

Heaton, Robert H.; pvt.; **C**; 2nd Regt. Infan.

Heckler, John M.; pvt.; **E**; 1st Regt. Infan.

Heiston, James P.; pvt.; **C**; 1st Battalion Infan.

Hemby, William R.; pvt.; **C**; 1st Regt. Infan.

Henderson, James A.; pvt.; **F**; 1st Regt. Infan.

Henderson, John H.; pvt.; **E**; 2nd Regt. Infan.

Henderson, John L.; pvt.; **I**; 1st Regt. Infan.

Henderson, Thomas W.; pvt.; **E**; 2nd Regt. Infan.

Hendricks, Jeremiah; pvt.; **A**; 2nd Regt. Infan.

Hendrix, Reuben; pvt.; **A**; 1st Battalion Infan.

Henry, Eli G.; 2nd, 1st Lieut.; **H**; 2nd Regt. Infan.

Henry, Ely I.; pvt.; **K**; 1st Regt. Infan.

Henry, James W.; pvt.; **I**; 2nd Regt. Infan.

Henry, Mathew M.; pvt.; **H**; 2nd Regt. Infan.

Henry, Robert A.; cpl., 2nd Sgt.; **B**; 2nd Regt. Infan.

Henry, Rufus; pvt.; **F**; 1st Regt. Infan.

Henry, Sidney; pvt.; **B**; 2nd Regt. Infan.

Henry, Timothy K.; pvt.; **D**; 2nd Regt. Infan.

Herald, William; pvt.; **A**; 1st Battalion Infan.

Herbert, John Q.; pvt.; **B**; 1st Regt. Infan.

Herring, Stephen G.; pvt.; **A**; 1st Battalion Infan.

Herrod, Andrew J.; pvt.; **A**; 1st Regt. Infan.

Heslip, James O.; pvt., 1st cpl.; **C**; 2nd Regt. Infan.

Hewitt, Edgar; pvt.; **G**; 2nd Regt. Infan.

Hewitt, John; pvt.; **A**; 1st Battalion Infan.

Hibble, Jacob; pvt.; **K**; 2nd Regt. Infan.

Hickey, William V.; cpl., 3rd Sgt.; **C**; 1st Regt. Infan.
Hicks, Joseph W.; pvt.; **C**; 1st Battalion Infan.
Hicks, Moses; pvt.; **A**; 1st Battalion Infan.
Higdon, Alexander; pvt.; **C**; 2nd Regt. Infan.
Higdon, James; pvt.; **E**; 1st Regt. Infan.
Higdon, Russell Benjamin; pvt.; **G**; 2nd Regt. Infan.
Higgason, John D.; pvt.; **K**; 1st Regt. Infan.
Higginbotham, Thomas T.; pvt., cpl., Sgt.; **A**; 1st Regt. Infan.
Higginbottom, Ransom C.; pvt.; **F**; 1st Regt. Infan.
Hight, Thomas B.; 1st cpl., Sgt.; **H**; 2nd Regt. Infan.
Hill, Albert P.; 2nd, 1st Sgt.; **A**; 1st Regt. Infan.
Hill, James; pvt.; **B**; 1st Regt. Infan.
Hill, John H.; pvt.; **Unknown**; 2nd Regt. Infan.
Hill, John W.; pvt.; **B**; 2nd Regt. Infan.
Hill, John W.; pvt.; **C**; 2nd Regt. Infan.
Hill, Richard; pvt.; **I**; 2nd Regt. Infan.
Hill, Richard H.; pvt.; **C**; 2nd Regt. Infan.
Hill, Sanford H.; pvt.; **H**; 1st Regt. Infan.
Hilliard, John C.; pvt.; **B**; 2nd Regt. Infan.
Hilliard, Thomas; pvt.; **Unknown**; 2nd Regt. Infan.
Hilton, Carl; pvt.; **I**; 2nd Regt. Infan.
Hindman, Robert Holt; pvt., 2nd Sgt.; **E**; 2nd Regt. Infan.
Hindman, Samuel; pvt.; **C**; 1st Regt. Infan.
Hindman, Thomas Carmichael; 2nd Lieut.; **E**; 2nd Regt. Infan.
Hindsley, John J.; pvt.; **K**; 1st Regt. Infan.
Hines, John; pvt.; **E**; 2nd Regt. Infan.
Hinkley, Henry; pvt.; **G**; 2nd Regt. Infan.
Hinton, William; pvt.; **D**; 2nd Regt. Infan.
Hipple, Henry; pvt.; **E**; 1st Regt. Infan.
Hise, George W.; pvt.; **H**; 1st Regt. Infan.
Hobbs, Calvin; mus. (Fifer), pvt.; **E**; 1st Regt. Infan. and **B**;
        1st Battalion Infan.
Hobbs, J. P.; 2nd cpl.; **F**; 1st Regt. Infan.
Hobbs, John S.; **Unknown**; 1st Battalion Infan.
Hobbs, William; pvt.; **I**; 1st Regt. Infan.
Hoburg, Edward G.; pvt.; **A**; 2nd Regt. Infan.
Hodge, Benjamin Louis; pvt., 2nd Lieut.; **D**; 1st Regt. Infan.
Hodge, Francis; pvt.; **H**; 2nd Regt. Infan.
Hodge, James; 2nd Sgt.; **C**; 1st Battalion Infan.
Hodge, James L.; pvt.; **B**; 1st Regt. Infan.
Hodge, William I.; pvt., 3rd cpl.; **B**; 1st Regt. Infan.
Hodnett, Thomas; pvt.; **I**; 2nd Regt. Infan.
Hogan, Timothy; pvt.; **K**; 2nd Regt. Infan.
Hoggany, Benjamin; 2nd Sgt.; **F**; 1st Regt. Infan.
Hoggatt, John; pvt.; **A**; 1st Battalion Infan.

Holcomb, J.; pvt.; **F**; 1st Regt. Infan.

Holden, William E.; pvt.; **B**; 2nd Regt. Infan.

Holdway, Howard DeCalb; pvt.; **I**; 1st Regt. Infan.

Holland, Charles; pvt.; **C**; 2nd Regt. Infan.

Holland, John M. M.; 1st Sgt.; **I**; 1st Regt. Infan.

Holland, Kemp S.; Assist.-Com., Capt.; **A/F&S**; 1st Regt. Infan.

Holland, William H.; pvt.; **C**; 2nd Regt. Infan.

Holland, William T.; pvt.; **Unknown**; 2nd Regt. Infan.

Hollingshead, Samuel B.; pvt.; **A**; 2nd Regt. Infan.

Hollingsworth, David M.; mus., 1st Sgt.; **A**; 1st Regt. Infan.

Hollingsworth, E.; pvt., 1st cpl., 2nd Sgt., 2nd Lieut.; **D**; 1st Regt. Infan.

Holloway, Lewis M.; pvt.; **C**; 1st Battalion Infan.

Hollowell, Edwin O.; pvt.; **B**; 2nd Regt. Infan.

Holmead, John; pvt., cpl.; **I**; 2nd Regt. Infan.

Holt, John Saunders; pvt. (Interpreter); **B**; 1st Regt. Infan.

Holt, John T.; pvt., cpl., 4th Sgt.; **B**; 1st Regt. Infan.

Holt, Josiah; pvt.; **C**; 1st Battalion Infan.

Holt, William; pvt.; **F**; 1st Regt. Infan.

Holtzhopfer, Jacob; pvt.; **K**; 2nd Regt. Infan.

Homer, George W.; pvt.; **D**; 2nd Regt. Infan.

Hood, Parker; pvt.; **D**; 1st Regt. Infan.

Hooker, John M.; pvt.; **E**; 1st Regt. Infan.

Hope, John S.; pvt.; **A/B**; 2nd Regt. Infan.

Hope, William Gready; pvt.; **B**; 1st Regt. Infan.

Hopkins, Richard; pvt., 2nd Lieut.; **H**; 1st Regt. Infan.

Hopper, Joseph W.; pvt.; **E**; 1st Battalion Infan.

Horn, Edward G.; pvt.; **B**; 1st Battalion Infan.

Horton, William; pvt.; **D**; 2nd Regt. Infan.

Hoskins, William H.; pvt.; **I**; 1st Regt. Infan.

Hous, Jesse B.; pvt.; **B**; 1st Battalion Infan.

Hovas, Christopher; 4th Sgt.; **H**; 2nd Regt. Infan.

Hovis, Adoniram J.; pvt.; **E**; 2nd Regt. Infan.

Howard, Bainbridge D.; Capt.; **D**; 1st Regt. Infan.

Howard, Calvin; pvt.; **C**; 1st Battalion Infan.

Howard, Cary; pvt.; **E**; 2nd Regt. Infan.

Howard, Harrison L.; pvt.; **K**; 1st Regt. Infan.

Howard, John; mus. (Drummer), pvt.; **K**; 2nd Regt. Infan.

Howard, Lewis T.; 2nd Lieut.; **D**; 1st Regt. Infan.

Howell, Benjamin L.; 1st cpl., 1st Sgt.; **D**; 2nd Regt. Infan.

Howell, James E.; pvt.; **Unknown**; 2nd Regt. Infan.

Howell, Joseph D.; pvt.; **C**; 1st Regt. Infan.

Hoyle, Solomon H.; pvt.; **E**; 1st Battalion Infan.

Hubbard, Napoleon W.; 4th cpl.; **K**; 2nd Regt. Infan.

Huddleston, James; Sgt.; **A**; 2nd Regt. Infan.

Hudgins, John; pvt.; **I**; 2nd Regt. Infan.

Hudson, Alfred; pvt.; **D**; 1st Regt. Infan.
Hudson, Nathaniel M.; pvt.; **D**; 1st Battalion Infan.
Hudspeth, John; pvt.; **I**; 1st Regt. Infan.
Huffman, Warren; pvt.; **D**; 1st Regt. Infan.
Hughes, Archibald M.; 2nd Sgt.; **E**; 1st Regt. Infan.
Hughes, Daniel; pvt.; **A**; 1st Regt. Infan.
Hughes, James H.; 2nd Lieut.; **E**; 1st Regt. Infan.
Hughes, Joseph A.; pvt.; **I**; 1st Regt. Infan.
Hulbert, Harris M.; 4th, 3rd Sgt.; **G**; 2nd Regt. Infan.
Hulsey, Joab A.; pvt.; **D**; 1st Battalion Infan.
Humber, John; pvt.; **E**; 1st Battalion Infan.
Humphreys, David W.; 1st Sgt.; **I**; 2nd Regt. Infan.
Humphries, David; pvt.; **E**; 2nd Regt. Infan.
Humphries, W. R.; pvt.; **F**; 1st Regt. Infan.
Hunt, Benjamin B.; pvt., 2nd cpl.; **F**; 2nd Regt. Infan.
Hunt, George; pvt.; **K**; 1st Regt. Infan.
Hunt, Thomas M.; mus., pvt.; **E**; 1st Battalion Infan.
Hunter, J. W.; pvt.; **E**; 1st Regt. Infan.
Hunter, Robert H.; mus., pvt., Aide; **I**; 2nd Regt. Infan.
Hunter, Samuel; 2nd Lieut.; **D**; 1st Battalion Infan.
Hunter, Stephen D.; pvt.; **F**; 1st Regt. Infan.
Hutchins, Nathan; pvt.; **F**; 2nd Regt. Infan.
Hutchins, William; pvt.; **B**; 2nd Regt. Infan.
Hutchinson, Irenius R.; pvt.; **B**; 1st Regt. Infan.
Hutchinson, William F.; pvt.; **A/G**; 1st Regt. Infan.
Hutten, William C.; pvt.; **A**; 1st Battalion Infan.
Hyneman, Henry C.; pvt.; **E**; 2nd Regt. Infan.
Ijams, Wilson; 2nd Lieut., Capt.; **B**; 2nd Regt. Infan.
Inabnet, William A.; pvt.; **C**; 1st Battalion Infan.
Ingole, Peter; pvt.; **H**; 2nd Regt. Infan.
Ingram, Henry D.; pvt.; **D**; 1st Battalion Infan.
Ingram, Newton; pvt.; **G**; 1st Regt. Infan.
Ingram, William W.; pvt., cpl., 3rd Sgt.; **A**; 1st Regt. Infan.
Irvin, David; pvt.; **D**; 2nd Regt. Infan.
Irvin, William; pvt.; **D**; 2nd Regt. Infan.
Irvine, Francis M.; pvt.; **D**; 2nd Regt. Infan.
Irvine, James; pvt.; **C**; 1st Regt. Infan.
Irvine, Tillmon J.; pvt.; **D**; 2nd Regt. Infan.
Irwin, Hugh L.; pvt.; **B**; 1st Battalion Infan.
Irwin, William T.; pvt.; **A**; 2nd Regt. Infan.
Ivy, Myrick; pvt.; **H**; 2nd Regt. Infan.
Ivy, Thomas; 2nd Lieut.; **A**; 1st Battalion Infan.
Ivy, Washington P.; pvt.; **A**; 1st Battalion Infan.
Jackson, Alexander Melvourne; Capt.; **E**; 2nd Regt. Infan.
Jackson, Andrew; pvt.; **I**; 2nd Regt. Infan.

Jackson, Daniel M.; pvt., 2nd Lieut.; **H**; 2nd Regt. Infan.
Jackson, Daniel N.; pvt.; **E**; 2nd Regt. Infan.
Jackson, George W.; pvt.; **E**; 2nd Regt. Infan.
Jackson, J. H.; pvt.; **B**; 1st Regt. Infan.
Jackson, Jasper; pvt.; **H**; 2nd Regt. Infan.
Jackson, John A.; 2nd Sgt., 2nd Lieut.; **H**; 2nd Regt. Infan.
Jackson, John W.; pvt.; **H**; 2nd Regt. Infan.
Jackson, William H.; 2nd Lieut.; **E**; 2nd Regt. Infan.
Jackson, William M.; pvt.; **E**; 2nd Regt. Infan.
James, Andrew J.; pvt., cpl.; **E**; 2nd Regt. Infan.
Jean, Thomas D.; pvt.; **C**; 1st Battalion Infan.
Jefferson, David W.; pvt.; **D**; 1st Regt. Infan.
Jenkins, Allen B.; pvt.; **B**; 1st Battalion Infan.
Jenkins, Carodine; pvt.; **A**; 1st Battalion Infan.
Jennings, John; pvt., 4th, 2nd cpl.; **K**; 2nd Regt. Infan.
Jeter, John; pvt.; **C**; 1st Regt. Infan.
Jimerson, David Reed; pvt.; **F**; 1st Regt. Infan.
Jobe, David M.; pvt.; **Unknown**; 2nd Regt. Infan.
Johns, Abijah; pvt.; **G**; 2nd Regt. Infan.
Johnson, Albert; pvt., teamster; **A**; 1st Regt. Infan.
Johnson, Blake; pvt.; **A**; 2nd Regt. Infan.
Johnson, Daniel B.; pvt.; **G**; 1st Regt. Infan.
Johnson, Duncan B.; pvt.; **E**; 2nd Regt. Infan.
Johnson, Ewing C.; pvt.; **E**; 1st Battalion Infan.
Johnson, James; pvt.; **C**; 1st Regt. Infan.
Johnson, James; pvt.; **D**; 1st Regt. Infan.
Johnson, James S.; pvt., 3rd, 2nd Sgt.; **C**; 2nd Regt. Infan.
Johnson, James T.; pvt.; **F**; 2nd Regt. Infan.
Johnson, John; pvt.; **A**; 1st Regt. Infan.
Johnson, Laban J.; pvt.; **G**; 2nd Regt. Infan.
Johnson, Nathaniel; pvt.; **K**; 1st Regt. Infan.
Johnson, Peter W.; pvt.; **C**; 1st Regt. Infan.
Johnson, Robert; pvt.; **A**; 2nd Regt. Infan.
Johnson, Sugan L.; pvt.; **K**; 2nd Regt. Infan.
Johnson, Wiley B.; pvt., 1st cpl.; **F**; 2nd Regt. Infan.
Johnson, William; pvt.; **H**; 2nd Regt. Infan.
Johnson, William F.; pvt.; **A**; 1st Battalion Infan.
Johnson, William R.; pvt.; **D**; 1st Battalion Infan.
Johnston, Isaac S.; pvt.; **H**; 1st Regt. Infan.
Joiner, Benjamin; pvt.; **F**; 1st Regt. Infan.
Joiner, William D.; 2nd Sgt.; **F**; 2nd Regt. Infan.
Joiner, William R.; pvt.; **E**; 1st Battalion Infan.
Jolly, Meridian; pvt.; **I**; 1st Regt. Infan.
Jones, David A.; pvt.; **G**; 1st Regt. Infan.
Jones, Francis A.; pvt.; **I**; 2nd Regt. Infan.

Jones, George H.; pvt.; **B**; 1st Regt. Infan.
Jones, James; pvt.; **F**; 2nd Regt. Infan.
Jones, James L.; pvt.; **C**; 2nd Regt. Infan.
Jones, John; pvt.; **F**; 2nd Regt. Infan.
Jones, John C.; pvt.; **C**; 1st Battalion Infan.
Jones, John L.; 2nd cpl.; **E**; 1st Battalion Infan.
Jones, Miles T.; pvt.; **A**; 2nd Regt. Infan.
Jones, Owen W.; pvt.; **D**; 1st Regt. Infan.
Jones, Richard D.; pvt.; **Unknown**; 2nd Regt. Infan.
Jones, Robert; pvt.; **C**; 2nd Regt. Infan.
Jones, Seaborne; pvt.; **B**; 1st Regt. Infan.
Jones, Stephen; pvt.; **F**; 1st Regt. Infan.
Jones, Stephen; pvt.; **E**; 2nd Regt. Infan.
Jones, Thomas L.; pvt.; **F**; 1st Regt. Infan.
Jones, Thomas L.; 2nd cpl.; **K**; 1st Regt. Infan.
Jones, William; pvt.; **B**; 1st Battalion Infan.
Jones, William H.; mus. (Drummer), pvt.; **D/F**; 1st Regt. Infan.
Jordan, Alfred; pvt.; **B**; 2nd Regt. Infan.
Josselyn, Robert; pvt.; **I**; 1st Regt. Infan.
Joyce, Robert A.; pvt.; **E**; 1st Regt. Infan.
Julian, William R.; 2nd cpl., Sgt.; **K**; 1st Regt. Infan.
Justice, Wallace; pvt.; **H**; 2nd Regt. Infan.
Kavanaugh, William W.; pvt.; **E**; 2nd Regt. Infan.
Kearsey, John J.; pvt.; **B**; 1st Regt. Infan.
Keegan, John; 3rd, 2nd, 1st Sgt.; **K**; 2nd Regt. Infan.
Keeling, David H.; pvt.; **I**; 1st Regt. Infan.
Keep, Henry V.; pvt.; **E**; 1st Regt. Infan.
Keith, Miller D.; pvt.; **Unknown**; 2nd Regt. Infan.
Kellebrew, Henry B.; 2nd cpl., 4th Sgt.; **I**; 2nd Regt. Infan.
Kelley, William H.; pvt.; **K**; 1st Regt. Infan.
Kelly, Zachariah; Prin. Mus.; **G**; 2nd Regt. Infan.
Kenna, Henry R.; pvt.; **A**; 1st Regt. Infan.
Kennedy, John; pvt.; **E**; 1st Regt. Infan.
Kennedy, William G.; 3rd cpl.; **D**; 1st Battalion Infan.
Kenner, Daniel F.; pvt.; **G**; 1st Regt. Infan.
Kenny, William; pvt.; **E**; 1st Regt. Infan.
Kercheval, Rufus; 3rd cpl.; **E**; 1st Battalion Infan.
Kern, William P.; pvt.; **B**; 1st Battalion Infan.
Kerr, Argyle A.; pvt., cpl.; **K**; 1st Regt. Infan.
Kerr, Jerome B.; pvt.; **I**; 1st Regt. Infan.
Kewen, Thomas; pvt., Sgt.; **A**; 2nd Regt. Infan.
Kewen, Thomas L.; pvt.; **K**; 1st Regt. Infan.
Kewer, I. W.; pvt.; **I**; 2nd Regt. Infan.
Key, Albert M.; pvt.; **G**; 1st Regt. Infan.
Keyes, William McCord; Capt.; **A**; 1st Battalion Infan.

Keywood, John T.; pvt.; **I**; 2nd Regt. Infan.
Keywood, Lockhart; pvt.; **I**; 2nd Regt. Infan.
Kilgore, Benjamin M.; 4th cpl.; **A**; 1st Battalion Infan.
Kilgore, Josiah G.; pvt.; **A**; 1st Battalion Infan.
Kilpatrick, Joseph H.; Capt., Lieut.-Col.; **B/F&S**; 2nd Regt. Infan.
Kilvey, James H.; pvt.; **E**; 1st Regt. Infan.
Kincaid, John M.; pvt.; **I**; 1st Regt. Infan.
Kincannon, James L.; pvt.; **A**; 2nd Regt. Infan.
Kinchloe, David Anderson; Asst. Surgeon; **I/F&S**; 2nd Regt. Infan.
King, Andrew J.; pvt.; **K**; 1st Regt. Infan.
King, Elias; pvt.; **K**; 2nd Regt. Infan.
King, Leonidas W.; pvt.; **A**; 2nd Regt. Infan.
King, Richard S.; lst Lieut.; **C**; 1st Battalion Infan.
King, Robert; 4th, 3rd, 2nd cpl., 4th Sgt.; **K**; 2nd Regt. Infan.
King, Thomas; pvt.; **I**; 2nd Regt. Infan.
King, Thomas; pvt.; **K**; 2nd Regt. Infan.
Kinnest, William; pvt.; **K**; 1st Regt. Infan.
Kinnis, Edward; pvt.; **K**; 1st Regt. Infan.
Kirk, J. W.; pvt.; **A**; 1st Regt. Infan.
Kirkland, Daniel; pvt.; **A**; 2nd Regt. Infan.
Kirkland, Oliver P.; pvt.; **A**; 2nd Regt. Infan.
Kirkland, Uriah; pvt.; **K**; 2nd Regt. Infan.
Kitchens, William; pvt.; **A**; 1st Battalion Infan.
Kittrell, Alexander; pvt.; **H**; 2nd Regt. Infan.
Knapp, David L.; pvt.; **G**; 2nd Regt. Infan.
Knapp, John; pvt.; **A**; 2nd Regt. Infan.
Knieff, Francis A.; pvt.; **A**; 1st Battalion Infan.
Knight, Abel E.; 1st cpl.; **C**; 2nd Regt. Infan.
Knight, Absolem; pvt.; **F**; 1st Regt. Infan.
Knight, Elijah; pvt.; **A**; 2nd Regt. Infan.
Knight, James K.; pvt.; **A**; 2nd Regt. Infan.
Knight, Raleigh J.; pvt.; **A**; 2nd Regt. Infan.
Knott, Elijah; pvt.; **C**; 1st Battalion Infan.
Krah, Elias E.; pvt.; **E**; 1st Battalion Infan.
Kremer, Andrew; pvt.; **H**; 1st Regt. Infan.
Kyle, J.; pvt.; **B**; 1st Regt. Infan.
Kyle, Joseph P.; pvt.; **E**; 1st Battalion Infan.
Kyle, Thomas J.; 2nd cpl., 2nd Sgt., 2nd Lieut.; **D**; 1st Regt. Infan.
Lackings, Benjamin; pvt.; **G**; 2nd Regt. Infan.
Lacy, Beverly M.; pvt.; **D**; 1st Battalion Infan.
Laird, Eli; pvt.; **F**; 2nd Regt. Infan.
Laird, George W.; pvt., cpl.; **E**; 1st Regt. Infan.
Laird, Hiram; pvt.; **F**; 2nd Regt. Infan.
Laird, Isham C.; pvt.; **E**; 1st Regt. Infan.
Laird, William D.; lst Lieut.; **F**; 2nd Regt. Infan.

Lairy, Jeremiah E.; pvt.; **E**; 1st Regt. Infan.
Lamb, Samuel; pvt.; **F**; 2nd Regt. Infan.
Lambertson, Henry; pvt.; **I**; 2nd Regt. Infan.
Lambright, George T.; pvt.; **I**; 2nd Regt. Infan.
Lamen, Felix G.; pvt.; **I**; 1st Regt. Infan.
Landers, William H.; 1st Lieut.; **B**; 1st Battalion Infan.
Landrum, Dyonisius; pvt.; **H**; 2nd Regt. Infan.
Lane (Lain), James H.; pvt., Sgt.; **D**; 2nd Regt. Infan.
Lane, Josiah; pvt.; **B**; 2nd Regt. Infan.
Lane, Samuel W.; pvt., 2nd cpl.; **E**; 1st Regt. Infan.
Lanehart, A. C.; pvt.; **B**; 1st Regt. Infan.
Lanehart, Adam; pvt.; **B**; 1st Regt. Infan.
Langford, Joseph H.; 4th Sgt.; **E**; 1st Regt. Infan.
Langford, William R.; 3rd cpl.; **E**; 1st Regt. Infan.
Langley, Samuel; pvt.; **C**; 1st Battalion Infan.
Langley, William H.; pvt.; **B**; 2nd Regt. Infan.
Langston, James; pvt.; **I**; 1st Regt. Infan.
Lanham, John M.; pvt.; **A**; 1st Battalion Infan.
Lanter, Thomas C.; pvt.; **I**; 2nd Regt. Infan.
Latham, Richard; pvt.; **E**; 1st Regt. Infan.
Lauderdale, William C.; 2nd Lieut.; **A**; 2nd Regt. Infan.
Lauell, Henry H.; pvt., cpl.; **H**; 1st Regt. Infan.
Laughter, George A.; pvt., cpl.; **H**; 2nd Regt. Infan.
Lavender, Solomon D.; pvt.; **A**; 1st Regt. Infan.
Law, Thomas H.; mus. (Drummer); **B**; 1st Regt. Infan.
Lawhon, John; pvt.; **K**; 1st Regt. Infan.
Lawrence, William A.; pvt.; **B**; 1st Regt. Infan.
Lawson, Charles; pvt.; **F**; 1st Regt. Infan.
Layden, James; pvt.; **B**; 2nd Regt. Infan.
Layne, William H.; 3rd Sgt.; **B**; 2nd Regt. Infan.
Leach, John R.; pvt.; **F**; 2nd Regt. Infan.
Leake, Charles Austin; pvt.; **A**; 1st Regt. Infan.
Leard, David E.; pvt.; **H**; 2nd Regt. Infan.
Leath, James; pvt.; **E**; 2nd Regt. Infan.
Leatherwood, Spencer; pvt.; **E**; 1st Battalion Infan.
Lee, James M.; pvt.; **A**; 2nd Regt. Infan.
Lee, Patrick; pvt.; **I**; 2nd Regt. Infan.
Lee, Patrick; pvt., 4th, 3rd cpl.; **I**; 1st Regt. Infan.
Leland, Columbus M.; 1st Lieut.; **D**; 1st Battalion Infan.
Leland, Stephen D.; pvt.; **D**; 1st Battalion Infan.
Lemaster, James R.; pvt.; **C**; 2nd Regt. Infan.
Lemaster, John; cpl.; **B**; 2nd Regt. Infan.
Lemay, John P.; pvt.; **I**; 1st Regt. Infan.
Lemay, Lewis A.; pvt.; **B**; 2nd Regt. Infan.
Lenoir, Whitman; pvt.; **K**; 2nd Regt. Infan.

LeSueur, Charles Marion; 2nd Lieut.; **B**; 2nd Regt. Infan.

Lesley, Andrew J.; pvt.; **E**; 2nd Regt. Infan.

Leunex, James; pvt.; **B**; 1st Regt. Infan.

Leverett, Jeremiah G.; pvt.; **A**; 2nd Regt. Infan.

Levy, Samuel H.; pvt.; **E**; 1st Battalion Infan.

Lewers, Charles A.; pvt.; **F**; 1st Regt. Infan.

Lewis, Alfred; pvt.; **C**; 1st Battalion Infan.

Lewis, Charles; pvt.; **C**; 2nd Regt. Infan.

Lewis, Daniel B.; pvt.; **K**; 1st Regt. Infan.

Lewis, Edward B.; pvt.; **K**; 1st Regt. Infan.

Lewis, Henry; pvt., 3rd, 2nd Sgt.; **C**; 1st Battalion Infan.

Lewis, Robert A.; pvt., cpl., 3rd Sgt.; **D**; 1st Regt. Infan.

Lewis, William; pvt.; **C**; 2nd Regt. Infan.

Liddell, Charles J.; pvt.; **C**; 2nd Regt. Infan.

Liddell, James M.; cpl., 2nd Lieut.; **C**; 2nd Regt. Infan.

Liddell, Phillip Franklin; 2nd Lieut., Capt.; **C**; 2nd Regt. Infan.

Liles, Alfred M.; pvt.; **F**; 1st Regt. Infan.

Liles, Richard; pvt.; **E**; 2nd Regt. Infan.

Lilly, John A.; 3rd Sgt.; **D**; 1st Battalion Infan.

Linder, Uriah; pvt.; **B**; 1st Battalion Infan.

Lindsey, Hugh N.; pvt.; **B**; 1st Regt. Infan.

Lindsey, William G.; mus., pvt.; **G**; 1st Regt. Infan.

Linsey, Moses; pvt.; **G**; 2nd Regt. Infan.

Lipscomb, George Hardwick; pvt., cpl., Q.M.S., Q.M..; **A**; 2nd Regt. Infan.

Lipsey, Ansylum G.; pvt.; **C**; 1st Battalion Infan.

Little, Henry S.; pvt.; **A**; 1st Regt. Infan.

Livesay, Cornelius; pvt.; **D**; 2nd Regt. Infan.

Livingston, G. H.; pvt.; **F**; 1st Regt. Infan.

Livingston, George H.; pvt., 1st Sgt.; **A/C**; 1st Battalion Infan.

Livingston, John; mus.; **F**; 1st Regt. Infan.

Locke, J. J.; pvt.; **H**; 1st Regt. Infan.

Locke, Matthew F.; pvt., cpl.; **F**; 1st Regt. Infan.

Locker, Andrew J.; pvt.; **E**; 2nd Regt. Infan.

Locker, Thomas B.; pvt.; **E**; 2nd Regt. Infan.

Logan, Andrew L.; pvt.; **D**; 2nd Regt. Infan.

Logan, William P.; pvt.; **H**; 2nd Regt. Infan.

Loghary, John; pvt.; **I**; 2nd Regt. Infan.

Long, Alfred V.; pvt.; **C**; 2nd Regt. Infan.

Long, John; pvt., 2nd Sgt.; **I**; 1st Regt. Infan.

Long, John C.; pvt.; **G**; 2nd Regt. Infan.

Longstreet, William D.; pvt.; **K**; 1st Regt. Infan.

Lopeman, Dennis; pvt.; **D**; 1st Battalion Infan.

Lott, William; pvt.; **D**; 1st Regt. Infan.

Lott, William H.; 2nd, 1st cpl., 4th Sgt.; **K**; 2nd Regt. Infan.

Love, Alfred L.; pvt.; **G**; 2nd Regt. Infan.

Love, David E.; 3rd Sgt.; **D**; 1st Regt. Infan.
Love, Thomas L.; pvt.; **A**; 2nd Regt. Infan.
Love, Thomas Neely; Surgeon; **A/F&S**; 2nd Regt. Infan.
Lowe, Frederick; pvt.; **H**; 2nd Regt. Infan.
Lowe, John C.; pvt.; **F**; 1st Regt. Infan.
Lowe, Thomas; pvt.; **B**; 2nd Regt. Infan.
Lowe, Luke; 2nd Lieut.; **B**; 1st Battalion Infan.
Lowe, William; pvt.; **E**; 1st Regt. Infan.
Lowery, Jefferson R.; pvt.; **D**; 2nd Regt. Infan.
Lowrey, John J.; pvt.; **B**; 1st Battalion Infan.
Lowrey, Mark Perrin; pvt.; **E**; 2nd Regt. Infan.
Lowry, James; pvt.; **E**; 1st Regt. Infan.
Lowry, James G.; pvt.; **B/E**; 2nd Regt. Infan.
Lowry, Robert H.; pvt.; **B**; 1st Regt. Infan.
Lucas, Sterling; pvt.; **D**; 1st Battalion Infan.
Lucken, Frederick W.; pvt.; **D**; 1st Battalion Infan.
Luckett, John; pvt.; **F**; 1st Regt. Infan.
Luckett, Samuel; pvt.; **F**; 1st Regt. Infan.
Luckin, John J.; pvt.; **H**; 1st Regt. Infan.
Lucky, William R.; pvt.; **F**; 2nd Regt. Infan.
Lunceford, Napoleon B.; pvt.; **B**; 1st Battalion Infan.
Lyerly, James B.; pvt.; **E**; 1st Regt. Infan.
Lynch, Isaac; pvt.; **K**; 2nd Regt. Infan.
Lyon, Henry P.; pvt.; **K**; 1st Regt. Infan.
Lytle, Armstrong; pvt., 1st cpl.; **H**; 1st Regt. Infan.
Maben, William; pvt.; **G**; 1st Regt. Infan.
Mabry, Erastus W.; pvt., cpl.; **C**; 2nd Regt. Infan.
Mabry, Thomas F.; pvt.; **G**; 1st Regt. Infan.
McAlister, Neal; pvt.; **D**; 1st Regt. Infan.
Macauley, George; pvt.; **H**; 2nd Regt. Infan.
McCanlass, John T.; pvt.; **D**; 2nd Regt. Infan.
McCannon, Michael; pvt.; **I**; 2nd Regt. Infan.
McCarroll, Alexander; 4th, 2nd Sgt.; **C**; 2nd Regt. Infan.
McCarty, James C.; pvt.; **A**; 2nd Regt. Infan.
McCauly, John; pvt.; **D**; 1st Regt. Infan.
McClanahan, Thadeus O.; pvt.; **I**; 1st Regt. Infan.
McClendon, Andrew J.; pvt.; **D**; 1st Regt. Infan.
McClung, Alexander Keith; Capt., Lieut.-Col.; **K/F&S**; 1st Regt. Infan.
McClure, David H.; pvt.; **H**; 1st Regt. Infan.
McClure, Joseph F.; pvt.; **B**; 1st Regt. Infan.
McConnell, Robert; 1st Sgt.; **B**; 1st Regt. Infan.
McCoy, James A.; pvt.; **D**; 1st Regt. Infan.
McCune, Thomas W.; pvt.; **E**; 2nd Regt. Infan.
McDonald, Hugh R.; pvt., 3rd cpl.; **K**; 2nd Regt. Infan.
McDonald, James; pvt.; **E**; 1st Battalion Infan.

McDonald, James Madison; pvt.; **F**; 2nd Regt. Infan.
McDonald, Pendleton; pvt.; **Unknown**; 2nd Regt. Infan.
McDonald, Robert S.; pvt.; **H**; 2nd Regt. Infan.
McDoniel, Alfred H.; pvt.; **A**; 1st Battalion Infan.
McDoniel, James; pvt.; **A**; 1st Battalion Infan.
McDuffie, William Stoker; pvt.; **K**; 1st Regt. Infan.
McFarland, Alexander B.; pvt.; **F**; 1st Regt. Infan.
McGary, Martin H.; pvt.; **C**; 2nd Regt. Infan.
McGaughey, Thomas H.; pvt.; **H**; 1st Regt. Infan.
McGee, William; pvt.; **E**; 2nd Regt. Infan.
McGeehee, David; pvt.; **C**; 1st Battalion Infan.
McGehee, Daniel R.; pvt.; **B**; 1st Regt. Infan.
McGimpsey, Charles P.; pvt.; **I**; 1st Regt. Infan.
McGraw, Wiley; pvt.; **K**; 2nd Regt. Infan.
McGregor, George; pvt.; **G**; 2nd Regt. Infan.
McGuin, John E. C.; pvt.; **K**; 1st Regt. Infan.
McGurk, John; pvt.; **D**; 2nd Regt. Infan.
McInnis, Malcolm; pvt.; **G**; 1st Regt. Infan.
McKay, Daniel A.; pvt.; **C**; 1st Regt. Infan.
McKee, William; pvt.; **Unknown**; 2nd Regt. Infan.
McKeever, Isaac; pvt.; **I**; 2nd Regt. Infan.
McKeever, Thomas; pvt.; **A/B**; 1st Battalion Infan.
McKenna, Edward A.; pvt.; **C**; 1st Battalion Infan.
McKenzie, John P.; pvt., cpl., Sgt.; **B**; 2nd Regt. Infan.
McKey, John S.; pvt.; **G**; 2nd Regt. Infan.
McKey, Robert; pvt.; **C**; 1st Regt. Infan.
McKie, Green; pvt.; **F**; 1st Regt. Infan.
McKinney, James M.; 2nd, 1st Sgt., 1st Lieut.; **I**; 2nd Regt. Infan.
McKinney, William; pvt.; **F**; 2nd Regt. Infan.
McKinney, William C.; pvt.; **E**; 1st Battalion Infan.
McKinney, William H.; pvt., cpl.; **H**; 1st Regt. Infan.
McKnight, Samuel B.; pvt.; **A**; 1st Battalion Infan.
McLain, James; pvt.; **I**; 2nd Regt. Infan.
McLaughlin, James A.; 4th cpl., 4th Sgt.; **C**; 1st Regt. Infan.
McLean, William D. V.; pvt.; **E**; 2nd Regt. Infan.
McLemore, William K.; pvt.; **H**; 2nd Regt. Infan.
McManus, John Lewis; Capt.; **E**; 1st Regt. Infan.
McMorrough, Theodore; mus.; **H**; 1st Regt. Infan.
McMullaen, James; pvt.; **K**; 2nd Regt. Infan.
McMullen, James H.; pvt.; **B**; 1st Battalion Infan.
McMurray, Moses; pvt.; **H**; 1st Regt. Infan.
McNair, Evander; 2nd cpl., 1st Sgt.; **E**; 1st Regt. Infan.
McNair, Neil M.; pvt.; **D**; 1st Battalion Infan.
McNair, Robert; mus.; **H**; 1st Regt. Infan.
McNeil, William E.; Sgt.-Maj.; **D/F&S**; 1st Battalion Infan.

McNelly, Zachariah; pvt.; **K**; 2nd Regt. Infan.
McNorris, John D.; pvt.; **K**; 1st Regt. Infan.
McNully, Z.; pvt.; **E**; 1st Regt. Infan.
McNulty, Francis J.; Ord. Sgt., Bvt. 2nd Lieut.; **G**; 1st Regt. Infan.
Macon, Henry; pvt.; **Unknown**; 2nd Regt. Infan.
McQuary, Jasper A.; pvt.; **C**; 2nd Regt. Infan.
McQueen, James A.; pvt.; **C**; 2nd Regt. Infan.
Macrery, John; 3rd, 2nd cpl.; **G**; 2nd Regt. Infan.
McVay, William T.; pvt.; **B**; 1st Battalion Infan.
McVey, James M.; pvt.; **Unknown**; 2nd Regt. Infan.
McWilliams, Wesley; pvt.; **E**; 1st Battalion Infan.
McWillie, Adam; pvt., Capt.; **H**; 1st Regt. Infan. and **H**; 2nd Regt. Infan.
Maddox, William E.; pvt.; **A**; 2nd Regt. Infan.
Mallet, Stephen; pvt.; **K**; 2nd Regt. Infan.
Mallett, James H.; pvt.; **G**; 1st Regt. Infan.
Mallett, William; pvt.; **K**; 1st Regt. Infan.
Mallory, William; pvt.; **A**; 2nd Regt. Infan.
Malone, Frederick James; pvt., 2nd Lieut.; **F**; 1st Regt. Infan.
Malone, Robert H.; pvt., 1st cpl.; **C/I**; 1st Regt. Infan.
Malone, Thomas; pvt.; **B**; 2nd Regt. Infan.
Mann, Cornelius W.; pvt.; **H**; 2nd Regt. Infan.
Mann, Metsalon A.; 2nd, 1st Lieut.; **D**; 2nd Regt. Infan.
Manner, James; pvt.; **E**; 2nd Regt. Infan.
Manning, Joseph W.; pvt.; **C**; 1st Battalion Infan.
Maples, John Wesley; pvt.; **C**; 1st Regt. Infan.
Mapp, Littleton J.; pvt.; **G**; 1st Regt. Infan.
Mardis, James T.; pvt.; **I**; 2nd Regt. Infan.
Markham, John B.; 2nd cpl.; **C**; 1st Regt. Infan.
Markham, Hugh Mercer; 2nd Lieut.; **H**; 1st Regt. Infan.
Marr, James S.; pvt.; **I**; 1st Regt. Infan.
Marr, James T.; pvt.; **D**; 1st Battalion Infan.
Marrs, William H.; pvt.; **E**; 1st Regt. Infan.
Marsh, Samuel W.; pvt.; **E**; 1st Regt. Infan.
Marshall, Andrew J.; pvt., cpl.; **B**; 2nd Regt. Infan.
Marshall, Humphrey; pvt., 2nd Sgt., Sgt.-Maj.; **H/F&S**; 1st Regt. Infan.
Marshall, Thomas W.; pvt.; **A**; 1st Battalion Infan.
Martin, Charles; pvt.; **K**; 1st Regt. Infan.
Martin, Francis Marion Sr.; pvt.; **G**; 1st Regt. Infan.
Martin, James; pvt.; **H**; 2nd Regt. Infan.
Martin, James M.; pvt.; **B**; 1st Regt. Infan.
Martin, John; 2nd Lieut.; **H**; 2nd Regt. Infan.
Martin, John A.; pvt., cpl.; **A/G**; 1st Regt. Infan.
Martin, Joseph; pvt.; **H**; 1st Regt. Infan.
Martin, Leroy C.; pvt.; **D**; 1st Battalion Infan.
Martin, M. J.; pvt.; **K**; 2nd Regt. Infan.

Martin, Plummer M.; pvt., 4th Sgt.; **I**; 1st Regt. Infan.
Martin, Richard; pvt.; **D**; 1st Regt. Infan.
Martin, Robert; 2nd Lieut.; **I**; 2nd Regt. Infan.
Martin, Robert G.; pvt.; **K**; 2nd Regt. Infan.
Martin, Robert M.; 4th cpl.; **H**; 1st Regt. Infan.
Martin, Russell M.; pvt.; **C**; 1st Regt. Infan.
Martin, S. D.; pvt.; **I**; 1st Regt. Infan.
Martin, Samuel N.; pvt.; **G**; 2nd Regt. Infan.
Martin, William A.; pvt.; **I**; 1st Regt. Infan.
Martin, William D.; pvt.; **D**; 1st Regt. Infan.
Martin, William S.; pvt.; **E**; 1st Regt. Infan.
Mason, John A.; pvt.; **E**; 1st Battalion Infan.
Mason, Madison M.; pvt.; **A**; 1st Regt. Infan.
Mason, Solomon; mus., pvt.; **C**; 1st Battalion Infan.
Massell, Eugene; 3rd Sgt.; **B**; 1st Regt. Infan.
Massey, Joseph V.; pvt.; **H**; 2nd Regt. Infan.
Massie, Nathaniel; pvt.; **I**; 1st Regt. Infan.
Mathews, Frederick; pvt.; **H**; 1st Regt. Infan.
Matlock, Andrew J.; 4th Sgt.; **C**; 1st Battalion Infan.
Matlock, Charles M.; mus., pvt.; **C**; 1st Battalion Infan.
Matlock, Manuel W.; pvt.; **E**; 2nd Regt. Infan.
Matlock, William B.; pvt.; **B**; 2nd Regt. Infan.
Matlock, William P.; pvt.; **B**; 2nd Regt. Infan.
Matthews, Beverly; 2nd Lieut., Aide; **A**; 2nd Regt. Infan.
Mattingly, John F.; pvt.; **H**; 1st Regt. Infan.
Maule, Joseph L.; 2nd, 1st cpl.; **G**; 2nd Regt. Infan.
Maum, James W.; pvt.; **E**; 1st Battalion Infan.
Maunday, Samuel S.; pvt.; **D**; 1st Regt. Infan.
Maxcel, William A.; pvt.; **B**; 1st Battalion Infan.
Maxwell, Charles D.; pvt.; **D**; 2nd Regt. Infan.
Mayers, James M.; pvt.; **A**; 1st Battalion Infan.
Mayers, Richard C.; pvt., 1st cpl.; **A**; 1st Battalion Infan.
Maza, Levi; pvt.; **F**; 1st Regt. Infan.
Meachem, Silas; pvt.; **E**; 1st Regt. Infan.
Meaders, Levi M.; pvt.; **F**; 1st Regt. Infan.
Medlock, John J.; 4th Sgt.; **E**; 2nd Regt. Infan.
Mellon, Thomas Armour; 4th Sgt.; **G**; 1st Regt. Infan.
Melvin, John J.; 4th Sgt.; **F**; 2nd Regt. Infan.
Merrill, Austin P.; pvt.; **E**; 1st Battalion Infan.
Merritt, John; pvt.; **F**; 2nd Regt. Infan.
Merryman, Willis W.; pvt.; **E**; 1st Battalion Infan.
Messer, James; pvt.; **E**; 2nd Regt. Infan.
Metcalf, George Edward; pvt.; **C**; 1st Regt. Infan.
Metlock, John; pvt.; **E**; 1st Battalion Infan.
Mican, James; pvt.; **D**; 1st Battalion Infan.

Mickey, Caius M. M.; pvt.; **H**; 2nd Regt. Infan.
Mickey, William A.; pvt.; **H**; 2nd Regt. Infan.
Middlebrooks, William S.; pvt.; **A**; 1st Battalion Infan.
Middleton, Holland; 1st Lieut.; **C**; 2nd Regt. Infan.
Middleton, Moses C.; 3rd cpl.; **C**; 2nd Regt. Infan.
Milam, Henry S. W.; pvt.; **D**; 1st Battalion Infan.
Milam, Isaac E.; pvt., 2nd Sgt.; **I**; 1st Regt. Infan.
Miles, William; pvt.; **E**; 1st Battalion Infan.
Miley, Andrew B.; pvt.; **H**; 2nd Regt. Infan.
Miller, Archibald W.; pvt.; **K**; 1st Regt. Infan.
Miller, Charles J.; pvt., cpl.; **A**; 1st Regt. Infan.
Miller, Horace H.; 1st Sgt., Sgt.-Maj.; **H/F&S**; 1st Regt. Infan.
Miller, James M.; pvt.; **A**; 1st Regt. Infan.
Miller, James Madison; pvt.; **B**; 1st Regt. Infan.
Miller, Joel; pvt.; **D**; 2nd Regt. Infan.
Miller, John; pvt.; **G**; 2nd Regt. Infan.
Miller, John; pvt.; **I**; 2nd Regt. Infan.
Miller, John A.; pvt.; **A**; 2nd Regt. Infan.
Miller, John P.; pvt.; **D**; 2nd Regt. Infan.
Miller, John R.; pvt.; **G**; 1st Regt. Infan.
Miller, Joseph; pvt.; **C**; 1st Regt. Infan.
Miller, O. P.; pvt., 4th, 1st cpl., Sgt.; **K**; 2nd Regt. Infan.
Miller, Oliver R.; pvt.; **E**; 2nd Regt. Infan.
Miller, Robert; 3rd cpl.; **B**; 1st Regt. Infan.
Miller, Stephen W.; 1st cpl.; **C**; 1st Battalion Infan.
Miller, Thomas; pvt.; **B**; 1st Battalion Infan.
Miller, Thomas G.; pvt., cpl.; **E**; 2nd Regt. Infan.
Miller, Thomas W.; pvt.; **E**; 2nd Regt. Infan.
Miller, William H.; pvt.; **B**; 1st Regt. Infan.
Miller, William J.; 4th cpl.; **A**; 1st Regt. Infan.
Milton, Hiram; pvt.; **Unknown**; 2nd Regt. Infan.
Milton, William F.; pvt.; **Unknown**; 2nd Regt. Infan.
Minga, Henry F.; pvt.; **C**; 2nd Regt. Infan.
Minney, James; pvt.; **C**; 2nd Regt. Infan.
Mitchell, Alexander; pvt.; **K**; 1st Regt. Infan.
Mitchell, John; pvt.; **C**; 2nd Regt. Infan.
Mitchell, John S.; pvt., 3rd cpl., 1st Sgt.; **B**; 2nd Regt. Infan.
Mitchell, Robert C.; pvt.; **B**; 2nd Regt. Infan.
Mobley, Middleton Rufus; pvt.; **A**; 1st Regt. Infan.
Moffitt, Allston; pvt.; **E**; 2nd Regt. Infan.
Mole, John; pvt.; **E**; 2nd Regt. Infan.
Money, Joseph; pvt.; **H**; 2nd Regt. Infan.
Monk, Menan; pvt.; **A**; 1st Battalion Infan.
Montgomery, Charles S.; pvt.; **E**; 1st Battalion Infan.
Montgomery, Jacob P.; pvt.; **A**; 1st Battalion Infan.

Montgomery, John H.; pvt.; **D**; 2nd Regt. Infan.
Montgomery, Robartis H.; pvt.; **H**; 2nd Regt. Infan.
Moody, Joseph E.; pvt., 1st Sgt., 2nd Lieut.; **B**; 2nd Regt. Infan.
Moody, Lewis; pvt.; **A**; 1st Battalion Infan.
Moore, Andrew J.; pvt.; **C**; 2nd Regt. Infan.
Moore, C.; pvt.; **F**; 1st Regt. Infan.
Moore, Elbert P.; pvt.; **A**; 2nd Regt. Infan.
Moore, Gamer; pvt.; **B**; 2nd Regt. Infan.
Moore, Henry; pvt.; **A**; 1st Battalion Infan.
Moore, Hugh; pvt.; **D**; 2nd Regt. Infan.
Moore, James; pvt.; **E**; 1st Regt. Infan.
Moore, James P.; pvt.; **I**; 1st Regt. Infan.
Moore, James S.; pvt.; **B**; 2nd Regt. Infan.
Moore, Robert E.; pvt.; **E**; 1st Battalion Infan.
Moore, Robert L.; 1st Lieut.; **H**; 1st Regt. Infan.
Moore, Thomas; pvt.; **H**; 2nd Regt. Infan.
Moore, William; pvt.; **A**; 1st Regt. Infan.
Moore, William; pvt.; **H**; 1st Regt. Infan.
Moore, William; pvt., 2nd cpl.; **B**; 1st Battalion Infan.
Moore, William M.; pvt.; **H**; 1st Regt. Infan.
Moore, William S.; 3rd Sgt.; **C**; 1st Battalion Infan.
Mootry, Lewis; pvt.; **B**; 1st Regt. Infan.
Morgan, Daniel T.; pvt.; **C**; 2nd Regt. Infan.
Morgan, Hiram; pvt.; **B**; 1st Regt. Infan.
Morgan, Waddy F.; pvt.; **C**; 1st Battalion Infan.
Morphew, Silas; pvt.; **E**; 1st Battalion Infan.
Morris, Howard; pvt., cpl.; **C**; 1st Regt. Infan.
Morris, James T.; pvt.; **F**; 1st Regt. Infan.
Morris, Joseph W.; pvt.; **F**; 1st Regt. Infan.
Morris, Mabry Ivy; pvt.; **B**; 1st Regt. Infan.
Morris, Pleasant; pvt.; **A**; 1st Battalion Infan.
Morris, Samuel; pvt.; **A**; 2nd Regt. Infan.
Morris, William K.; 1st Lieut.; **E**; 2nd Regt. Infan.
Morrison, John; pvt., 3rd cpl.; **D**; 1st Battalion Infan.
Morrow, William; pvt.; **D**; 1st Battalion Infan.
Morton, Joseph W.; pvt.; **A**; 1st Regt. Infan.
Mosby, Robert G.; pvt.; **K**; 1st Regt. Infan.
Moseley, Lewis; pvt.; **A**; 1st Battalion Infan.
Mosely, John P.; pvt.; **G**; 1st Regt. Infan.
Moss, Jesse W.; pvt.; **E**; 1st Regt. Infan.
Moss, Stephen; pvt.; **E**; 2nd Regt. Infan.
Mott, Christopher Haynes; 1st Lieut.; **I**; 1st Regt. Infan.
Mulcare, Thomas; pvt.; **C**; 1st Battalion Infan.
Muldoon, Philip; pvt.; **H**; 1st Regt. Infan.
Mullen, Peter A.; pvt.; **K**; 2nd Regt. Infan.

Mullens, Elgen A.; mus.; **I**; 1st Regt. Infan.

Mullenix, William M.; pvt.; **A**; 1st Battalion Infan.

Mullinax, James P.; pvt.; **F**; 1st Regt. Infan.

Munce, Josiah S.; pvt.; **G**; 2nd Regt. Infan.

Munce, Thomas S.; 1st Lieut., Adjut.; **A/G/F&S**; 2nd Regt. Infan.

Mundon, Benjamin; pvt.; **E**; 2nd Regt. Infan.

Murphree (Murphrie), Leonard H.; pvt.; **I**; 1st Regt. Infan.

Murphy, James; pvt.; **B**; 2nd Regt. Infan.

Murphy, John; pvt.; **G**; 2nd Regt. Infan.

Murphy, Sidney R.; pvt.; **B**; 2nd Regt. Infan.

Murray, David; pvt.; **B**; 1st Regt. Infan.

Murry, John L.; pvt.; **G**; 2nd Regt. Infan.

Murtough, Barney; pvt.; **B**; 1st Regt. Infan.

Mustin, William C.; pvt.; **D**; 1st Battalion Infan.

Myrick, J. M.; pvt.; **E**; 1st Regt. Infan.

Myrick, M. G.; pvt.; **E**; 1st Regt. Infan.

Nabrous, Christopher R.; pvt.; **B**; 1st Battalion Infan.

Nail, Montgomery; pvt.; **I**; 1st Regt. Infan.

Nash, Charles B.; pvt.; **C**; 1st Battalion Infan.

Nash, Madison G.; pvt.; **H**; 2nd Regt. Infan.

Nash, Washington B.; pvt.; **A**; 2nd Regt. Infan.

Navon, James; pvt.; **I**; 2nd Regt. Infan.

Neal, Montgomery; pvt.; **B**; 2nd Regt. Infan.

Neel, Francis M.; pvt.; **A**; 1st Battalion Infan.

Neel, James R.; pvt.; **A**; 1st Battalion Infan.

Neeland, Robert H.; pvt.; **B**; 1st Regt. Infan.

Neely, Andrew J.; pvt.; **G**; 1st Regt. Infan.

Neilson, Charles A.; pvt.; **A**; 2nd Regt. Infan.

Nelson, Charles.; pvt.; **A**; 2nd Regt. Infan.

Nelson, Thomas W.; pvt.; **K**; 2nd Regt. Infan.

Newman, Albert M.; 4th Sgt.; **H**; 1st Regt. Infan.

Newman, Alexander; pvt.; **B**; 1st Regt. Infan.

Newman, Henry; pvt.; **D**; 2nd Regt. Infan.

Newman, James; pvt.; **B**; 1st Battalion Infan.

Newman, John; pvt.; **K**; 2nd Regt. Infan.

Newman, Solomon; pvt.; **B**; 1st Regt. Infan.

Newman, William B.; 2nd Lieut.; **G**; 2nd Regt. Infan.

Newman, William K.; cpl., 4th Sgt.; **D**; 2nd Regt. Infan.

Newson, John; pvt.; **F**; 2nd Regt. Infan.

Nichols, John W.; pvt.; **A**; 1st Battalion Infan.

Nicholson, Ira O.; pvt.; **A**; 1st Battalion Infan.

Nicholson, James H.; pvt.; **B**; 1st Regt. Infan.

Nicholson, William; pvt.; **E**; 1st Battalion Infan.

Nixon, Ceasar L.; pvt., 4th Sgt.; **D**; 1st Regt. Infan.

Noland, Avery; pvt.; **H**; 1st Regt. Infan.

Norman, Benjamin F.; pvt.; **D**; 1st Regt. Infan.
Norman, Hiram G.; pvt.; **D**; 1st Regt. Infan.
Norwood, Alexander T.; pvt.; **B**; 1st Battalion Infan.
Norworthy, William; pvt.; **H**; 1st Regt. Infan.
Nutter, William Mason; pvt.; **C**; 1st Regt. Infan.
O'Brien, William; pvt.; **C**; 1st Battalion Infan.
O'Bryant, James; pvt.; **A**; 1st Regt. Infan.
O'Flannegan, Peter; pvt.; **B**; 1st Battalion Infan.
O'Neal, Henry F.; pvt.; **B**; 1st Regt. Infan.
O'Neal, John C.; pvt.; **A**; 1st Battalion Infan.
O'Rourke, Patrick; pvt.; **I**; 2nd Regt. Infan.
O'Rourke, William; pvt.; **K**; 1st Regt. Infan.
O'Sullivan, Cornelius; pvt.; **A**; 1st Regt. Infan.
Oaks, James F.; pvt.; **D**; 2nd Regt. Infan.
Obarr, Jesse; pvt.; **D**; 1st Battalion Infan.
Odoms, Jesse; pvt.; **G**; 1st Regt. Infan.
Ogden, Lorenzo D.; pvt., 1st Sgt.; **B**; 1st Battalion Infan.
Ogilvie, Philip S. Smith; pvt.; **E/H**; 2nd Regt. Infan.
Oldham, Jesse; pvt.; **I**; 1st Regt. Infan.
Oliver, James M.; pvt.; **A**; 1st Battalion Infan.
Orr, Daniel B.; pvt.; **I**; 2nd Regt. Infan.
Orr, John; pvt.; **D**; 2nd Regt. Infan.
Orr, Valentine B.; pvt.; **I**; 1st Regt. Infan.
Orr, William; pvt.; **D**; 1st Regt. Infan.
Orr, William J.; pvt.; **I**; 2nd Regt. Infan.
Orrell, Robert; pvt.; **K**; 2nd Regt. Infan.
Osborn, Lewdy B.; pvt.; **F**; 2nd Regt. Infan.
Osburn, John; pvt.; **C**; 2nd Regt. Infan.
Otis, Allen; pvt.; **B**; 2nd Regt. Infan.
Ott, Peter W.; pvt.; Briscoe's Co. Mtd. Louisiana Volunteers
Overbey, Edmund P.; pvt.; **A**; 1st Battalion Infan.
Overstreet, John R.; pvt.; **F**; 2nd Regt. Infan.
Overton, Alfred A.; Capt.; **I**; 1st Regt. Infan.; and I, 2nd Regt. Infan.
Overton, Horatio; pvt.; **K**; 1st Regt. Infan.
Owens, Ethedreal; pvt.; **F**; 2nd Regt. Infan.
Owens, William; mus. (Fifer), pvt.; **F**; 2nd Regt. Infan.
Owens, William H.; pvt.; **F**; 1st Regt. Infan.
Owings, John D.; pvt.; **D**; 2nd Regt. Infan.
Owings, Jonathan Lafayette; pvt.; **D**; 1st Battalion Infan.
Ownley, James W.; pvt.; **H**; 2nd Regt. Infan.
Pace, Thomas; pvt.; **E**; 2nd Regt. Infan.
Pack, James D.; pvt.; **C**; 1st Regt. Infan.
Page, Francis M.; pvt.; **D**; 2nd Regt. Infan.
Palmer, William; pvt.; **G/I**; 2nd Regt. Infan.
Pamplin, Robert H.; pvt.; **F**; 2nd Regt. Infan.

Parham, Allen B.; pvt.; **B**; 2nd Regt. Infan.
Parish, Issac W.; pvt.; **C**; 2nd Regt. Infan.
Parish, Robert T.; pvt.; **F**; 2nd Regt. Infan.
Parker, Samuel O.; pvt.; **A**; 1st Regt. Infan.
Parker, William S.; pvt.; **A**; 2nd Regt. Infan.
Parker, William S.; **F**; 1st Regt. Infan.
Parr, Giles S.; pvt.; **C**; 2nd Regt. Infan.
Parr, Richard E.; pvt.; **G**; 1st Regt. Infan.
Parrish, Joel T.; pvt.; **K**; 1st Regt. Infan.
Parsons, James R.; pvt.; **I**; 2nd Regt. Infan.
Paschal, Richard A.; pvt.; **Unknown**; 2nd Regt. Infan.
Patrick, David A.; pvt.; **I**; 2nd Regt. Infan.
Patton (Patten), Thomas S.; pvt.; **E**; 2nd Regt. Infan.
Patterson, Andrew B.; pvt., 1st Sgt.; **E**; 1st Regt. Infan.
Patterson, D. E.; pvt., **F**; 1st Regt. Infan.
Patterson, William H. H.; 1st Lieut.; **K**; 1st Regt. Infan.
Patton, Alfred; pvt.; **G**; 1st Regt. Infan.
Paul, Peter A.; pvt.; **A**; 1st Regt. Infan.
Payne, Joshua; pvt.; **C**; 1st Battalion Infan.
Peace, John; pvt.; **I**; 1st Regt. Infan.
Pearson, John M.; pvt.; **A**; 2nd Regt. Infan.
Peaster, William H.; pvt.; **A**; 1st Regt. Infan.
Peaterson, G.; pvt.; **F**; 1st Regt. Infan.
Peery, James; pvt.; **C**; 2nd Regt. Infan.
Peery, John; pvt.; **C**; 2nd Regt. Infan.
Penny, Joseph H.; pvt.; **A**; 1st Regt. Infan.
Penny, Thomas; pvt., cpl.; **A**; 2nd Regt. Infan.
Perkins, I. Camp; pvt.; **E**; 1st Regt. Infan.
Perkins, John; pvt.; **A**; 2nd Regt. Infan.
Perkins, William M.; pvt.; **A**; 1st Battalion Infan.
Perrett, Mathew; pvt.; **K**; 2nd Regt. Infan.
Perritt, Wiley A.; pvt.; **K**; 2nd Regt. Infan.
Perry, Bryant; pvt.; **K**; 1st Regt. Infan.
Perry, Elihu I.; pvt.; **D**; 1st Battalion Infan.
Perry, James; pvt.; **B**; 2nd Regt. Infan.
Perry, John B.; pvt., 4th cpl.; **B**; 2nd Regt. Infan.
Perryman, Felix G.; pvt., cpl.; **I**; 2nd Regt. Infan.
Perryman, Presley P.; pvt.; **I**; 2nd Regt. Infan.
Peyton, Elijah A.; pvt.; **H**; 1st Regt. Infan.
Peyton, John C.; pvt.; **H**; 1st Regt. Infan.
Phares, Henry J.; pvt.; **C**; 2nd Regt. Infan.
Phares, John C.; pvt.; **C**; 2nd Regt. Infan.
Pharris, Joseph; pvt.; **B**; 1st Battalion Infan.
Philips, Lorenzo D.; pvt.; **F**; 2nd Regt. Infan.
Phillips, Frederick; pvt.; **H**; 2nd Regt. Infan.

Phillips, George; pvt.; **E;** 1st Regt. Infan.
Phillips, Rufus Eldridge; pvt.; **I;** 1st Regt. Infan.
Phillips, Seaborne Moses; cpl., 4th Sgt., 2nd Lieut.; **A;** 1st Regt. Infan.
Phillips, William W.; 3rd Sgt.; **E;** 1st Regt. Infan.
Phips, David; pvt.; **G;** 2nd Regt. Infan.
Pierce, Hugh W.; pvt.; **E;** 1st Regt. Infan.
Pierce, Simeon; pvt.; **A;** 2nd Regt. Infan.
Pierce, William H.; pvt.; **K;** 2nd Regt. Infan.
Pigg, John; pvt.; **B;** 1st Battalion Infan.
Pilkington, John A.; pvt.; **E;** 1st Battalion Infan.
Pippins, John E.; pvt.; **D;** 1st Battalion Infan.
Pitman, John; pvt.; **I;** 1st Regt. Infan.
Pittman, William H.; pvt.; **D;** 1st Battalion Infan.
Pitts, Bartley; pvt.; **E;** 1st Battalion Infan.
Pitts, John B.; pvt.; **D;** 1st Battalion Infan.
Pitts, John C.; pvt.; **D;** 1st Battalion Infan.
Pleasants, Frank P.; pvt.; **D;** 1st Regt. Infan.
Poag, Samuel G. W.; pvt.; **C;** 1st Battalion Infan.
Poe, Levi; mus.; **C;** 2nd Regt. Infan.
Poindexter, John J.; pvt., cpl., 2nd Lieut.; **H;** 1st Regt. Infan.
Pomroy, Henry; pvt.; **E;** 1st Regt. Infan.
Poole, Equilla M.; Sgt.; **I;** 2nd Regt. Infan.
Pope, William; pvt.; **B;** 2nd Regt. Infan.
Porch, John B.; pvt.; **D;** 2nd Regt. Infan.
Porter, David H.; pvt.; **D;** 1st Battalion Infan.
Porter, George C.; pvt.; **I;** 2nd Regt. Infan.
Porter, Hancock; pvt.; **A;** 1st Battalion Infan.
Porter, James; pvt.; **D;** 1st Battalion Infan.
Porter, William; pvt.; **D;** 1st Battalion Infan.
Porter, William C.; 3rd, 1st Sgt.; **H;** 1st Regt. Infan.
Portis, James P.; pvt.; **E;** 2nd Regt. Infan.
Posey, Carnot; 1st Lieut., Capt.; **B;** 1st Regt. Infan.
Postlethwaite, Stephen D.; pvt., 3rd, 2nd, 1st Sgt.; **G;** 2nd Regt. Infan.
Potts, Samuel; pvt.; **G;** 1st Regt. Infan.
Potts, Zachary H.; pvt.; **E;** 2nd Regt. Infan.
Powell, Andrew T.; pvt.; **D;** 1st Regt. Infan.
Powell, Alfred; pvt.; **I;** 2nd Regt. Infan.
Powell, James L.; pvt.; **F;** 1st Regt. Infan.
Powell, Robert V.; pvt.; **H;** 2nd Regt. Infan.
Powell, Wiley; pvt.; **I;** 2nd Regt. Infan.
Power, Francis; pvt.; **C;** 2nd Regt. Infan.
Powers, Stephen F.; pvt.; **G;** 2nd Regt. Infan.
Preston, John; pvt.; **C;** 1st Regt. Infan.
Prestridge, William A.; pvt.; **A;** 1st Regt. Infan.
Prewett, Emory; pvt.; **A;** 1st Regt. Infan.

Prewitt, Josiah; pvt.; **C**; 2nd Regt. Infan.
Prewitt, Wilson M.; pvt., 2nd cpl., Sgt.; **C**; 2nd Regt. Infan.
Price, Archibald G.; pvt., cpl.; **E**; 1st Regt. Infan.
Price, Charles M.; Q.M..; **F&S**; 2nd Regt. Infan.
Price, David B.; pvt.; **H**; 2nd Regt. Infan.
Price, Ezra R.; Lieut.; **E**; 4th Regt. LA Infan. and Maj.;
        F&S; 2nd Regt. Infan.
Price, Pierre; 1st cpl., Sgt.; **G**; 2nd Regt. Infan.
Price, Thomas W.; pvt.; **Unknown**; 2nd Regt. Infan.
Prickett, William; pvt.; **B**; 2nd Regt. Infan.
Priest, Edward; pvt.; **I**; 2nd Regt. Infan.
Prior, Belfield W.; pvt.; **C**; 1st Battalion Infan.
Pritchet, Bryant S.; pvt.; **F**; 2nd Regt. Infan.
Pritchet, William; pvt., **F**; 2nd Regt. Infan.
Proctor, Collin B.; pvt.; **D**; 1st Battalion Infan.
Proctor, Harris J. M.; pvt.; **I**; 1st Regt. Infan.
Puckett, Anthony B.; pvt., 3rd cpl.; **E**; 1st Regt. Infan.
Puckett, Henry L.; 4th, 3rd Sgt.; **C**; 1st Regt. Infan.
Pue, Thomas; pvt.; **I**; 2nd Regt. Infan.
Pugh, David R.; pvt.; **F**; 2nd Regt. Infan.
Pugh, Edworth; pvt.; **Unknown**; 2nd Regt. Infan.
Pulliam, Robert W.; mus., pvt.; **A**; 1st Battalion Infan.
Pulliem, Thomas W. W.; pvt.; **A**; 1st Battalion Infan.
Pybus, Benjamin N.; pvt.; **A**; 2nd Regt. Infan.
Pyles, Milton; pvt.; **A/G**; 1st Regt. Infan.
Quinan, Michael J.; pvt.; **I**; 2nd Regt. Infan.
Quinn, John A.; pvt.; **D**; 2nd Regt. Infan.
Quinn, Peter; pvt.; **D**; 2nd Regt. Infan.
Quitman, John Anthony; Brig. Gen., Maj. Gen.,
        Military Gov. Of Mexico City
Ragan, Robartus; pvt.; **H**; 2nd Regt. Infan.
Rages, Magdelena; Matron; **Unknown**; 2nd Regt. Infan.
Ragsdale, James O.; pvt.; **K**; 1st Regt. Infan.
Ragsdale, James O.; pvt.; **E**; 1st Battalion Infan.
Raimey, Preston G.; pvt.; **D**; 2nd Regt. Infan.
Raine, Henry T.; pvt.; **H**; 1st Regt. Infan.
Rainey, James B.; pvt.; **I**; 2nd Regt. Infan.
Rainwater, John P.; pvt.; **A**; 1st Battalion Infan.
Rainwaters, Edwin N.; pvt.; **H**; 2nd Regt. Infan.
Rainy, James M.; pvt.; **G**; 2nd Regt. Infan.
Rakestraw, William; pvt.; **A**; 2nd Regt. Infan.
Ramey, William C.; pvt.; **B**; 2nd Regt. Infan.
Ramsey, George W.; pvt.; **D**; 1st Regt. Infan.
Ramsey, James M.; 4th Sgt.; **D**; 1st Regt. Infan.
Ramsey, Simeon D.; pvt.; **B**; 1st Battalion Infan.

Ramsey, Thomas J.; 2nd Lieut.; **B**; 1st Battalion Infan.
Randolph, Thadeus D.; pvt., Sgt.; **I**; 1st Regt. Infan.
Raney, Samuel M.; pvt.; **G**; 2nd Regt. Infan.
Rapplee, William; pvt.; **C**; 1st Battalion Infan.
Rariden, Patrick; pvt.; **H**; 1st Regt. Infan.
Ratliff, William; pvt.; **H**; 2nd Regt. Infan.
Rawlings, James; pvt.; **E**; 1st Regt. Infan.
Ray, Chesley; pvt.; **B**; 2nd Regt. Infan.
Ray, Ephraim; pvt.; **B**; 2nd Regt. Infan.
Ray, Wiley; pvt.; **Unknown**; 2nd Regt. Infan.
Ray, William H.; pvt.; **E**; 2nd Regt. Infan.
Rayburn, William R.; pvt.; **B**; 2nd Regt. Infan.
Rea, Hampton M.; pvt.; **A**; 1st Battalion Infan.
Rea, William R.; pvt.; **B**; 1st Regt. Infan.
Read, Jesse; pvt.; **A**; 1st Regt. Infan.
Read, Licurgos D.; Sgt.; **A**; 1st Regt. Infan.
Real, Joseph P.; 2nd Lieut.; **C**; 2nd Regt. Infan.
Redden, Harmon; pvt.; **A**; 1st Battalion Infan.
Redden, Stephen W.; pvt.; **D**; 2nd Regt. Infan.
Redding, William W.; pvt., 2nd Lieut.; **F**; 1st Regt. Infan.
Redus, James W.; pvt.; **A**; 1st Battalion Infan.
Reed, Edward; pvt.; **E**; 2nd Regt. Infan.
Reed, Israel M.; pvt.; **D**; 2nd Regt. Infan.
Reed, Thomas W.; pvt.; **D**; 2nd Regt. Infan.
Reed, William C.; pvt.; **E**; 1st Regt. Infan.
Reedy, John; pvt.; **E**; 1st Battalion Infan.
Rees, Joshua C.; pvt.; **I**; 2nd Regt. Infan.
Reese, Hugh M.; pvt.; **K**; 1st Regt. Infan.
Reese, Isham I.; pvt.; **G**; 2nd Regt. Infan.
Reese, James G.; 3rd cpl., Sgt.; **K**; 1st Regt. Infan.
Reid, Hugh James; pvt.; **Comstock's Co.**, 3rd LA Infan.
Reid, Wiley J.; pvt.; **B**; 1st Battalion Infan.
Reneau, John; pvt.; **K**; 1st Regt. Infan.
Reno, John D.; pvt.; **E**; 2nd Regt. Infan.
Revell, Joseph C.; pvt.; **E**; 1st Regt. Infan.
Reynolds, Hugh A.; pvt., 4th cpl.; **D**; 1st Regt. Infan.
Reynolds, John H. C.; pvt.; **I**; 1st Regt. Infan.
Reynolds, John Q.; pvt.; **D**; 1st Regt. Infan.
Reynolds, Sherod; pvt.; **D**; 1st Regt. Infan.
Reynolds, Thomas P.; pvt.; **E**; 2nd Regt. Infan.
Rhoades, John; 1st cpl., 3rd Sgt.; **I**; 2nd Regt. Infan.
Rhodes, Andrew E.; pvt.; **I**; 2nd Regt. Infan.
Rhodes, Benjamin B.; pvt.; **D**; 1st Regt. Infan.
Rhyne, John R.; pvt.; **I**; 2nd Regt. Infan.
Rice, Hilton P.; pvt., 1st Sgt.; **B**; 1st Battalion Infan.

Rice, John; pvt.; **B**; 1st Battalion Infan.
Rich, Edward C.; 4th cpl.; **A**; 2nd Regt. Infan.
Richards, Andrew L.; pvt.; **C**; 1st Regt. Infan.
Richards, James; pvt.; **A**; 1st Regt. Infan.
Richardson, George P.; pvt.; **B**; 1st Regt. Infan.
Richardson, Robert E.; pvt.; **C**; 1st Regt. Infan.
Richardson, Samuel J.; pvt.; **B**; 1st Regt. Infan.
Riddle, James; pvt.; **B**; 1st Regt. Infan.
Ridge, James W.; pvt.; **E**; 1st Battalion Infan.
Ridley, Benjamin F.; pvt.; **A**; 1st Regt. Infan.
Riley, Hugh; pvt.; **H**; 1st Regt. Infan.
Riley, John S.; pvt.; **E**; 2nd Regt. Infan.
Riley, Terrills; pvt.; **H**; 2nd Regt. Infan.
Rimes, John F.; pvt.; **G**; 1st Regt. Infan.
Rimes, William L.; pvt.; **G**; 1st Regt. Infan.
Ringo, William; pvt.; **B**; 1st Battalion Infan.
Ripley, Hiram D.; pvt.; **G**; 1st Regt. Infan.
Ripley, William E.; pvt.; **G**; 1st Regt. Infan.
Ripley, Zeno R.; mus., pvt.; **K**; 2nd Regt. Infan.
Risher, Jacob; pvt.; **A**; 1st Battalion Infan.
Ritch, John; pvt.; **E**; 1st Regt. Infan.
Ritchey, Stephen W.; pvt.; **G**; 2nd Regt. Infan.
Rivercomb, George; pvt., 4th cpl.; **B**; 1st Regt. Infan.
Roach, Dobson; pvt.; **A**; 1st Battalion Infan.
Roan, Carter; pvt.; **E**; 1st Battalion Infan.
Roberson, Caleb R.; pvt.; **D**; 1st Battalion Infan.
Roberts, Benjamin F.; pvt.; **H**; 1st Regt. Infan.
Roberts, E. W.; pvt.; **E**; 1st Regt. Infan.
Roberts, Joseph M.; 2nd Sgt.; **G**; 1st Regt. Infan.
Roberts, Simeon; pvt.; **C**; 2nd Regt. Infan.
Robertson, William J.; pvt., 4th cpl.; **F**; 2nd Regt. Infan.
Robins, George W.; pvt.; **F**; 2nd Regt. Infan.
Robins, Mitchell M.; pvt.; **H**; 1st Regt. Infan.
Robinson, Alexander H.; pvt.; **Unknown**; 2nd Regt. Infan.
Robinson, D. H.; pvt.; **E**; 1st Regt. Infan.
Robinson, Francis M.; 1st cpl.; **E**; 1st Regt. Infan.
Robinson, George W.; pvt.; **K**; 2nd Regt. Infan.
Robinson, Jerome B.; 3rd Sgt.; **B**; 1st Battalion Infan.
Robinson (Roberson ?), John; pvt.; **B**; 1st Regt. Infan.
Robinson, William D.; pvt.; **H**; 1st Regt. Infan.
Robinson, William M.; pvt.; **B**; 1st Battalion Infan.
Robinson, Young; pvt.; **B**; 1st Battalion Infan.
Roddon, James; pvt.; **A**; 2nd Regt. Infan.
Roden, Carter; pvt.; **E**; 1st Battalion Infan.
Rogers, George W.; pvt.; **H**; 2nd Regt. Infan.

Rogers, James; pvt.; **H**; 2nd Regt. Infan.
Rogers, Jefferson C.; pvt.; **E**; 2nd Regt. Infan.
Rogers, Joseph; pvt.; **B**; 1st Battalion Infan.
Rogers, William E.; pvt.; **E**; 2nd Regt. Infan.
Rogers, William P.; 1st Lieut., Capt.; **K**; 1st Regt. Infan.
Rondenburg, John; pvt.; **G**; 2nd Regt. Infan.
Rose, William; pvt.; **A**; 1st Battalion Infan.
Rose, William; pvt.; **Unknown**; 2nd Regt. Infan.
Ross, Alfred; 3rd cpl.; **A**; 1st Battalion Infan.
Ross, John; pvt.; **H**; 1st Regt. Infan.
Ross, Ravenna; pvt.; **H**; 1st Regt. Infan.
Rosseau, John F.; pvt.; **A/B**; 1st Battalion Infan.
Rotrammel, William Simpson; pvt.; **B**; 1st Regt. Infan.
Rowe, A. Govan; pvt., 3rd, 2nd cpl.; **D**; 1st Regt. Infan.
Runnels, Ellis J.; pvt.; **E**; 1st Regt. Infan.
Russell, C. H.; pvt.; **C**; 1st Regt. Infan.
Russell, Daniel R.; 1st Lieut., Capt.; **D**; 1st Regt. Infan.
Russell, Ellis; pvt.; **I**; 2nd Regt. Infan.
Russell, James H.; pvt.; **E**; 1st Battalion Infan.
Russell, John G.; 4th cpl.; **B**; 1st Battalion Infan.
Russell, L. H.; pvt., cpl., Sgt.; **D**; 1st Regt. Infan.
Russell, Oscar; pvt.; **I**; 2nd Regt. Infan.
Russell, Reuben; pvt.; **A/G**; 1st Regt. Infan.
Russell, Street; pvt.; **K**; 2nd Regt. Infan.
Saffell, Amos H.; pvt.; **C**; 2nd Regt. Infan.
Saffell, James T.; pvt.; **C**; 2nd Regt. Infan.
St. John, Arthur; pvt.; **F**; 2nd Regt. Infan.
Sample, William A.; pvt.; **C**; 2nd Regt. Infan.
Sanders, Benjamin F.; pvt., cpl., Sgt.; **H**; 1st Regt. Infan.
Sanders, Daniel B.; pvt.; **D**; 2nd Regt. Infan.
Sanders, Edward I.; pvt.; **G**; 2nd Regt. Infan.
Sanders, John M.; pvt.; **H**; 2nd Regt. Infan.
Sanders, Robert H.; pvt.; **H**; 2nd Regt. Infan.
Sanders, William; pvt., **G**; 2nd Regt. Infan.
Sandifir, Daniel J.; pvt.; **B**; 1st Battalion Infan.
Saunders, James; pvt.; **Unknown**; 2nd Regt. Infan.
Saunders, Romulus M.; pvt.; **G**; 1st Regt. Infan.
Saunders, Thaddeus W.; pvt.; **G**; 1st Regt. Infan.
Savage, John; pvt.; **A**; 1st Battalion Infan.
Sawyer, William C.; pvt.; **E**; 2nd Regt. Infan.
Scales, Stephen D.; pvt.; **C**; 2nd Regt. Infan.
Schad, William; pvt.; **E**; 1st Regt. Infan.
Schmaling, Joseph; 1st cpl., Sgt.; **H**; 1st Regt. Infan.
Schmidt, John; pvt.; **H**; 2nd Regt. Infan.
Schnebely, Calvin; pvt.; **A**; 1st Regt. Infan.

Schultis, Lawrence; pvt.; **K**; 2nd Regt. Infan.

Scoggins, William S.; pvt.; **Unknown**; 2nd Regt. Infan.

Scott, Hines; pvt.; **H**; 2nd Regt. Infan.

Scott, James; pvt.; **A**; 2nd Regt. Infan.

Scott, Joseph; pvt.; **I**; 2nd Regt. Infan.

Scott, William; pvt.; **F**; 2nd Regt. Infan.

Scott, William Henry; 2nd, 1st Sgt.; **C**; 1st Regt. Infan.

Scott, William R.; pvt.; **C**; 2nd Regt. Infan.

Scrivener, Andrew J.; pvt.; **K**; 2nd Regt. Infan.

Scroggins, William; pvt.; **A**; 1st Battalion Infan.

Scruggs, Samuel; pvt.; **E**; 1st Regt. Infan.

Seale, Benajah B.; pvt.; **A**; 2nd Regt. Infan.

Seaman, Joel; pvt.; **B**; 1st Battalion Infan.

Seater, Robert Y.; pvt.; **K**; 2nd Regt. Infan.

Seay, William M.; pvt.; **G**; 1st Regt. Infan.

Selby, James E.; pvt.; **B**; 2nd Regt. Infan.

Sellers, James M.; pvt.; **G**; 2nd Regt. Infan.

Sellers, William; pvt.; **E**; 1st Regt. Infan.

Sellman, Eli; pvt.; **G**; 1st Regt. Infan.

Sellman, Thomas B.; pvt.; **G**; 1st Regt. Infan.

Sessions, James H.; pvt.; **A**; 1st Battalion Infan.

Sessions, John H.; pvt.; **E**; 1st Battalion Infan.

Setzler, George A.; pvt.; **D**; 1st Battalion Infan.

Sevier, Granville S. T.; pvt.; **B**; 2nd Regt. Infan.

Shackelford, Josephus; 2nd cpl.; **D**; 1st Battalion Infan.

Shackelford, Richard D.; pvt.; **H**; 1st Regt Infan.

Shaddock, Samuel; pvt.; **H**; 2nd Regt. Infan.

Shaifer, George Wilson Humphreys; pvt.; **H**; 1st Regt. Infan.

Shallies, Melvin H.; pvt.; **A**; 1st Battalion Infan.

Shandt, Benjamin K.; pvt.; **I**; 2nd Regt. Infan.

Shannon, Joseph P.; pvt.; **H**; 1st Regt. Infan.

Shannon, Sydneyham; pvt.; **A**; 1st Battalion Infan.

Sharman, James A.; pvt.; **K**; 1st Regt. Infan.

Sharp, John McNitt; Capt.; **A**; 1st Regt. Infan.

Sharp, William T.; 2nd Lieut.; **B**; 1st Battalion Infan.

Shaw, Franklin; pvt.; **Unknown**; 2nd Regt. Infan.

Shaw, Gustavis M.; pvt., 2nd cpl.; **D**; 2nd Regt. Infan.

Shaw, Robert J.; pvt., 3rd Sgt.; **F**; 1st Regt. Infan.

Shaw, Samuel; pvt.; **H**; 1st Regt. Infan.

Shaw, William G.; pvt.; **G**; 2nd Regt. Infan.

Sheehorn, William; pvt.; **F**; 1st Regt. Infan.

Shelling, Francis M.; pvt.; **D**; 2nd Regt. Infan.

Shelton, Calvin A.; pvt.; **E**; 1st Regt. Infan.

Shelton, Edward B.; 1st Sgt., 2nd Lieut.; **F**; 2nd Regt. Infan.

Shelton, James M.; pvt.; **E**; 1st Regt. Infan.

Shelton, John; pvt.; **D**; 1st Battalion Infan.
Shelton, Obadiah; pvt.; **D**; 2nd Regt. Infan.
Shelton, Redden; pvt.; **D**; 1st Battalion Infan.
Shields, R. W.; pvt.; **G**; 1st Regt. Infan.
Shields, Richard; pvt.; **H**; 2nd Regt. Infan.
Shilby, Isaac M.; pvt.; **I**; 1st Regt. Infan.
Shockley, James H.; 3rd Sgt.; **D**; 2nd Regt. Infan.
Shook, Robert L.; pvt.; **A**; 1st Regt. Infan.
Shooke, John; pvt.; **D**; 1st Regt. Infan.
Shope, Thomas J.; pvt.; **F**; 2nd Regt. Infan.
Short, Aaron B.; pvt.; **D/G**; 2nd Regt. Infan.
Shrives, Baker S.; pvt; **I**; 1st Regt. Infan.
Shy, Osborne; pvt.; **I**; 2nd Regt. Infan.
Sillers, Joseph; pvt.; **H**; 1st Regt. Infan.
Simmons, Jeremiah; pvt.; **D**; 2nd Regt. Infan.
Simms, William; pvt.; **F**; 2nd Regt. Infan.
Simpson, Charles T.; pvt.; **D**; 2nd Regt. Infan.
Simpson, James G.; pvt., cpl.; **H**; 2nd Regt. Infan.
Simpson, T. L.; pvt.; **F**; 1st Regt. Infan.
Sims, Benjamin M.; pvt.; **C**; 1st Regt. Infan.
Sims, David; pvt.; **C**; 1st Regt. Infan.
Sinclair, Peter; 4th, 1st cpl., 4th Sgt.; **G**; 1st Regt. Infan.
Singleton, Perry H.; pvt.; **E**; 2nd Regt. Infan.
Singleton, William; pvt.; **E**; 2nd Regt. Infan.
Singly, William G.; pvt.; **I**; 2nd Regt. Infan.
Siples, Lewis; pvt.; **E**; 1st Regt. Infan.
Skelton, William Redding; pvt.; **C**; 1st Regt. Infan.
Skidmore, Allen; pvt.; **K**; 1st Regt. Infan.
Slade, Thomas Pugh; 2nd Lieut.; **A**; 1st Regt. Infan.
Sloan, Rankin; pvt.; **C**; 1st Battalion Infan.
Small, Samuel; pvt.; **B**; 1st Regt. Infan.
Smedes, Charles E.; pvt.; **H**; 1st Regt. Infan.
Smith, Andrew C.; pvt.; **D**; 2nd Regt. Infan.
Smith, E. W.; pvt.; **G**; 1st Regt. Infan.
Smith, Erastus; pvt.; **A**; 2nd Regt. Infan.
Smith, Francis; pvt.; **C**; 2nd Regt. Infan.
Smith, Franklin; Capt., Asst. Surgeon; **F&S**; 1st Regt. Infan.
Smith, George A.; pvt.; **B**; 1st Regt. Infan.
Smith, Hampton H.; pvt.; **B**; 1st Regt. Infan.
Smith, Harrison; pvt.; **I**; 2nd Regt. Infan.
Smith, Harvey N.; pvt.; **E**; 2nd Regt. Infan.
Smith, Henry T.; pvt.; **K**; 2nd Regt. Infan.
Smith, James G.; pvt.; **E**; 2nd Regt. Infan.
Smith, James L.; pvt.; **B**; 1st Regt. Infan.
Smith, John; pvt.; **H**; 1st Regt. Infan.

Smith, John C.; pvt.; **A/G**; 2nd Regt. Infan.
Smith, John F.; pvt.; **B**; 1st Battalion Infan.
Smith, John H.; pvt.; **I**; 1st Regt. Infan.
Smith, John R.; pvt.; **A/B**; 1st Battalion Infan.
Smith, Johnson W.; pvt.; **E**; 1st Battalion Infan.
Smith, Joshua T.; pvt.; **G**; 2nd Regt. Infan.
Smith, Marshall Madison; pvt.; **E**; 1st Regt. Infan.
Smith, Migamon W.; pvt.; **Unknown**; 2nd Regt. Infan.
Smith, Nathaniel; pvt.; **G**; 2nd Regt. Infan.
Smith, Peter; pvt.; **B**; 1st Regt. Infan.
Smith, Richard H.; pvt.; **B**; 1st Battalion Infan.
Smith, Samuel; pvt.; **B**; 2nd Regt. Infan.
Smith, Stephen F.; 2nd mus., pvt.; **E**; 1st Battalion Infan.
Smith, Thaddeus C.; pvt.; **G**; 1st Regt. Infan.
Smith, Thomas; pvt.; **C**; 2nd Regt. Infan.
Smith, William A.; pvt.; **F**; 2nd Regt. Infan.
Smith, William F.; pvt.; **B**; 1st Battalion Infan.
Smith, William S.; pvt.; **A**; 1st Battalion Infan.
Smith, William T.; pvt.; **K**; 2nd Regt. Infan.
Smithwick, Ed. W.; pvt.; **F**; 2nd Regt. Infan.
Smithy, Abram; pvt.; **B**; 2nd Regt. Infan.
Smoot, John B.; pvt.; **I**; 1st Regt. Infan.
Snap, Nathaniel; pvt.; **B**; 1st Battalion Infan.
Snead, John; pvt.; **H**; 2nd Regt. Infan.
Snedicor, Platt; pvt.; **K**; 1st Regt. Infan.
Snow, James C.; pvt.; **E**; 2nd Regt. Infan.
Snyder, F. M.; pvt.; **B**; 1st Regt. Infan.
Sojourner, Sylvester D.; pvt.; **G**; 1st Regt. Infan.
Somerville, James; pvt.; **D**; 1st Regt. Infan.
Sones, Thomas S.; pvt.; **F**; 2nd Regt. Infan.
Sorsby, Thaddeus T.; pvt.; **E**; 1st Regt. Infan.
Spalding, Eugene A.; pvt., 3rd cpl.; **A**; 2nd Regt. Infan.
Sparks, James P.; pvt., Sgt.; **G**; 2nd Regt. Infan.
Speed, James; pvt.; **Unknown**; 2nd Regt. Infan.
Speed, William; pvt.; **I**; 2nd Regt. Infan.
Spencer, Edward; pvt.; **D**; 1st Battalion Infan.
Spencer, William P.; pvt.; **E**; 1st Regt. Infan.
Spinks, William B.; pvt.; **I**; 1st Regt. Infan.
Spurlock, Allen; pvt.; **B**; 1st Battalion Infan.
Spurlock, James; pvt.; **B**; 1st Battalion Infan.
Spurlock, Walter; pvt.; **B**; 1st Regt. Infan.
Stacy, William L.; pvt.; **E**; 1st Regt. Infan.
Stafford, John; pvt.; **E**; 1st Regt. Infan.
Stafford, Stephen B.; pvt.; **G**; 1st Regt. Infan.
Staggs, Thomas; pvt.; **A**; 1st Battalion Infan.

Stalions, Spencer B.; pvt.; **I**; 1st Regt. Infan.
Stamps, Franklin R.; pvt.; **K**; 2nd Regt. Infan.
Standin, John; pvt.; **A**; 1st Regt. Infan.
Starns, W. W.; pvt.; **B**; 1st Regt. Infan.
Starnes, John; pvt.; **C**; 2nd Regt. Infan.
Stedman, Daniel P.; 4th Sgt.; **K**; 1st Regt. Infan.
Steele, James J. V.; pvt.; **H**; 1st Regt. Infan.
Steele, Jesse G.; 1st Lieut.; **F**; 2nd Regt. Infan.
Steele, Newton A.; pvt., 1st Sgt.; **A**; 1st Battalion Infan.
Steele, Robert J.; pvt.; **E**; 1st Regt. Infan.
Steele, Thomas I.; pvt.; **Unknown**; 2nd Regt. Infan.
Stephens, Daniel; pvt.; **A**; 1st Regt. Infan.
Stephens, Joseph H.; pvt., 2nd cpl.; **F**; 2nd Regt. Infan.
Stephenson, J. N. Jr.; pvt.; **C**; 1st Regt. Infan.
Stevens, James N.; pvt.; **C**; 1st Regt. Infan.
Stevens, Samuel M.; pvt.; **E**; 1st Battalion Infan.
Stevens, William; pvt.; **K**; 2nd Regt. Infan.
Stevenson, James W.; pvt.; **H**; 1st Regt. Infan.
Steward, James D.; pvt.; **B**; 1st Regt. Infan.
Stewart, Adkinson; pvt.; **K**; 1st Regt. Infan.
Stewart, Benjamin E.; pvt.; **E**; 1st Battalion Infan.
Stewart, George E.; Capt.; **E**; 1st Battalion Infan.
Stewart, James E.; pvt., cpl., 1st Lieut.; **H**; 1st Regt. Infan.
Stewart, James J.; pvt.; **C**; 2nd Regt. Infan.
Stewart, James M.; pvt.; **K**; 2nd Regt. Infan.
Stewart, John; pvt.; **K**; 1st Regt. Infan.
Stewart, John H.; pvt., 4th Sgt.; **G**; 1st Regt. Infan.
Stewart, John W.; 2nd Lieut.; **D**; 1st Battalion Infan.
Stewart, Malcomb; pvt.; **E**; 1st Battalion Infan.
Stewart, Robert E.; pvt.; **B**; 1st Battalion Infan.
Stewart, Wesley; mus. (Fifer); **B**; 1st Regt. Infan.
Stiner, Calvin C.; 3rd, 2nd Sgt.; **D**; 2nd Regt. Infan.
Stockard, H.; pvt.; **F**; 1st Regt. Infan.
Stockard, John P.; pvt., 2nd Lieut.; **F**; 1st Regt. Infan.
Stockard, Joseph C.; pvt.: **F**; 1st Regt. Infan.
Stockton, James S.; pvt.; **B**; 2nd Regt. Infan.
Stokes, Redden; pvt.; **C**; 2nd Regt. Infan.
Stokes, Samuel A.; pvt.; **C**; 2nd Regt. Infan.
Stone, Joshua; pvt., 3rd, 1st Sgt.; **G**; 1st Regt. Infan.
Stone, William F.; pvt.; **A**; 2nd Regt. Infan.
Stonehouse, Sebastian; pvt.; **K**; 2nd Regt. Infan.
Stout, Henry; pvt.; **C**; 1st Regt. Infan.
Stout, John; pvt.; **C**; 1st Regt. Infan.
Stovall, William A.; pvt.; **C**; 2nd Regt. Infan.
Stratton, Jesse K.; pvt., 2nd cpl.; **K**; 2nd Regt. Infan.

Straugher, Calvin J.; pvt.; **B**; 1st Regt. Infan.
Straughn, John; pvt.; **H**; 1st Regt. Infan.
Street, William G.; pvt.; **C**; 1st Regt. Infan.
Stribbling, Clayton; pvt.; **B**; 2nd Regt. Infan.
Strickland, Jesse; mus. (Fifer); **D**; 1st Regt. Infan.
Strickland, John W.; pvt.; **H**; 2nd Regt. Infan.
Strong, John; pvt.; **F**; 1st Regt. Infan.
Strong, William; pvt.; **B**; 1st Battalion Infan.
Strong, William Miller; pvt.; **F**; 1st Regt. Infan.
Strother, William; 1st Lieut.; **K**; 2nd Regt. Infan.
Stroud, Thomas I.; pvt.; **F**; 2nd Regt. Infan.
Strouse, Charles; pvt.; **H**; 1st Regt. Infan.
Stubblefield, Adolphus H. M.; pvt., 2nd cpl.; **E**; 2nd Regt. Infan.
Stubblefield, Stephen Potts; pvt.; **A**; 1st Regt. Infan.
Stubblefield, William H.; pvt.; **E**; 2nd Regt. Infan.
Stubblefield, William Henry; pvt.; **A**; 1st Regt. Infan.
Strubeck, F. J.; pvt.; **C**; 1st Regt. Infan.
Suit, Samuel C.; pvt., cpl.; **C**; 1st Regt. Infan.
Sullivan, William; pvt.; **B**; 2nd Regt. Infan.
Sullivan, William; pvt.; **I**; 2nd Regt. Infan.
Sumner, Thomas I.; pvt.; **E**; 1st Battalion Infan.
Sumrall, Thomas S.; pvt.; **G**; 1st Regt. Infan.
Sutterly, John; pvt.; **B**; 2nd Regt. Infan.
Sutton, Stephen S.; pvt.; **G**; 2nd Regt. Infan.
Sutton, William; pvt.; **B**; 1st Battalion Infan.
Swann, Thomas; pvt., 2nd Sgt.; **F**; 1st Regt. Infan.
Sweeney, John; pvt.; **C**; 1st Battalion Infan.
Sweeten, Samuel M.; pvt.; **E**; 2nd Regt. Infan.
Swepston, Thomas S.; pvt., 4th, 3rd cpl.; **D**; 2nd Regt. Infan.
Swisher, Robert; pvt.; **A**; 1st Regt. Infan.
Tankley, John; pvt.; **D/G**; 2nd Regt. Infan.
Tanner, David; pvt.; **K**; 2nd Regt. Infan.
Tanner, James C.; pvt.; **K**; 1st Regt. Infan.
Tanner, Thomas A.; pvt.; **B**; 2nd Regt. Infan.
Tanner, William M.; pvt.; **D**; 2nd Regt. Infan.
Tapscott, Addison; pvt.; **D**; 1st Battalion Infan.
Tate, Arthur; pvt.; **E**; 1st Battalion Infan.
Tatum, Josephus J.; 4th Sgt., 2nd Lieut.; **F**; 1st Regt. Infan.
Taylor, Benjamin F.; pvt., 3rd cpl.; **D**; 1st Regt. Infan.
Taylor, George; pvt.; **I**; 1st Regt. Infan.
Taylor, Green B.; pvt.; **C**; 1st Regt. Infan.
Taylor, James H. R.; pvt., Capt.; **I**; 1st Regt. Infan.
Taylor, James I.; pvt., cpl.; **A**; 2nd Regt. Infan.
Taylor, John; pvt.; **G**; 2nd Regt. Infan.
Taylor, Memory; pvt.; **D**; 1st Regt. Infan.

Taylor, Wilson; pvt.; **F**; 1st Regt. Infan.

Teague, A. W.; pvt.; **A/G**; 1st Regt. Infan.

Teague, Hardy J.; pvt.; **A**; 2nd Regt. Infan.

Templeton, James H.; pvt.; **I**; 2nd Regt. Infan.

Terry, Lampkin Straughn; pvt., hospital steward, Sgt.; **H**; 2nd Regt. Infan.

Thames, Washington; pvt.; **C**; 1st Regt. Infan.

Tharpe, James M.; pvt.; **E**; 2nd Regt. Infan.

Thomas, Alfred B.; pvt.; **E**; 1st Battalion Infan.

Thomas, Daniel; pvt.; **A**; 1st Battalion Infan.

Thomas, James; pvt.; **B**; 1st Battalion Infan.

Thomas, James W.; pvt.; **A**; 1st Regt. Infan.

Thomas, James W.; pvt.; **E**; 1st Battalion Infan.

Thomas, Samuel Beuchamp; pvt., 3rd, 2nd Sgt., 2nd Lieut.; **G**; 1st Regt. Infan.

Thomas, Westley H.; 2nd, 1st Sgt.; **K**; 2nd Regt. Infan.

Thomas, Wyatt; pvt.; **K**; 2nd Regt. Infan.

Thompson, Cephas; pvt.; **B**; 1st Battalion Infan.

Thompson, Henry B.; pvt.; **C**; 1st Regt. Infan.

Thompson, James; pvt.; **K**; 1st Regt. Infan.

Thompson, James; pvt.; **E**; 1st Battalion Infan.

Thompson, James; pvt.; **K**; 2nd Regt. Infan.

Thompson, James O.; pvt.; **A**; 1st Battalion Infan.

Thompson, John; Asst. Surgeon; **A**; 1st Regt. Infan.

Thompson, John K.; pvt.; **B**; 2nd Regt. Infan.

Thompson, John L.; pvt.; **K**; 1st Regt. Infan.

Thompson, John L.; pvt.; **E**; 2nd Regt. Infan.

Thompson, Joseph H.; pvt., 3rd cpl.; **G**; 1st Regt. Infan.

Thompson, Joshua F.; pvt.; **B/E**; 2nd Regt. Infan.

Thompson, Nelson; pvt.; **K**; 2nd Regt. Infan.

Thompson, Robert E.; pvt.; **K**; 1st Regt. Infan.

Thompson, Walter Alvis; pvt.; **I**; 1st Regt. Infan.

Thompson, William; pvt., 1st Sgt.; **F**; 1st Regt. Infan.

Thompson, William; pvt.; **D**; 2nd Regt. Infan.

Thompson, William B.; pvt.; **C**; 2nd Regt. Infan.

Thompson, William P.; pvt.; **C**; 1st Battalion Infan.

Thornton, Thomas; 2nd Sgt.; **E**; 1st Battalion Infan.

Thurman, James; pvt.; **A**; 2nd Regt. Infan.

Thweatt, Elbert G.; pvt.; **H**; 2nd Regt. Infan.

Thweatt, James; pvt., 4th, 3rd cpl.; **D**; 2nd Regt. Infan.

Thweatt, Uriah W.; pvt.; **H**; 2nd Regt. Infan.

Tidwell, Francis R.; pvt.; **B**; 2nd Regt. Infan.

Tierce, Tucker Richard; pvt.; **K**; 1st Regt. Infan.

Tigner, Clarke H.; pvt.; **B**; 1st Regt. Infan.

Tilden, Thomas Ware; pvt.; **C**; 1st Regt. Infan.

Tillman, John C.; pvt.; **Unknown**; 2nd Regt. Infan.

Tillman, Louis; pvt.; **C**; 1st Regt. Infan.
Tindall, Henry; 2nd Sgt.; **K**; 1st Regt. Infan.
Tindsley, Calvin; pvt.; **K**; 1st Regt. Infan.
Tiner, William R.; pvt.; **B**; 2nd Regt. Infan.
Tinnin, Hugh Perry; pvt.; **E**; 1st Regt. Infan.
Tippett, Martin C.; pvt.; **I**; 2nd Regt. Infan.
Title(y?), Thomas H.; pvt.; **B**; 1st Regt. Infan.
Toomer, Benjamin Franklin; pvt.; **B**; 1st Battalion Infan.
Townsend, Littleton M.; pvt.; **B**; 1st Battalion Infan.
Townsend, William Purnell; pvt., 2nd Lieut.; **K**; 1st Regt. Infan.
Treadaway, William M.; pvt.; **D**; 2nd Regt. Infan.
Trotter, Henry G.; pvt.; **I**; 1st Regt. Infan.
Trotter, John; pvt., cpl.; **D**; 2nd Regt. Infan.
Trousdale, Leonidas; pvt., cpl., 2nd Lieut.; **D**; 1st Regt. Infan.
Truly, John H.; pvt.; **G**; 2nd Regt. Infan.
Truly, Philip H.; pvt.; **G**; 2nd Regt. Infan.
Trussell, Andrew Jackson; 2nd Lieut.; **F**; 2nd Regt. Infan.
Tucker, James Harvey; pvt.; **F**; 1st Regt. Infan.
Tucker, Marsden S.; pvt.; **B**; 2nd Regt. Infan.
Tucker, William D.; pvt.; **I**; 1st Regt. Infan.
Tunnill, Joseph P.; pvt.; **H**; 1st Regt. Infan.
Turberville, Benjamin Lewis; pvt.; **B**; 1st Regt. Infan.
Turnbull, John E.; pvt.; **F**; 1st Regt. Infan.
Turner, Asa; pvt.; **Unknown**; 2nd Regt. Infan.
Turner, Eaton B.; pvt.; **D**; 1st Battalion Infan.
Turner, Fielding; pvt.; **G**; 2nd Regt. Infan.
Turner, John R.; 2nd mus.; **D**; 1st Battalion Infan.
Turner, Joshua H.; pvt.; **F**; 1st Regt. Infan.
Turner, L. M.; pvt.; **C**; 1st Regt. Infan.
Tyler, Calvin C.; pvt.; **A**; 2nd Regt. Infan.
Tyree, John M.; pvt.; **K**; 1st Regt. Infan.
Tyson, James C.; pvt.; **A/F**; 2nd Regt. Infan.
Umphlett, Job; pvt.; **K**; 1st Regt. Infan.
Underwood, Ripley C.; pvt.; **F**; 2nd Regt. Infan.
Upson, Gad E.; mus.; **E**; 1st Regt. Infan.
Ussrey, Thomas J.; pvt.; **G**; 1st Regt. Infan.
Valentine, Charles T.; 2nd Sgt.; **K**; 1st Regt. Infan.
Van Dorn, Earl; Capt.; U.S. Dragoons
Van Norman, Stephen R.; pvt.; **B**; 1st Battalion Infan.
Van Wagener, John W.; pvt.; **C**; 1st Battalion Infan.
Vance, George W.; pvt.; **D**; 1st Regt. Infan.
Vance, John D. Gray; pvt.; **D**; 1st Regt. Infan.
Vandivure, John E.; pvt.; **H**; 1st Regt. Infan.
Vaughn, William G.; pvt.; **F**; 1st Regt. Infan.
Ventress, Edward L.; pvt.; **C**; 1st Regt. Infan.

Vest, George; pvt.; **D**; 2nd Regt. Infan.
Vincent, William; pvt.; **A**; 1st Battalion Infan.
Vinson, James W.; pvt.; **I**; 1st Regt. Infan.
Waddill, Anderson M.; mus., pvt.; **G**; 1st Regt. Infan.
Wade, Nathaniel T.; pvt.; **H**; 2nd Regt. Infan.
Wade, William; pvt.; **E**; 1st Regt. Infan.
Wade, William Bartee; pvt., 2nd Lieut.; **K**; 1st Regt. Infan.
Wadsworth, Alexander; pvt.; **E**; 2nd Regt. Infan.
Wadsworth, William W.; pvt.; **H**; 1st Regt. Infan.
Waganon, Daniel; pvt.; **D**; 1st Regt. Infan.
Wagers, James G.; pvt.; **D**; 1st Battalion Infan.
Wagner, John; pvt.; **B**; 2nd Regt. Infan.
Wainger, Casper; pvt.; **G**; 2nd Regt. Infan.
Waldern, William; pvt.; **B**; 2nd Regt. Infan.
Waldrop, John W.; pvt.; **E**; 1st Regt. Infan.
Walker, James M.; pvt.; **D**; 2nd Regt. Infan.
Walker, John M.; pvt.; **C**; 1st Battalion Infan.
Walker, Joseph W.; pvt.; **D**; 1st Battalion Infan.
Walker, Lawrence F.; pvt.; **D**; 1st Battalion Infan.
Walker, Robert B.; cpl.; **I**; 2nd Regt. Infan.
Walker, William K.; pvt.; **H**; 1st Regt. Infan.
Walker, William S.; lst Sgt.; **H**; 2nd Regt. Infan.
Wallace, E. D.; pvt.; **F**; 1st Regt. Infan.
Wallace, Edward; pvt.; **B**; 2nd Regt. Infan.
Wallace, James; pvt., 4th Sgt.; **I**; 2nd Regt. Infan.
Wallace, William C.; pvt., 4th Sgt.; **K**; 2nd Regt. Infan.
Walsh, James; pvt.; **E**; 1st Regt. Infan.
Walters, John H.; pvt.; **D**; 2nd Regt. Infan.
Walton, George W.; pvt.; **C**; 2nd Regt. Infan.
Ward, Amos F.; pvt.; **A**; 2nd Regt. Infan.
Ward, Hiram; pvt.; **K**; 2nd Regt. Infan.
Ward, James; pvt.; **E**; 1st Regt. Infan.
Ward, James G.; pvt.; **D**; 2nd Regt. Infan.
Ward, Werter; pvt.; **F**; 2nd Regt. Infan.
Ware, John R.; pvt.; **A**; 1st Regt. Infan.
Ware, Robert; pvt.; **C**; 2nd Regt. Infan.
Ware, Wilson; pvt.; **A/G**; 1st Regt. Infan.
Warren, William E.; pvt., Aide, Q.M.S.; **A/F&S**; 2nd Regt. Infan.
Washer, Thomas I.; pvt., 2nd Lieut.; **K**; 1st Regt. Infan. and **E**;
        2nd Regt. Infan.
Wasson, James; pvt.; **G**; 2nd Regt. Infan.
Watkins, Ichabod; pvt.; **K**; 2nd Regt. Infan.
Watlington, John M.; pvt.; **E**; 1st Battalion Infan.
Watson, James M.; pvt.; **G**; 1st Regt. Infan.
Watson, Kyran; pvt.; **I**; 2nd Regt. Infan.

Watson, Morgan; pvt.; **E/K**; 1st Regt. Infan.
Watson, William B.; 4th Sgt.; **A**; 1st Battalion Infan.
Watters, S. A.; pvt.; **D**; 2nd Regt. Infan.
Watts, J. J.; pvt.; **A/G**; 1st Regt. Infan.
Watts, N. G.; 3rd, 2nd, lst Sgt.; **C**; 1st Regt. Infan.
Waugh, James; pvt.; **E**; 1st Regt. Infan.
Way, William J. D.; pvt.; **B**; 1st Regt. Infan.
Weaver, Alexander W.; pvt., cpl., lst Lieut.; **C**; 2nd Regt. Infan.
Weaver, Asa H.; pvt.; **I**; 2nd Regt. Infan.
Weaver, Benjamin F.; pvt.; **C**; 2nd Regt. Infan.
Weaver, Hartwell R.; pvt.; **D**; 2nd Regt. Infan.
Weaver, John G.; pvt.; **D**; 2nd Regt. Infan.
Webb, George; pvt.; **E**; 2nd Regt. Infan.
Webb, George M.; pvt.; **A**; 2nd Regt. Infan.
Webb, Henry C.; pvt.; **K**; 2nd Regt. Infan.
Webb, James; pvt.; **Unknown**; 2nd Regt. Infan.
Webb, John; pvt.; **F**; 1st Regt. Infan.
Webster, George H.; 4th Sgt.; **B**; 1st Battalion Infan.
Webster, Martin; pvt.; **F**; 2nd Regt. Infan.
Wedekin, Christopher; pvt.; **A**; 1st Regt. Infan.
Weeks, John S.; pvt.; **D**; 2nd Regt. Infan.
Weems, Daniel L.; pvt., 2nd Lieut.; **F**; 2nd Regt. Infan.
Welch, Francis S.; pvt.; **F**; 1st Regt. Infan. and **B**; 2nd Regt. Infan.
Wellons, Marcus C.; 2nd Sgt.; **D**; 1st Regt. Infan.
Wells, John; pvt.; **B**; 1st Battalion Infan.
Wells, Joseph; pvt.; **B**; 2nd Regt. Infan.
West, Douglass; 2nd Sgt.; **B**; 1st Regt. Infan.
West, George; pvt.; **D**; 2nd Regt. Infan.
West, Harvey (aka Hervey); pvt.; **A**; 1st Regt. Infan.
West, Mitchell A.; pvt.; **D**; 2nd Regt. Infan.
West, Osborne F.; pvt., cpl.; **B**; 2nd Regt. Infan.
West, William D.; pvt.; **D**; 2nd Regt. Infan.
West, William L.; pvt.; **D**; 2nd Regt. Infan.
Westbrooks, John W.; pvt., cpl.; **K**; 1st Regt. Infan.
Weston, Robert B.; pvt.; **F**; 2nd Regt. Infan.
Westrope, James Monroe; pvt.; **B**; 1st Regt. Infan.
Wharton, Samuel; pvt.; **C**; 1st Regt. Infan.
Whatley, Elijah; pvt.; **C**; 2nd Regt. Infan.
Whatley, William H.; pvt., cpl.; **A**; 2nd Regt. Infan.
White, Archibald H.; pvt.; **K**; 1st Regt. Infan. and **E**; 1st Battalion Infan.
White, Martin S.; 2nd, 1st Lieut.; **D**; 2nd Regt. Infan.
White, Samuel Warren; pvt., Q.M.S.; **A/G/F&S**; 1st Regt. Infan.
White, Theodore W.; pvt.; **B**; 1st Regt. Infan.
White, Thomas; pvt.; **H**; 1st Regt. Infan.
White, Thomas C.; pvt.; **F**; 2nd Regt. Infan.

White, William A.; pvt.; **D**; 2nd Regt. Infan.
Whitehead, Calvin; pvt.; **Unknown**; 2nd Regt. Infan.
Whitman, James W.; pvt.; **A**; 1st Regt. Infan.
Whitman, Ulysses; pvt.; **A**; 1st Regt. Infan.
Whittington, John J.; pvt.; **B**; 1st Battalion Infan.
Whittington, Kenyon R.; pvt.; **B**; 1st Regt. Infan.
Wiatt, William M.; pvt.; **D**; 1st Battalion Infan.
Wigington, Henry J.; pvt.; **F**; 2nd Regt. Infan.
Wilburn, John A.; pvt.; **B**; 1st Battalion Infan.
Wilcox, John Allen; 1st Lieut., Lieut.-Col.; **D/F&S**; 2nd Regt. Infan.
Wilder, Sanford J.; pvt.; **A**; 1st Battalion Infan.
Wiley, Benjamin T.; pvt.; **C**; 2nd Regt. Infan.
Wilgus, David; pvt.; **D**; 1st Regt. Infan.
Wilkerson, Elijah J.; pvt., 4th Sgt.; **B**; 2nd Regt. Infan.
Wilkerson, Stephen P.; pvt.; **A**; 1st Battalion Infan.
Wilkerson, Thomas T.; pvt.; **I**; 1st Regt. Infan.
Wilkerson, Wiley M.; pvt.; **D**; 2nd Regt. Infan.
Wilkins, James L.; pvt.; **F**; 2nd Regt. Infan.
Wilkinson, William H.; pvt.; **B**; 1st Regt. Infan.
Willeford, John W.; pvt.; **A**; 2nd Regt. Infan.
Willett, John C.; pvt.; **K**; 1st Regt. Infan. and **E**; 1st Battalion Infan.
Williams, Allen; pvt.; **C**; 1st Battalion Infan.
Williams, Benjamin T.; pvt.; **K**; 2nd Regt. Infan.
Williams, Charles H.; 1st cpl.; **D**; 1st Battalion Infan.
Williams, Charles S.; pvt.; **G**; 1st Regt. Infan.
Williams, Eli; pvt.; **F**; 2nd Regt. Infan.
Williams, George; pvt., mus.; **A/G**; 1st Regt. Infan.
Williams, Gideon; pvt.; **I**; 1st Regt. Infan.
Williams, James N.; mus. (Drummer), pvt.; **D**; 2nd Regt. Infan.
    and **E**; 1st Battalion Infan.
Williams, James W.; pvt.; **E**; 1st Regt. Infan.
Williams, John; pvt.; **I**; 1st Regt. Infan.
Williams, John; pvt.; **C**; 1st Battalion Infan.
Williams, John; pvt.; **K**; 2nd Regt. Infan.
Williams, John H.; pvt.; **H**; 2nd Regt. Infan.
Williams, John M.; pvt.; **H**; 1st Regt. Infan.
Williams, John N.; pvt.; **E**; 1st Regt. Infan.
Williams, John R.; pvt.; **E**; 1st Regt. Infan.
Williams, Richard; pvt.; **D**; 1st Regt. Infan.
Williams, Robert Fitzgerald; 4th Sgt.; **A**; 1st Regt. Infan.
Williams, Samuel D.; pvt.; **H**; 2nd Regt. Infan.
Williams, Simon; pvt.; **C**; 1st Battalion Infan.
Williams, Stephen C. L.; pvt.; **D**; 2nd Regt. Infan.
Williams, Valerius R.; pvt.; **E**; 1st Battalion Infan.
Williams, William; pvt.; **D**; 1st Battalion Infan.

Williams, William A. I.; pvt.; **E**; 1st Battalion Infan.
Williams, William W.; pvt., 2nd Sgt.; **D**; 2nd Regt. Infan.
Williamson, Albert; pvt.; **H**; 2nd Regt. Infan.
Williamson, George D.; pvt.; **C**; 1st Regt. Infan.
Williamson, Isham; 3rd cpl.; **F**; 2nd Regt. Infan.
Williamson, James; pvt.; **G**; 1st Regt. Infan.
Williamson, John N. B.; pvt.; **D**; 1st Regt. Infan.
Williamson, Joseph A.; pvt.; **F**; 2nd Regt. Infan.
Williamson, Rufus R.; pvt.; **H**; 1st Regt. Infan.
Willis, John C.; Capt.; **C**; 1st Regt. Infan.
Willis, Pyatt A.; pvt.; **B**; 2nd Regt. Infan.
Wills, George; pvt.; **D**; 1st Regt. Infan.
Wills, James Austin Jr.; pvt.; **D**; 2nd Regt. Infan.
Wilson, Basil H.; pvt.; **C**; 2nd Regt. Infan.
Wilson, George A.; pvt.; **B**; 1st Battalion Infan.
Wilson, George H.; pvt.; **B**; 2nd Regt. Infan.
Wilson, Giles L.; pvt.; **C**; 2nd Regt. Infan.
Wilson, J.; pvt.; **D**; 2nd Regt. Infan.
Wilson, James C.; 1st Sgt., Sgt.-Maj.; **D/F&S**; 2nd Regt. Infan.
Wilson, James R.; pvt.; **I**; 2nd Regt. Infan.
Wilson, John; pvt.; **E**; 1st Battalion Infan.
Wilson, John G.; 3rd cpl.; **B**; 2nd Regt. Infan.
Wilson, Josiah; pvt.; **E**; 2nd Regt. Infan.
Wilson, Richard; pvt.; **D**; 2nd Regt. Infan.
Wilson, Samuel; pvt.; **C**; 2nd Regt. Infan.
Wiltshire, George W.; mus., cpl.; **C**; 2nd Regt. Infan.
Winans, William; pvt.; **H**; 1st Regt. Infan.
Winn, John C.; pvt.; **C**; 1st Regt. Infan.
Winn, Joseph A.; pvt.; **H**; 2nd Regt. Infan.
Winn, Osborne; pvt.; **B**; 2nd Regt. Infan.
Winston, Joseph W.; pvt., 4th cpl.; **E**; 2nd Regt. Infan.
Winston, William; 4th cpl.; **D**; 1st Battalion Infan.
Winters, Benjamin F.; pvt.; **C**; 1st Battalion Infan.
Wiseman, John F.; pvt.; **A**; 1st Battalion Infan.
Wolcott (Walcott), Carlton Luke; pvt.; **C**; 1st Battalion Infan.
Wolf, Francis A.; 3rd Sgt.; **I**; 1st Regt. Infan.
Wolfe, Alexander D.; pvt.; **D**; 1st Battalion Infan.
Wood, Augustus; pvt.; **H**; 1st Regt. Infan.
Wood, James B.; pvt.; **C**; 2nd Regt. Infan.
Wood, James N.; pvt.; **C**; 1st Regt. Infan.
Wood, Malam; pvt.; **A**; 1st Battalion Infan.
Wood, William W. W.; **E**; 4th Regt. LA Infan.
Woodall, Alexander R.; 2nd Sgt.; **A**; 1st Battalion Infan.
Woodard, Abijah; pvt.; **G**; 2nd Regt. Infan.
Woodburn, John; pvt.; **C**; 2nd Regt. Infan.

Woodliff, William C.; pvt.; **K**; 1st Regt. Infan.

Woodruff, J. O.; pvt.; **C**; 1st Regt. Infan.

Woods, Andrew; pvt.; **C**; 2nd Regt. Infan.

Wooldridge, Samuel D.; 1st cpl.; **G**; 1st Regt. Infan.

Woolridge, John; pvt.; **A**; 1st Regt. Infan.

Woosley, William; pvt.; **B**; 1st Regt. Infan.

Word, Charles Sullivan; 4th cpl.; **F**; 1st Regt. Infan.

Word, Cuthbert B.; pvt.; **E**; 2nd Regt. Infan.

Workman, Benjamin F.; pvt.; **K**; 2nd Regt. Infan.

Worsham, Henry; pvt.; **D**; 1st Battalion Infan.

Woulger, Charles; pvt.; **B**; 1st Regt. Infan.

Wray, John F.; Capt.; **D**; 1st Battalion Infan.

Wright, Michael; pvt.; **I**; 2nd Regt. Infan.

Wright, R. H.; pvt.; **G**; 1st Regt. Infan.

Wurmser, George; pvt.; **D/E**; 2nd Regt. Infan.

Wyatt, David P.; pvt., cpl., 4th, 3rd, 2nd Sgt.; **G**; 2nd Regt. Infan.

Wyatt, Willford D.; pvt.; **B**; 1st Battalion Infan.

Wynn, Richard; pvt.; **A**; 2nd Regt. Infan.

Wynns, Robert P.; pvt., cpl.; **D**; 1st Regt. Infan.

Yancey, Joseph T.; 1st cpl., 4th Sgt.; **I**; 1st Regt. Infan.

Yancey, Simon B.; 2nd cpl.; **I**; 1st Regt. Infan.

Yancey, Tryon Milton; pvt.; **I**; 1st Regt. Infan.

York, Daniel; pvt.; **A**; 1st Battalion Infan.

Young, Albert; pvt.; **D**; 1st Regt. Infan.

Young, Andrew J.; pvt.; **I**; 2nd Regt. Infan.

Young, Benjamin; pvt.; **D**; 2nd Regt. Infan.

Young, Jackson; pvt.; **I**; 2nd Regt. Infan.

Young, Jacob T.; pvt.; **D**; 1st Regt. Infan.

Young, Mathew A.; pvt.; **E**; 1st Battalion Infan.

Young, Pearleamon J.; pvt.; **B**; 1st Battalion Infan.

Young, Samuel A.; 1st Sgt.; **D**; 1st Regt. Infan.

Zolicoffer, Oscar M.; pvt.; **F**; 1st Regt. Infan.

Soldiers
★ Listed By Company ★
1st Regiment Mississippi Volunteers

Field & Service Staff

Bradford, Alexander Blackburn   Major
Davis, Jefferson Finis   Colonel
Dodds, Stephen V.   Drum-Major
Griffith, Richard   Adjutant
Halsey, Seymour   Surgeon
Harlan, Charles T.   Sergeant-Major
Holland, Kemp S.   Assistant-Commissary
McClung, Alexander Keith   Lieutenant-Colonel
Marshall, Humphrey   Sergeant-Major
Miller, Horace H.   Sergeant-Major
Smith, Franklin   Assistant-Surgeon
White, Samuel Warren   Quartermaster

Company A, Yazoo Volunteers
(Yazoo County)

Aiken, John   pvt.
Bailey, David F.   pvt.
Banks, Winston   pvt.
Batton, Daniel H.   pvt., cpl.
Bell, James H.   pvt., 2nd cpl.
Bisbee, Noah   pvt.
Bostick, Ferdinand   Sgt., 1st Lieut.
Bowman, Edward   3rd cpl., Sgt.
Bradley, John   pvt.
Brooke, George   pvt.
Brown, Alonzo L.   pvt.
Burrus, Philip J.   1st Lieut.
Caldwell, Samuel S.   musician
Capshaw, A. C.   pvt.
Capshaw, William W.   pvt.
Carter, Samuel K.   pvt.
Cason, John A.   3rd Sgt.
Clark, Henry D.   pvt.
Colton, Francis   pvt.
Conger, Jeptha   pvt.

Corwine, Amos Breckinridge   pvt., 2nd, 1st Lieut.
Cowart, Andrew J.   pvt.
Dillon, John   pvt.
Dixon, Elijah   pvt.
Ellis, Thomas J.   pvt.
Fisher, Robert   pvt., Sgt.
Floyd, Elijah   pvt.
Floyd, Henry   pvt.
Forbes, Daniel   pvt.
Fox, Edwin   pvt.
Gardner, Solomon   pvt.
Gerrald, Richard S.   pvt.
Gerrald, William G.   pvt.
Gordon, Charles R.   pvt.
Green, Richard   pvt.
Griffin, Robert Henderson   pvt.
Griffin, Thomas R.   pvt., cpl.
Grimes, Caleb   pvt.
Hart, Meredith   pvt.

Herrod, Andrew J. pvt.
Higginbotham, Thomas T. pvt., cpl., Sgt.
Hill, Albert P. 2nd, 1st Sgt.
Holland, Kemp S. Asst. Comsy., Capt.
Hollingsworth, David M. musician, 1st Sgt.
Hughes, Daniel pvt.
Hutchinson, William F. pvt.
Ingram, William W. pvt., cpl., 3rd Sgt.
Johnson, Albert pvt., Teamster
Johnson, John pvt.
Kenna, Henry R. pvt.
Kirk, J. W. pvt.
Lavender, Solomon D. pvt.
Leake, Charles Austin pvt.
Little, Henry S. pvt.
Martin, John A. pvt., cpl.
Mason, Madison M. pvt.
Miller, Charles J. pvt., cpl.
Miller, James M. pvt.
Miller, William J. 4th cpl.
Mobley, Middleton Rufus pvt.
Moore, William pvt.
Morton, Joseph W. pvt.
O'Bryant, James pvt.
O'Sullivan, Cornelius pvt.
Parker, Samuel O. pvt.
Paul, Peter A. pvt.
Peaster, William H. pvt.
Penny, Joseph H. pvt.

Phillips, Seaborne Moses cpl., 4th Sgt., 2nd Lieut.
Prestridge, William A. pvt.
Prewett, Emory pvt.
Pyles, Milton pvt.
Read, Jesse pvt.
Read, Licurgos D. Sgt.
Richards, James pvt.
Ridley, Benjamin F. pvt.
Russell, Reuben pvt.
Schnebely, Calvin pvt.
Sharp, John McNitt Capt.
Shook, Robert L. pvt.
Slade, Thomas Pugh 2nd Lieut.
Standin, John pvt.
Stephens, Daniel pvt.
Stubblefield, Stephen Potts pvt.
Stubblefield, William Henry pvt.
Swisher, Robert pvt.
Teague, A. W. pvt.
Thomas, James W. pvt.
Thompson, John Assistant-Surgeon
Ware, John R. pvt.
Ware, Wilson pvt.
Watts, J. J. pvt.
Wedekin, Christopher pvt.
West, Harvey (aka Hervey) pvt.
White, Samuel Warren pvt., Q.M.S.
Whitman, James W. pvt.
Whitman, Ulysses pvt.
Williams, George musician, pvt.
Williams, Robert Fitzgerald 4th Sgt.
Woolridge, John pvt.

Company B, Wilkinson Volunteers
(Wilkinson County)

Anderson, John L. pvt.
Baird, James B. pvt.
Best, Francis 1st cpl., 3rd Sgt.
Bragg, Thomas Z. pvt.
Bryant, William J. pvt.
Cage, Albert G. Jr. pvt.
Cage, Benjamin M. pvt., 2nd cpl.

Cage, William L. pvt.
Calhoun, James 2nd Lieut.
Carriger, Ido pvt.
Caulfield, James Douglas pvt.
Chance, Reuben W. pvt.
Clampett, Richard F. pvt.
Conner, Thomas G. pvt.

Cooper, Douglas Hancock Capt.
Cotton, William A. pvt.
Dixon, Noland S. pvt.
Donnelly, James W. pvt.
Erambert, Charles 2nd cpl., 4th Sgt.
Farish, Claiborne 4th, 2nd Sgt.
Fuqua, Joseph S. pvt.
Gayden, Iverson Greene pvt.
Hampton, Thomas H. pvt.
Harris, David B. pvt.
Harrison, Samuel R. pvt., Bvt. 2nd
   Lieut.
Herbert, John Q. pvt.
Hill, James pvt.
Hodge, James L. pvt.
Hodge, William I. pvt., 3rd cpl.
Holt, John Saunders pvt.
Holt, John T. pvt., cpl., 4th Sgt.
Hope, William Gready pvt.
Hutchinson, Irenius R. pvt.
Jackson, J. H. pvt.
Jones, George H. pvt.
Jones, Seaborne pvt.
Kearsey, John J. pvt.
Kyle, J. pvt.
Lanehart, A. C. pvt.
Lanehart, Adam pvt.
Law, Thomas H. musician
   (Drummer)
Lawrence, William A. pvt.
Leunex, James pvt.
Lindsey, Hugh N. pvt.
Lowry, Robert H. pvt.
McClure, Joseph F. pvt.
McConnell, Robert 1st Sgt.
McGehee, Daniel R. pvt.
Martin, James M. pvt.
Massell, Eugene 3rd Sgt.
Miller, James Madison pvt.
Miller, Robert 3rd cpl.
Miller, William H. pvt.

Mootry, Lewis pvt.
Morgan, Hiram pvt.
Morris, Mabry Ivy pvt.
Murray, David pvt.
Murtough, Barney pvt.
Neeland, Robert H. pvt.
Newman, Alexander pvt.
Newman, Solomon pvt.
Nicholson, James H. pvt.
O'Neal, Henry F. pvt.
Posey, Carnot 1st Lieut., Capt.
Rea, William R. pvt.
Richardson, George P. pvt.
Richardson, Samuel J. pvt.
Riddle, James pvt.
Rivercomb, George pvt., 4th cpl.
Robinson (Roberson?), John pvt.
Robinson, William D. pvt.
Rotrammel, William Simpson pvt.
Small, Samuel pvt.
Smith, George A. pvt.
Smith, Hampton H. pvt.
Smith, James L. pvt.
Smith, Peter pvt.
Snyder, F. M. pvt.
Spurlock, Walter pvt.
Starns, W. W. pvt.
Steward, James D. pvt.
Stewart, Wesley musician (Fifer)
Straugher, Calvin J. pvt.
Tigner, Clarke H. pvt.
Title(y?), Thomas H. pvt.
Turberville, Benjamin Lewis pvt.
Way, William J. D. pvt.
West, Douglass 2nd Sgt.
Westrope, James Monroe pvt.
White, Theodore W. pvt.
Whittington, Kenyon R. pvt.
Wilkinson, William H. pvt.
Woosley, William pvt.
Woulger, Charles pvt.

Company C, Vicksburg Southrons
(Warren County)

Abbott, Richard H. pvt.
Armour, Henry L. musician
Arthur, Rufus K. 1st Sgt., 2nd Lieut.
Banks, Robert B. pvt.
Barnes, Charles pvt.
Barnes, John M. pvt.
Bass, Benjamin pvt.
Batts, Theodore D. pvt.
Bradford, Charles T. pvt.
Bradford, Ira Oscar pvt.
Bright, William H. pvt.
Brown, George W. pvt.
Brownlee, Adam pvt.
Clark, Francis pvt.
Clements, William H. pvt.
Collier, Jonathan Nichols pvt., cpl.
Collins, Samuel P. pvt.
Conn, James W. pvt.
Connor, Benjamin G. pvt.
Cook, Henry Felix 1st Lieut.
Couch, William pvt.
Cowan, J. C. pvt.
Craft, John pvt.
Culverton, Robert pvt.
Currie, Edward pvt.
Daughtry, John M. pvt.
Davis, Robert H. pvt.
Denson, John S. musician (Fifer)
Dixon, A. L. pvt.
Dodds, Stephen V. musician (Drum Major), pvt.
Dugan, John pvt.
Dunn, George W. pvt.
Eggleston, Dick H. pvt.
Ellis, Charles H. pvt.
Ford, Henry F. pvt.
Forkes, Benjamin pvt,
Forkes, James L. pvt.
Friar, William J. pvt.
Gaffney, Edward pvt.
Godwin, Josiah H. cpl.
Gray, George H. pvt.
Grey, J. W. pvt.
Griffith, Richard 2nd Lieut., Adjut.
Guy, J. M. pvt.
Gwinn, James musician
Harris, William E. pvt.
Harrod, John pvt.
Hartley, A. pvt.
Hemby, William R. pvt.
Hickey, William V. cpl., 3rd Sgt.
Hindman, Samuel pvt.
Howell, Joseph D. pvt.
Irvine, James pvt.
Jeter, John pvt.
Johnson, James pvt.
Johnson, Peter W. pvt.
McKay, Daniel A. pvt.
McKey, Robert pvt.
McLaughlin, James A. 4th cpl., 4th Sgt.
Malone, Robert H. pvt., 1st cpl.
Maples, John Wesley pvt.
Markham, John B. 2nd cpl.
Martin, Russell M. pvt.
Metcalf, George Edward pvt.
Miller, Joseph pvt.
Morris, Howard pvt., cpl.
Nutter, William Mason pvt.
Pack, James D. pvt.
Preston, John pvt.
Puckett, Henry L. 4th, 3rd Sgt.
Richards, Andrew L. pvt.
Richardson, Robert E. pvt.
Russell, C. H. pvt.
Scott, William Henry 2nd, 1st Sgt.
Sims, Benjamin M. pvt.
Sims, David pvt.
Skelton, William Redding pvt.
Stephenson, J. N. Jr. pvt.
Stevens, James N. pvt.
Stout, Henry pvt.
Stout, John pvt.
Street, William G. pvt.

Strubeck, F. J. pvt.
Suit, Samuel C. pvt., cpl.
Taylor, Green B. pvt.
Thames, Washington pvt.
Thompson, Henry B. pvt.
Tilden, Thomas Ware pvt.
Tillman, Louis pvt.
Turner, L. M. pvt.

Ventress, Edward L. pvt.
Watts, N. G. 3rd, 2nd, 1st Sgt.
Wharton, Samuel pvt.
Williamson, George D. pvt.
Willis, John C. Capt.
Winn, John C. pvt.
Wood, James N. pvt.
Woodruff, J. O. pvt.

Company D, Carroll County Volunteers
(Carroll County)

Adair, Francis Marion pvt.
Adair, Isaac Granger pvt., cpl., 2nd
  Sgt.
Adkinson, J. G. pvt.
Adkinson, Pinkney G. pvt.
Applegate, Richard pvt.
Beall, Egbert F. pvt., 4th Sgt.
Beard, Harrison B. pvt.
Benthall, John C. pvt.
Blake, J. W. pvt., 4th cpl.
Brown, Thomas pvt.
Buckholts, John A. pvt.
Burrell, James H. pvt.
Burwell, James pvt.
Capshaw, Daniel C. pvt.
Carr, Young pvt.
Clark, Robert pvt.
Coakley, John pvt., cpl.
Cobb, Alpheus pvt.
Cocke, Daniel P. pvt., 3rd, 2nd cpl.
Colburn, Samuel G. pvt.
Creamer, Henry pvt.
Davidson, Thomas B. pvt.
Doyle, David R. pvt.
Durden, Jonathan 3rd cpl., 3rd Sgt.
Durham, W. T. S. pvt.
Elliott, John G. pvt.
Erwin, John W. pvt.
Ewing, Andrew pvt.
Ferguson, Samuel T. pvt.
Fields, Ripley pvt.
Forbes, Joel pvt.
Forster, Charles A. musician

(Bugler)
Gage, James D. M. pvt.
George, James Zachariah pvt.
Gray, William P. pvt.
Gunter, William M. pvt.
Hall, Harmon Y. pvt.
Hanks, Marion pvt.
Hanks, Talliaferro pvt.
Harper, John R. pvt.
Harrell, Wells C. pvt., 1st Sgt.
Heath, J. B. pvt.
Hodge, Benjamin Louis pvt., 2nd
  Lieut.
Hollingsworth, E. pvt., 1st cpl , 2nd
  Sgt., 2nd Lieut.
Hood, Parker pvt.
Howard, Bainbridge D. Capt.
Howard, Lewis T. 2nd Lieut.
Hudson, Alfred pvt.
Huffman, Warren pvt.
Jefferson, David W. pvt.
Johnson, James pvt.
Jones, Owen W. pvt.
Jones, William H. musician
  (Drummer), pvt.
Kyle, Thomas J. 2nd cpl., 2nd Sgt.,
  2nd Lieut.
Lewis, Robert A. pvt., cpl., 3rd Sgt.
Lott, William pvt.
Love, David E. 3rd Sgt.
McAlister, Neal pvt.
McCauly, John pvt.
McClendon, Andrew J. pvt.

McCoy, James A. pvt.
Martin, Richard pvt.
Martin, William D. pvt.
Maunday, Samuel S. pvt.
Nixon, Ceasar L. pvt., 4th Sgt.
Norman, Benjamin F. pvt.
Norman, Hiram G. pvt.
Orr, William pvt.
Pleasants, Frank P. pvt.
Powell, Andrew T. pvt.
Ramsey, George W. pvt.
Ramsey, James M. 4th Sgt.
Reynolds, Hugh A. pvt., 4th cpl.
Reynolds, John Q. pvt.
Reynolds, Sherod pvt.
Rhodes, Benjamin B. pvt.
Rowe, A. Govan pvt., 3rd, 2nd cpl.
Russell, Daniel R. 1st Lieut., Capt.
Russell, L. H. pvt., cpl., Sgt.

Shooke, John pvt.
Somerville, James pvt.
Strickland, Jesse musician (Fifer)
Taylor, Benjamin F. pvt., 3rd cpl.
Taylor, Memory pvt.
Trousdale, Leonidas pvt., cpl., 2nd
  Lieut.
Vance, George W. pvt.
Vance, John D. Gray pvt.
Waganon, Daniel pvt.
Wellons, Marcus C. 2nd Sgt.
Wilgus, David pvt.
Williams, Richard pvt.
Williamson, John N. B. pvt.
Wills, George pvt.
Wynns, Robert P. pvt., cpl.
Young, Albert pvt.
Young, Jacob T. pvt.
Young, Samuel A. 1st Sgt.

Company E, State Fencibles
(Hinds County)

Bowman, John H. pvt., 4th cpl., Sgt.
Bradford, Charles MacPherson pvt.,
  2nd Lieut.
Bryan, Henry Herbert pvt.
Burnham, A. P. pvt.
Butler, William A. pvt.
Campbell, John pvt.
Clariday, Richard pvt.
Cohea, Edward U. pvt.
Coleman, John pvt.
Conner, Daniel pvt.
Coulter, Solomon M. pvt.
Deigman (Degnan), Patrick pvt.
Donald, James pvt.
Edwards, Benjamin Harrison pvt.
Estis, William E. 4th cpl., 3rd Sgt.
Farrar, George Harding pvt.
Fauntleroy, Frederick W. pvt.
Finley, George P. pvt.
Fleming, William H. pvt.
Fletcher, Crawford 1st Lieut.
Foute, Marcellus A. 4th, 2nd cpl.

Fox, Robert pvt.
Frazier, David pvt.
Fredericks, Jacob pvt.
Gourley, Hugh pvt.
Gourley, Milton F. pvt.
Green, F. G. pvt.
Green, Girault pvt.
Griffin, James T. pvt.
Harrison, John pvt.
Hasty, William H. pvt.
Heckler, John M. pvt.
Higdon, James pvt.
Hipple, Henry pvt.
Hobbs, Calvin musician (Fifer), pvt.
Hooker, John M. pvt.
Hughes, Archibald M. 2nd Sgt.
Hughes, James H. 2nd Lieut.
Hunter, J. W. pvt.
Joyce, Robert A. pvt.
Keep, Henry V. pvt.
Kennedy, John pvt.
Kenny, William pvt.

Kilvey, James H. pvt.
Laird, George W. pvt., cpl.
Laird, Isham C. pvt.
Lairy, Jeremiah E. pvt.
Lane, Samuel W. pvt., 2nd cpl.
Langford, Joseph H. 4th Sgt.
Langford, William R. 3rd cpl.
Latham, Richard pvt.
Lowe, William pvt.
Lowry, James pvt.
Lyerly, James B. pvt.
McManus, John Lewis Capt.
McNair, Evander 2nd cpl., 1st Sgt.
McNully, Z. pvt.
Marrs, William H. pvt.
Marsh, Samuel W. pvt.
Martin, William S. pvt.
Meachem, Silas pvt.
Moore, James pvt.
Moss, Jesse W. pvt.
Myrick, J. M. pvt.
Myrick, M. G. pvt.
Patterson, Andrew B. pvt., 1st Sgt.
Perkins, I. Camp pvt.
Phillips, George pvt.
Phillips, William W. 3rd Sgt.
Pierce, Hugh W. pvt.
Pomroy, Henry pvt.
Price, Archibald G. pvt., cpl.
Puckett, Anthony B. pvt., 3rd cpl.
Rawlings, James pvt.

Reed, William C. pvt.
Revell, Joseph C. pvt.
Ritch, John pvt.
Roberts, E. W. pvt.
Robinson, D. H. pvt.
Robinson, Francis M. 1st cpl.
Runnels, Ellis J. pvt.
Schad, William pvt.
Scruggs, Samuel pvt.
Sellers, William pvt.
Shelton, Calvin A. pvt.
Shelton, James M. pvt.
Siples, Lewis pvt.
Smith, Marshall Madison pvt.
Sorsby, Thaddeus T. pvt.
Spencer, William P. pvt.
Stacy, William L. pvt.
Stafford, John pvt.
Steele, Robert J. pvt.
Tinnin, Hugh Perry pvt.
Upson, Gad E. musician
Wade, William pvt.
Waldrop, John W. pvt.
Walsh, James pvt.
Ward, James pvt.
Watson, Morgan pvt.
Waugh, James pvt
Williams, James W. pvt.
Williams, John N. pvt.
Williams, John R. pvt.

Company F, Lafayette Volunteers
(Lafayette County)

Ater, H. C. pvt.
Bigby (Bigbie), James N. pvt.
Blakely, James Witherspoon pvt.,
    1st cpl.
Boyd, J. pvt.
Boyd, James pvt.
Brittain, D. A. pvt.
Broach, William H. pvt.
Brown, William N. 1st Lieut.
Browning, Alfred G. pvt.

Browning, James C. pvt.
Buie, Thomas J. pvt.
Burks, A. T. pvt.
Butler, Damascus L. pvt., cpl.
Campbell, James pvt.
Carger, J. H. pvt., cpl.
Carloss, M. D. C. 1st Sgt.
Carr, Madison H. pvt.
Carr, William A. Jr. pvt.
Chester, Jacob R. musician

Childres, James M. pvt.
Cloak, William G. pvt.
Coatney, Thomas pvt.
Conner, John pvt.
Davis, Thomas A. pvt.
Davis, Waller pvt.
Delay, William Henry Capt.
Dixon, Almaron S. 3rd Sgt.
Dunevant, Peter J. pvt.
Eaton, William W. pvt.
Gardner, D. Mc. pvt.
Garrott, Enos pvt.
Gee, William H. pvt.
Goodwin, Crawford pvt.
Goodwin, George W. pvt.
Hancock, John A. G. pvt.
Henderson, James A. pvt.
Henry, Rufus pvt.
Higginbottom, Ransom C. pvt.
Hobbs, J. P. 2nd cpl.
Hoggany, Benjamin 2nd Sgt.
Holcomb, J. pvt.
Holt, William pvt.
Humphries, W. R. pvt.
Hunter, Stephen D. pvt.
Jimerson, David Reed pvt.
Joiner, Benjamin pvt.
Jones, Stephen pvt.
Jones, Thomas L. pvt.
Jones, William H. musician
(Drummer), pvt.
Knight, Absolem pvt.
Lawson, Charles pvt.
Lewers, Charles A. pvt.
Liles, Alfred M. pvt.
Livingston, G. H. pvt.
Livingston, John musician
Locke, Matthew F. pvt., cpl.
Lowe, John C. pvt.
Luckett, John pvt.

Luckett, Samuel pvt.
McFarland, Alexander B. pvt.
McKie, Green pvt.
Malone, Frederick James pvt., 2nd
Lieut.
Maza, Levi pvt.
Meaders, Levi M. pvt.
Moore, C. pvt.
Morris, James T. pvt.
Morris, Joseph W. pvt.
Mullinax, James P. pvt.
Owens, William H. pvt.
Parker, William S. pvt.
Patterson, D. E. pvt.
Peaterson, G. pvt.
Powell, James L. pvt.
Redding, William W. pvt., 2nd
Lieut.
Shaw, Robert J. pvt., 3rd Sgt.
Sheehorn, William pvt.
Simpson, T. L. pvt.
Stockard, H. pvt.
Stockard, John P. pvt., 2nd Lieut.
Stockard, Joseph C. pvt.
Strong, John pvt.
Strong, William Miller pvt.
Swann, Thomas pvt., 2nd Sgt.
Tatum, Josephus J. 4th Sgt., 2nd
Lieut.
Taylor, Wilson pvt.
Thompson, William pvt., 1st Sgt.
Tucker, James Harvey pvt.
Turnbull, John E. pvt.
Turner, Joshua H. pvt.
Vaughn, William G. pvt.
Wallace, E. D. pvt.
Webb, John pvt.
Welch, Francis S. pvt.
Word, Charles Sullivan 4th cpl.
Zolicoffer, Oscar M. pvt.

Company G, Raymond Fencibles
(Hinds County)

Ainsworth, William D. pvt.

Alexander, J. M. pvt., 4th cpl.

Anderson, Thomas Jefferson pvt.

Atkinson, Asa B. pvt., 3rd, 1st cpl.

Bird, George J. W. pvt.

Bond, Joseph S. pvt.

Bowen, Robert pvt.

Boyd, James pvt.

Bradley, Thomas pvt.

Brown, James S. pvt.

Burland, Charles M. pvt.

Burnett, Phillip pvt.

Burnett, V. S. pvt.

Burney, Elonzo Pleasant pvt.

Champion, Sidney Smith pvt.

Chapman, John A. pvt.

Chapman, Theodore C. pvt., 4th cpl.

Charlton, Edward Francis pvt.

Charlton, Edward S. 2nd cpl., 1st Sgt.

Clarke, Watson E. pvt.

Conger, Jephta pvt.

Cooper, Louis A. pvt.

Cooper, William G. Jr. pvt.

Coorpender, Lewis pvt.

Coorpender, William F. pvt.

Downing, Reuben Newman Capt.

Dunlap, Elijah pvt.

Edwards, Benjamin F. pvt.

Eilbott, Leon F. pvt.

Fairchild, Joseph B. pvt.

Felts, Robert pvt.

Fondran, S. R. pvt.

Gallman, William B. pvt.

Gibbs, Charles Hanson pvt.

Graves, James H. pvt.

Greaves, Stephen Arne Decatur 1st Lieut.

Grisham, Vincent S. pvt., 4th cpl.

Hammond, Job pvt.

Hampton, William Henry 2nd Lieut.

Harrison, George W. 3rd, 2nd cpl.

Hays, James C. 3rd Sgt.

Hays, May pvt.

Hutchinson, William F. pvt.

Ingram, Newton pvt.

Johnson, Daniel B. pvt.

Jones, David A. pvt.

Kenner, Daniel F. pvt.

Key, Albert M. pvt.

Lindsey, William G. musician, pvt.

Maben, William pvt.

Mabry, Thomas F. pvt.

McInnis, Malcolm pvt.

McNulty, Francis J. Ord. Sgt., Bvt. 2nd Lieut.

Mallett, James H. pvt.

Mapp, Littleton J. pvt.

Martin, Francis Marion Sr. pvt.

Martin, John A. pvt., cpl.

Mellon, Thomas Armour 4th Sgt.

Miller, John R. pvt.

Mosely, John P. pvt.

Neely, Andrew J. pvt.

Odoms, Jesse pvt.

Parr, Richard E. pvt.

Patton, Alfred pvt.

Potts, Samuel pvt.

Pyles, Milton pvt.

Rimes, John F. pvt.

Rimes, William L. pvt.

Ripley, Hiram D. pvt.

Ripley, William E. pvt.

Roberts, Joseph M. 2nd Sgt.

Russell, Reuben pvt.

Saunders, Romulus M. pvt.

Saunders, Thaddeus W. pvt.

Seay, William M. pvt.

Sellman, Eli pvt.

Sellman, Thomas B. pvt.

Shields, R. W. pvt.

Sinclair, Peter 4th, 1st cpl., 4th Sgt.

Smith, E. W. pvt.

Smith, Thaddeus C. pvt.

Sojourner, Sylvester D. pvt.
Stafford, Stephen B. pvt.
Stewart, John H. pvt., 4th Sgt.
Stone, Joshua pvt., 3rd, 1st Sgt.
Sumrall, Thomas S. pvt.
Teague, A. W. pvt.
Thomas, Samuel Beauchamp pvt.,
    3rd, 2nd Sgt., 2nd Lieut.
Thompson, Joseph H. pvt., 3rd cpl.
Ussrey, Thomas J. pvt.
Waddill, Anderson M. musician,

pvt.
Ware, Wilson pvt.
Watson, James M. pvt.
Watts, J. J. pvt.
White, Samuel Warren pvt., Q.M.S.
Williams, Charles S. pvt.
Williams, George musician, pvt.
Williamson, James pvt.
Wooldridge, Samuel D. 1st cpl.
Wright, R. H. pvt.

Company H, Vicksburg Volunteers
(Warren County)

Allen, Edward C. pvt., cpl.
Barefield, Ervin pvt.
Bird, Daniel A. pvt.
Bobb, John Jr. pvt., 2nd Lieut.
Brown, Simeon pvt.
Burney, Richard S. pvt.
Carson, Stephen D. pvt.
Chaffin, William pvt.
Clendenin, John S. 2nd cpl., Bvt.
    2nd Lieut., Capt.
Coe, Thomas J. pvt.
Cox, Edward pvt.
Crump, George P. Capt.
Dart, John Paul pvt.
Davidson, Thomas Jefferson pvt.
Davis, James C. pvt.
Dubose, Daniel D. pvt.
Dunlop, Daniel pvt.
Dunn, Edward pvt.
Dupree, James H. pvt.
Edwards, Samuel M. pvt.
Finch, John pvt.
Gregg, Robert pvt.
Groves, Benjamin L. pvt.
Hackler, George H. pvt.
Hackler, James pvt.
Harlan, Charles T. 2nd Sgt., Sgt.-
    -Maj.
Harris, John A. pvt.
Harrison, William D. F. pvt.

Harvey, William H. pvt.
Hatton, Benjamin pvt.
Hill, Sanford H. pvt.
Hise, George W. pvt.
Hopkins, Richard pvt., 2nd Lieut.
Johnston, Isaac S. pvt.
Kremer, Andrew pvt.
Lauell, Henry H. pvt., cpl.
Locke, J. J. pvt.
Luckin, John J. pvt.
Lytle, Armstrong pvt., 1st cpl.
McClure, David H. pvt.
McGaughey, Thomas H. pvt.
McKinney, William H. pvt., cpl.
McMorrough, Theodore musician
McMurray, Moses pvt.
McNair, Robert musician
McWillie, Adam pvt., Capt.
Markham, Hugh Mercer 2nd Lieut.
Marshall, Humphrey pvt., 2nd Sgt.,
    Sgt.-Maj.
Martin, Joseph pvt.
Martin, Robert M. 4th cpl.
Mathews, Frederick pvt.
Mattingly, John F. pvt.
Miller, Horace H. 1st Sgt., Sgt.-Maj.
Moore, Robert L. 1st Lieut.
Moore, William pvt.
Moore, William M. pvt.
Muldoon, Phillip pvt.

Newman, Albert M. 4th Sgt.
Noland, Avery pvt.
Norworthy, William pvt.
Peyton, Elijah A. pvt.
Peyton, John C. pvt.
Poindexter, John J. pvt., cpl., 2nd
  Lieut.
Porter, William C. 3rd, 1st Sgt.
Raine, Henry T. pvt.
Rariden, Patrick pvt.
Ratliff, William pvt.
Riley, Hugh pvt.
Roberts, Benjamin F. pvt.
Robins, Mitchell M. pvt.
Ross, John pvt.
Ross, Ravenna pvt.
Sanders, Benjamin F. pvt., cpl., Sgt.
Schmaling, Joseph 1st cpl., Sgt.
Shackelford, Richard D. pvt.
Shaifer, George Wilson Humphreys
  pvt.

Shannon, Joseph P. pvt.
Shaw, Samuel pvt.
Sillers, Joseph pvt.
Smedes, Charles E. pvt.
Smith, John pvt.
Steele, James J. V. pvt.
Stevenson, James W. pvt.
Stewart, James E. pvt., cpl., 1st
  Lieut.
Straughn, John pvt.
Strouse, Charles pvt.
Tunnill, Joseph P. pvt.
Vandivure, John E. pvt.
Wadsworth, William W. pvt.
Walker, William K. pvt.
White, Thomas pvt.
Williams, John M. pvt.
Williamson, Rufus R. pvt.
Winans, William pvt.
Wood, Augustus pvt.

Company I, Marshall Guards
(Marshall County)

Abston, Albert L. pvt.
Allen, Samuel M. pvt., hospital
  steward
Anderson, Garland pvt., 3rd Sgt.
Bass, John E. pvt.
Best, Berry O. pvt.
Branch, John S. pvt.
Bridges, Joseph L. pvt.
Brown, Leonidas B. pvt.
Burton, Alexander S. pvt.
Clark, John M. pvt.
Cole, Andrew J. pvt.
Cole, Samuel M. pvt.
Collingsworth, Addison pvt.
Cotton, Charles F. pvt.
Craft, William H. pvt.
Crawford, John H. pvt.
Davis, Spotswood H. pvt.
Delap, Alfred 1st musician
  (Drummer)

Dickerson, Isaac D. pvt.
Dill, Samuel H. 2nd Lieut.
Dorman, Perry pvt.
Downing, Joseph A. pvt.
Eddins, Robert J. pvt.
Edmondson, Charles M. pvt.
Eppes, William E. pvt., Bvt. 2nd
  Lieut.
Evans, James pvt.
Evans, Joseph pvt.
Floyd, George W. pvt.
Foreman, Andrew Jackson pvt., 4th
  cpl.
Glenn, John W. pvt.
Greer, Elkanah Brackin pvt.
Griffith, Peter O. D. pvt.
Grisham, William H. pvt., 3rd cpl.
Hall, Samuel S. pvt.
Hamilton, Wiley pvt.
Heaton, Joseph pvt.

Henderson, John L. pvt.
Hobbs, William pvt.
Holdway, Howard DeCalb pvt.
Holland, John M. M. 1st Sgt.
Hoskins, William H. pvt.
Hudspeth, John pvt.
Hughes, Joseph A. pvt.
Jolly, Meridian pvt.
Josselyn, Robert pvt.
Keeling, David H. pvt.
Kellebrew, Henry B. 2nd cpl., 4th
  Sgt.
Kerr, Jerome B. pvt.
Kincaid, John M. pvt.
Lamen, Felix G. pvt.
Langston, James pvt.
Lee, Patrick pvt., 4th, 3rd cpl.
Lemay, John P. pvt.
Long, John pvt., 2nd Sgt.
McClanahan, Thadeus O. pvt.
McGimpsey, Charles P. pvt.
Malone, Robert H. pvt., 1st cpl.
Marr, James S. pvt.
Martin, Plummer M. pvt., 4th Sgt.
Martin, S. D. pvt.
Martin, William A. pvt.
Massie, Nathaniel pvt.
Milam, Isaac E. pvt., 2nd Sgt.
Moore, James P. pvt.
Mott, Christopher Haynes 1st Lieut.
Mullens, Elgen A. musician

Murphree (Murphie), Leonard H.
  pvt.
Nail, Montgomery pvt.
Oldham, Jesse pvt.
Orr, Valentine B. pvt.
Overton, Alfred A. Capt.
Peace, John pvt.
Phillips, Rufus Eldridge pvt.
Pitman, John pvt.
Proctor, Harris J. M. pvt.
Randolph, Thadeus D. pvt., Sgt.
Reynolds, John H. C. pvt.
Shilby, Isaac M. pvt.
Shrives, Baker S. pvt.
Smith, John H. pvt.
Smoot, John B. pvt.
Spinks, William B. pvt.
Stalions, Spencer B. pvt.
Taylor, George pvt.
Taylor, James H. R. pvt., Capt.
Thompson, Walter Alvis pvt.
Trotter, Henry G. pvt.
Tucker, William D. pvt.
Vinson, James W. pvt.
Wilkerson, Thomas T. pvt.
Williams, Gideon pvt.
Williams, John pvt.
Wolf, Francis A. 3rd Sgt.
Yancey, Joseph T. 1st cpl., 4th Sgt.
Yancey, Simon B. 2nd cpl.
Yancey, Tryon Milton pvt.

Company K, Tombigbee Volunteers
(Lowndes County)

Allen, Robert J. pvt.
Ames, Thomas G. musician
Astin, Samuel C. pvt., 1st Lieut.
Bartee, James L. pvt., cpl.
Bell, Richard pvt.
Bell, William Henry 1st Sgt.
Brand, John pvt.
Brazeale, Edward E. pvt.
Broom, George W. pvt.
Campbell, George W. pvt.

Carey, Green B. pvt.
Cook, Henry Mansfield pvt.
Covington, Joseph L. 3rd, 1st Sgt.
Cravens, John E. pvt.
Creight, William pvt.
Cummings, John W. pvt.
Davis, Benjamin F. pvt.
Davis, Charles F. pvt.
Day, John E. pvt.
Dockery, Tolbert pvt.

Dowsing, Fielding L. pvt.
Dunn, John W. pvt.
Echols, Moses D. pvt.
Evans, James A. pvt., 4th cpl.
Feltman, Jacob J. pvt.
Fisher, George pvt., 2nd cpl.
Flanagan, James pvt.
Flanagan, William A. pvt.
Frazee, Carman pvt.
Gillian, William P. cpl.
Gregory, Edward H. pvt.
Grugett, Benjamin F. pvt., 4th Sgt.
Hale, James M. pvt.
Harrison, Thomas pvt.
Hartman, John W. musician
Henry, Ely I. pvt.
Higgason, John D. pvt.
Hindsley, John J. pvt.
Howard, Harrison L. pvt.
Hunt, George pvt.
Johnson, Nathaniel pvt.
Jones, Thomas L. 2nd cpl.
Julian, William R. 2nd cpl., Sgt.
Kelley, William H. pvt.
Kerr, Argyle A. pvt., cpl.
Kewen, Thomas L. pvt.
King, Andrew J. pvt.
Kinnest, William pvt.
Kinnis, Edward pvt.
Lawhon, John pvt.
Lewis, Daniel B. pvt.
Lewis, Edward B. pvt.
Longstreet, William D. pvt.
Lyon, Henry P. pvt.
McClung, Alexander Keith Capt.,
  Lieut. Col.
McDuffie, William Stoker pvt.
McGuin, John E. C. pvt.
McNorris, John D. pvt.
Mallett, William pvt.

Martin, Charles pvt.
Miller, Archibald W. pvt.
Mitchell, Alexander pvt.
Mosby, Robert G. pvt.
O'Rourke, William pvt.
Overton, Horatio pvt.
Parrish, Joel T. pvt.
Patterson, William H. H. 1st Lieut.
Perry, Bryant pvt.
Ragsdale, James O. pvt.
Reese, Hugh M. pvt.
Reese, James G. 3rd cpl., Sgt.
Reneau, John pvt.
Rogers, William P. 1st Lieut., Capt.
Sharman, James A. pvt.
Skidmore, Allen pvt.
Snedicor, Platt pvt.
Stedman, Daniel P. 4th Sgt.
Stewart, Adkinson pvt.
Stewart, John pvt.
Tanner, James C. pvt.
Thompson, James pvt.
Thompson, John L. pvt.
Thompson, Robert E. pvt.
Tierce, Tucker Richard pvt.
Tindall, Henry 2nd Sgt.
Tindsley, Calvin pvt.
Townsend, William Purnell pvt.,
  2nd Lieut.
Tyree, John M. pvt.
Umphlett, Job pvt.
Valentine, Charles T. 2nd Sgt.
Wade, William Bartee pvt., 2nd
  Lieut.
Washer, Thomas I. pvt., 2nd Lieut.
Watson, Morgan pvt.
Westbrooks, John W. pvt., cpl.
White, Archibald H. pvt.
Willett, John C. pvt.
Woodliff, William C. pvt.

Company Unknown

Dixon, Philip B. pvt.

How to Access Service Records
of
Mississippi's Mexican War Soldiers

Service Records for Mississippi's Mexican War soldiers can be located in either the National Archives (Washington, D.C.), or Mississippi Department of Archives and History (Jackson, MS). These records are listed under the title: "Compiled Service Records of Volunteer Soldiers Who Served During the Mexican War in Organizations from Mississippi." (RG 58):

Unit	Alphabet	Roll Number
1st Infantry	(A-G)	1-National Archives
		1596-MDAH
1st Infantry	(H-O)	2-National Archives
		4838-MDAH
1st Infantry	(P-Z)	3-National Archives
		4037-MDAH
2nd Infantry	(A-E)	4-National Archives
		1544-MDAH
2nd Infantry	(F-K)	5-National Archives
		2419-MDAH
2nd Infantry	(L-Q)	6-National Archives
		103-MDAH
2nd Infantry	(R-Z)	7-National Archives
		3428-MDAH
Anderson's Rifles	(A-L)	8-National Archives
		1609-MDAH
Anderson's Rifles	(M-Z)	9-National Archives
		2015-MDAH

2nd Regiment Volunteer Infantry

Field & Service Staff

Bagby, Charles H. Acting Sergeant-Major
Barksdale, William A.C.S.
Baughn, William P. Sergeant-Major
Davis, Reuben Colonel
Kilpatrick, Joseph H. Lieutenant-Colonel
Kinchloe, David Anderson Assistant-Surgeon
Love, Thomas Neely Surgeon
Munce, Thomas S. Adjutant
Price, Charles M. Q.M.
Price, Ezra R. Major
Warren, William E. Aide, Q.M.S.
Wilcox, John Allen Lieutenant-Colonel
Wilson, James C. Sergeant-Major

Company A, Lowndes Guards
(Lowndes County)

Adams, John R. pvt.
Archer, Joseph pvt.
Bagby, Charles H. 1st Sgt., Act.
  Sgt.-Maj.
Beckham, Caswell D. pvt.
Bekeart, Julius Francis pvt.
Bennett, Isaac M. pvt.
Blair, George W. pvt.
Blythe, Andrew K. Capt.
Branch, William pvt.
Burge, Beverly B. pvt.
Burnett, William pvt.
Cabler, Alexander pvt.
Cayce, Joseph A. pvt.
Coakley, William B. pvt.
Collins, Hiram W. pvt.
Coor, Fleet M. pvt.
Covington, James B. pvt., Sgt.
Curry, John B. pvt., 3rd Sgt.
Doss, Washington L. pvt., cpl., Sgt.
Dowsing, Everard 1st Lieut.
Dowsing, Jeremiah 2nd Sgt.
Drake, Benjamin W. pvt.

Dyche, Samuel pvt., cpl.
Ellis, John M. pvt.
Ellis, William L. pvt.
Fanning, William P. pvt.
Fields, Elias D. pvt.
Fields, John pvt.
Ford, John J. pvt.
Frazee, Carman pvt.
Frederick, Abraham C. pvt.
Freeman, William A. cpl.
Gill, William E. pvt.
Glass, Thomas C. pvt.
Goodman, James M. pvt.
Goodman, Joseph 2nd Sgt.
Gray, Robert pvt.
Green, William B. pvt.
Greenlee, Francis M. pvt.
Hamilton, Archibald pvt., cpl.
Hamilton, Henry T. pvt.
Harman, Theodore E. pvt.
Harrison, Aaron pvt.
Hendricks, Jeremiah pvt.
Hoburg, Edward G. pvt.

Hollingshead, Samuel B. pvt.
Hope, John S. pvt.
Huddleston, James Sgt.
Irwin, William T. pvt.
Johnson, Blake pvt.
Johnson, Robert pvt.
Jones, Miles T. pvt.
Kewen, Thomas pvt., Sgt.
Kincannon, James L. pvt.
King, Leonidas W. pvt.
Kirkland, Daniel pvt.
Kirkland, Oliver P. pvt.
Knapp, John pvt.
Knight, Elijah pvt.
Knight, James K. pvt.
Knight, Raleigh J. pvt.
Lauderdale, William C. 2nd Lieut.
Lee, James M. pvt.
Leverett, Jeremiah G. pvt.
Lipscomb, George Hardwick pvt.,
  cpl., Q.M.S., Q.M.
Love, Thomas L. pvt.
Love, Thomas Neely Surgeon
McCarty, James C. pvt.
Maddox, William E. pvt.
Mallory, William pvt.
Matthews, Beverly Aide, 2nd
Lieut.
Miller, John A. pvt.
Moore, Elbert P. pvt.
Morris, Samuel pvt.

Munce, Thomas S. 1st Lieut., Adjt.
Nash, Washington B. pvt.
Neilson, Charles A. pvt.
Nelson, Charles pvt.
Parker, William S. pvt.
Pearson, John M. pvt.
Penny, Thomas pvt., cpl.
Perkins, John pvt.
Pierce, Simeon pvt.
Pybus, Benjamin N. pvt.
Rakestraw, William pvt.
Rich, Edward C. 4th cpl.
Roddon, James pvt.
Scott, James pvt.
Seale, Benajah B. pvt.
Smith, Erastus pvt.
Smith, John C. pvt.
Spalding, Eugene A. pvt., 3rd cpl.
Stone, William F. pvt.
Taylor, James I. pvt., cpl.
Teague, Hardy J. pvt.
Thurman, James pvt.
Tyler, Calvin C. pvt.
Tyson, James C. pvt.
Ward, Amos F. pvt.
Warren, William E. pvt., Aide,
  Q.M.S.
Webb, George M. pvt.
Whatley, William H. pvt., cpl.
Willeford, John W. pvt.
Wynn, Richard pvt.

Company B, Marshall Relief Guards
(Marshall County)

Adams, John L. C. pvt.
Akin, R. T. 2nd cpl.
Allen, James W. pvt.
Allen, John A. pvt.
Andrews, O. H. pvt.
Bailey, Thomas pvt.
Barden, John pvt.
Bibb, Benjamin F. pvt.
Bomar, John N. O. pvt.
Box, Loving pvt.

Boyd, John 2nd cpl.
Brown, Leonidas pvt.
Carter, Green B. pvt.
Childers, Alfred pvt.
Childers, David M. pvt.
Chinn, Christopher C. 1st Lieut.
Clark, Martin pvt.
Clarke, Walton G. pvt.
Clarke, William G. pvt.
Cocke, John Q. A. pvt.

Conavey, Lawrence   pvt., cpl.
Cook, Robert W.   2nd Lieut.
Craddock, William B.   pvt.
Curtis, Cornelius   pvt.
Curtis, Sanford   pvt.
Darden, Uriah M.   pvt.
Davis, Anderson   pvt.
Davis, Edward A. C.   Sgt.
Davis, John F.   pvt.
Davis, William L.   pvt.
Delap, Alford   pvt.
Feely, Daniel   pvt.
Fogg, William   2nd Sgt.
Frazee, Carman   pvt.
Giddings, James D.   pvt.
Giddins, Robert C.   pvt.
Gill, William   pvt.
Gill, William E.   pvt.
Glenning, Patrick   pvt.
Gordon, James J.   pvt.
Gorman, John   pvt.
Graham, John   pvt.
Gregory, Alston   pvt., 2nd Lieut.
Hackworth, Francis M.   2nd Lieut.
Hays, Henry   pvt.
Henry, Robert A.   cpl., 2nd Sgt.
Henry, Sidney   pvt.
Hill, John W.   pvt.
Hilliard, John C.   pvt.
Holden, William E.   pvt.
Hollowell, Edwin O.   pvt.
Hope, John S.   pvt.
Hutchins, William   pvt.
Ijams, Wilson   2nd Lieut., Capt.
Jordan, Alfred   pvt.
Kilpatrick, Joseph H.   Capt., Lieut.
   Col.
Lane, Josiah   pvt.
Langley, William H.   pvt.
Layden, James   pvt.
Layne, William H.   3rd Sgt.
Lemaster, John   cpl.
Lemay, Lewis A.   pvt.
LeSueur, Charles Marion 2nd Lieut.
Lowe, Thomas   pvt.
Lowry, James G.   pvt.

McKenzie, John P.   pvt., cpl., Sgt.
Malone, Thomas   pvt.
Marshall, Andrew J.   pvt., cpl.
Matlock, William B.   pvt.
Matlock, William P.   pvt.
Mitchell, John S.   pvt., 3rd cpl., 1st
   Sgt.
Mitchell, Robert C.   pvt.
Moody, Joseph E.   pvt., 1st Sgt.,
   2nd Lieut.
Moore, Gamer   pvt.
Moore, James S.   pvt.
Murphy, James   pvt.
Murphy, Sidney R.   pvt.
Neal, Montgomery   pvt.
Otis, Allen   pvt.
Parham, Allen B.   pvt.
Perry, James   pvt.
Perry, John B.   pvt., 4th cpl.
Pope, William   pvt.
Prickett, William   pvt.
Ramey, William C.   pvt.
Ray, Chesley   pvt.
Ray, Ephraim   pvt.
Rayburn, William R.   pvt.
Selby, James E.   pvt.
Sevier, Granville S. T.   pvt.
Smith, Samuel   pvt.
Smithy, Abram   pvt.
Stockton, James S.   pvt.
Stribbling, Clayton   pvt.
Sullivan, William   pvt.
Sutterly, John   pvt.
Tanner, Thomas A.   pvt.
Thompson, John K.   pvt.
Thompson, Joshua F.   pvt.
Tidwell, Francis R.   pvt.
Tiner, William R.   pvt.
Tucker, Marsden S.   pvt.
Wagner, John   pvt.
Waldern, William   pvt.
Wallace, Edward   pvt.
Welch, Francis S.   pvt.
Wells, Joseph   pvt.
West, Osborne F.   pvt., cpl.
Wilkerson, Elijah J.   pvt., 4th Sgt.

Willis, Pyatt A. pvt.

Wilson, George H. pvt.

Wilson, John G. 3rd cpl.

Winn, Osborne pvt.

Company C, Choctaw Volunteers
(Choctaw County)

Acee, William B. pvt.

Aldridge, Jasper N. cpl.

Alverson, Elias pvt.

Barfield, W. M. pvt.

Barfield, William F. pvt.

Barnett, William pvt.

Barnett, William pvt.

Barron, Ezekiel pvt.

Bays, Henry pvt., 4th, 3rd Sgt.

Bays, James M. pvt.

Benedict, Jacob pvt.

Binion, Ananias O. pvt.

Bowen, John pvt.

Bowen, William H. pvt., cpl.

Caperton, James S. pvt.

Caperton, William G. pvt.

Childers, James T. pvt.

Childers, Robert S. pvt.

Cochran, William F. pvt.

Cook, William M. pvt.

Cooper, George W. pvt.

Cooper, Thomas C. pvt.

Cox, Allen pvt.

Crenshaw, Cornelius M. pvt.

Crenshaw, Nathaniel M. pvt.

Cromer, Richard S. Sgt., 2nd Lieut.

Dennehy, John pvt.

Dick, John W. N. 1st Sgt.

Dunn, Richard W. pvt.

Dunn, Thomas G. pvt.

Dyer, Alexander H. 3rd Sgt.

Dyer, Christopher C. pvt.

Elder, David M. pvt.

Elder, Enos Capt.

Elder, William H. pvt.

Evans, Oliver C. pvt.

Fox, Isaac pvt.

Fox, Thomas J. pvt.

Garland, Edward W. pvt.

Hall, William C. pvt.

Hancher, John pvt.

Hart, Jesse D. pvt.

Hearn, William C. pvt.,1st cpl., Sgt.

Heaton, Robert H. pvt.

Heslip, James O. pvt., 1st cpl.

Higdon, Alexander pvt.

Hill, John W. pvt.

Hill, Richard H. pvt.

Holland, Charles pvt.

Holland, William H. pvt.

Johnson, James S. pvt.,3rd, 2nd Sgt.

Jones, James L. pvt.

Jones, Robert pvt.

Knight, Abel E. 1st cpl.

Lemaster, James R. pvt.

Lewis, Charles pvt.

Lewis, William pvt.

Liddell, Charles J. pvt.

Liddell, James M. cpl., 2nd Lieut.

Liddell, Phillip Franklin 2nd Lieut.,
    Capt.

Long, Alfred V. pvt.

Mabry, Erastus W. pvt., cpl.

McCarroll, Alexander 4th, 2nd Sgt.

McGary, Martin H. pvt.

McQuary, Jasper A. pvt.

McQueen, James A. pvt.

Middleton, Holland 1st Lieut.

Middleton, Moses C. 3rd cpl.

Minga, Henry F. pvt.

Minney, James pvt.

Mitchell, John pvt.

Moore, Andrew J. pvt.

Morgan, Daniel T. pvt.

Osburn, John pvt.

Parish, Isaac W. pvt.

Parr, Giles S. pvt.

Peery, James pvt.

Peery, John pvt.
Phares, Henry J. pvt.
Phares, John C. pvt.
Poe, Levi musician
Power, Francis pvt.
Prewitt, Josiah pvt.
Prewitt, Wilson M. pvt., 2nd cpl.,
   Sgt.
Real, Joseph P. 2nd Lieut.
Roberts, Simeon pvt.
Saffell, Amos H. pvt.
Saffell, James T. pvt.
Sample, William A. pvt.
Scales, Stephen D. pvt.
Scott, William R. pvt.
Smith, Francis pvt.
Smith, Thomas pvt.
Starnes, John pvt.
Stewart, James J. pvt.

Stokes, Redden pvt.
Stokes, Samuel A. pvt.
Stovall, William A. pvt.
Thompson, William B. pvt.
Walton, George W. pvt.
Ware, Robert pvt.
Weaver, Alexander W. pvt., cpl.,
   1st Lieut.
Weaver, Benjamin F. pvt.
Whatley, Elijah pvt.
Wiley, Benjamin T. pvt.
Wilson, Basil H. pvt.
Wilson, Giles L. pvt.
Wilson, Samuel pvt.
Wiltshire, George W. musician,
   cpl.
Wood, James B. pvt.
Woodburn, John pvt.
Woods, Andrew pvt.

Company D, Monroe Volunteers
(Monroe County)

Abbott, William H. pvt.
Acker, Joel M. Capt.
Albertus, Bruno pvt.
Alexander, Jeremiah pvt.,2nd Lieut.
Alverson, Elias pvt.
Anglin, William C. pvt.
Atkins, Robert M. pvt.
Austin, John pvt.
Baker, Thomas pvt.
Bass, James N. pvt.
Baughn, William P. cpl., 1st Sgt.,
   Sgt.-Maj.
Beston, Patrick pvt.
Bright, Alfred pvt.
Brown, Elijah pvt.
Brown, Samuel pvt.
Burgess, Thomas pvt.
Butler, Joshua W. pvt.
Cheshire, Watson L. pvt.
Clary, Newton pvt.
Clayton, Charles M. pvt.
Coleman, George A. pvt.

Collins, Thomas R. pvt.
Conley, Andrew pvt.
Cook, William pvt.
Culton, Samuel D. pvt., cpl.
Cummings, William pvt.
Daniel, John pvt.
Davis, C. David pvt.
Davis, James M. A. pvt.
Dobbs, Andrew J. cpl., 2nd Sgt.
Dodge, Hamilton pvt.
Flyn, Zachariah K. pvt.
Franks, Gabriel M. pvt.
Franks, James A. pvt.
Galloway, George M. pvt.
Gillis, John M. pvt.
Gore, Rufus pvt.
Gray, John pvt.
Grizzle, Wilson P. pvt.
Hamilton, Alexander S. pvt., 1st
   Sgt., 2nd Lieut.
Harden, Nicholas pvt.
Harrison, William K. pvt., 4th Sgt.

Harvey, John W. pvt.
Henry, Timothy K. pvt.
Hinton, William pvt.
Homer, George W. pvt.
Horton, William pvt.
Howell, Benjamin L. 1st cpl., 1st
 Sgt.
Irvin, David pvt.
Irvin, William pvt.
Irvine, Francis M. pvt.
Irvine, Tillmon J. pvt.
Lane (Lain), James H. pvt., Sgt.
Livesay, Cornelius pvt.
Logan, Andrew L. pvt.
Lowery, Jefferson R. pvt.
McCanlass, John T. pvt.
McGurk, John pvt.
Mann, Metsalon A. 2nd, 1st Lieut.
Maxwell, Charles D. pvt.
Miller, Joel pvt.
Miller, John P. pvt.
Montgomery, John H. pvt.
Moore, Hugh pvt.
Newman, Henry pvt.
Newman, William K. cpl., 4th Sgt.
Oaks, James F. pvt.
Orr, John pvt.
Owings, John D. pvt.
Page, Francis M. pvt.
Porch, John B. pvt.
Quinn, John A. pvt.
Quinn, Peter pvt.
Raimey, Preston G. pvt.
Redden, Stephen W. pvt.
Reed, Israel M. pvt.
Reed, Thomas W. pvt.
Sanders, Daniel B. pvt.
Shaw, Gustavis M. pvt., 2nd cpl.
Shelling, Francis M. pvt.
Shelton, Obadiah pvt.
Shockley, James H. 3rd Sgt.
Short, Aaron B. pvt.

Simmons, Jeremiah pvt.
Simpson, Charles T. pvt.
Smith, Andrew C. pvt.
Stiner, Calvin C. 3rd, 2nd Sgt.
Swepston, Thomas S. pvt., 4th, 3rd
 cpl.
Tankley, John pvt.
Tanner, William M. pvt.
Thompson, William pvt.
Thweatt, James pvt., 4th, 3rd cpl.
Treadaway, William M. pvt.
Trotter, John pvt., cpl.
Vest, George pvt.
Walker, James M. pvt.
Walters, John H. pvt.
Ward, James G. pvt.
Watters, S. A. pvt.
Weaver, Hartwell R. pvt.
Weaver, John G. pvt.
Weeks, John S. pvt.
West, George pvt.
West, Mitchell A. pvt.
West, William D. pvt.
West, William L. pvt.
White, Martin S. 2nd, 1st Lieut.
White, William A. pvt.
Wilcox, John Allen 1st Lieut.,
 Lieut.-Col.
Wilkerson, Wiley M. pvt.
Williams, James N. musician
 (Drummer)
Williams, Stephen C. L. pvt.
Williams, William W. pvt., 2nd
Sgt.
Wills, James Austin Jr. pvt.
Wilson, J. pvt.
Wilson, James C. 1st Sgt., Sgt.-
Maj.
Wilson, Richard pvt.
Wurmser, George pvt.
Young, Benjamin pvt.

Company E, Tippah Guards
(Tippah County)

Alexander, Barton W. 3rd, 2nd Sgt.
Anderson, Joseph M. pvt.
Askew, James pvt.
Boone, Jordan R. pvt.
Boone, Joseph T. pvt.
Buchanan, John H. pvt.
Buchanan, Samuel T. 2nd Sgt.
Burriss, William H. pvt.
Coakley, William B. pvt.
Coke, Addison pvt.
Coleman, James S. pvt.
Cook, Thomas E. pvt.
Coyle, Peter pvt.
Crawford, Thomas F. pvt.
Crunk, Joseph Wright pvt.
Davis, John L. W. pvt.
Davis, John S. pvt.
Dugan, Michael pvt.
Edwards, William pvt.
Falkner, Joseph pvt.
Falkner, Thomas pvt.
Falkner, William C. 1st Lieut.
Flournoy, Jesse pvt.
Gallaher, David L. cpl.
Goforth, James L. pvt., 2nd Sgt.
Gray, James W. 2nd Sgt.
Griffin, William N. cpl., 1st Sgt.
Gunn, John B. pvt.
Gunnells, Joseph W. pvt., 1st cpl.
Harlan, Columbus C. pvt.
Harlan, Dutton S. pvt.
Harris, William H. 1st Sgt., 1st
   Lieut.
Henderson, John H. pvt.
Henderson, Thomas W. pvt.
Hindman, Robert Holt pvt., 2nd Sgt.
Hindman, Thomas Carmichael 2nd
   Lieut.
Hines, John pvt.
Hovis, Adoniram J. pvt.
Howard, Cary pvt.
Humphries, David pvt.

Hyneman, Henry C. pvt.
Jackson, Alexander Melvourne
   Capt.
Jackson, Daniel N. pvt.
Jackson, George W. pvt.
Jackson, William H. 2nd Lieut.
Jackson, William M. pvt.
James, Andrew J. pvt., cpl.
Johnson, Duncan B. pvt.
Jones, Stephen pvt.
Kavanaugh, William W. pvt.
Leath, James pvt.
Lesley, Andrew J. pvt.
Liles, Richard pvt.
Locker, Andrew J. pvt.
Locker, Thomas B. pvt.
Lowery, Mark Perrin pvt.
Lowry, James G. pvt.
McCune, Thomas W. pvt.
McGee, William pvt.
McLean, William D. V. pvt.
Manner, James pvt.
Matlock, Manuel W. pvt.
Medlock, John J. 4th Sgt.
Messer, James pvt.
Miller, Oliver R. pvt.
Miller, Thomas G. pvt., cpl.
Miller, Thomas W. pvt.
Moffitt, Allston pvt.
Mole, John pvt.
Morris, William K. 1st Lieut.
Moss, Stephen pvt.
Mundon, Benjamin pvt.
Ogilvie, Philip S. Smith pvt.
Pace, Thomas pvt.
Patton (Patten), Thomas S. pvt.
Portis, James P. pvt.
Potts, Zachary H. pvt.
Ray, William H. pvt.
Reed, Edward pvt.
Reno, John D. pvt.
Reynolds, Thomas P. pvt.

Riley, John S. pvt.
Rogers, Jefferson C. pvt.
Rogers, William E. pvt.
Sawyer, William C. pvt.
Singleton, Perry H. pvt.
Singleton, William pvt.
Smith, Harvey N. pvt.
Smith, James G. pvt.
Snow, James C. pvt.
Stubblefield, Adolphus H. M. pvt.,
  2nd cpl.
Stubblefield, William H. pvt.

Sweeten, Samuel M. pvt.
Tharpe, James M. pvt.
Thompson, John L. pvt.
Thompson, Joshua F. pvt.
Wadsworth, Alexander pvt.
Washer, Thomas I. pvt., 2nd Lieut.
Webb, George pvt.
Wilson, Josiah pvt.
Winston, Joseph W. pvt., 4th cpl.
Word, Cuthbert B. pvt.
Wurmser, George pvt.

Company F, Lauderdale Volunteers
(Lauderdale County)

Adams, Jackson pvt.
Adams, John pvt.
Anderson, Hartley pvt.
Bankston, Thomas I. (J.?) pvt.
Barefield, Elias pvt.
Barnes, Jasper N. pvt.
Bennett, Thomas pvt.
Bibb, Benjamin F. pvt.
Blum, George pvt.
Boutwell, Chappel Spencer pvt.
Bradley, Joseph pvt.
Bragg, Thomas Z. pvt.
Brooks, William pvt.
Busby, George pvt.
Calhoun, Louchlin pvt.
Calhoun, Richmond N. pvt., 5th,
  3rd Sgt.
Carlisle, Ellet pvt.
Chambers, James P. pvt., cpl.
Chaney, Archibald 3rd, 2nd Lieut.
Cheesman, Joseph H. musician, pvt.
Coe, Ezra pvt.
Connell, John pvt.
Cook, James I. pvt.
Cross, Franklin A. pvt., 2nd cpl.
Cross, William I. pvt.
Daniels, William I. Capt.
Davis, Anderson pvt.
Davis, Benjamin E. pvt.

Davis, John H. pvt.
Dozier, Edwin M. pvt.
Easterling, Simeon pvt.
Eastland, James pvt., 1st Sgt.
Eastland, William D. 3rd, 2nd Lieut.
Folly, Acy pvt.
Ford, William F. cpl.
Fowler, Adrian pvt.
Francis, James A. pvt.
Futch, Isham T. 4th cpl.
Gardner, John pvt.
Gibson, Amos pvt.
Gossett, Barnett pvt.
Gray, James pvt.
Guest, Isaac N. pvt.
Gynn, Chisley R. pvt.
Hall, James pvt.
Harper, William E. 3rd cpl.
Hunt, Benjamin B. pvt., 2nd cpl.
Hutchins, Nathan pvt.
Johnson, James T. pvt.
Johnson, Wiley B. pvt., 1st cpl.
Joiner, William D. 2nd Sgt.
Jones, James pvt.
Jones, John pvt.
Laird, Eli pvt.
Laird, Hiram pvt.
Laird, William D. 1st Lieut.
Lamb, Samuel pvt.

Leach, John R. pvt.
Lucky, William R. pvt.
McDonald, James Madison pvt.
McKinney, William pvt.
Melvin, John J. 4th Sgt.
Merritt, John pvt.
Newson, John pvt.
Osborn, Lewdy B. pvt.
Overstreet, John R. pvt.
Owens, Ethedreal pvt.
Owens, William musician (Fifer),
  pvt.
Pamplin, Robert H. pvt.
Parish, Robert T. pvt.
Philips, Lorenzo D. pvt.
Pritchet, Bryant S. pvt.
Pritchet, William pvt.
Pugh, David R. pvt.
Robertson, William J. pvt., 4th cpl.
Robins, George W. pvt.
St. John, Arthur pvt.
Scott, William pvt.
Shelton, Edward B. 1st Sgt., 2nd

Lieut.
Shope, Thomas J. pvt.
Simms, William pvt.
Smith, William A. pvt.
Smithwick, Ed. W. pvt.
Sones, Thomas S. pvt.
Steele, Jesse G. 1st Lieut.
Stephens, Joseph H. pvt., 2nd cpl.
Stroud, Thomas I. pvt.
Trussell, Andrew Jackson 2nd Lieut.
Tyson, James C. pvt.
Underwood, Ripley C. pvt.
Ward, Werter pvt.
Webster, Martin pvt.
Weems, Daniel L. pvt., 2nd Lieut.
Weston, Robert B. pvt.
White, Thomas C. pvt.
Wigington, Henry J. pvt.
Wilkins, James L. pvt.
Williams, Eli pvt.
Williamson, Isham 3rd cpl.
Williamson, Joseph A. pvt.

Company G. Thomas Hinds Guards
(Hinds County)

Adams, James pvt.
Babb, James D. pvt.
Baldridge, William F. pvt.
Barclay, Joseph C. pvt., cpl.
Bass, James N. pvt.
Bethea, Thomas I. pvt.
Biddle, Marks J. 1st Sgt., 2nd Lieut.
Black, Augustus H. pvt.
Braselton, James H. pvt.
Brice, Presley pvt.
Brill, Philip pvt.
Bust, Luke S. pvt., 3rd Sgt.
Cade, James pvt.
Caraway, Adam H. pvt.
Carter, Thomas T. 1st Sgt., 2nd
  Lieut.
Clark, Charles Capt., Col.
Clark, Levi W. pvt.

Clinton, John H. pvt., 2nd Sgt.
Coe, Milford G. pvt.
Coffey, Chesley Sheldon 2nd
  Lieut., Capt.
Cook, Joseph B. pvt.
Currie, John H. pvt., cpl.
Dabney, John H. pvt.
Davenport, Thomas pvt., cpl.
Davidson, George W. pvt.
Davis, Henry J. pvt.
Davis, John E. pvt.
Dixon, Robert C. pvt.
Ewing, William M. 4th cpl.
Fleming, William pvt.
Flowers, Ephraim A. pvt.
Flowers, Graham H. pvt.
Ford, Canaday pvt.
Foster, William pvt.

Fry, David B. pvt.
Gillis, John M. pvt.
Groves, William A. pvt.
Harman, Theodore E. pvt.
Hart, Dominick pvt.
Hays, Matthew pvt.
Hewitt, Edgar pvt.
Higdon, Russell Benjamin pvt.
Hinkley, Henry pvt.
Hulbert, Harris M. 4th, 3rd Sgt.
Johns, Abijah pvt.
Johnson, Laban J. pvt.
Kelly, Zachariah Principal Musician
Knapp, David L. pvt.
Lackings, Benjamin pvt.
Linsey, Moses pvt.
Long, John C. pvt.
Love, Alfred L. pvt.
McGregor, George pvt.
McKey, John S. pvt.
Macrery, John 3rd, 2nd cpl.
Martin, Samuel N. pvt.
Maule, Joseph L. 2nd, 1st cpl.
Miller, John pvt.
Munce, Josiah S. pvt.
Munce, Thomas G. 1st Lieut.,Adjut.
Murphy, John pvt.
Murry, John L. pvt.
Newman, William B. 2nd Lieut.
Palmer, William pvt.

Phips, David pvt.
Postlethwaite, Stephen D. pvt., 3rd, 2nd, 1st Sgt.
Powers, Stephen F. pvt.
Price, Pierre 1st cpl., Sgt.
Rainy, James M. pvt.
Raney, Samuel M. pvt.
Reese, Isham I. pvt.
Ritchey, Stephen W. pvt.
Rondenburg, John pvt.
Sanders, Edward I. pvt.
Sanders, William pvt.
Sellers, James M. pvt.
Shaw, William G. pvt.
Short, Aaron B. pvt.
Smith, John C. pvt.
Smith, Joshua T. pvt.
Smith, Nathaniel pvt.
Sparks, James P. pvt., Sgt.
Sutton, Stephen S. pvt.
Tankley, John pvt.
Taylor, John pvt.
Truly, John H. pvt.
Truly, Philip H. pvt.
Turner, Fielding pvt.
Wainger, Casper pvt.
Wasson, James pvt.
Woodard, Abijah pvt.
Wyatt, David P. pvt., cpl., 4th, 3rd, 2nd Sgt.

Company H. Union Grays
(Attala County)

Ambrose, John 3rd, 1st Sgt.
Amyx, Flemming 1st Lieut., Capt.
Arnold, Solomon A. pvt.
Beall, John M. pvt., cpl.
Bell, Richard D. pvt.
Blake, John H. pvt.
Boles, Samuel W. pvt.
Boyd, David W. pvt.
Boyd, John L. cpl.
Boyett, Robert T. pvt.
Byram, Jackson C. pvt.

Campbell, Robert Bond pvt.
Carter, Edward B. pvt.
Chambers, James R. 3rd cpl.
Charleville, John pvt.
Cole, John R. pvt.
Cole, Robert A. pvt.
Corbin, Vincent pvt.
Cox, Reuben T. pvt.
Craft, John pvt.
Daniel, James P. pvt.
Davis, Zachariah V. pvt.

Dearing, Joseph S. pvt.
Durham, James J. pvt.
Eakin, John G. pvt.
East, Anderson pvt.
Edrington, George W. pvt.
Ellis, Benjamin T. pvt.
Fletcher, Lorenzo Dow pvt.
Fox, Edwin pvt.
Gage, John J. 2nd cpl., Sgt.
Gilliland, John G. pvt.
Green, William B. pvt.
Haley, Isaac N. pvt.
Hare, Martin pvt.
Harper, William B. pvt.
Henry, Eli G. 2nd, 1st Lieut.
Henry, Mathew M. pvt.
Hight, Thomas B. 1st cpl., Sgt.
Hodge, Francis pvt.
Hovas, Christopher 4th Sgt.
Ingole, Peter pvt.
Ivy, Myrick pvt.
Jackson, Daniel M. pvt., 2nd Lieut.
Jackson, Jasper pvt.
Jackson, John A. 2nd Sgt., 2nd
  Lieut.
Jackson, John W. pvt.
Johnson, William pvt.
Justice, Wallace pvt.
Kittrell, Alexander pvt.
Landrum, Dyonisius pvt.
Laughter, George A. pvt., cpl.
Leard, David E. pvt.
Logan, William P. pvt.
Lowe, Frederick pvt.
Macauley, George pvt.
McDonald, Robert S. pvt.
McLemore, William K. pvt.
McWillie, Adam Capt.
Mann, Cornelius W. pvt.

Martin, James pvt.
Martin, John 2nd Lieut.
Massey, Joseph V. pvt.
Mickey, Caius M. M. pvt.
Mickey, William A. pvt.
Miley, Andrew B. pvt.
Money, Joseph pvt.
Montgomery, Robartis H. pvt.
Moore, Thomas pvt.
Nash, Madison G. pvt.
Ogilvie, Philip S. Smith pvt.
Ownley, James W. pvt.
Phillips, Frederick pvt.
Powell, Robert V. pvt.
Price, David B. pvt.
Ragan, Robartus pvt.
Rainwaters, Edwin N. pvt.
Riley, Terrills pvt.
Rogers, George W. pvt.
Rogers, James pvt.
Sanders, John M. pvt.
Sanders, Robert H. pvt.
Schmidt, John pvt.
Scott, Hines pvt.
Shaddock, Samuel pvt.
Shields, Richard pvt.
Simpson, James G. pvt., cpl.
Snead, John pvt.
Strickland, John W. pvt.
Terry, Lampkin Straughn pvt.,
  hospital steward, Sgt.
Thweatt, Elbert G. pvt.
Thweatt, Uriah W. pvt.
Wade, Nathaniel T. pvt.
Walker, William S. 1st Sgt.
Williams, John H. pvt.
Williams, Samuel D. pvt.
Williamson, Albert pvt.
Winn, Joseph A. pvt.

Company I, Panola Boys
(Panola County)

Abrams, Emanuel pvt.
Allen, William pvt.

Allen, William R. pvt.
Andrews, James D. pvt.

Andrews, Lemuel J. pvt., 4th cpl.
Banks, Paul C. pvt.
Bickerstaff, Marcas D. pvt.
Black, Martin pvt.
Bowman, James pvt.
Brosius, Daniel K. Sgt.
Buchanan, Perry J. pvt., 3rd cpl.,
  Sgt.
Burton, Madison J. pvt., cpl.
Byars, Wiley Thomas 4th, 1st Sgt.
Calvert, William pvt.
Campbell, James B. pvt.
Clark, William H. pvt., cpl.
Clelland, Robert 2nd Lieut.
Cobb, William L. pvt.
Cosby, James R. pvt.
Cosby, Morris pvt.
Crouch, Levi pvt.
Davanay, James pvt.
Dickerson, Henry C. pvt.
Earp, Mason N. pvt.
Erskins, John pvt.
Estelle, William M. 1st Lieut., Capt.
Evans, Joshua W. pvt.
Falkner, Edmund G. pvt.
Finch, John pvt.
Flowers, Ephraim A. pvt.
Flowers, Graham H. pvt.
Fort, Marcus L. pvt.
Gaff, Felix W. cpl., 2nd Lieut.
Ganong, William L. pvt.
Garrett, Bartholomew pvt.
Gotsel (Godsil?), Patrick pvt.
Grogan, George J. pvt.
Guffee, Benjamin W. pvt.
Hall, John pvt.
Harley, Thomas pvt.
Harrison, Hilry pvt.
Henry, James W. pvt.
Hill, Richard pvt.
Hilton, Carl pvt.
Hodnett, Thomas pvt.
Holmead, John pvt., cpl.
Hudgins, John pvt.
Humphreys, David W. 1st Sgt.
Hunter, Robert H. musician, pvt.,

Aide
Jackson, Andrew pvt.
Jones, Francis A. pvt.
Kewer, I. W. pvt.
Keywood, John T. pvt.
Keywood, Lockhart pvt.
Kinchloe, David A. Asst. Surgeon
King, Thomas pvt.
Lambertson, Henry pvt.
Lambright, George T. pvt.
Lanter, Thomas C. pvt.
Lee, Patrick pvt.
Loghary, John pvt.
McCannon, Michael pvt.
McKeever, Isaac pvt.
McKinney, James M. 2nd, 1st Sgt.,
  1st Lieut.
McLain, James pvt.
Mardis, James T. pvt.
Martin, Robert 2nd Lieut.
Miller, John pvt.
Navon, James pvt.
O'Rourke, Patrick pvt.
Orr, Daniel B. pvt.
Orr, William J. pvt.
Overton, Alfred A. Capt.
Palmer, William pvt.
Parsons, James R. pvt.
Patrick, David A. pvt.
Perryman, Felix G. pvt., cpl.
Perryman, Presley P. pvt.
Poole, Equilla M. Sgt.
Porter, George C. pvt.
Powell, Alfred pvt.
Powell, Wiley pvt.
Priest, Edward pvt.
Pue, Thomas pvt.
Quinan, Michael J. pvt.
Rainey, James B. pvt.
Rees, Joshua C. pvt.
Rhoades, John 1st cpl., 3rd Sgt.
Rhodes, Andrew E. pvt.
Rhyne, John R. pvt.
Russell, Ellis pvt.
Russell, Oscar pvt.
Scott, Joseph pvt.

Shandt, Benjamin K. pvt.
Shy, Osborne pvt.
Singly, William G. pvt.
Smith, Harrison pvt.
Speed, William pvt.
Sullivan, William pvt.
Templeton, James H. pvt.
Tippett, Martin C. pvt.

Walker, Robert B. cpl.
Wallace, James pvt., 4th Sgt.
Watson, Kyran pvt.
Weaver, Asa H. pvt.
Wilson, James R. pvt.
Wright, Michael pvt.
Young, Andrew J. pvt.
Young, Jackson pvt.

Company K, Capt. Buckley's Company
(Lawrence County)

Arandes (Allinder, Armanders, Oranders?), John pvt.
Barrows, George pvt., 2nd Lieut.
Bixler, William pvt.
Blount, Benjamin pvt.
Bowen, William pvt.
Bowen, William B. pvt.
Boyd, Oliver H. P. pvt.
Buckley, Benjamin C. Capt.
Burge, Beverly pvt.
Carlisle, William pvt.
Carloss, Robert pvt.
Carr, William S. pvt.
Carson, James H. pvt.
Carvin, Arthur pvt.
Crawford, A. G. H. pvt.
Crosland, Alexander pvt.
Crossin, John pvt., 1st cpl., 4th, 3rd Sgt.
Crowder, James C. pvt.
David, James pvt.
Davis, James pvt.
Dawson, Joseph pvt.
Deason, John B. 3rd, 2nd Lieut., Capt.
Deason, Joseph L. pvt.
Dickson, David H. pvt., 1st Sgt.
Elliott, George W. pvt., cpl.
Flippin, William pvt.
Foil, David pvt.
Foil, John C. pvt.
Fortner, George W. pvt.
Garner, George W. pvt.

Garner, Ransom pvt.
Gentry, Merenether T. pvt.
Gibson, Ralph pvt.
Goubeneaux, Charles 2nd Lieut.
Grant, Alhaney pvt.
Griffis, Pleasant A. pvt.
Hall, John A. pvt.
Hamilton, William C. pvt.
Harley, Thomas pvt.
Harris, Lewis B. pvt., 3rd, 2nd, 1st cpl., Sgt.
Hays, James C. 3rd, 2nd Sgt.
Hibble, Jacob pvt.
Hogan, Timothy pvt.
Holtzhopfer, Jacob pvt.
Howard, John musician (Drummer), pvt.
Hubbard, Napoleon W. 4th cpl.
Jennings, John pvt., 4th, 2nd cpl.
Johnson, Sugan L. pvt.
Keegan, John 3rd, 2nd, 1st Sgt.
King, Elias pvt.
King, Robert 4th, 3rd, 2nd cpl., 4th Sgt.
King, Thomas pvt.
Kirkland, Uriah pvt.
Lenoir, Whitman pvt.
Lott, William H. 2nd, 1st cpl., 4th Sgt.
Lynch, Isaac pvt.
McDonald, Hugh R. pvt., 3rd cpl.
McGraw, Wiley pvt.
McMullaen, James pvt.

McNelly, Zachariah pvt.
Mallet, Stephen pvt.
Martin, M. J. pvt.
Martin, Robert G. pvt.
Miller, O. P. pvt., 4th, 1st cpl., Sgt.
Mullen, Peter A. pvt.
Nelson, Thomas W. pvt.
Newman, John pvt.
Orrell, Robert pvt.
Perrett, Mathew pvt.
Perritt, Wiley A. pvt.
Pierce, William H. pvt.
Ripley, Zeno R. musician, pvt.
Robinson, George W. pvt.
Russell, Street pvt.
Schultis, Lawrence pvt.
Scrivener, Andrew J. pvt.
Seater, Robert Y. pvt.
Smith, Henry T. pvt.

Smith, William T. pvt.
Stamps, Franklin R. pvt.
Stevens, William pvt.
Stewart, James M. pvt.
Stonehouse, Sebastian pvt.
Stratton, Jesse K. pvt., 2nd cpl.
Strother, William 1st Lieut.
Tanner, David pvt.
Thomas, Westley H. 2nd, 1st Sgt.
Thomas, Wyatt pvt.
Thompson, James pvt.
Thompson, Nelson pvt.
Wallace, William C. pvt., 4th Sgt.
Ward, Hiram pvt.
Watkins, Ichabod pvt.
Webb, Henry C. pvt.
Williams, Benjamin T. pvt.
Williams, John pvt.
Workman, Benjamin F. pvt.

Companies Unknown

Adams, John pvt.
Austin, James M. pvt.
Ayes (Ayers), Charles pvt.
Bartle, John G. pvt.
Bell, James A. pvt.
Bolin, Jacob pvt.
Briedlove, Isaac F. pvt.
Busby, James pvt.
Buson, Samuel pvt.
Cameron, John pvt.
Carothers, Henry pvt.
Cozart (Coyart?), George A. pvt.
Craig, Robert A. pvt.
Crook, Martin D. pvt.
Cumberland, Samuel pvt.
Deheart, Lenbron pvt.
Dhenny, John P. pvt.
Dobbins, John W. pvt.
Edge, Julien O. pvt.
Ellis, Thomas pvt.
Estelle, Preston pvt.
Evans, William pvt.
Fortner, Joseph pvt.
Graham, James W. pvt.

Graves, John C. pvt.
Green, Luther D. pvt.
Griffin, Mack pvt.
Hill, John H. pvt.
Hilliard, Thomas pvt.
Holland, William T. pvt.
Howell, James E. pvt.
Jobe, David M. pvt.
Jones, Richard D. pvt.
Keith, Miller D. pvt.
McDonald, Pendleton pvt.
McKee, William pvt.
Macon, Henry pvt.
McVey, James M. pvt.
Milton, Hiram pvt.
Milton, William F. pvt.
Paschal, Richard A. pvt.
Price, Thomas W. pvt.
Pugh, Edworth pvt.
Rages, Magdelena Matron
Ray, Wiley pvt.
Robinson, Alexander H. pvt.
Rose, William pvt.
Saunders, James pvt.

Scoggins, William S. pvt.
Shaw, Franklin pvt.
Smith, Migamon W. pvt.
Speed, James pvt.
Steele, Thomas I. pvt.

Tillman, John C. pvt.
Turner, Asa pvt.
Webb, James pvt.
Whitehead, Calvin pvt.

1st Battalion Infantry

Field & Service Staff

Anderson, James Patton Lieutenant-Colonel
Anderson, John A. Adjutant
Dickson, Joseph P. Q.M.S.
McNeil, William E. Sergeant-Major

Company A, Capt. Keyes' Company (Chickasaw County)

Adams, John G. pvt.
Anglin, Jasper musician, pvt.
Appling, Edward R. 3rd Sgt.
Austin, William pvt.
Bennett, John W. pvt.
Brown, William pvt.
Carithers, John M. pvt.
Cartledge, Jesse pvt.
Cocke, William T. Bvt. 2nd Lieut.
Crimm, James F. pvt.
Currie, Alexander M. pvt.
Davis, Benjamin musician, pvt.
Davis, John A. pvt.
Davis, William pvt.
Deen, William D. pvt.
Dickinson, Joseph C. pvt.
Donathan, James W. 1st cpl.
Evans, Ezekiel W. 1st Lieut.
Franklin, George W. pvt.
Freeland, James pvt.
Garrett, Samuel pvt.
Gibbons, Seth pvt.
Gilleland, Samuel M. pvt.
Glaze, William pvt.
Goode, George B. pvt.

Goode, Obadiah pvt.
Hague, Sydney F. pvt.
Hall, James T. pvt.
Hawkins, John L. pvt.
Hayes, Garland H. 2nd cpl.
Hazlewood, Calvin T. pvt.
Hearn, Madison H. pvt.
Hendrix, Reuben pvt.
Herald, William pvt.
Herring, Stephen G. pvt.
Hewitt, John pvt.
Hicks, Moses pvt.
Hoggatt, John pvt.
Hutten, William C. pvt.
Ivy, Thomas 2nd Lieut.
Ivy, Washington P. pvt.
Jenkins, Carodine pvt.
Johnson, William F. pvt.
Keyes, William McCord Capt.
Kilgore, Benjamin M. 4th cpl.
Kilgore, Josiah G. pvt.
Kitchens, William pvt.
Knieff, Francis A. pvt.
Lanham, John M. pvt.
Livingston, George H. pvt., 1st Sgt.

McDoniel, Alfred H. pvt.
McDoniel, James pvt.
McKeever, Thomas pvt.
McKnight, Samuel B. pvt.
Marshall, Thomas W. pvt.
Mayers, James M. pvt.
Mayers, Richard C. pvt., 1st cpl.
Middlebrooks, William S. pvt.
Monk, Menan pvt.
Montgomery, Jacob P. pvt.
Moody, Lewis pvt.
Moore, Henry pvt.
Morris, Pleasant pvt.
Moseley, Lewis pvt.
Mullenix, William M. pvt.
Neel, Francis M. pvt.
Neel, James R. pvt.
Nichols, John W. pvt.
Nicholson, Ira O. pvt.
O'Neal, John C. pvt.
Oliver, James M. pvt.
Overbey, Edmund P. pvt.
Perkins, William M. pvt.
Porter, Hancock pvt.
Pulliam, Robert W. musician, pvt.
Pulliem, Thomas W. W. pvt.
Rainwater, John P. pvt.

Rea, Hampton M. pvt.
Redden, Harmon pvt.
Redus, James W. pvt.
Risher, Jacob pvt.
Roach, Dobson pvt.
Rose, William pvt.
Ross, Alfred 3rd cpl.
Rosseau, John F. pvt.
Savage, John pvt.
Scroggins, William pvt.
Sessions, James H. pvt.
Shallies, Melvin H. pvt.
Shannon, Sydneyham pvt.
Smith, John R. pvt.
Smith, William S. pvt.
Staggs, Thomas pvt.
Steele, Newton A. pvt., 1st Sgt.
Thomas, Daniel pvt.
Thompson, James O. pvt.
Vincent, William pvt.
Watson, William B. 4th Sgt.
Wilder, Sanford J. pvt.
Wilkerson, Stephen P. pvt.
Wiseman, John F. pvt.
Wood, Malam pvt.
Woodall, Alexander R. 2nd Sgt.
York, Daniel pvt.

Company B. Capt. Crowson's Company (Copiah County)

Anglin, Jasper musician, pvt.
Ashley, Thomas pvt.
Bankston, William M. 4th Sgt.
Barker, James pvt.
Barker, William A. pvt.
Bates, Marshall P. 1st cpl.
Beale, Thomas I. 2nd Sgt.
Braden, John G. pvt.
Bridges, Bird 2nd Sgt.
Britt, Joseph pvt.
Broomley (Bromley), William C.
  pvt.
Brown, Henry F. pvt.
Brown, Joseph E. pvt.

Brown, William G. pvt.
Butler, James G. pvt.
Cain, William L. pvt.
Campbell, Samuel pvt.
Corbell, John R. pvt.
Courtney, Thomas W. pvt.
Crowson, Elisha Capt.
Dampier, William G. pvt.
Dickens, Elijah pvt.
Elder, James I. pvt.
Eubanks, James 3rd cpl., 3rd Sgt.
Giffin, Robert pvt.
Goss, George H. pvt.
Guynes, Bryant F. pvt.

Guynes, John pvt.
Hobbs, Calvin musician (Fifer),
  pvt.
Horn, Edward G. pvt.
Hous, Jesse B. pvt.
Irwin, Hugh L. pvt.
Jenkins, Allen B. pvt.
Jones, William pvt.
Kern, William P. pvt.
Landers, William H. 1st Lieut.
Linder, Uriah pvt.
Lowe, Luke 2nd Lieut.
Lowrey, John J. pvt.
Lunceford, Napoleon B. pvt.
McKeever, Thomas pvt.
McMullen, James H. pvt.
McVay, William T. pvt.
Maxcel, William A. pvt.
Miller, Thomas pvt.
Moore, William pvt., 2nd cpl.
Nabrous, Christopher R. pvt.
Newman, James pvt.
Norwood, Alexander T. pvt.
O'Flannegan, Peter pvt.
Ogden, Lorenzo D. pvt., 1st Sgt.
Pharris, Joseph pvt.
Pigg, John pvt.
Ramsey, Simeon D. pvt.
Ramsey, Thomas J. 2nd Lieut.
Reid, Wiley J. pvt.
Rice, Hilton P. pvt., 1st Sgt.
Rice, John pvt.

Ringo, William pvt.
Robinson, Jerome B. 3rd Sgt.
Robinson, William M. pvt.
Robinson, Young pvt.
Rogers, Joseph pvt.
Rosseau, John F. pvt.
Russell, John G. 4th cpl.
Sandifir, Daniel J. pvt.
Seaman, Joel pvt.
Sharp, William T. 2nd Lieut.
Smith, John F. pvt.
Smith, John R. pvt.
Smith, Richard H. pvt.
Smith, William F. pvt.
Snap, Nathaniel pvt.
Spurlock, Allen pvt.
Spurlock, James pvt.
Stewart, Robert E. pvt.
Strong, William pvt.
Sutton, William pvt.
Thomas, James pvt.
Thompson, Cephas pvt.
Toomer, Benjamin Franklin pvt.
Townsend, Littleton M. pvt.
Van Norman, Stephen R. pvt.
Webster, George H. 4th Sgt.
Wells, John pvt.
Whittington, John J. pvt.
Wilburn, John A. pvt.
Wilson, George A. pvt.
Wyatt, Willford D. pvt.
Young, Pearleamon J. pvt.

Company C, Capt. Anderson's Company (DeSoto County)

Agee, David G. pvt.
Anderson, James Patton Capt.,
  Lieut.-Col.
Anderson, Jesse pvt.
Anderson, John A. Adjut.
Anderson, Thomas S. 1st Sgt.
Anderson, William pvt.
Barnes, John P. pvt.
Bee, James pvt.

Benthall, Washington O. pvt.
Booth, George W. P. pvt.
Bradley, Jefferson C. pvt.
Bradley, John Franklin pvt.
Carter, William B. musician
  (Bugler), pvt.
Clough, Zebulon M. P. pvt., 3rd
  cpl.
Cobb, Bayless E. 4th cpl.

Cobb, Josiah pvt.
Cox, William R. pvt.
Crumby, Absalom L. pvt.
Crumby, Walter K. pvt.
Dalton, David L. musician
Dickson, Joseph P. pvt., Q.M.S.
Dorsey, Hilliard pvt., Capt.
Douglass, Jeremiah M. pvt.
Eason, Ashley D. pvt.
Edmonson, Archibald S. pvt.
Ellis, Andrew I. pvt.
Fisher, George S. pvt.
Fisher, John pvt.
Forrest, Hardeman C. 2nd Lieut.
Forrest, John M. pvt.
Garrett, John S. pvt.
Griffin, James T. pvt.
Gwaltney, Leonidas pvt.
Hancock, George W. pvt., 3rd cpl.
Harrell, Jesse M. pvt., 2nd cpl.
Haynes, Granville O. pvt., 2nd cpl.
Heiston, James P. pvt.
Hicks, Joseph W. pvt.
Hodge, James 2nd Sgt.
Holloway, Lewis M. pvt.
Holt, Josiah pvt.
Howard, Calvin pvt.
Inabnet, William A. pvt.
Jean, Thomas D. pvt.
Jones, John C. pvt.
King, Richard S. 1st Lieut.
Knott, Elijah pvt.

Langley, Samuel pvt.
Lewis, Alfred pvt.
Lewis, Henry pvt., 3rd, 2nd Sgt.
Lipsey, Ansylum G. pvt.
Livingston, George H. pvt., 1st Sgt.
McGeehee, David pvt.
McKenna, Edward A. pvt.
Manning, Joseph W. pvt.
Mason, Solomon musician, pvt.
Matlock, Andrew J. 4th Sgt.
Matlock, Charles M. musician, pvt.
Miller, Stephen W. 1st cpl.
Moore, William S. 3rd Sgt.
Morgan, Waddy F. pvt.
Mulcare, Thomas pvt.
Nash, Charles B. pvt.
O'Brien, William pvt.
Payne, Joshua pvt.
Poag, Samuel G. W. pvt.
Prior, Belfield W. pvt.
Rapplee, William pvt.
Sloan, Rankin pvt.
Sweeney, John pvt.
Thompson, William P. pvt.
Van Wagener, John W. pvt.
Walker, John M. pvt.
Williams, Allen pvt.
Williams, John pvt.
Williams, Simon pvt.
Winters, Benjamin F. pvt.
Wolcott (Walcott), Carlton Luke
  pvt.

Company D. Pontotoc Avengers
(Pontotoc County)

Andrews, William pvt.
Arnold, William 1st musician
Barnett, John A. pvt.
Billings, Charles E. pvt.
Black, Oliver H. P. pvt.
Bourk, Peter pvt.
Bradford, Edmund pvt.
Burton, Edmund pvt.
Carricer, Marton pvt.

Carson, Eli B. pvt.
Carson, William G. pvt.
Cary, Nathaniel Robert 1st Lieut.,
  Capt.
Cobb, George H. 1st Sgt.
Collins, Abraham pvt.
Collins, Joel pvt.
Collins, Robert A. 4th Sgt.
Cornelius, James A. pvt.

Crumpton, William A. 2nd Sgt.
Delaney, Joseph pvt.
Delany, Edward pvt.
Denton, Jerry W. pvt.
Dillahunty, Henry I. pvt.
Downing, William R. pvt.
Edwards, Thomas pvt.
Falkner, Kelly pvt.
Fullerton, Elijah M. pvt.
Fullerton, George W. pvt.
Googer, Martin pvt.
Goss, George H. pvt.
Harris, Daniel C. pvt.
Hudson, Nathaniel M. pvt.
Hulsey, Joab A. pvt.
Hunter, Samuel 2nd Lieut.
Ingram, Henry D. pvt.
Johnson, William R. pvt.
Kennedy, William G. 3rd cpl.
Lacy, Beverly M. pvt.
Leland, Columbus M. 1st Lieut.
Leland, Stephen D. pvt.
Lilly, John A. 3rd Sgt.
Lopeman, Dennis pvt.
Lucas, Sterling pvt.
Lucken, Frederick W. pvt.
McNair, Neil M. pvt.
McNeil, William E. Sgt.-Maj.
Marr, James F. pvt.
Martin, Leroy C. pvt.
Mican, James pvt.
Milam, Henry S. W. pvt.
Morrison, John pvt., 3rd cpl.

Morrow, William pvt.
Mustin, William C. pvt.
Obarr, Jesse pvt.
Owings, Jonathan Lafayette pvt.
Perry, Elihu I. pvt.
Pippins, John E. pvt.
Pittman, William H. pvt.
Pitts, John B. pvt.
Pitts, John C. pvt.
Porter, David Henry pvt.
Porter, James pvt.
Porter, William pvt.
Proctor, Collin B. pvt.
Roberson, Caleb R. pvt.
Setzler, George A. pvt.
Shackelford, Josephus 2nd cpl.
Shelton, John pvt.
Shelton, Redden pvt.
Spencer, Edward pvt.
Stewart, John W. 2nd Lieut.
Tapscott, Addison pvt.
Turner, Eaton, B. pvt.
Turner, John R. 2nd musician
Wagers, James G. pvt.
Walker, Joseph W. pvt.
Walker, Lawrence F. pvt.
Wiatt, William M. pvt.
Williams, Charles H. 1st cpl.
Williams, William pvt.
Winston, William 4th cpl.
Wolfe, Alexander D. pvt.
Worsham, Henry pvt.
Wray, John F. Capt.

Company E, Capt. Stewart's Company
(Monroe County)

Astin, Samuel C. 1st Lieut.
Barton, Benjamin F. pvt.
Belt, David B. pvt.
Bennett, Robert E. pvt.
Bettersworth, William A. 1st Sgt.
Branch, Michael pvt.
Brown, Samuel W. pvt.
Brownley, Henry F. 4th Sgt.

Burnett, Willis 3rd Sgt.
Byrns, Calvin pvt.
Calvit, Joseph pvt.
Cassel, Gardiner B. pvt.
Cheek, Isaiah V. pvt.
Coleman, Reuben pvt.
Coleman, William pvt.
Cooper, Little I. B. musician

Coopwood, John   pvt.
Coopwood, Thomas B.   4th, 3rd cpl.
Cothran, William G.   1st cpl.
Curren, Robert   pvt.
Davis, Benjamin   pvt.
Dement, Thomas C.   pvt.
Dickerson, Richard B.   pvt.
Dillingham, William H.   Add'l. 2nd Lieut.
East, William I.   pvt.
Ellison, John B.   pvt.
Feltman, Jacob J.   pvt.
Fortenberry, James R.   pvt.
George, James H.   pvt.
Gibbons, George W.   pvt.
Goos, Frederick   pvt.
Gore, Ashford   pvt.
Grant, James   pvt.
Grove, William   pvt.
Guess, Walker   pvt.
Hall, William A.   pvt.
Hardin, Green B.   pvt.
Harrison, William H.   pvt.
Hopper, Joseph W.   pvt.
Hoyle, Solomon H.   pvt.
Humber, John   pvt.
Hunt, Thomas M.   musician, pvt.
Johnson, Ewing C.   pvt.
Joiner, William R.   pvt.
Jones, John L.   2nd cpl.
Kercheval, Rufus   3rd cpl.
Krah, Elias E.   pvt.
Kyle, Joseph P.   pvt.
Langford, Joseph H.   4th Sgt.
Langford, William R.   3rd cpl.
Leatherwood, Spencer   pvt.
Levy, Samuel H.   pvt.
McDonald, James   pvt.
McKinney, William C.   pvt.
McWilliams, Wesley   pvt.

Mason, John A.   pvt.
Maum, James W.   pvt.
Merrill, Austin P.   pvt.
Merryman, Willis W.   pvt.
Metlock, John   pvt.
Miles, William   pvt.
Montgomery, Charles S.   pvt.
Moore, Robert E.   pvt.
Morphew, Silas   pvt.
Nicholson, William   pvt.
Pilkington, John A.   pvt.
Pitts, Bartley   pvt.
Ragsdale, James O.   pvt.
Reedy, John   pvt.
Ridge, James W.   pvt.
Roan, Carter   pvt.
Roden, Carter   pvt.
Russell, James H.   pvt.
Sessions, John H.   pvt.
Smith, Johnson W.   pvt.
Smith, Stephen F.   2nd musician, pvt.
Stevens, Samuel M.   pvt.
Stewart, Benjamin E.   pvt.
Stewart, George E.   Capt.
Stewart, Malcomb   pvt.
Sumner, Thomas I.   pvt.
Tate, Arthur   pvt.
Thomas, Alfred B.   pvt.
Thomas, James W.   pvt.
Thompson, James   pvt.
Thornton, Thomas   2nd Sgt.
Watlington, John M.   pvt.
White, Archibald H.   pvt.
Willett, John C.   pvt.
Williams, James N.   musician (Drummer), pvt.
Williams, Valerius R.   pvt.
Williams, William A. I.   pvt.
Wilson, John   pvt.
Young, Mathew A.   pvt.

Companies Unknown

Hobbs, John S.

Mississippi Mexican War Pension List

The following is a list of Mexican War veterans who drew their pensions while residing within the State of Mississippi. Not all of these soldiers/sailors/marines served in Mississippi units.

Abrams, Washington H., WC - 4793, 1 Jun 1887, MS ser Co. K, 1st TX Foot Vols as a Musician.
Acker, Joel M., Annie E., WC - 8538, 14 Apr 1893 & SC - 2196, both MS, srv Co. D, 2nd Regt. MS Vols as a Pvt. In 1847-8, BLW # 7028 - 160 - 50, sol. died 5 Dec 1892.
Acklin, Morris, SA - 10847, 16 Apr 1887, MS, srv in the Qtr. Mstr. Dept.
Adair, Isaac G., SC - 16584, 30 Jul 1887, MS, Howard's Co., 1st MS Vols.
Adams, L. C., Dillie, WC - 15363, 5 Mar 1909 & SC - H642, both AR, srv Co. B, 2nd MS Vols as Pvt., OW IA - # 24162 Rej, also See XC - 2660510.
Agee, David G., Susan, WC - 11209, 7 Aug 1897, AR, srv Co. C, 1st Bttn 2nd MS Vols as a Pvt.
Aiken (Also listed as Akin), Roland T., SC - 10492, 6 Jul 1887, MS, srv Co. B, 2nd MS Vols.
Alburgen, John P., Mary L., WA - 6918, 26 Jul 1888, MO, srv in the MS Vols.
Alexander, A. Jeptha, Sarah E., WC - 12598, 29 Jun 1900 & SC - 928, both MS, srv Co. C, U.S. Voltiguers.
Alexander, Barton W., SC - 6716, 18 May 1887, TX, srv Co. E, 2nd MS Vols.
Alexander, David W., SC - 16831, 14 Aug 1888, MS, srv as Qtr. Mstr. Sgt. & 1st Sgt. Co. D, 1st TN Mtd. Vols.
Alexander, Theodore L., Sarah M., WA - 14807, 16 Nov 1898 & SC - 19167, both MS, srv as Teamster in Qtr. Mstr. Dept.
Alexander, W., SC - 6716, 18 May 1887, TX, srv Co. E, 2nd MS Vols.
Allen, Andrew J., Emma, WA - 16606, 30 Apr 1902, MO & SA - 19888 in TX, srv Bradford's Co., 1st MS Vols as a Pvt. in 1846, BLW # 79391 - 160 - 47, sol died 29 Jan 1902.
Allen, James N., Olympia C., WC - 1057, 11 Feb 1887, MS, srv Co. K, 1st AR Mtd. Vols.
Allen, Samuel M., SC - 8738, 10 Aug 1887, AR, srv Co., I 1st MS Vols.
Allinder, John W., SA - 24405, 14 Aug 1893, TX, srv Capt. Jno D. Bradford's MS Vols, BLW # 53302 - 160- 47.
Anderson, Garlin, Rhoda, WA - 3698, 9 Jun 1887, TX, srv Capt. Bradford's Pontotoc Rovers in MS Vols as a Pvt. in 1846, BLW # 77423 - 160 - 47, sol. died 1 Sep 1884.
Anderson, Hartley, Sarah E., WC - 9224, 4 Nov 1893 & SC 5497, both TN, srv Co. F, 2nd MS Infan.
Anderson, Henry H., SC - 8056, 24 Mar 1887, MS, srv Co. G, 4th LA Vols.
Anderson, J. Patton, Getta Adair, WC - 1064, 11 Feb 1887, KY, srv as a Lt. Col. in a Bttn MS Vols.
Anderson, John C., Sarah R. N., WA - 12774, 3 Jun 1895, KY, srv Hamilton's

Co., MS Vols.

Anderson, John H., SA - 24648, 3 Dec 1894, OH, srv Wasker's Co., 1st MS Vol Rifles.

Anderson, Joseph M., Rhoda J. C., WC - 4708, 26 Apr 1888 & SC - 35, both TX, srv Co. E, 2nd MS Vols.

Andrews, Lemuel J., SC - 8957, 19 Mar 1887, AR, srv Capt. Estell's Co., 2nd MS Vols.

Anglin, Jasper, SC - 11587, 4 Feb 1887, LA, srv Co. B, 3rd MS Vols.

Anglin, William C., SC - 76, 11 Mar 1887, MS, srv Co., 2nd MS Vols.

Appling, Edwin R., Rebecca J., WC - 14423, 25 Oct 1905 & SC - 12239, both CA, srv Key's Co., 1st MS Vols.

Archer, Joseph, SA - 24973, 30 Aug 1897, MS, srv Capt. Blythe's Co., 2nd MS.

Arnold, Solomon A., SC - 13008, 2 Feb 1888, MS, srv Co. H, 2nd MS Vols.

Arthur, Jasper Newton, Phoeba Ann, WC - 1902, May 1887, MS, srv Co., G 13th U.S. Infan.

Ashcraft, Brown M., Jane N., WC - 1062, 30 Mar 1887, MS, srv Co. F, 3rd U.S. Dragoons.

Atkins, James J., SC - 11395, 10 Sep 1887, MS, srv Thompson's Co., 2nd KY Infan.

Auglin, William C., SC - 4568, 27 Apr 1887, MS, srv Co. D, 2nd MS Vols, dupl. of C - # 76.

Austin, James M., SA - 23574, 21 Sep 1891, AR, srv as a Recruit in 2nd MS Vol. Infan.

Ayers, Daniel G., SA - 24812, 27 Apr 1896, MN, srv Capt. Ader's 2nd MS Vols. as a Recruit.

Baird, James B., Caroline A. Manghan, WA - 17792, 17 Oct 1904, TX, srv Cooper's Co. B, 1st MS Rifles.

Baker, Isaac, SC - 12644, 15 Nov 1887, MS, srv Morris' Co., 4th IL.

Baker, James H., Harriet C., WC - 1372, 2 Mar 1887, MS, srv Bullen's Co., Ist KY Vols.

Ball, G. Henderson, Gertrude, SC - 32, 17 Mar 1887, MS, srv Co. I, 3rd US Dragoons.

Ball, Joseph C., SC - 333, 15 Feb 1887, MS, srv Co. C, 3rd and F 1st U.S. Arty.

Banks, Winston, Adela, WC - 3543, 1 Sep 1887, TN, srv Sharp's Co. A, 1st MS Foot Vols.

Bankston, Thomas J., Jane, WC - 2520, 12 Aug 1887, MS, srv Co. F, 2nd MS Vols.

Barden, John, Mary J., WC - 10246, 2 Mar 1896 & SC - 182, both MS, srv Co. B, 2nd MS Vols.

Barefield, Elias, Mary D. T., WC - 1104, 7 Apr 1887, MS, srv Co. F, 2nd MS Vols.

Barefield, Ervin, Wincey C., WC - 6356, 24 Sep 1888, MS, srv Co. H, 1st MS Vols.

Barnes, Edwin W., Virginia C., WA - 9516, 11 Dec 1890, MS, srv Co. A, 3rd LA Vols.

Barnes, M., SA - 24660, 31 Dec 1894, MO, srv McMilla's Co., MS Vols.

Barnett, Starling Willis, SA - 18067, 5 Jan 1888, MS, srv Dennis' Co., 1st AL

Vols.

Barnett, William, Elizabeth, WC - 8717, 3 Jul 1892 & SC - 702, both MS, srv Co. C, 2nd MS Vols.

Barnett, William N., Louisa Adline, WA - 15232, 15 Aug 1899, MS, srv in AL Vols as Pvt in 1846, BLW # 97219 - 160 - 55, Indian War WO - 8255 for srv Capt. Cook's AL Vols 1836 (alledged) sol died 11 Jul 1860.

Barron, Ezekiel, wid J. C., WC - 3449, 9 Mar 1887, MS, srv Co. C, 2nd MS Vols.

Barrows, George, Julia F., WC - 7494, 19 May 1891 & SC - 188, both MS, srv Deason's Co., 2nd MS Vols. as Lt.

Barth, William G., Maria, WC - 5643, 6 Apr 1888, MS, srv Phelps' Co. H, 4th US Arty.

Bass, Benjamin, Eliza, WC - 29, 29 Mar 1887, MS, srv Co. B, 1st MS Rifles.

Bates, John R., Amanda I., WA - 10049, 14 Aug 1891, MS, srv Co. F, 6th LA Vols. BLW # 52324 - 160 - 55, died 1878.

Bates, Marshall P., Cornelia, WC - 12564, 5 Mar 1901 & SC - 19537, both MS, srv Co. B, 3rd MS Riflemen as a Cpl.

Bates, William H., Zilpha, WA - 6294, 14 Apr 1888, MS, srv Howard's Co., 1st MS Rifles.

Batts, Theodore D., SC - 106, 14 Mar 1887, MS, srv Co. C, 1st MS Rifles.

Baughman, John B., SA - 361, 15 Feb 1887, MS, srv as a Teamster in the Qtr. Mstr. Dept.

Baughn, William T., SC - 110, 4 Feb 1887, TX, srv as a Sgt.-Maj. In Co. D, 2nd MS Vols.

Beall, John M., Martha A., WC - 9187, 2 Nov 1893, TN or TX & SC - 310 in MS, srv Co. H, 2nd MS Vol Infan as a Cpl.

Beasley, John H., Mary B., WA - 17331, 23 Oct 1903, AL, srv as a Pvt in MS Vol Rifles in 1847 - 8.

Beattie, John D., Susan E., WC - 12397, 5 Jun 1901 & SC - 16463, both MS, srv Cook's Co., 2nd TN Vol Infan as a Sgt.

Becker, Jacob, Regina, WC - 8502, 12 May 1896, MO & SC - 8393 in MS, srv Co. C, Gilpin's Bttn MO Vols as a Pvt in 1847 - 8, BLW # 55148 - 160 - 47, sol. died 18 Apr 1893.

Beesley, John S., Martha L., WC - 12072, 2 Mar 1900, MO & SC - 8591 in MS, srv Shiver's Co., 1st TX Vols.

Bekeart, Julius F., SC - 11218, 2 Aug 1887, CA, srv Co. A, 2nd MS Vols.

Bell, Alexander U., Sarah M., WC - 3211, 28 Dec 1887, MS, srv Ligon's Co., Raiford's Bttn AL Vols.

Bell, Dary, SA - 23763, 23 Dec 1891, MS, srv in 2nd OH Vols, BLW # 79141 - 160 - 47.

Bell, Samuel H., Elizabeth, WC - 12502, 30 Nov 1900 & SC - 7890, both MS, srv Co. D, 1st Battn AL Vols as a Cpl.

Bell, William H., Elizabeth, WC - 2776, 13 Sep 1887, CA, srv Co. K 1st MS Vols as 1st Sgt., OW IC - 413 file 596.

Bellenger, Charles E., Antonia M., WC - 13305, MS, 4 Feb 1901, srv Co. D, Anderson's Bttn MS Vols.

Best, Berry O., Narcissa, WC - 13017, 18 Jul 1901 & SC - 16386, both MS, srv Co.

I, 1st MS Vols as a Pvt.

Bettersworth, Atkinson J., Emily E., WC - 7573, 17 Oct 1889 & SC - 10908, both MS, srv Watson's Co. 1st TN Vols as a Musician.

Bigbie, James N., Mary C., WC - 14538, 28 May 1906, GA, srv Delay's Co., 1st MS Infan as a Pvt.

Bigelow, Lewis A., Emily A., WA - 13696, 23 Dec 1896, MS, srv as Recruit unassigned in US Army.

Billingsley, James C., Sarah C., WA - 15313, 5 Oct 1899, AR, srv in the 2nd MS Vols.

Bird, Charles P. alias Charles Volgher, SC - 9604, 4 Feb 1887, UT, srv Co. B, 1st MS Vols.

Black, Oliver H. P., Amanda, WC - 13869, 18 Feb 1904 & SC - 8194, both MS, srv Co. D, 1st Bttn MS Rifles as a Pvt.

Blackford, Mark, SC - 1091, 2 Mar 1887, WI, srv Co. C, 1st MS Vols.

Blagg, Jesse, Nancy C., WC - 14456, 30 Aug 1902, OK & SC - 14359 in MS, srv Co. C, 3rd TX Mtd. Vols as a Pvt.

Blair, George W., Alise, WA - 7033, 20 Aug 1888, IL, srv Co. A, 2nd MS Vols.

Blanton, William O. or D., SC - 6494, 18 Apr 1887, MS, srv Co. G, 1st US Infan.

Bledsoe, Benjamin S., Mary Anne, WC - 3733, 13 Jun 1887, MS, srv Jones' Co., 5th TN Vols.

Blount, Benjamin F., Mary V., WC - 2105, 18 May 1887, MS, srv Co. K, 2nd MS Vols.

Boardman, Daniel A., Martha, WA - 3223, 17 May 1887, MS, srv on US Transport *Gen'l Hamer*.

Bobb, John, Isabella, WC - 6798, 31 Jan 1890 & SC - 237, both MS, srv Crump's Co., 1st MS Vols as a 2nd Lt.

Bodley, John F., Sarah H., WA - 7901, 10 Apr 1889, MS, srv as Adj in 4th LA Vols.

Boggs, John, Lucia, WC - 1907, 2 May 1887, MS, srv McKellop's Co., 1st MO Inf.

Booth, George W. P., Eliza F., WC - 9021, 19 Oct 1893 & SC - 4931, both MS, srv Co. C, 1st Bttn MS Rifles.

Bossel, John H., Anna G., WA - 5417, 25 Nov 1887, MS, srv in the 1st MS Vols.

Boswell, James M. alias William M. Boswell, Mary B., WA - 13849, 1 Apr 1897, MS, srv Co. H, 3rd KY Inf as a Pvt.

Boswell, Thomas J., Cornelia F., WA - 13237, 24 Mar 1896, MS, srv Hale's TX Vols.

Boutwell, Chappel Spencer, Eliza A., WC - 6291, 27 Apr 1889 & SC 6274, both TX, srv Co. F, 2nd MS Rifles.

Bowen, William B., Mary, WC - 4503, 30 Apr 1888, SC, srv Co. K, 2nd MS Vols.

Bowman, John H., SC - 7860, 25 Feb 1887, WA Terr, srv Co. E, 1st MS Rifles, sol. died 25 Jan 1914.

Bowman, William H., Sarah C., WC - 10295, 30 Dec 1895, MS, srv Co. A, 3rd LA Mtd. Vols.

Boyd, John R., SA - 18491, 14 Feb 1888, MS, srv Bradford's Co., 1st MS Vols as a Lt.

Bradbury, James R., Jane, WC - 674, 11 Feb 1887, MS, srv Downman's Co.,

Raiford's Bttn AL Vols.

Braddock, William A., Lucinda, WC - 10215, 12 Mar 1896 & SC 12270, both MS, srv B, Battalion GA Vol. Inf.

Bradford, Charles M., Amelia D., WC - 1460, 12 Jul 1887, LA, srv Co. E, 1st MS Vols as a 2nd Lt.

Bradford, Ira O., Priscilla, WC - 2308, 17 Mar 1887, TN, srv in the 1st MS Vols.

Bradley, Jefferson C., Mary, WC - 9145, 10 Apr 1887, CA, srv Dorsey's Co., 1st Bttn MS Inf.

Bradley, John Franklin, SC - 20451, 1 Nov 1897, TX, srv Co. C, 1st Bttn MS Vol Rifles.

Bradley, Robert N., Sarah A., WA - 17748, 22 Aug 1904 & SC - 673, both MS, srv Wither's Co., AL Vols as a Pvt.

Bragg, Benjamin, Mary, WC - 15767, 3 May 1911 & SC 18180, both MS, srv Co. F, 13th U.S. Inf as a Pvt.

Brantley, William P., SC - 17459, 8 Dec 1888, MS, srv Curtis' Co., Raiford's Bttn AL Vols.

Brazier, James H., SC - 14612, 18 Jan 1888, MS, srv Lewis' Co., LA Mtd. Vols.

Brewer, Francis M., Margaret E., WC - 15407, 9 Apr 1904 & SC - 12472, both MS, srv Co. L, 2nd KY Vols as a Pvt.

Brice, Jacob, Rosanna, WC - 1470, 17 Mar 1887, MS, srv Co. G, 4th U.S. Art.

Bridges, Joseph, Sarah L., WC - 4069, 17 Mar 1887, AR, srv Taylor's Co., 1st MS Rifles.

Bright, William H., Rebecca M., WC - 7838, 21 Jan 1891, KY, srv Co. C, 1st MS Rifles.

Britt, John Henry, Jane, WC - 10712, 23 Mar 1897, MS, SC - 4053, srv Co. C, 14th U.S. Vols.

Bromley, William C., Josephine, WC - 5507, 14 Jul 1888 & SC - 8519, both TX, srv Co. B, 1st Bttn MS Rifles.

Brame, Charles E., Euma, WC - 8766, 20 Oct 1892, MS & SC - 6763 in MO, srv Co. D, 1st AL Vols.

Brown, Alonzo L., Agnes E., WC - 5052, 4 Mar 1887, MS, srv Co. A, 1st MS Inf as a Pvt 1846-7, BLW # 13567 - 160 - 47 sol. died 2 Feb 1873.

Brown, Daniel, Louisa C., WC - 11598, 6 Jan 1899 & SC - 15683, both MS, srv Ligon's Co., Raiford's Bttn LA Vols.

Brown, James S., Susan M., WC - 12385, 2 Nov 1900 & SC 235, both LA, srv Co. G, 1st MS Rifles as a Pvt.

Brown, John M., Etta L., WA - 16213, 25 May 1901 & SC 14751, both MS, srv Gibbs' Co. C, in Bttn AL Vols as Cpl.

Brown, Leonidas B., Mary Jane, WC - 5630, 16 Jan 1888, MS, srv Co. B, 2nd MS Vols.

Brown, Richard L, Caroline, WC - 11340, 3 Aug 1896, MS, srv Co. H, 3rd LA Vols as a Pvt.

Brown, Samuel W., Cynthia C., WC - 10212, 21 Feb 1896 & SC - 9915, both AL, srv Co. E, 1st Bttn MS Rifles.

Browning, Alfred G., SC - 12638, 15 Nov 1887, TX, srv Co. F, 1st MS Inf, sol. died 27 Jan 1916.

Browning, James C., SC - 3614, 7 Apr 1887, MS, srv Capt. Delay's Co., 1st MS Vols.

Bryan, Henry H., Harriett E., WC - 528, 19 Mar 1887, NC, srv Co. E, 1st MS Inf.

Bryant, John, SA - 25340, 24 Apr 1903, MS, srv Capt. May's Indpt. Co.

Buckholts, John A., Drucilla W., WC - 11482, 25 Jul 1898 & SC - 13040, both TX, srv Co. D, 1st MS Vol Inf.

Buerckley, Lawrenz, SC - 321, 4 Feb 1887, MS, srv Co. C, 4th LA Vols.

Buford, William, SA - 21928, 1 Aug 1889, MS, srv Barrow's Co. A in AL Bttn.

Buie, Owen, SC - 13050, 6 Dec 1887, MS, srv Co. I, 1st NC Vols.

Bull, Edward, Lucretia E., WA - 2751, 22 Apr 1887, MS, srv in the MS Vols.

Bunting, John, Nancy A., WC - 13987, 27 Jun 1905 & SC - 20060, both MS, srv Co. F, 6th LA Vols.

Burkley, Lawrence, SC - 312, 14 Feb 1887, MS, srv Co. C, 4th LA Vols.

Burney, Elonzo P., Alice M., WC - 5043, 4 Feb 1888, MS, srv Downing's Co., 1st MS Vols.

Burnitt, Lucy W., WC - 10231, 30 Sep 1895, TX, srv Co. A, 2nd MS Vol. Infan.

Burrell, James H., Sallie D., WC - 13587, 28 Mar 1904 & SC - 328, both MS, srv Co. D, 1st MS Rifles as a Pvt.

Burton, Madison T., SC - 16922, 11 Sep 1888, TX, srv Co. I, 2nd MS Vols as a Cpl.

Bush, Levi, Adelaide, WC - 16205, 22 Sep 1916 & SC - 11394, both MS, srv Co. D, 5th LA Vols died 10 Aug 1916.

Busser, Jacob, SA - 15701, 6 Aug 1887, MS, srv as a mechanic in Qtr Mstr Dept.

Butler, Jabez W., Elizabeth, WC - 2524, 24 Jun 1887, MS, srv Co. A, 6th LA Vols.

Byram, Jackson C., Eliza S., WC - 14762, 22 May 1905 & SC - 11017, both LA, srv Co. H, 2nd MS Vols as a Pvt.

Cage, William L., Josephine, WC - 6743, 22 Mar 1887, LA, srv Cooper's Co., 1st MS Rifles.

Caldwell, John K., Susan W., WC - 621, 20 Apr 1887, MS, srv Coleman's Co., 1st AL Vols.

Calhoun, Richmond N., Sarah J., WC - 5890, 3 Jan 1888, TX, srv Co. F, 2nd MS Vols.

Cameron, Watts, Mary T., WC - 14352, 2 Apr 1906, MS & SC - 19618 in UT, srv Co. G, 1st TX Mtd. Vols as a Pvt., also see contesting widow **Elizabeth M.**, WO - 17673, 27 Jun 1904 filed in TX.

Camp, John T. alias **John Taylor**, SA - 25444, 14 Apr 1905, AR, srv Co. D, 2nd MS Vols.

Campbell, George, Leonora, WC - 1964, 19 May 1887, TX, srv Co. K, 1st MS Vols.

Caperton, William G., Permelia J., WA - 19774, 4 May 1911, MS, srv Co. C, 2nd MS Vols as a Pvt.

Capshaw, Daniel C., Millie C., WC - 4924, 28 May 1888 & SC - 16234, both Indian Terr. srv 1st MS Infan.

Caraway, Adam H., SC - 369, 4 Feb 1887, TX, srv Co. G, 2nd MS Rifles.

Carcand, Thomas alias **Thomas Concord**, SA - 23059, 23 Sep 1890, MD, srv in 1st MS Rifles.

Cardin, Shackelford W., Harriet, WC - 4923, 8 Feb 1888, MS, srv Coleman's Co., 1st AL Vols.

Carr, Madison H., SC - 8078, 4 Feb 1887, MS, srv Co. F, 1st MS Inf.

Carr, William or William S., Adaline, WC - 14042, 30 Sep 1903 & SC - 13423, both LA, srv Co. K, 2nd MS Vols.

Carraway, William B. Or William B. Conoway, SA - 24767, 18 Nov 1895, LA, srv Clay's Co., 1st MS Vols.

Carre, Henry W., SA - 15802, 10 Aug 1887, MS, srv in Qtr Mstr Dept of U.S. Army

Carriger, Ido, SC - 5745, 18 Apr 1887, TX, srv Cooper's Co. B, 1st MS Vols.

Carroll, Charles C., Orpha M., WA - 7533, 27 Dec 1888, MS, srv Pike's Co. Yell's Regt AR Mtd Vols, OW IA - 23031R.

Carroll, Zachariah H., Mary Rebecca, WC - 9899, 26 Jun 1893, MS & SC - 16232 in AL, srv Co. A, 12th U.S. Inf.

Carson, William G., SC - 15547, 30 Apr 1888, MS, srv Co. D, 1st MS Bttn.

Carter, Henry P., SA - 11436, 10 Mar 1887, MS, srv as a Teamster in Qtr Mstr Dept, OW IA - 20220 Rej.

Carter, Thomas T., Eliza W., WA - 7894, 8 Apr 1888, MS, srv Co. G, 2nd MS Vols as a Lt.

Cason, John A., SC - 337, 3 Mar 1887, MS, srv Co. A, 1st MS Rifles.

Caston, Samuel, SC - 11640, 26 Mar 1887, MS, srv in Palmetto Regt of SC Vols.

Cayce, Joel A. alias **Joseph A. Cayce, Isabella**, WC - 8868, 12 Dec 1888, AR, srv Co. A, 2nd MS Vols.

Cayce, Joseph A. (See **Joel A. Cayce**)

Cayton, William W., Ellaise, WA - 16026, 18 Feb 1901, MS & SC - 9708 in NY, srv Co G, 3rd IL Vols as a Pvt.

Champlon, Sidney S., Mary M., WC - 6842, 30 Oct 1889, MS, srv Co. G, 1st MS Vols.

Chandler, Early M., Adelia A., WC - 13066, 17 Jun 1901 & SC - 6517, both MS, srv Green's Co., 1st TX Rangers (Vols.).

Chaney, Archibald, SC - 11064, 3 Aug 1887, MS, srv Co. F, 2nd MS Rifle Vols.

Chaney, William T., SA - 25132, 11 Aug 1899, MS, srv Jones' Co., 1st AL Vols.

Chapman, Llewelleyn G., Elizabeth N., WC - 14325, 23 Aug 1904, LA & SC-5506 in MS, srv Co. A, 3rd LA Vols as Pvt.

Charlton, Edward F., Isabella J. Bankston, WA - 18231, 18 Nov 1905, MS, srv Co. G, 1st MS Vols.

Chester, Jacob R., Louisa E., WC - 7722, 25 Aug 1891 & SC - 1278, AR, srv Co F, 1st MS Vols.

Childress, James M., Eliza Ann, WC - 3384, 12 Jun 1888 & SC - 10398, TX, srv Co. F, 1st MS Vols.

Chrisholm, John R., Nancy V., WC - 2109, 3 Jan 1887, MS, srv Chase's Co., 2nd LA Vols.

Clardy, Richard, Margaret, WC - 2825, 3 Oct 1887, MS, srv Co. E, 1st MS Vols.

Clark, Felix G., Matilda D., WC - 12435, 21 Jan 1901 & SC - 380, both MS, srv Co. A, 67th (?) LA Vols.

Clark, John M., SC - 13055, 29 Nov 1887, MS, srv Estelle's Co., 2nd MS Vols.

Clark, Robert, Pauline, WC - 15560, 15 Aug 1910 & SC - 20117, both TX, srv Co. D, 1st MS Vols as Pvt XC - 2660438.

Clark, William Henry, Mary McD., WC - 4773, 7 May 1887, TX, srv Co. C, 2nd MS Vols.

Clauton, Albert B., SC - 10709, 26 Jul 1887, MS, srv Co. D, 1st Bttn AL Inf as a 2nd Lt.

Clement, George W. alias Alex McCarroll, SA - 1175, 4 Feb 1887, MS, srv Co. K, MS Rifle Vols.

Clement, George W., SA - 23148, 24 Oct 1890, TX, srv Willie's Co., 4th (?) MS Inf dupl of # 1175.

Clements, James H., Margaret C., WC - 13918, 29 Oct 1910, VA & SC - 18232 in MS, srv Fairfax's Co. L, 1st VA Vols.

Clements, William H., Loula I., WC - 532, 22 Mar 1887, MS, srv Co. C, 1st MS Rifles.

Clendening, John, Susan E., WC - 15061, 14 Apr 1906, LA & SC - 17274 in MS, srv Co. H, 1st PA Vol. Inf.

Cloak, Meresa, SA - 15771, 9 Aug 1887, IA, srv Delay's Co., 1st MS Vols.

Cloak, William G., Theresa, WC - 5029, 9 Aug 1887, IA, srv Delay's Co., 1st MS Vols.

Clough, Zebulon M. P., Lucinda E., WC - 13712, 14 Dec 1903 & SC - 17447, both CA, srv Co. C, 1st Bttn MS Rifles.

Coakley, John, Elizabeth, WA - 10693, 13 Jun 1892, MS, srv Davis' Co., 1st MS Vols.

Cobb, Bayles E., Emma R., WC - 15163, 20 Oct 1908 & SC - 16527, both TX, srv Co. C, 1st Bttn MS Rifles as a Cpl.

Cocke, William T. alias William T. Coke, Victoria L., WC - 8881, 7 Oct 1893 & SC - 15590, both TX, srv as 2nd Lt in Co. A, 1st Bttn MS Vols (Key's Co.).

Cody, James W., SA - 21360, 14 Mar 1889, TX, srv Acker's Co., 2nd MS Vols., Indian War WC - 1858.

Coe, Thomas J., Martha W., WC - 4365, 22 Apr 1887, LA, srv Co. H, 1st MS Vols OW WA - 21736.

Coke, William H., SA - 20407, no filing date shown, KY, srv Key's Co., Anderson's Bttn MS Vols as 2nd Lt.

Coke, William T., see William T. Cocke.

Cole, Andrew J., Eleanor D., WC - 9721, 26 Nov 1894 & SC - 6734, both MS, srv Taylor's Co., 1st MS Vol Inf.

Coleman, Reuben, SC - 5802, 23 Mar 1887, MS, srv Co. E, Anderson's Bttn MS Rifles.

Collier, Benjamin W., Anna Maria, WC - 9153, 4 Dec 1893 & SC - 402, both MS, srv Co., 1st VA Vols as a 2nd Lt.

Collier, John W., Temperance A., WC - 6118, 17 Feb 1887, MS, srv Gouldings's Co., Calhoun's Bttn GA Vols.

Collier, Jonathan N., SC - 487, 4 Feb 1887, MS, srv Co. C, 1st MS Vols.

Collingsworth, Adison, Anna, WA - 9619, 3 Feb 1891, IN, SC - 22765, srv Gillins' Co., 1st MS Rifles.

Collins, Absalom, Parmelia A., WC - 9947, 30 Sep 1895, AR, srv Co. D, 1st Bttn

MS Rifles.

Collins, Jacob D., SA - 25294, 19 Jul 1902, MS, srv Winnberly's AL Regt.

Collins, Joel, Mary A., WC - 13039, 17 Dec 1901 & SC - 14361, both TX, srv Co. H, Anderson's Bttn MS Vol Rifles.

Collins, Lafayette K., Silvinia M., WA - 7295, 26 Oct 1888, MO, srv in the 1st MS Vols.

Collins, Robert A., wid E. A., WC - 3862, 20 Mar 1888, MS, srv Co. D, Jackson's Bttn MS Vols.

Collins, Samuel P., Sarah R., WC - 9192, 26 Dec 1893 & SC - 15176, both LA, srv Willis' Co., 1st MS Rifles as Cpl.

Collinsworth, Adison, SA - 22765, 29 May 1890, IN, WA - 9619, srv Gillens' Co., 1st MS Vols.

Colsen, Evin or Ervin W., SA - 15507, 30 Jul 1887, FL, srv Co. A, 4th MS Vols.

Concord, Thomas alias Thomas Carcand, SA - 23059, 23 Sep 1890, MD, srv 1st MS Rifles.

Conder, Shadrach B. A., SA - 25636, 7 Sep 1912, MS, srv Co. D, 6th US Inf, BLW # 47087 - 160 - 47, CW IC - 287340 for srv Co. E, 66th Inf as 1st Lt & in Band of 14th US Inf, sol died 22 Sep 1918 State Line MS.

Conger, Jeptha, Cary Ann, WC - 10818, 24 Oct 1896 & SC - 546, both AR, srv Downing's Co., G 1st MS Rifles.

Conlar, Shadrach B. A., SA - 25636, 7 Sep 1912, MS, srv Co. D 6th U.S. Inf, CW - 287340 srv 66th IN Inf.

Conn, James W., SC - 6732, 18 May 1887, MS, srv Co. C, 1st MS Vols.

Conner, Michael, SC - 10177, 21 May 1887, MS, srv Co. C, 1st US Arty.

Conner, Thomas G., Elizabeth L., WC - 7077, 2 Jun 1888, LA, srv Co. B, 1st MS Rifles.

Connor, Daniel, Mary, WC - 56, 29 Mar 1887, MS, srv Co. E, 1st MS Vols.

Conoway, William B. or William Carraway, SA - 24767, 18 Nov 1895, LA, srv Clay's Co., 1st MS Vols.

Cook, Henry F., Eliza B., WC - 5639, 4 Aug 1888 & SC 490, both MS, srv Co. C, 1st MS Rifles as a Lt.

Cook, Henry M., SC - 12767, 4 Feb 1887, TX, srv Co. K, 1st MS Rifles

Cook, James, Sarah, WC - 118, 31 Mar 1887, MS, srv Co. H, 2nd US Dragoons OW IF - # 10126.

Cook, Miles J., SA - 25318, 21 Nov 1902, MS, srv Lt George Neal's Co. TX Vols as a Pvt, (alleged).

Cook, William, Caroline, WA - 18612, 6 Feb 1907, MS, srv Co. B, 22 US Inf as a Pvt.

Cook, William T., SC - 19417, 21 Jan 1888, TX, srv Co. D, 2nd MS Inf.

Cooper, Douglas H., Frances M., WC - 149, 23 Mar 1887, DC, srv Co. B, 1st MS Rifles.

Cooper, William G., SC - 11182, 17 Aug 1887, MS, srv Co. G, 1st MS Vols.

Coopewood, John, wid M. A., WC - 1911, 16 May 1887, TX, srv Stewart's Co. E, Andrews Bttn MS Rifles.

Coopewood, Thomas B., Minerva, WC - 4690, 22 Mar 1888, TX, srv Stewart's Co., Anderson's Bttn MS Vols.

Coorpender, Lewis C., Alice A., WC - 2380, 13 Jun 1887, TX, srv Downing's Co., 1st MS Vols.

Coorpender, William F., Anna E., WC - 6692, 14 Aug 1889, VA, srv Downing's Co., 1st MS Vols.

Corbitt, John M., SC - 8908, 8 Apr 1887, MS, srv Co. K, 1st TN Vols.

Corwine, Amos B., Caroline A., WC - 3221, 25 Nov 1887, NY, srv Sharp's Co. A, 1st MS Vol. Inf as a 1st Lt.

Cothrum, William G., SC - 12770, 31 Oct 1887, TX, srv Co. E, in Bttn MS Vols.

Cotten, William A., Alathea A., WC - 2714, 17 Aug 1889, MS, Co. B, 1st MS Rifles.

Coulter, Solomon M., SC - 592, 4 Feb 1887, MS, srv Co. E, 1st MS Vols.

Courtney, Thomas, Eliza, WC - 12877, 19 Feb 1902, TX & SC - 5067 in KY, srv Co. B, 3rd Bttn MS Rifles as Pvt.

Cowger, Jacob H., Elizabeth, WC - 4642, 29 Feb 1888, AR, srv Delay's Co., 1st MS Vols.

Cox, Gilbert, SC - 13419, 4 Feb 1887, MS, srv Co. G, 4th LA Vols.

Cox, John Q. A., SA - 1393, 4 Feb 1887, TX, srv Co. B 2nd MS Vols. LW WC - 381593 for srv 4th AR Cav.

Cox, William R., Annie E., WC - 12159, 9 Jan 1900 & SC - 5541, both LA, srv Co. C, Anderson's Bttn MS Vol Rifles.

Craft, William H., Mary, WC - 1453, 11 Feb 1887, TN, srv Co. I, in 1st MS Vols.

Crane, George S. or George Simmons, Sarah, WA - 7140, 14 Sep 1888, IN, srv McClung's Co., 1st MS Vols.

Crawford, Thomas F., SC - 6973, 23 May 1887, TN, srv Co. E, 2nd MS Vols.

Creed, Cornelius, SC - 10235, 2 Jun 1887, MS, srv Gibbs' Co. C, Seibels' Bttn AL Vols as a Pvt.

Creed, Stephen, SA - 24714, 28 May 1895, MS, srv Fremont's AL Vols.

Creel, Burton, SA - 24602, 17 Aug 1894, LA, srv Findlay's Co,. MS Vols.

Creight, William, Martha, WC - 5134, 8 Jun 1888, SC, srv Roger's Co. K, 1st MS Vols.

Crenshaw, Nathaniel M., SC - 2085, 4 Feb 1887, TX, srv Capt. Elder's Co., 2nd MS Vols.

Cromer, Richard S., Nancy S., WC - 15236, 1 Mar 1909, TX & SC - 7581 in MS, srv Co., C 2nd MS Rifles as a Lt.

Crosland, Alexander, Nancy B., SC - 5944, 31 Oct 1888 & SC - 4629, both in SC, srv Co. K, 2nd MS Rifles.

Crosland, John A., Martha L., WC - 1200, 4 Feb 1887, MS, srv Co. B, 2nd TN Vols.

Cross, Franklin A., Isabell, WC - 3453, 18 Jul 1887, MS, srv Co. F, 2nd MS Vols.

Cross, William J., Mary P., WC - 11607, 24 Feb 1899 & SC - 11539, both TX, srv Co. F, 2nd MS Vols as a Pvt.

Crumby, Absalom L., SC - 11614, 4 Feb 1887, MS, srv Capt. Dorsey's Co., MS Rifles.

Crumby, Albert L. W. alias **Walter K. Crumby, Mary Ann**, WC - 10969, 17 Dec 1896, TN, srv Anderson's Co. C, 1st Bttn MS Rifles & Dorsey's Co. C, 1st Bttn MS Rifles, BLW # 27011 - 160 - 47 issued to Walter K. Crumby, sol. died 19 Jan 1880 in Right TN.

Crumby, Walter K., see **Albert L. W. Crumby**.

Crumpton, William A., Amanda J., WC - 12935, 13 Nov 1900, CA & SC - 12480 in TX, srv Anderson's Bttn 1st MS Rifles in Co. D as a Sgt., OW IA - 22043 Rej.

Crunk, Joseph Wright, Susan M., WC - 7638, 24 Jun 1891 & SC - 4610, both TX, srv Jackson's Co. 2nd MS Vol Inf.

Cuden, John, Sa - 1521, 7 Mar 1887, MS, srv on the *U.S.S. Constitution*.

Cummins, Sanford, Demaris, WC - 12038, 16 Oct 1899 & SC - 9124, both MS, srv Co. B, 4th IN Vols as a Sgt.

Cundiff, Isaac H., SC - 569, 17 Jul 1887, MS, srv Co. H, 16th U.S. Inf.

Cuny, Richard H., Mary E., WC - 7226, 28 Jul 1890 & SC - 16686, both MS, srv Graham's Co. 3 LA Vols.

Curl, William L., Sarah A., WA - 11670, 21 Oct 1893, CA, srv Cos. I & B, MS Rifles as a Capt (alleged) sol. died 21 Apr 1892.

Currie, Edward, Margaret V., WC - 1190, 2 Mar 1887, TX, srv Co. C, 1st MS Vols.

Curry, Milton, Sallie J., WC - 11748, 3 Nov 1898, AR & SC - 6282 in MS, srv Platt's Co., AL Vols attch to 5th LA.

Daily, Josiah, Mary, WC - 9926, 11 Feb 1895 & SC - 12060, both MS, srv Co. I, 13th U.S. Inf.

Dampier, William G., Mahana T., WC - 6303, 29 Apr 1889, MS, srv Crowson's Co., 1st Bttn MS Rifles.

Dart, John alias **John P., Edith P.**, WA - 11139, 16 Feb 1893 & SC - 10752, both CA, srv Co. H, 1st MS Vols.

Davaney, James, Sarah A., WA - 9251, 23 Aug 1890, TX, srv Overton's Co., 2nd MS Rifles.

Davis, Abraham H., SC - 7946, 1 Apr 1887, MS, srv Co. D, 12th U.S. Inf.

Davis, Henry J., SC - 2205, 23 Mar 1887, AZ, srv Co. G 2nd MS Vols.

Davis, James, SA - 25055, 11 May 1898, MS, srv Col. Thomas' TN Vols.

Davis, James M. A., Elizabeth Jane, WC - 8610, 9 May 1893 & SC - 2557, both MS, srv Co. D, 2nd MS Vols.

Davis, Jerry P., Susan, WA - 11067, 13 Jan 1893, MS, srv Moore's Co., Coffey's Regt. AL Vols.

Davis, Joe (alias), SA - 11012, 14 Apr 1887, MS, srv Co. A Briscoe's Co., LA Mtd. Vols., dupl of # 2885.

Davis, John J., Martha S., WA - 12125, 6 Jun 1894, MS, srv as a Pvt. In LA Vols.

Davis, John L. W., Polly A., WC - 13797, 24 Oct 1902, MS, srv Co. E, 2nd MS Vols. as a Pvt., OW IC-7317 file 45795.

Davis, Joseph alias **Thomas Hargrove, Julia Ann**, WC - 10887, 14 Dec 1895 & SC - 16482, both MS, srv Co. A, 1st Bttn LA Mtd. Vols.

Davis, Owen C., 21 Feb 1887, MS, srv Ligon's Co., Raiford's Bttn AL Vols.

Davis, Reuben, Sallie V., WC - 7404, 6 Mar 1891 & SC - 609, both MS, srv as a Col in 2nd MS Vols.

Davis, Warles, Mary E., WC - 8719, 28 Apr 1887 & SC - 12786, both MS, srv Delay's Co., 1st MS Vols.

Davis, William, May, WC - 5790 & WA - 7093, 3 Sep 1888, MS, srv Co. A, 1st

Bttn MS Rifles, OW IA - 13591 Rej.

Davis, William L., Fannie M., WA - 4231, 19 Jul 1887, MS, srv Kilpatrick's Co., 2nd MS Vols.

Deason, John B., SC - 650, 8 Mar 1887, MS, srv Co. K, 2nd MS Rifles as a Capt.

Deason, Joseph L., Athelia B., WC - 2964, 22 Oct 1887, MS, srv Co. K, 2nd MS Inf.

Deblieux, Benjamin, SC - 13626, 31 Dec 1887, MS, srv Stewart's Co., 3rd LA Vols.

Degnan, Patrick, SC - 10108, 4 Feb 1881, CA, srv Co. E, 1st MS Vols.

Denman, Enoch J., Rebecca, WA - 6416, 2 May 1888, MS, srv Gibbs' Co., Bttn AL Vols., also see as Dunman.

Denman, Frederick J., Nannie, WA - 13482, 29 Jul 1896, MS, srv Co. I, 1st U.S. Inf as a 1st Lt.

Dennis, Joseph G., SC - 646, 11 Feb 1887, MS, srv Capt. Coleman's Co., 1st AL Vols.

Denny, Alexander, Mary Ann, WC - 15848, 8 Jul 1912, MO & SC - 17023 in MS, srv Co. A, 1st MO Mtd Inf as a Pvt, also see XC - 2660367, sol also in CW Co. F, 46th MO Mil.

Devenport, Thomas, SC - 8268, 15 Mar 1887, MS, srv Co. G, 2nd MS Vols.

Dickens, Elijah, Samantha L., WC - 11993, 19 Sep 1896 & SC - 8176, both MS, srv Co. B, Bttn 3rd MS Rifles.

Dickerson, Isaac D., Elizabeth J., WC - 10198, 11 Feb 1895, LA, SC - 8909, srv Co. I, 1st MS Vols., OW IA - 22064 Rej.

Dickinson, Isaac D., SC - 8909, 26 Feb 1887, LA, WA - 12553, srv Co. I, 1st MS Vols., OW IA - 22064 Rej.

Dickinson, Joseph C., Rachel, WA - 17514, 8 Mar 1904, AR, srv A, Bttn MS Vol. Rifles as a Pvt., CW C - #672176 for srv Co. B, 14th KS Vol Cav.

Dickinson, Richard B., SC - 8372, 5 Apr 1887, MS, srv Co. E, 3rd MS Vols.

Dickson, Almaron S., Ursula A., WC - 1205, 11 Feb 1887, MS, srv Co. F, 1st MS Vols.

Dickson, David H., Marion, WC - 75, 29 Mar 1887, MS, srv Co. K, 2nd MS Vols.

Dickson, Nolan S., Annie E., WC - 11624, 5 Oct 1889, MS, srv Cooper's Co., 1st MS Vols as a Pvt.

Dillingham, William H., SC - 791, 4 Feb 1887, Indian Terr., srv Co. E, 3rd MS Rifles.

Dixon, Elijah, Francis E., WC - 6396, 29 Apr 1889, TX, srv Sharpe's Co., 1st MS Vols.

Dixon, Philip B., SC - 8523, 2 Apr 1887, CA, srv Co. C, 1st MS Inf.

Dobson, Blackman C., SC - 8086, 17 Feb 1887, MS, srv Co. C, 3rd TN Vols.

Dockerey, Tolbert, Ann Hellen, WC - 1211, 8 Mar 1887, MS, srv Co. K, 1st MS Inf.

Dodds, Stephen, Catherine, WC - 94, 28 Feb 1887, NY, srv as a Drum Maj. In 1st Regt. MS Rifles.

Doss, Washington L., Noraline A., WC - 12266, 18 Jul 1900 & SC - 2432, both MS, srv Co. A, 2nd MS Vols.

Dotson, William M. alias **William M. Ilsley**, SC - 19768, 20 May 1889, MS, srv on *U.S.S. McLane* as Marine died 28 Jul 1921 Jackson, MS.

Dougherty, Edward alias **Edward Sitley** or **Sibley, Julia C.**, WC - 10676, 27 Jul 1896 & SC - 16403, both MS, srv on the *USS Columbus* under Capt Wyman as a Landsman.

Douglas, Jeremiah M., SC - 3963, 25 Apr 1887, AR, WC - 5980, srv Co. C, 1st MS Vol. Rifles.

Douglass, James B., SC - 15879, 18 May 1888, MS, srv Co. C in NC Vols as a Musician.

Douglass, Jeremiah M., Amanda H., WC - 5980, 2 Jan or Jun 1889, AR, srv Dorsey's Co., 1st Bttn MS Rifles.

Douglass, Robert, Mary, WA - 19566, 19 May 1910, GA & SC - 18442 in MS, srv Co. E, Palmetto Regt. of SC Vols as a Pvt also see OW IA - 22078 Rej.

Dowsing, Jeremiah, Rebecca, WC - 9750, 27 Oct 1890 & SC - 728, both MS, srv Co. A, 2nd MS Inf as a Sgt.

Doyle, Moses, SA - 8087, 4 Apr 1887, MS, srv in 6th IL Vols.

Duke, Ensley A., SC - 696, 8 Mar 1887, MS, srv Co. G Palmetto Regt. of SC Vols.

Dunkin, Phillip, SA - 24263, 8 Mar 1893, MS, srv (Downing's) Co., MS Vols.

Dunlap, Jonathan Dickey, Clara L. or **S.**, WA - 20565, 22 Mar 1920, CA, srv 2nd MS Rifles 1846-8, sol died 24 June 1904 Los Angeles CA, see IW - WO #15048 as wid of Albert W. B. Crooks who srv Co. B, 32nd US Inf in 1865-8.

Dunnam, Enoch J., Rebecca, WC - 4955, 2 May 1888, MS, srv Gibbs' Co., AL Inf.

Dupree, James H., SC - 12667, 7 Nov 1887, MS, srv Co. H, 1st MS Vols.

Durdin, Jonathan, Eliza J., WC - 6129, 31 Oct 1888, TN, srv Co. D, 1st MS Vols.

Easterling, Simeon, Seletha, WC - 12660, 2 May 1901 & SC - 10762, both MS, srv Co. F, 2nd MS Inf.

Eastland, James, Emily, WC - 15668, 10 Feb 1911 & SC - 18632, both TX, srv Co. F, 2nd MS Vols as a Sgt.

Eastland, William D., Helen M., WC - 3620, 11 Mar 1887, TX, srv Co. F, 2nd MS Vols.

Eaton, William W., Sarah A., WC - 12979, 18 Nov 1901 & SC - 9051, both AR, srv Co. F, 1st MS Rifles as a Pvt.

Eddins, Robert J., Harriet, WC - 4303, 15 Mar 1888, TX, srv Taylor's Co., 1st MS Rifles.

Edington, James M., SA - 25307, 12 Aug 1902, MS, srv in Pontotoc Rovers in MS Vols.

Edmonson, Charles M., Eliza A., WA - 18177, 9 Oct 1905 & SC - 777, both MS, srv Co. I, MS Vols as a Pvt.

Edmonston, Archibald S., Julia A., WA - 601, 15 Feb 1887, AR, srv Co. C, 1st Bttn MS Rifles as a Pvt.

Edwards, Benjamin F., Carrie S., WC - 2429, 16 Jul 1887, MS, srv Co. G, 1st MS Vols.

Edwards, Benjamin H., Mariah E., WC - 15507, 25 May 1910 & SC - 2433, both MS, srv Co. E, 1st MS Inf as a Pvt.

Eggleston, John R., Sarah D., WC - 15999, 15 Oct 1913 & SC - 20162, both MS, srv as a Lt in U.S.N. 1847-61 (resigned), BLW #69807-160-44, sailor died 19 Sep 1913 Raymond MS.

Elkins, Woodford M., SA - 23442, 9 Apr 1891, MS, srv Crump's Co., 1st MS

Rifles.

Ellerbee, Boggan, Cintha, WA - 4628, 26 Aug 1887, MS, srv as a Teamster in Qtr. Master Dept of US Army.

Ellington, Jamerson, Mary L., WC - 3042, 9 Nov 1887, MS, srv Loyal's Indpt. Co., GA Mtd Vols.

Elliott, George W., Mary H., WA - 10027, 6 Aug 1891, MS, srv Co. K, 2nd MS Vols.

Ellis, William L., Elizabeth P., WC - 1236, 23 Mar 1887, MS, srv Blythe's Co., 2nd MS Vols.

English, Archy D., Marthy E., WA - 13227, 14 Mar 1896, MS, srv as a Pvt. in the USMC.

Enochs, Edgar Romley, SC - 8857, 19 Feb 1887, MS, srv Co. B, 2nd TN Vols.

Erwin, John W., SC - 2209, 1 Apr 1887, MS, srv Co. D, 1st MS Vols.

Erwin, William T., Mary, WC - 5066, 21 Mar 1887, MS, srv Blythe's Co., 2nd MS Vols.

Estelle, John, SC - 19988, 5 Sep 1892, MS, srv Co. E, 1st TN Vols, OW IF - #20349.

Estes, William E., Jane, WC - 13284, 19 Nov 1902 & SC - 12669 in TX, srv Co. E, 1st MS Rifles.

Evans, James, SC - 891, 7 Mar 1887, MS, srv Co. I, 2nd MS Vols.

Evans, James A., Lucy, WC - 3145, 1 Dec 1887, MS, srv Rogers' Co., 1st MS Vols.

Evans, James H., SC - 841, 19 Feb 1887, MS, srv as a Capt in Co. I, 4th TN Vols.

Fairchild, Joseph B., Mary E., WC - 2470, 30 Jul 1887, MS, srv Co. G, 1st MS Vols.

Falkner, Edmond G., Margaret M., WC - 15629, 17 Nov 1909, AL & SC - 10948 in MS, srv Co. I, 2nd MS Vol Inf.

Falkner, William C., Lizzie H., WC - 8504, 11 Nov 1890, TN & SC - 5523 in MS, srv Co. E, 2nd MS Vol Rifles as a 1st Lt, OW IF - #5374.

Farish, Claiborne, Anna A., WC - 6717, 18 Dec 1889 & SC - 1131, both MS, srv Co. B, 1st MS Vols as a Sgt.

Farrar, Edgar D., SC - 7208, 9 Apr 1887, MS, srv Lawrence's Co. E, 5th LA Vols.

Farrar, Joseph S., Nancy F., WC - 5220, 11 May 1888, MS, srv Co. K, 1st TX Vols.

Fauntleroy, Fred alias Frederick W., Mary A., WC - 12668, 8 Mar 1901 & SC - 12301, both TX, srv Co. E, 1st MS Vols, Indian War WO - # 13421.

Featherston, Edward, Rebecca W., WC - 3297, 18 Jan 1888, MS, srv in the 6th LA Vols.

Fee, William, SA - 25481, 10 May 1906, no place of filing shown on the card, srv under Capt. Jeff Davis MS.

Ferguson, A., SA - 24694, 27 Mar 1895, MS, srv Martin's Co., MS Vols.

Ferguson, James H., SA - 24912, 24 Feb 1897, MS, srv Co. G, 1st MS Vols.

Ferguson, Jeremiah, SC - 13733, 30 Dec 1887, MS, srv in the SC Vols.

Ferguson, Samuel T., SC - 2443, 4 Apr 1887, MS, srv Co. D, 1st MS Vols.

Fewell, Edmund M., Jane D., WC - 8443, 1 Jun 1892 & SC - 974, both MS, srv Co. F, 3rd U.S. Dragoons as a Pvt. in 1847-8, BLW # 50877 - 160 - 47.

Fields, Edmond I., SC - 3053, 4 Apr 1887, MS, srv Co. H, 1st KY Cav.

Fields, Ripley, SC - 2793, 6 Apr 1887, GA, srv Co. D, 1st MS Vols.

Finklea, James, WC - 3972, 8 Apr 1887, MS, srv Co. H, 5th LA Vols.

Finlay, George P., Carrie R., WC - 15674, 11 Apr 1911 & SC - 19780, both TX, srv McMann's Co., 1st MS Vols.

Fisher, Robert, SC - 3052, 23 Mar 1887, MS, srv Co. A, 1st MS Vols.

Fisher, Robert, Mary, WC - 4074, 1 Mar 1888, MS, srv Sharp's Co. A, 1st MS Vol. Inf.

Fitzgerald, Edmund W., Mary A., WC - 13782, 14 Nov 1903, TX & SC - 2104 in MS, srv Co. E, 1st VA Vol Inf.

Fitzsimmons, William T., Melissa, WC - 15958, 28 Oct 1905 & SC - 7588, both MS, srv Co. F, Calhoun's Mtd GA Vols as a Pvt. 1847-8, OW IA - 21426 Rej., sol died 24 Sep 1905.

Fletcher, Crawford, Sallie, WC - 2687, 18 Aug 1887, AR, srv McManus' Co., 1st MS Vols.

Fletcher, Lorenzo Dow, SC - 10257, 15 Feb 1887, MS, srv Co. H, 2nd MS Vols.

Flournoy, John G., Sallie L., WC - 9513, 11 Jan 1894 & SC - 2567, both MS, srv Barbee's Co., 2nd MO Cav as a 2 Lt. OW IA - 14203 Rej.

Flowers, Ephraim A., Kate, WC - 12619, 12 Jun 1901 & SC - 13011, both MS, srv Co. G, 2nd MS Vol Rifles as a Pvt.

Flowers, Graham H., Julia, WC - 11473, 26 May 1898 & SC - 9607, both MS, srv Co. G, 2nd MS Vol Rifles, OW IA - 14204R.

Floyd, Elijah, Mary Ann, WC - 7891, 21 Sep 1891 & SC - 1013, both TN, srv Co. A, 1st MS Vol Rifles.

Flynn, William P., Mary, WC - 11798, 30 Nov 1898, MS, srv Co. E, 1st LA Vols.

Flynn, Zachariah K., Eliza C., WC - 16133, 29 Apr 1910 & SC - 13057, both MS, srv Co. D, 2nd MS Inf as a Pvt.

Foil, John C., Mary Ann, WC - 4645, 17 Apr 1888, no place of filing given, Buckley's Co., 2nd MS Vols.

Folen, Edward, Jane, WA - 684, 1 Apr 1887, MS, srv Co. F, Calhoun's Bttn GA Vols.

Folkes, Benjamin, SC - 2338, 21 Mar 1887, MS, srv Willis' Co., 1st MS Vol Rifles.

Folkes, James L., Lillie L., WC - 2973, 26 Oct 1887, OR, srv Co. C, 1st MS Rifles.

Fongel, Charles alias **Charles Volgher** or **Charles P. Bird**, SC - 9604, 4 Feb 1887, UT, srv 1st MS Vols.

Foot (Ford), Marcus L. or **Marcus L. Fort**, SC - 18679, 2 Apr 1889, TX, WC - 9189, srv Co. I, 2nd MS Vols.

Ford, Charles, Elizabeth C., WA - 8792, 8 Mar 1890, NV, srv Co. D, 1st MS Inf.

Ford, Henry F., Emily C., WC - 12210, 18 Aug 1898 & SC - 13224, both TX, srv Willis' Co., 1st MS Vols as a Pvt.

Ford, James F., Mary R., WC - 1360, 25 Feb 1887, MS, srv Co. B, 14th US Inf.

Foreman, Andy alias **Jesse A. J.**, SC - 14159, 19 Sep 1887, KS, WA - 18251, srv Co. I, 1st MS Vols.

Forgay, William H., SA - 19785, 30 Jun 1888, TX, srv Youngblood's Co. in MS Vols.

Forman, Andy alias **Jesse A. J., Permelia A.**, WA - 18251, 16 Dec 1905, KS, SC - 14159, srv Co. I, 1st MS Vols.

Forman, Jesse A. J., see Andy Forman.

Forrest, Hardeman C., SC - 17407, 4 Feb 1887, TX, srv Co. C, Anderson's Bttn MS Rifles as a 2nd Lt.

Fort, Marcus L., Nannie J., WC - 9189, 18 Jan 1893, & SC - 18679, both TX, srv Co. I, 2nd MS Vols.

Fortenberry, James R., Cynthia, WC - 8794, 17 Jul 1889 & SC - 11770, both MS, srv Stewart's Bttn MS Vols.

Foster, John, SA - 16098, 23 Aug 1887, MS, srv on the *U.S.S. Col. Clay.*

Foster, John, SA - 24681, 14 Feb 1895, MS, srv as Asst Engr on Transport in Qtr Mstr Dept of U.S.N.

Fougel, Charles, SA - 499, 4 Feb 1887, UT Terr. Srv Co. B, 1st MS Vols, see Charles Bird.

Fox, Thomas J., SC - 4639, 23 Mar 1887, AR, srv Co. C, 2nd MS Vols, CW IC - 649011 & MC - 526506 for srv Co. D 6th TX Cav.

Foy, Frederick W., SA - 8285, 17 Mar 1887, MS, srv as a Teamster in Qtr Mstr Dept of US Army.

Franklin, Jeremiah, SA - 8288, 2 Apr 1887, MS, srv Shelly's Co., 2nd AL Vols.

Frazee, Carman, SC - 8561, 4 Feb 1887, TX, srv Co. K ,1st MS Rifles.

Frazer, William, SA - 18763, 12 Mar 1888, MS, srv McManus' Co., 1st MS Vols.

Free, Thomas R., Elizabeth, WC - 8349, 30 Dec 1891 & SC - 907, both MS, srv Co. G, 1st TN Vols, also see WO - #15154 for Icy Free (contesting wid).

Freeland, Hiram A., Elizabeth, WC - 1208, 4 Apr 1887, MS, srv Johnson's Co., TX Mtd Vols.

Freeland, James, Sarah, WA - 14224, 27 Oct 1897, LA, srv Key's Co., 2nd MS Vols.

Freeman, Samuel D., Minerva, WA - 6556, 17 May 1888, MS, srv Co. I, 8th U.S. Inf as a Pvt, OW W - #23153.

Freeman, William A., SC - 2570, 23 Mar 1887, AL, srv Co. A, 2nd MS Vols.

Friar, William J., Sarah Ann, WC - 2707, 16 May 1887, MS, srv Willis' Co., 1st MS Rifles.

Fulcher, Jesse H., SA - 25276, 22 Mar 1902, MS, srv Capt. Bennett's Co. A, 1st TX Vols.

Fuller, Samuel P. B., SC - 9397, 11 Feb 1887, MS, srv Co. C, 1st AL Vols.

Fulson, John K., Emma J., WC - 14334, 1 Sep 1905 & SC - 15979, both MS, 1st MI Vol Inf.

Gabel, Elias P. Or Elias P. Gabrel, SA - 24444, 8 Nov 1893, MS, srv Allen's Co., 1st TN Vols.

Gabriel, Philip, SA - 14324, 20 Jun 1887, MS, srv Seible's Co., 2nd AL Vols.

Gage, James D. M., SC - 1530, 24 Feb 1887, TX, srv Co. D, 1st MS Vols.

Gage, John J., SC - 13801, 22 Dec 1887, MS, WA - 721, srv Co. H, 2nd MS Vols.

Gallaway, George M., Louisa T., WC - 16216, 22 Jan 1915 & SC - 18162, both ID, srv Co. D, 2nd MS Inf as a Pvt 1846-8, BLW # 43689 - 160 - 47, also CW srv Co. B, 1st Bttn AR Inf 1862, died 29 Nov 1914 White Bird.

Ganong, Luther M., SA - 2400, 4 Feb 1887, MS, srv as a Teamster in Qtr Mstr Dept.

Ganong, William L., Manetta F., WC - 295, 11 Feb 1887, MS, srv Co. I, 2nd MS

Rifles.

Gardner, Alvin N., Violet L., WA - 8254, 8 Aug 1889, MS, srv Co. K, 6th US Inf.

Gardner, Solomon, Sallie B., WC - 9399, 5 Jun 1894 & SC - 1544, both AR, srv Co. A, 1st MS Inf.

Garland, Edward W., Julia R., WC - 11421, 7 Mar 1898 & SC - 1532, both TX, srv Co. C, 2nd MS Rifles (Vols.).

Garrett, John S., Rebecca, WC - 4731, 7 May 1888, TX, srv Co. C, 1st Bttn MS Vol Rifles.

George, James Z., SC - 17214, 9 Oct 1888, DC, srv Howard's Co., 1st MS Vols.

Gibbins, William Evans, Eliza, WC - 196, 11 Feb 1887, MS, srv Co. C, 15th US Inf.

Gibbons, Seth, Martha V., WA - 8417, 8 Oct 1889, CA, srv Co. A, 1st MS Vols.

Gibbs, Charles H., Ellen L., WC - 297, 12 Mar 1887, MS, srv Co. G, 1st MS Rifles.

Gibson, Ralph J., Louisa C., WC - 6170, 14 Nov 1888, MS, srv Co. K, 2nd MS Vols.

Gibson, Thomas J., Mary S., WC - 2028, 27 Apr 1887, MS, srv in the TN Vols.

Gillespie, John E. alias **John G. Elliott,** SC - 12340, 31 Oct 1887, KY, srv Co. D, 1st MS Vols.

Gilliland, John G., SC - 2226, 17 Mar 1887, MS, srv Co. B, 2nd MS Vols.

Gilliland, Samuel M., Julia A. E., WC - 9594, 16 Sep 1890 & SC - 7809, both TX, srv Co. A, 1st Bttn MS Vols (Rifles).

Glenn, John W., Sallie, WC - 4543, 4 Jan 1888, LA, srv Co. I, 1st MS Vols.

Goff, Felix W., SC - 2220, 4 Apr 1887, KY, srv Co. I, 2nd MS Vols. as a 2nd Lt.

Goforth, James L., Amanda F., WC - 10585, 23 Nov 1896, TX, SC - 2456, srv Co. E, 2nd MS Vols as a Sgt.

Gofoth, James L., see **James L. Goforth.**

Goldson, John, Mary F., WC - 16195, 28 Jun 1916, MS & SC - 15783 in TN, srv Co. B, 1st AL Inf as a Pvt. in 1846-7, sol died 21 May 1916 Ecru, MS.

Goode, Obadiah, Martha H., WA - 4581, 22 Aug 1887, TX, srv Capt. Key's Co. B, Bttn MS Rifles as a Pvt.

Goodman, James M., Louisa A., WC - 6065, 17 Apr 1888, LA, srv Blythe's Co., 2nd MS Vols.

Goodwin, Crofford, Sarah F., WC - 13575, 8 May 1902, TN & SC - 1184 in MS, srv Co. F, 1st MS Vols.

Goodwin, George W., SC - 6301, 12 Apr 1887, TX, srv Co. F, 1st MS Vols.

Googer, John M., SC - 2802, 18 Mar 1887, MS, srv Co. D, 1st Bttn MS Rifles.

Gore, Ashford, SC - 16857, 29 Aug 1888, CA, srv Stewart's Co., 1st Bttn MS Vols.

Gore, Rufus, Margaret, WC - 4646, 1 Jun 1887, MS, srv Co. D, 2nd MS Vols.

Graham, Charles D., Rebecca M., WC - 1125, 9 Mar 1887, MS, srv Co. D, 1st AL Vols OW W - #21236 Rej.

Gray, George H., Carrie A., WC - 8706, 23 Sep 1892 & SC - 18241, both TX, srv Co. C, 1st MS Vol Rifles as a Pvt.

Gray, Peter, SC - 9673, 28 Feb 1887, MS, srv as a Recruit in the 1st US Dragoons.

Gray, William or William Grey, Elizabeth, WA - 13303, 23 Apr 1896, MS, srv in the TN Vols.

Greaves, Stephen A. D., Jennie B., WC - 2779, 26 Sep 1887, MS, srv Co. G, 1st

MS Vols.

Green, David L. alias **William B. Green**, SA - 25601, 5 Jun 1911, MS, srv Co. H, 2nd MS Inf.

Green, James E., Belinda C., WC - 10435, 24 Jul 1895 & SC - 13865, both MS, srv Davis' Co., 2nd TN Vols.

Green, John B., Martha A., WA - 20025, 29 Nov 1912, MS, srv Co. B, Seymour's Bttn GA Vols.

Green, Luther D. alias **Luther D. Tobe**, SA - 25039, 22 Mar 1898, MS, srv Blythe's Co., 2nd MS Vols.

Green, Richard, Nancy E., WC - 15485, 11 Mar 1910 & SC - 11275, both CA, srv Co. A, 1st MS Vol Inf as a Pvt.

Green, William B. alias **David L. Green**, SA - 25601, 5 Jun 1911, MS, srv Co. H, 2nd MS Inf.

Greer, Elkanah, Anna E., WC - 5804, 23 Jun 1887, TX, srv Taylor's Co., 1st MS Vols.

Gregg, Robert, SC - 10769, 27 Jul 1887, LA, srv Co. H, 1st MS Rifles.

Grey, William or **William Gray, Elizabeth**, WA - 13303, 23 Apr 1896, MS, srv in TN Vols, IW - WO #6816.

Griffin, John W., SC - 11598, 27 Jun 1887, MS, srv Colman's Co., 4th AL Vols.

Griffin, Robert Henderson, Sarah A., WC - 15027, 2 Mar 1908 & SC - 11551, both TX, srv Co. A, 1st MS Inf as a Pvt.

Griffin, Thomas M., SC - 2341, 26 Mar 1887, MS, srv Co. C, 4th IN Inf, sol. dead (last paid 4 Nov 1916).

Griffin, Thomas M., SA - 8448, 26 Mar 1887, MS, srv Capt. Payne's Co., 4th IN Vols.

Griffin, Thomas R., SC - 6758, 17 Feb 1887, MS, srv Co. A, 1st MS Vols.

Grimes, Richard, SA - 8447, 24 Mar 1887, MS, srv Co. H, 2nd US Inf.

Grisham, Vinston S., Elizabeth C., WC - 15697, 7 Feb 1911 & SC - 18136, both AR, srv Co. I, 1st MS Inf as a Cpl.

Grissom, Charles, SA - 25593, 22 Jun 1910, MS, no other data on the card.

Guess, Walker, Nancy, WC - 637, 10 May 1887, MS, srv Co. E, 1st Bttn MS Rifle Vols.

Guest, Isaac N., Sallie, WC - 16235, 20 Feb 1917, CA & SC - 12965 in TX, srv Co. F, 2nd MS Vols as a Pvt in 1847-8, BLW #21743 - 160 - 47, XC - 948024, sol died 31 Dec 1916 Pomona CA.

Guinn, Chesley R., SA - 24165, 9 Dec 1892, AR, srv Daniel's Co., 2nd MS Vols dupl #21758.

Guinn, Chesley R., Eliza Jane, WC - 14106, 18 Mar 1905 & SC - 20256, both AR, srv Co. F, 2nd MS Inf see # 24165.

Hague, Sidney F., SA - 23975, 20 Jun 1892, MS, srv Keye's Co., Anderson's Regt. MS Rifles as a Pvt.

Hall, Harman Y. or **Harmon G., Martha**, WC - 6324, 20 Nov 1888, TX, srv Howard's Co., 1st MS Rifles.

Hall, John A., Mary A., WA - 17525, 16 Mar 1904, TX, srv in the 1st MS Rifles.

Hall, William A., Lorrita, WC - 10072, 6 Jun 1892, TN, srv Co. E, Bttn 1st MS Rifles Inf. (Anderson's).

Hall, William H., SC - 12605, 2 Apr 1887, MS, srv Howe's Co. 1st MA Inf CW Army I - #517893 for srv Co. B, 2nd ME Cav & 6th ME Inf.

Hamilton, William, Sophia C., WC - 8958, 16 Jun 1892, MS, srv Co. C, Bttn AL Inf as a Pvt.

Hamilton, William C., SC - 11717, 18 Oct 1887, TX, srv Buckley's Co., 2nd MS Vols.

Hampton, Thomas H., SC - 4382, 7 Apr 1887, LA, srv Co. B, 1st MS Rifles.

Hancher, John, Elizabeth J., WC - 10964, 5 Mar 1897, SC, srv Co. C, 2nd MS Inf as a Pvt.

Hancock, John A. G., Mary E., WC - 12915, 29 Jun 1905, LA & SC - 8630 in MS, srv Co. F, 1st MS Vols, see contesting widow Ida, Mex War WO - 15180.

Hankins, William Albert, SA - 25246, 26 Sept 1901, MS, srv Capt Dill's Co. as a Pvt., no other srv data given.

Hanks, Toliver, Emeline, WC - 14447, 24 Jan 1906 & SC 3071, both MS, srv Co. D, 1st MS Inf Riflemen as a Pvt.

Hargrave, Thomas alias Joseph Davis, SC - 16482, 9 Mar 1887, MS, WC - 10887, srv Co. A, 1st Bttn LA Mtd Vols.

Hargrove, Thomas alias Joseph Davis, Julia Ann, WC - 10887, 14 Dec 1895, MS, SC - 16482, srv Co. A, 1st Bttn LA Mtd.

Harney, William S., Mary E., WC - 8022, 7 Oct 1890, MO & SC - 17762 in MS, srv as Col & Brig Gen'l 2nd US Drgns.

Harper, William B., SC - 4984, 7 May 1887, MS, srv Co. H, 2nd MS Rifles.

Harper, William J., Harriette, WC - 14149, 17 Jul 1905 & SC - 11646, both MS, srv Co. G, 1st LA Vols, XC - 2660487.

Harpole, James, SC - 1023, 4 Feb 1887, MS, srv Co. A, 1st AL Vols.

Harpole, James, Mary A., WC - 252, 7 Mar 1887, MS, srv Co. A, 1st AL Vols.

Harrell, Jesse M., Martha A., WC - 10381, 21 Feb 1893 & SC - 9439, both MS, srv Co. C, 1st Bttn MS Rifles.

Harrell, Wells, C., Dolly L., WC - 9727, 22 Apr 1895 & SC - 4378, both MS, srv Howard's Co. D, 1st MS Rifles as Sgt.

Harrell, William J., SC - 16954, 7 Jan 1888, MS, srv Lomax's Co. D, 1st AL Vols.

Harrington, David R., SC - 15217, 19 Nov 1887, TX, srv Co. B, 1st MS Vols.

Harris, James F., Eliza E., WC - 3668, 9 Apr 1887 (WI or MS ?), srv Haden's Co., 4th IN Inf.

Harris, John N., Elizabeth, WC - 8699, 23 Feb 1893 & SC - 9109, both AR, srv Co. H, 1st MS Vol Inf.

Harris, Joseph W., SA - 25054, 11 May 1898, MS, srv Shiver's Co., 6th MS Vols as a Pvt.

Harris, Lewis B., Lucy Ella, WC - 7740, 26 Oct 1891 & SC - 18266, both MS, srv Deason's Co., 2nd MS Vols.

Harris, Robert Armistead, SC - 7488, 7 Feb 1887, MS, srv Co. B, 1st LA Vols.

Harris, William H., SC - 10262, 7 Jan 1887, OR, srv Co. E, 2nd MS Rifles.

Harrison, Aaron, Mary, WA - 2916, 22 Apr 1887, NY, srv Blythe's Co., 2nd MS Vols as a Pvt.

Harrison, Richard, SC - 14488, 3 Jan 1888, MS, srv Barry's Co. in MD & DC Vols.

Harrison, Samuel R., Jennie McC., WC - 1988, 14 May 1887, TX, srv Co. B, 1st MS Vols as a 2nd Lt.

Harrison, Thomas, SC - 12111, 17 Jun 1887, TX, srv Rodger's Co., 1st Regt MS Rifles.

Hartgraves, William M., Mary M., WA - 13290, 4 Apr 1896, MS, srv Delay's Co., 1st MS Vols.

Hasty, William, Susie, WC - 10220, 28 Dec 1895 & SC - 17963, both MS, srv McManus' Co. E, 1st MS Inf.

Hatcock, Charles W., Missouri, WC - 14826, 10 Sep 1907, AR & SC - 11774 in MS, srv as Sgt Co. D 3rd US Arty, also see XC - 2660399, sol also srv Co. B, 3 US Arty 1848-51 & 1852-7.

Hatton, Benjamin, Elizabeth, WC - 7545, 11 Feb 1891, TN, srv Crump's Co., 1st MS Rifles.

Haynes, Granville O., Ann A., WC - 894, 22 Mar 1887, TX, srv Co. C, in Bttn MS Rifles.

Hays, May, Juliana alias Julianita M. de, WC - 12674, 9 Feb 1900 & SC - 11120, both NM, srv Downing's Co., 1st MS Vol Rifles.

Hazlewood, Calvin T., Martha, WC - 15018, 5 Nov 1907 & SC - 8658, both TX, srv Co. A, 1st Bttn MS Rifles.

Hearn, William C., SC - 6330, 1 Mar 1887, AL, srv Co. A, 2nd MS Vols & Peatt's AL Vols.

Heatwole, Gabriel, SC - 11407, 3 Sep 1887, MS, srv Harper's Co. VA Inf.

Heim, Frederick, Anna, WA - 14158, 14 Sep 1897 & SA - 23670, both MS, srv as Asst Overseer in Qtr Mstr Dept of US Army.

Heise, John, Annie, WA - 7677, 8 Feb 1889, Wash DC, srv in 1 MS Rifles.

Henley, John, Elizabeth, WC - 11137, 21 Aug 1896, LA & SC - 5595 in MS, srv Co. G, 6th LA Vols as a Sgt.

Henry, Charles J., SA - 19950, 24 Jul 1888, IL, srv Hays Co., 2nd MS Vols.

Henry, Robert A., Amanda E., WC - 10359, 15 Jul 1896 & SC - 17121, both MS, srv Co. B, 2nd MS Vols as a Sgt.

Henry, Rufus C., SC - 9610, 4 Feb 1887, MS, srv Co. F, 1st MS Inf.

Hensley, James, SA - 24028, 11 Aug 1892, MA or MS ?, srv as a Pvt in 1st IL Inf.

Herald, William, Samantha E., WC - 8962, 15 Aug 1893 & SC - 11909, both MS, srv Key's Co., 1st Bttn MS Rifles.

Herndon, Joseph F., SC - 10342, 15 Jan 1887, MS, srv Co. C, 1st Bttn AL Vols.

Herod, Andrew J., Texia C., WC - 15887, 19 Aug 1911 & SC - 16973, both MS, srv Co. A, 1st MS Inf as a Pvt.

Herridge, Tillman T., SC - 1434, 9 Mar 1887, MS, srv Co. B, 16th U.S. Inf.

Hewitt, John C., Mary S., WC - 12048, 8 Aug 1899 & SC - 16479, both CA, srv Keye's Co., 1st Bttn MS Rifles as Pvt.

Hicks, Joseph W., SC - 1028, 9 Feb 1887, TN, srv Co. C, 1st Bttn MS Rifles BLW # 22626 - 160 - 47.

Higdon, James, Mary Ann, WC - 2319, 7 Mar 1887, MS, srv 1st MS Vols.

Higgason, John D., SC - 14509, 3 Jan 1888, no place of filing on this card, srv Roger's Co., 1st MS Vols.

Hight, Thomas B., Mary E., WC - 7848, 28 Apr 1891 & SC - 7244, both MS, srv

Co. H, 2nd MS Vols as a Sgt.

Hill, Albert P., Margaret A., WC - 7665, 19 Mar 1889, MS, srv Sharp's Co., 1st MS Vols as a Sgt.

Hill, Elijah B., SA - 8543, 30 Mar 1887, MS, srv Capt Roger's Co., 1st MS Rifles.

Hill, George W., Nancy M., WC - 14396, 25 Jul 1904, LA & SC - 8131 in MS, srv Co. C, 1st Bttn AL Vols.

Hill, Larkin, SC - 14903, 30 Mar 1887, MS, srv Co. B, 1st AR Vols.

Hill, Richard H., WC - 4307, 11 Apr 1887, MS, srv James' Co., 2nd MS Vols.

Hill, Richard, Margaret L., WA - 7605, 21 Jan 1889, MS, srv Overton's & Estelle's Cos., 2nd MS Vols, also see Old War file #5526.

Hilliard, Thomas alias Thomas Hilyard, SC - 15216, 4 Feb 1887, TX, srv Lt. Steele's Detch 2nd MS Vols, sol died 23 Nov 1916 Rogers TX.

Hindsley, John J. or John J. Hinsley, Mary, WA - 11591, 8 Sep 1893, TX, srv Co. K, 1st MS Vols as a Pvt.

Hinson, James P., Mary A., WA - 8389, 26 Sep 1889, MS, no srv shown on the card.

Hobbs, Calvin, Thetus R., WC - 8404, 15 Feb 1892 & SC - 4657, both MS, srv Co. E, 1st MS Vols as a Musician.

Hobbs, William, Mary E., WC - 10652, 29 Apr 1896 & SC - 9333, both NC, srv Co. I, 1st MS Vol Rifles.

Hodge, William J., Margaret P., WC - 1468, 29 Mar 1887, MS, srv Co. B, 1st MS Vols as a Cpl.

Hoggatt, Jacob, Mary E., WC - 8205, 28 Mar 1892 & SC - 19241, both TX, srv Keye's Co., 3rd MS Vols.

Holdaway, Howard D., SC - 11002, 1 Aug 1887, AR, srv Co. F, 1st MS Rifles as Pvt. 1846-7, BLW #1681 - 160 - 47.

Holland, Andrew J., SC - 19234, 22 Mar 1890, MS, srv Sims' Co., Hayes' TX Mtd Vols, sol. died 13 Oct 1920.

Holland, Charles, Clarinda, WC - 1482, 19 Mar 1887, MS, srv Co. C, 2nd MS Vols.

Holland, William H., Elizabeth, WC - 3570, 2 May 1887, MS, srv Liddell's Co., 2nd MS Vols as a Pvt.

Holland, William Thomas, Celia A., WC - 15769, 16 Dec 1907 & SC - 15489, both MS, srv as unassigned Recruit in 2nd MS Vols.

Hollingsworth, David M., Rosina, WC - 7703, 5 Aug 1891 & SC - 11777, both LA, srv Sharp's Co., 1st MS Vol. Rifles.

Hollowell, Edward B., Maggie Eliza, WC - 4487, 11 Mar 1887, MS, srv Jones' Co., 2nd MS Vols, also see XC - 2660355.

Holmead, John, SC - 11498, 16 Sep 1887, MT Terr, srv Overton's Co., 2nd MS Vols.

Holmes, Henry C., Nancy E., WA - 17945, 8 Mar 1905, MS, srv in the MS Vols.

Holt, John S., Mary L., WC - 4989, 2 Jun 1887, MS, srv Co. B, 1st MS Vols as a Pvt.

Holt, John T., Cassandra, WC - 2318, 17 Mar 1887, MS, srv Co. B, 1st MS Rifles.

Hooker, J. M., Elizabeth, WC - 2699, 31 Aug 1887, AR, srv McManus' Co., 1st MS Inf.

Hope, William G., SC - 10191, 14 Jun 1887, TX, srv Co. B, 1st MS Vols.

Hopkins, Benjamin C. alias **L. C. Hopkins**, SA - 23749, 11 Dec 1891, MS, srv Co. B, 2nd MS Vols.

Hopkins, William F., SA - 25330, 4 Mar 1903, MS, srv Capt. Gordon's Co. in AL unit.

Hopper, David James, SC - 4373, 4 Feb 1887, MS, srv Co. A, 1st AL Vols.

Horne, Edward G., Nancy C., WC - 13976, 15 Aug 1904, Ind Terr & SC - 12796 in TX, srv B Bttn MS Rifles as a Pvt.

Hoskins, William A. H., SC - 8740, 10 Aug 1887, AR, srv Co. I, 1st MS Vols.

House, Buckner L, Charlotte J., WA - 13772, 9 Feb 1897, MS, srv Capt Gibbs' Co., 1st AL Vols as a Pvt.

Hovas, Christopher C., Martha J., WC - 1822, 23 Mar 1887, MS, srv Co. H, 2nd MS Vols.

Hovis, Hugh L. B., Laura S., WA - 4937, 26 Sep 1887, MS, srv Cos. K & M, 3rd US Arty.

Howard, Cary, Rachel, WC - 12610, 9 May 1910 & SC - 5125, both AR, srv Co. E, 2nd MS Vols as a Pvt.

Howard, James M., Elizabeth E., WC - 2320, 2 Jun 1887, MS, srv Edward's Co., U.S. Voltiguers.

Howard, John D., Martha, WC - 2368, 18 Jun 1887, TX, srv in 2nd MS Vols.

Howell, William W., Susan J., WC - 15319, 8 Sep 1909 & SC - 9870, both MS, srv Co. B, 1st OH as a Sgt.

Hubert, W., Elizabeth, WC - 1874, 14 May 1887, MS, srv Deason's Co., 2nd MS Inf.

Huddleston, James, Eugenie, WC - 8555, 13 Jun 1893 & SC - 6556, both LA, srv Co. A, Steed's Bttn 17th MS Vol Cav., also see Old War I - #22622 Rej.

Hudson, Nathaniel M., SC - 9405, 19 Mar 1887, LA, srv Co. D, 3rd MS Vols.

Hughes, Archibald M., SC - 13749, 29 Dec 1887, TX, srv Co. E, 1st MS Vols as a Sgt.

Hughes, James F., SA - 25117, 9 Jun 1899, MS, srv Co. A, Knox's LA Vols.

Hughes, James H., Marie P., WC - 7074, 28 Mar 1890 & SC - 11121, both TX, srv Co. E, 1st MS Vols as a 1st Lt.

Hulsey, Joab A., Martha, WC - 2273, 28 Mar 1887, TX, srv Co. D, 1st Bttn MS Vols.

Humber, John H., Nancy, WC - 9916, 26 Feb 1895 & SC - 6080, both MS, srv Co. E, 3rd MS Vol Rifles.

Hunt, Benjamin B., Loduska M. A., WC - 11064, 1 May 1897 & SC - 7230, both AL, srv Co. F, 2nd MS Vol Inf as a Cpl, OW I - #19576 Rej.

Hunter, Burrell E., SA - 16376, 6 Sep 1887, MS, srv Hoag's Co. C in IL Inf.

Hunter, D. W., SA - 24372, 17 Jun 1893, MS, srv Roger's Co., 1st MS Inf.

Hunter, Samuel, SC - 5590, 7 Apr 1887, TX, srv Cary's Co., 1st Bttn MS Rifles as a 2nd Lt.

Hunter, Stephen D., Ellen C., WC - 1786, 20 Apr 1887, AR, srv Delay's Co., 1st MS Vols.

Hutchins, Anthony C., Annie T., WA - 7338, 6 Nov 1888, MS, srv under Gen'l Quitman, no other srv shown.

Hutchison, Junius R., Zoe Anna, WC - 4508, 25 Nov 1887, TX, srv Cooper's Co., 1st MS Rifles.

Hutchison, William F., Sarah A., WC - 2722, 6 Sep 1887, KY, srv Downing's Co., 1st MS Vols, BLW #1491 - 160 - 47.

Hyde, John Dillard or Dillow, Alay E., WC - 13818, 2 Jan 1904 & SC - 6082, both MS, srv Co. A, 1st NC Vols.

Hyneman, Hy C., Susan, WC - 1501, 17 Feb 1887, MS, srv Co. E, 2nd MS Vols.

Ilsley, William M., alias **William M. Dotson**, SC - 19768, 20 May 1889, MS, srv on the *U.S.S. Lane* as a Revenue Marine.

Ingold, Peter, Nancy, WC - 14319, 12 Oct 1905 & SC - 15131, both MS, srv Co. K, 2nd MS Vols as a Pvt.

Ingram, Newton, SC - 1068, 4 Feb 1887, AZ Terr, srv Co. G, 1st MS Inf.

Irvin, David, Ellen, WC - 16374, 28 Dec 1925 & SC - 20407, both TX, srv Co. D, 2nd MS Inf as a Pvt 1847-8, BLW #56250 - 160 - 47, also see XC - 2660458 sol died 10 Nov 1925 Pilgrim TX.

Irvin, Francis M., SC - 2823, 4 Apr 1887, MS, srv Co. D, 2nd MS Vol Inf.

Irvin, Tilman J., Lettie M., WC - 14562, 24 Jul 1906, AL & SC - 2595 in MS, srv Co. D, 2nd MS Vol Inf as a Pvt.

Irvin, William E., WC - 5440, 1 Aug 1888, TX, srv Acker's Co., 2nd MS Vols.

Jackson, Alexander M., SC - 2608, 15 Mar 1887, TX, srv Co. E, 2nd MS Vols.

Jackson, Daniel M., Mary R., WC - 9221, 27 Jan 1894 & SC - 1125, both TX, srv 2nd MS Vol Inf as a 2nd Lt.

Jackson, Daniel N., SC - 16245, 29 May 1888, CA, srv Co. E, 2nd MS Vols.

Jackson, John A., Susan A., WC - 974, 4 Apr 1887, MS, srv Co. H, 2nd MS Vols.

Jackson, William H., Juriah, WC - 5680, 11 Sep 1888, MS, srv Pickens' Co., Coffey's Regt. AL Vols.

Jackson, William Hilton, SC - 11874, 28 Jun 1887, CA, srv Co. E, 2nd MS Vols as a 2nd Lt.

Jacquot, Blaise, Catherine, WC - 14686, 18 Dec 1906, MS & SC - 9440 in LA, srv Co. E, 2nd LA Mtd. Vol Inf.

Jakeway, Jesse M., SA - 11730, 30 Apr 1887, MO, srv Mitchell's Co., 3rd MS Vols.

Jamison, Henry, SC - 8153, 15 Mar 1887, MS, srv Newman's Co., 1st TN Cav.

Jean, Derias Thomas, Fannie L., WC - 14577, 30 Jul 1906 & SC - 12245, both TX, srv Co. C, 1st Bttn MS Rifles.

Jennings, John J., Sarah R., WC - 2790, 9 Aug 1887, MS, Deason's Co., MS Vols.

Jermyn, James, Semantha, WA - 4662, 23 Apr 1888, MS, srv Huffy's Co., 6th LA Inf.

Jeter, John, Mary E., WC - 8673, 20 Oct 1888, MS, srv Co. C, 1st MS Vols.

Jobson, David alias Henry Myers, Catharine Myers, WC - 7294, 18 Jun 1889, MS, srv Kerr's Co., LA Mtd Vols.

Johnson, Benjamin F., Mary Ann, WC - 10451, 19 Sep 1896 & SC - 1117, both MS, srv Co. E, Palmetto Regt of SC Vols.

Johnson, Duncan B., SC - 11783, 26 Feb 1887, AR, srv Co. E, 2nd MS Vols.

Johnson, George W. alias Thomas W. Farrin, Angeline, WA - 8983, 12 May 1890 & SA - 21738, MI, srv as Teamster in 1st MS Rifles, also see LW WC - 122254 as wid of Isaac Mullin who srv Co. H, 33rd IL Inf.

Johnson, Peter W., Eliza A., WC - 422, 15 Feb 1887, MS, srv Co. K, 1st MS Vols.

Johnson, Samuel W., Mary, WC - 8291, 3 Mar 1891, MS, srv Co. F, 3rd U.S. Dragoons, Ind War WO - 9728 for srv SC Mil.

Johnson, Wiley B., SC - 12363, 16 Aug 1887, TX, srv Daniels' Co., 2nd MS Inf.

Johnson, William, SC - 11280, 22 Aug 1887, MS, srv Co. K in Palmetto Regt. of SC Vols.

Johnson, William, SC - 12280, 22 Aug 1887, MS, srv Co. K in Palmetto Regt. of SC Vols.

Johnson, William H., Lou J., WA - 9611, 29 Jan 1891, MS, srv Shever's Co., 1st TX Vols.

Johnson, William R., Martha S., WC - 7487, 23 Jan 1891 & SC - 13876, both TX, srv Cary's Co., 1st Bttn MS Vol Inf.

Johnston, Daniel B., Catharine A., WC - 5892, 9 Oct 1888, MS, srv Downing's Co., 1st MS Rifles.

Johnston, Isaac S., SC - 11563, 24 Sep 1887, MS, srv Co. H, 1st MS Rifles.

Joiner, Addison M., Katherine, WC - 5706, 26 Nov 1887, MS, srv Co. C, 1st NC Vols.

Jokson, David alias Henry Myers, Catherine Myers, WC - 7294, 18 Jun 1889, MS, srv Co. C, 1st LA Mtd. Vols.

Jolly, Meridian, Martha Jane, WC - 2700, 23 Aug 1887, AR, srv Taylor's Co., 1st MS Rifles.

Jones, James, Liza A., WC - 12179, 8 Feb 1900 & SC - 12033, both KY, srv Co. F, 2nd MS Vols. as a Pvt.

Jones, James L., Tabitha, WC - 3980, 1 Jul 1887, MS, srv Elder's Co., 2nd MS Vols.

Jones, John, Nannie, WC - 15345, 19 Jan 1909 & SC - 18052, both MS, srv Co. F, 2nd MS Vols as a Pvt.

Jones, John L., Josephine, WA - 11868, 2 Feb 1894 & SC - 14370, both TX, srv Dorsey's Co. in Bttn MS Vols.

Jones, Philenzo, Mary A., WA - 6423, 1 May 1888, TX, srv in the MS Vols.

Jones, Thomas, SA - 21472, 2 Apr 1889, MS, srv Bell's Co., 1st AL Vols.

Jones, Thomas, Elizabeth, WA - 11353, 20 May 1893, KY, srv in the MS Rifles.

Jones, William H., Nancy, WA - 11308, 20 Apr 1893, TX, srv in the MS Vols.

Jones, William S., Elizabeth, WC - 2849, 17 Oct 1887, MS, srv under White, no other srv on the card.

Jopes, Henry S., Harriet, WA - 18475, 11 Aug 1906, MS, no srv shown on the card.

Jordan, Harrison, SC - 15418, 4 Feb 1887, MS, srv Co. A, 1st IL Vols.

Joyner, Reddick A., Amanthey P., WC - 9938, 3 Jul 1895 & SC - 6342, both MS, srv Co. G, 4th LA Vols as a 2nd Lt.

Julian, William R., Bettie M., WC - 6745, 27 Nov 1889 & SC - 13693, both AL, srv Co. K, 1st MS Inf Vols.

Kelley, George W., Martha A., WA - 13157, 3 Jan 1896 & SA - 14110, both MS, srv Vaughn's Co., 2nd MS Inf, Teamster.

Kelly, Zachariah, Martha J., WC - 16029, Apr 1913 & SC - 6345, both MS, srv

Co. G, MS Foot Vols as a Pvt & Drum Maj 1846-8, BLW #78677 - 160 - 47, sol died 8 Feb 1913.

Kenedy, William G., Susan E., WC - 11022, 28 Jan 1897, TX, srv Co. E in Bttn MS Rifles.

Kenmar, John A., SA - 19059, 12 Apr 1888, MS, srv on Transport *Breath.*

Kercheval, Rufus, Elizabeth B., WC - 3998, 29 Apr 1887, AR, srv Co. E, in MS Rifles.

Kerr, Jerome B., Jane E., WC - 4344, 26 Jan 1888, SC, srv Taylor's Co., 1st MS Rifles.

Kile, James L., Susan Elizabeth, WC - 5488, 11 Apr 1888, TX, srv Davis' Co., MS Vols.

Kilgore, Benjamin M., SC - 4690, 23 Mar 1887, MS, srv Capt Key's Co., MS Bttn.

Killebrew, Henry B., Martha M., WC - 1516, 11 Feb 1887, MS, srv Co. I, 2nd MS Vols.

Kilpatrick, Ebeneezer N., Rachel Ann, WC - 5244, 3 Sep 1887, MS, srv Co. E, 13th US Inf.

Kilpatrick, Joseph H., Eliza W., WC - 5703, 11 Mar 1887, TX, srv as a Lt Col in 2nd MS Vols.

Kilpatrick, William, Margaret H., WA - 19922, 6 Mar 1912, MS, no srv shown on the card.

Kincannon, James, Minerva A., WC - 14566, 6 Sep 1906 & SC - 18519, both MS, srv Co. A, 2nd MS Vols as a Pvt.

Kinchloe, David Anderson, Laura J., WC - 3612, 27 Mar 1888, MS, srv Overton's Co., 2nd MS Rifles.

King, George W., Sarah F., WC - 4097, 14 Dec 1887, MS, srv Frasier's Co., 1st TN Vols.

King, James W. G., SA - 25490, 14 Sep 1906, GA, srv Co. G, 1st MS Rifles.

King, John A., Mary A., WC - 3641, 22 Apr 1887, MS, srv Scott's Co., 1st VA Vols.

King, Robert, SC - 10454, 7 Jul 1887, VA, srv Co. K, 2nd MS Rifles.

King, Rufus B., SA - 3697, 27 Jan 1887, MS, srv Parker's Co., 1st AL Vols.

Kirk, John W., Catherine L., WC - 5261, 3 Jul 1888, MS, srv Co. A, 1st MS Vols as a Pvt.

Kirkland, Uriah, Elizabeth, WC - 4201, 29 Feb 1888, AL, srv in the MS Vols.

Klein, Julius N., Mary T., WA - 8111, 17 Jun 1889, MS, srv Kerr's Co. C in LA Mtd Vols.

Knapp, David L., SC - 4689, 18 Mar 1887, MS, srv Co. G, 2nd MS Vols.

Knapp, John, Hannah, WC - 7315, 6 Jun 1890, IA, srv Barksdale's Co. A, in MS Vols.

Knight, James K., SC - 16904, 5 Sep 1888, AR, srv Co. F, 2nd MS Rifles.

Knight, John R. alias Raleigh J., Marinda, WC - 9615, 1 Aug 1894, MS, srv Co. A, 2nd MS Vol Inf.

Kraus, Frederick, SC - 3273, 8 Mar 1887, MS, srv Seibel's Bttn AL Inf.

Kyle, Thomas J., Charlotte C., WC - 425, 4 Apr 1887, MS, srv Co. D, 1st Ms Vols.

Lacey, Beverly McK., SC - 17896, 26 Dec 1888, TX, srv Co. D, 1st Bttn MS Rifles.

Lacey, Felix, SA - 25167, 12 Feb 1900, MS, srv Downing's Co., 1st MS Vols.

Lafferty, Allen, SA - 3919, 17 Feb 1887, MS, srv Co. E, 7th US Inf.

Laird, Eli, Frances, WA - 15309, 30 Sep 1899 & SC 19261, both MS, srv Co. F, 2nd MS Vol Rifles as a Pvt.

Lambright, George T., Mary J., WC - 13854, 15 Oct 1904 & SC - 16554, both MS, srv Co. I, 2nd MS Rifles, Pvt.

Landers, William H., Jane A., WC - 5075, 12 Feb 1887, MS, srv Co. B, Bttn MS Riflemen as a 1st Lt.

Lane, Samuel W., Ann Mary, WC - 8664, 10 Jul 1893, TX, srv Co. E, 1st MS Vols.

Lanel, Henry H., Sarah A., WA - 1204, 18 Mar 1887, LA, srv Co. H, 1st MS Rifles as a Cpl.

Langley, William A., Mary E., WA - 4572, 20 Aug 1887, MS, srv Fisher's Indpt Co., FL Vols.

Lanham, John M., Sabra C., WC - 2222, 14 May 1887, MS, srv Keye's Co., Anderson's Bttn MS Vols.

Lary, Jeremiah E., Sarah Jane, WC - 14101, 24 Feb 1905 & SC - 13526, both TX, srv Co. C, 1st MS Vols & or Capt. McManus's Co. E 1st MS Vol Inf as a Pvt.

Latimer, Edwin R., Mary E., WC - 2223, 17 Feb 1887, MS, srv Hufty's Co., LA Vols.

Laurel, Henry H., Sarah A., WC - 1509, 18 Mar 1887, LA, srv Co. H, 1st MS Vols.

Lavender, Samuel D. alias **Solomon D., Annie M.**, WC - 11515, 7 Sep 1892, AL, srv Co. A, 1st MS Vol. Inf.

Lavender, Solomon D., see **Samuel D.**

Lawhon, John, Jane, WC - 2282, 9 Jun 1887, TX, srv Co. K, 1st MS Vols.

Lawrence, Robert J., Mary L., WA - 9967, 6 Jul 1891 & SA - 17499, both MS, srv Gibbs' Co., 1st AL Vols.

Layton, James, SA - 16050, 20 Aug 1887, MS, srv as a Cook on the *U.S.S. Massachusetts*.

Lea, James Madison, SA - 23400, 12 Mar 1891, AR, srv Blythe's Co., 2nd MS Vols.

Leeth, James M., Mary C., WC - 6073, 23 Jul 1888, MS, srv Co. E, 2nd MS Rifles.

Leland, Columbus M., SC - 11236, 23 Jun 1887, CA, srv Co. D, in MS Rifle Bttn.

Lemaster, James R., Ann, WC - 2483, 13 Jul 1887, TX, srv Liddell's Co., 2nd MS Vols.

Lepard, Humphrey P., Emily C., WC - 7260, 22 Jul 1890 & SC - 15189, both MS, srv Co. A, 13 U.S. Inf as a Pvt, old War I - #22545 Rej.

Leslie, Henry, Mary J., WC - 1531, 29 Mar 1887, MS, srv Co. F, 13th US Inf.

LeSueur, Charles Marion, SC - 7278, 3 Mar 1887, TX, WA - 13173, srv Co. B, 2nd MS Rifles.

LeSueur, Charles M., Annie E., WC - 10554, 24 Feb 1896, TX, SC - 7278, srv Co. D, 2nd MS Rifles as a 2nd Lt.

Leverett, Harrison D., SC - 1671, 29 Mar 1887, MS, srv Loyall's Indpt. Co., GA Mtd Vols., OW I - #21958 Rej.

Levy, Samuel H., Grace S., WC - 2853, 17 Sep 1887, LA, srv Stewart's Co., 3rd MS Rifles.

Lewis, Robert A., Martha A., WC - 9887, 17 Aug 1895 & SC - 1372, both MI, srv Co. D, 1st MS Rifle Vols as a Sgt.

Liddel, James Monroe, Sallie Y., WC - 12086, 12 Sep 1892 & SC - 3740, both MS, srv Co. C, 2nd MS Vols.

Lilly, John A., SC - 3113, 15 Mar 1887, TX, srv Cary's Co. D in MS Vols.

Lime, James, Eliza Jane, WC - 5610, 12 May 1888, MS, srv Co. K, 3rd KY Vols as a Pvt 1847-8, BLW # 28013 - 160 - 47, Civil War Army IC - 57061 & WO - 399366 for srv Co. G, 81st IN Inf 1865, sol died Nov 1887.

Linecum, Haywood H., SC - 14259, 13 Jul 1887, MS, srv Armstrong's & Evans' Cos., TX Rangers.

Lindsey, John, Susan, WC - 3695, 1 Jul 1887, MS, srv Co. C, 7th U.S. Inf as a Pvt.

Linfield, William E. M., Sophronia J., WC - 5951, 20 Dec 1888, MS, srv Co. E, 13th U.S. Inf.

Lippmins, Marcus H., Prudence E., WA - 13680, 12 Dec 1896, LA, srv Col. McClung's Co., MS Vols.

Lipsey, Ansylum G., Sarah Ann, WC - 6157, 2 Feb 1889, LA, srv Dorsey's Co., 1st Bttn MS Vols.

Liscomb, William J., SC - 9139, 4 Feb 1887, MS, srv 1st AL Vols & or Jones' Co., 4th AL Vols.

Little, Joseph E., SA - 9110, 2 Apr 1887, MS, srv Shiver's Indpt Co., TX Vols.

Locke, John C., Emily, WC - 9532, 8 Mar 1893 & SC - 3133, both MS, srv Ballard's Co., 3rd TX Cav (Mtd. Vols.).

Lofton, Thomas, SC - 8776, 4 Feb 1887, MS, srv Co. A, Seibel's Bttn AL Vols.

Lofton, Thomas, Sophronia, WC - 4885, 24 Mar 1888, MS, srv Co. A, Seibel's Bttn AL Vols.

Logan, Gaines F., SA - 22167, 15 Oct 1889, MS, srv Co. E, 1st AL Vols.

Long, Alfred V., SC - 3120, 4 Feb 1887, MS, srv Co. C, 2nd MS Vols. Old War I - #21279 Rej.

Long, Henry W., SA - 4150, 4 Feb 1887, AR, srv Co. B, 1st MS Vols.

Long, John, Emily P., WC - 96703, 13 Dec 1894 & SC - 2234, both MS, srv Co. I, 1st MS Rifles as a Sgt.

Long, John W., Prudence, WA - 1264, 14 Mar 1887, MS, srv Tucker's Co., 1st MS Vols.

Long, Robert M., Elizabeth F., WA - 5765, 23 Jan 1888, MS, srv Capt. Richardson's Co. as a Lt.

Long, Thomas W., SA - 25349, 19 May 1903, MS, srv as a Teamster in Qtr Mstr Dept, Ind War SO - #5424.

Longstreet, William D., Mary B., WC- 7648, 26 Dec 1889 & SC - 2086, both MS, srv Co. K, 1st MS Rifle Vols.

Lorenz, Martin, Margaretha, WC - 13317, 2 May 1903, MO & SC - 3810 in MS, srv Co. B, 1st MO Vols (Easton's Bttn) as a Pvt., Civil War srv Co. D 2nd MO Vol Arty.

Lott, George W., Mary Jordan, WA - 8728, 14 Feb 1890, MS, srv Staple's Co., 4th LA Vols.

Lott, William, Caroline, WC - 844, 14 May 1887, MS, srv Co. D, 1st MS Vols.

Love, David E., Emily F., WC - 9255, 28 Nov 1888, LA, srv Co. D, 1st MS Rifles.

Love, Robert C., Mary A., WA - 20196, 8 Apr 1914, TX, srv 1st MS Vols 1846-7, sol. died 23 Oct 1881.

Low, Thomas B., Samson A., WA - 9575, 10 Jan 1891, AR & SC- 12900 in MO, srv Gregory's Co., 2nd MS Vols.

Lowe, Aaron, SA - 13213, 19 May 1887, NC, srv Davis' Co., 1st MS Vols.

Lowery, J. G. or **James G., Margaret**, WC - 7044, 28 Apr 1890 & SC - 2231, both MS, srv Co. E, 2nd MS Rifle Vols.

Lowery, Mark P., Sarah R., WC - 6811, 2 Sep 1889, MS, srv Co. E, 2nd MS Vols.

Lowry, Robert H., wid **C. D.**, SC - 7779, 7 Jun 1887, TX, WA - 9960, srv Co. B, 1st MS Vols.

Luckett, Samuel, Sarah, WA - 17869, 7 Jan 1905 & SC - 19101, both AR, srv Co. F, 1st MS Vols as a Pvt.

Luckin, John J., SC - 11284, 22 Aug 1889, MS, WC - 12206, srv Co. H, 1st MS Rifles.

Lyerly, James B., Sarah Jane, WA - 9697, 5 Mar 1891 & SC - 8000, both TN, srv Co. E, 1st MS Rifles.

Lyle, Lewis, SA - 4228, 9 Jun 1886, MS, srv Dennis' Co., Bryant's Regt. AL Vols.

Lyman, C. H. or **Charles H., Mary**, WA - 15818, 8 Oct 1900 & SC - 14624, both MS, srv on *U.S.S. Mississippi* as a 1st Class Boy.

Lyon, John W., SA - 25556, 18 Feb 1908, AL, srv Co. A in MS unit as a Pvt.

Mabry, Thomas Fletcher, Mary Matilda, WC - 1526, 4 Feb 1887, LA, srv Co. G, 1st MS Vols.

McAlpin, Robert A., SA - 20190, 29 Aug 1888, MS, srv on the *U.S.S.s Tray* and *Rough and Ready.*

McAnally, Benjamin F., SA - 22732, 17 May 1890, MS, srv Musgrove's Co. A of AL Vols.

McCall, John W., Hannah D., WC - 7011, 22 Apr 1890, IL, SC - 12177, 4 Feb 1887, MS, srv Co. F, 13th U.S. Inf.

McCannon, Isaac, SA - 4453, 24 Feb 1887, TN, srv in Priest's Co., MS Vols.

McCarroll, Alex alias **George W. Clement**, SA - 1175, 4 Feb 1887, MS, srv Co. K, 1st MS Vol Rifles.

McCauley, William, SA - 16836, 4 Oct 1887, MS, srv as Seaman on *U.S.S. Alleghany*, Navy SA - 1048148, 24 May 1915, LA, sailor died 23 Mar 1911, Ft. Leavenworth, KS, BLW reg # 336740 - 35.

McClain, James, SC - 1927, 18 Feb 1887, MS, srv Co. I, 2nd MS Vols.

McClatchy, William H. alias **Billy Wilkins**, SA - 24996, 10 Nov 1897, TX, srv 1st MS Vols.

McCondy, Andrew, Mary, WA - 14139, 2 Sep 1897 & SC - 5150, both MS, srv Co. L, 1st NY or U.S. Arty.

McCrory, Thomas, SC - 9745, 24 Feb 1887, MS, srv Co. M, 1st TN Vols.

McCullen, Lewis M., SA - 11887, 19 Apr 1887, NC, srv Hunt's Co., 1st MS Vols.

McDaniel, Alfred H., Lucy J., WC - 3078, 5 Apr 1887, AL, srv Co. A, Anderson Bttn MS Rifle Vols.

McDaniel, Henry D., Margana, WC - 716, 4 Feb 1887, MS, srv Co. F, 6th LA Vols.

McDonald, James M., Elizabeth R., WA - 18508, 26 Sep 1906 & SC - 1922, both MS, srv Co. F, 2nd MS Rifles.

McDonald, Pendleton, Louisa, WC - 6628, 28 Oct 1889 & SC - 15511, both MS, srv Co. F, 2nd MS Rifles, OW IA - 21301 Rej.

McDonough, James, Malissa, WC - 13324, 15 May 1903 & SC - 4704, both MS, srv Co. A, 10th U.S. Inf as Sgt., OW IA - 21496R.

McDuffie, William S., SC - 4398, 5 Feb 1887, TX, srv Co. K, 1st MS Vols, OW IA - 22101 Rej.

McElroy, Jackson C., Mary Ann Frances, WC - 16064, 4 Feb 1914 & SC - 18202, both MS, srv Co. E, 3rd TN Vols. sol died 7 Dec 1913 BLW #75957 - 160 - 47.

McGee, William R., wid **J. L.,** WC - 10519, 12 Aug 1896, TX & SC - 11313 in MS, srv Co. K, 1st TN Cav (Frierson's).

McGinnis, Joseph alias Joseph L. Maganos, Bertha G., WC - 11895, 5 May 1899 & SC - 8607, both MS, Co. K, 1st TX Vols.

McGinty, Eli H., SA - 9351, 24 Feb 1887, MS, srv as a Teamster in the Qtr Mstr Dept of US Army.

McGraw, Wiley, Hanah, WC - 188, 4 Mar 1887, TX, srv Co. K, 2nd MS Vols.

McGregor, George, SC - 3303, 11 Apr 1887, AR, srv Co. G, 2nd MS Rifles.

McGuire, John E., Sarah B., WC - 374, 8 Feb 1887, MS, srv Co. K, 1st MS Vols.

McIlvain, James, Mariah, WC - 7635, 4 May 1891 & SC - 17867, both MS, srv Marshall's Co. E, Palmetto Regt. SC Vols.

McKay, Daniel A., Elizabeth A., WC - 13774, 4 Apr 1904 & SC - 12178, both MS, srv Co. C, 1st MS Vols as a Pvt.

McKee, Andrew J., SA - 22785, 2 Jun 1890, TX, srv Jackson's Co., 2nd MS Rifles.

McKee, James, Lucinda, WC - 5461, 20 Jul 1888, MS, srv Sparks' Co., TX Mtd Vols.

McKinney, William C., SC - 19595, 27 May 1891, AL, srv Co. E, 1st MS Bttn Vols.

McKnight, Samuel B., Sarah C., WA - 14424, 1 Mar 1898 & SC - 7616, both TX, srv Co. A, 1st MS Vols.

McKowen, Alexander, wid **L. B. T.,** WC - 5379, 16 May 1888, LA, srv Blackburn's MS Vols.

McLean, William D. T., Olive E., WC - 12110, 31 Jan 1899 & SC - 9828, both TX, srv Co. E, 2nd MS Vols.

McLemore, William K., Drucilla A., WC - 7295, 13 May 1890 & SC - 14135, both TX, srv Co. A (McWillie's), 2nd MS Rifles.

McLeon, Hugh A., SC - 4000, 8 Mar 1887, MS, srv Davis' 1st GA Vols.

McManus, John L., Mary A., WC - 10080, 2nd Dec 1895 & SC - 3455, both LA, srv Co. E, 1st MS Vols as a Capt.

McMatchy, William H. alias Billy Wilkins, SA - 24996, 10 Nov 1897, TX, srv 1st MS Rifles.

McMillan, J. M., SA - 25616, 15 Jun 1912, MS, no other data on the card.

McMorrough, Theodore J., SC - 11339, 3 Sep 1887, MS, srv Co. H, 1st MS Vols.

McNair, Evander, SC - 7872, 12 May 1887, MS, srv Co. E, 1st MS Vols.

McPeak, Elihu, SA - 25322, 2 Feb 1903, MS, srv Capt. Bledsoe's Co. E in TN Regt.

McPherson, Thomas, SC - 3686, 12 Mar 1887, MS, srv Dill's Co. in Regt. of GA Vols.

McQueen, James A., Mattie W., WC - 7479, 31 Mar 1891, TN & SC - 2481 in TX, srv Co. C, 2nd MS Vols.

McVey, James N., Tresa I., WA - 8313, 28 Aug 1889, MS, srv Lt. Lauderdale's Co., 2nd MS Vols.

McVey, William T., Tabitha D., WA - 11462, 28 Jun 1893, LA, srv 1st MS Vol. Infan.

McWilliams, Wesley, Elizabeth, WC - 14906, 22 Jul 1907 & SC - 6233, both TX, srv Co. E, in Bttn MS Rifles as a Pvt.

McWillie, Adam, Lucy A., WC - 1549, 10 Feb 1887, MS, srv Co. H, 2nd MS Vols.

Maffett, Silas L., Mary E., WA - 15452, 22 Jan 1900, MS, srv Co. D, 1st Bttn MS Rifles as a Pvt.

Maganos, Joseph L., Bertha G., WC - 11895, 5 May 1899 & SC - 8607, both MS, srv Co. K, 1st TX Vols. as Pvt., also see as Joseph L. McGinnis.

Magee, Laurin R., SC - 10038, 23 Apr 1887, MS, srv Co. D, 1st GA Vols.

Mahoney, Dennis, Bridget, WC - 4148, 18 Feb 1888, MS, srv in U.S.M.C.

Mallett, James H., Sarah R., WC - 15107, 27 Jul 1908, TX & SC - 2039 in FL, srv Co. G, 1st MS Vols.

Mallette, Stephen R., Olive, WA - 2988, 11 May 1887, TX, srv Straunder's Co., 1st MS Vols.

Malloy, John A., SC - 12702, 20 Jul 1887, MS, srv Elmore's Co., 5th LA Vols.

Malone, Frederick, Abigail, WC - 8060, 19 Apr 1892 & SC - 16958, both TX, srv Co. E (Delay's), 1st MS Vol. Inf.

Malone, Robert H., SC - 2132, 26 Feb 1887, MS, srv Co. I, 1st MS Rifles.

Malone, Thomas B., Mary E., WC - 16309, 7 Jun 1904 & SC - 13528, both TX, srv Co. B, 2nd MS Vols as a Pvt 1847-8, soldier died 11 Nov 1900 Mineral TX.

Manning, J. William, SC - 17130, 4 Feb 1887, TX, WA - 10067, srv Co. C, 3rd MS Inf.

Manning, Joseph W., Mary J., WC - 10187, 25 Aug 1891, TX, SC - 17130, srv Dorsey's Co., 1st Bttn MS Rifles.

Maples, John W., Mary Ann, WC - 495, 15 Apr 1887, MS, srv Co. C, 1st MS Vols.

Marble, John K., Martha, WC - 8702, 13 Jun 1889, MS, srv Co. A, 5th LA Vols.

Mardis, Abner G., Mary A., WC - 15492, 30 Sep 1909 & SC - 16966, both MS, srv Co. E, 5th LA Vols as a Sgt., Spc War IO - 1239999 & Mother's O - #737057 (Mother of Allen A. Mardis), srv Co. B, 1st MS Inf.

Markham, Hugh M., Catherine P., WC - 5988, 31 Dec 1888, MS, srv Crump's Co., 1st MS Vols.

Marks, Mathias D., Bertha, WA - 8819, 17 Mar 1890, MS, srv in 1st LA Vols.

Marshall, Andrew J., SC - 16679, 23 Feb 1888, TX, srv Co. B, 9th MS Inf, last paid 4 Aug 1912.

Marshall, Humphrey, SC - 17923, 21 Jan 1889, NM Terr, srv Crump's Co., 1st MS Rifles as a Sgt.

Martin, Charles, Letha Jane, WC - 2274, 7 May 1887, MS, srv Rodger's Co., 1st MS Vols., OW - 5738.

Martin, Francis M., Sarah E., WC - 10702, 6 Oct 1896, MS, srv Co. G, 1st MS Vols, OW IF - #46188.

Martin, H. P., SA - 24631, 16 Oct 1894, AR, srv Flenoy's Co., MS Vols.

Martin, James, Letitia, WC - 4003, 6 Aug 1887, MO, srv Cooper's Co., 1st MS Vols as a Cpl.

Martin, Joseph, Martha E., WC - 10042, 20 Jan 1896 & SC - 18216, both AR, srv Co. H, 1st MS Vols.

Martin, Joseph, Margaret J., WA - 16663, 24 May 1902, MS, srv Co. H, 1st MS Inf.

Martin, Leroy C., Lizzie T., WC - 15403, 28 Apr 1899, MS, srv Co. D, Bttn MS Rifles as a Pvt.

Mason, Joseph C., Liddy J., WC - 14469, 20 Jan 1906 & SC - 4829, both MS, srv Co. F, 1st AL Vols.

Mason, Solomon, SC - 6581, 12 May 1887, TX, srv Co. C, 1st MS Vols.

Mathews, Frederick, Adaline, WC - 3879, 15 Feb 1887, MO, srv Crump's Co., 1st MS Vols, OW IA - 29315.

Matlock, Gabriel S., Lucy I., WC - 9761, 15 Nov 1893 & SC - 2876, both MS, srv Co. L, 1st TN Vols.

Mattox, William B., SA - 24373, 17 Jun 1893, LA, srv Reed's Co., MS Vols.

Maum, James W., SC - 6829, 18 Feb 1887, MS, srv Co. E, Bttn MS Vols.

Maxey, Thomas R., Elizabeth, WC - 5436, 31 Jul 1888, MS & SC - 10815 in MO, srv Shelby's Co., Coffey's AL Vols.

Medlock, John J., Mary, WC - 13 Feb 1891 & SC - 2650, both TX, srv Co. E, 2nd MS Vols.

Meek, William H., SA - 21134, 30 Jan 1889, MS, srv Pettus' Co., 1st AL Vols.

Melcher, Lawson A., SC - 2919, 19 Feb 1887, MS, srv Co. C, 1st NC Inf.

Mellard, Wesley, wid **C. A.**, WC - 3807, 7 May 1887, MS, srv Ligon's Co., Raiford's Bttn AL Vols.

Mellon, John, SC - 5867, 4 Feb 1887, MS, srv Co. K, 11th US Inf.

Melton, Hiram, SA - 24984, 27 Sep 1897, TX, srv Capt. Lauderdale's Co., 2nd MS Vols.

Melton, John, SA - 22792, 9 Jun 1890, MS, srv Rodgers' Co., 1st MS Rifles.

Melvin, John J., SC - 12812, 4 Feb 1887, GA, srv Co. F, 2nd MS Vols as a Sgt.

Merrall, Austin P., Esther E., WA - 1562559, 15 Nov 1926, KS & SC - 8256 in MO, srv Co. E, Bttn MS Vols, BLW #21617-160 - 47, sol died 1 June 1911, Nesosho, MO.

Metcalf, George, SC - 13438, 4 Feb 1887, MS, srv Willis' Co., 1st MS Vols.

Middlebrook, William S., Mary V., WA - 15429, 5 Jan 1900, TX, srv Co. D, 2nd MS Vols.

Milam, William, SA - 4667, 25 Feb 1887, AR, srv Bradford's Indpt. Co. MS Vols.

Miles, William A., SC - 19359, 8 Oct 1890, TX, srv Co. E, Bauh's or Baul's MS Rifle Vols.

Miller, Caleb B., SA - 24745, 6 Sep 1895, TX, srv Pruitt's MS Vols., LW IC - 989946 for srv Co. C, 79th, Co. K, 1st & 210th PA Inf., also see WO - 942362 for John C. West srv. Co. H, 1st PA Inf MC - 144935 srv 135th PA Inf.

Miller, Daniel S., SA - 24453, 27 Nov 1893, MS, srv Martin's Co., 1st AL Vols.

Miller, James M., Frances Ann, WC - 1348, 26 Feb 1887, MS, srv Co. B, 1st MS Vols.

Miller, Joel, Mary, WC - 3175, 9 Dec 1887, MS, srv Co. D, 2nd MS Vols.

Miller, Joseph, wid **Juan**, WC - 11256, 19 Mar 1898 & SC 2250, both KY, srv Co. C, 1st MS Vols as a Pvt.

Miller, Silas H., SA - 25597, 23 Feb 1911, MS, srv Co. D, 2nd MS Inf as a Pvt.

Miller, William H., Nancy M., WC - 6451, 24 May 1889, KY, srv Cooper's Co., 1st MS Vols., OW - WA - 23829 Rej.

Miner, James R., Margaret, WA - 6567, 23 May 1888, MS, srv Col. Fay's Regt. NY Vols.

Minga, Henry F., Fannie, WC - 5584, 17 Feb 1888, MS, srv Co. C, 2nd MS Rifles.

Mitcham, William L. or **William L. Mitchell, Carrie**, WC - 10483, 24 Oct 1895 & SC - 11043, both MS, srv Elmore's Indpt. Co., 5th AL Vols., OW - IA - 24936 Rej.

Mitchell, Bird, SA - 24032, 15 Aug 1892, MS, srv Co. C, 2nd MS Vols.

Mitchell, John S., SC - 3161, 4 Feb 1887, MS, srv Co. B, 2nd MS Vols. as a 1st Sgt. OW IA - 21306.

Mitchell, Robert C., Mary A., WC - 4699, 28 Feb 1888, TN, srv Co. B, 2nd MS Vols.

Mitchell, William C., Sarah A., WA - 9683, 26 Feb 1861, MS, srv Davis' Co., 14th US Mtd. Rifles.

Mitchell, William L., or **William L. Mitcham, Carrie**, WC - 10483, 24 Oct 1895, MS, SC - 11043, srv Elmore's Indpt. Co. AL Vols., OW IA - 24936 Rej.

Mobley, Middleton R., SC - 2672, 1 Apr 1887, MS, srv Co. A, 1st MS Rifles.

Mobley, Middleton R., Carrie E., WC - 5579, 21 Aug 1888, LA, srv Sharp's Co., 1st MS Vols.

Monk, Menan, Sarah M., WC - 14245, 12 Jul 1892, AR, srv Co. A, Bttn MS Rifles as a Pvt.

Montgomery, Jacob P., SC - 2869, 8 Apr 1887, MS, srv King's Co. A, in MS Rifles.

Montgomery, Robartus H., Martha, WC - 2800, 26 Sep 1887, MS, srv McWillie's Co., 2nd MS Vols.

Moore, Benjamin B., SC - 19765, 28 Jul 1890, MS, srv Co. A, 1st AL Vols.

Moore, Conner, Mary, WC - 312, 7 Mar 1887, MS, srv Co. E, 1st MS Vols.

Moore, Henry, SA - 24400, Aug, 1893, MS, srv Co. A, 2nd LA Vols as a Pvt.

Moore, Henry, SA - 15685, 5 Aug 1887, MS, srv Keyes' Co., 1st Bttn MS Vols.

Moore, James P., Sarah, WC - 7308, 26 May 1890, MS, srv Co. I, 1st MS Vols.

Moore, Robert E., WC - 19743, 25 Jul 1891, TX, srv Co. E, MS Bttn.

Moore, William H. S., Morgiana, WC - 1578, 11 Feb 1887, MS, srv Co. F, 1st AL Vols.

Moore, William M., Cordelia L., WC - 1581, 11 Feb 1887, AL, srv Co. A, 1st MS Vols.

Moorland, James Pinkney, Matilda A., WC - 12288 (13288?), 4 Nov 1899 & SC - 11509, both MS, 1st AL Vols.

Morehead, Pleasant F., Rina T., WA - 13304, 29 Apr 1896, MS, srv Moore's Co., Coffey's Regt. AL Vols.

Morey, Albion K. P., SA - 24093, 12 Oct 1892, MS, srv Arnold's Co., 2nd U.S. Dragoons.

Morgan, Daniel T., Virginia T., WC - 14476, 1st Dec 1903, AR & SC - 8821 in TN, srv Co. C, 2nd MS Vols as a Pvt.

Morgan, Hiram, Augusta E., WC - 5441, 14 Jul 1888, MS, srv Cooper's Co., 1st

MS Vols.

Morgan, William H., Mary, WC - 8559, 9 Jun 1892 & SC - 7063, both MS, srv Co. A, 1st Bttn AL Vols.

Morphew, Silas, Sophronia A., WC - 14962, 21 Apr 1906 & SC - 15424, both AR, srv Co. E, Bttn MS Rifle Vols.

Morris, Howard, Eliza A., WC - 10912, 24 Apr 1897, MO, srv Co. C, 1st MS Rifles as a Cpl., OW IF - #9797.

Morris, Joseph W., Lavinia, WA - 9866, 18 May 1891, AR, SC - 5656, srv Delay's Co., 1st MS Vols., OW IF -#5991.

Morris, Mabry I., SC - 7050, 16 Apr 1887, MS, srv Co. B, 1st MS Vols.

Morrison, John, Mary, WC - 2874, 8 Sep 1887, MS, srv Cary's Co., 1st MS Rifles.

Morrison, Samuel F., SA - 21418, 21 Mar 1889, TN, srv Bradford's Co., 1st MS Vols.

Mosby, DeWitt C., Virginia A., WA - 15973, 5 Jan 1901, MS, no service shown on card.

Moses, Abraham alias **Nelson L. Stevens**, SC - 16255, 7 May 1888, MS, srv Co. C, 2nd LA Vols.

Mott, Christopher H., Sally G., WA - 20432, 1 Nov 1916, MS, srv as a 1st Lt. in the 1st MS Inf 1846-7, BLW #20625 - 160 - 50, soldier died 5 May 1862 in Williamsburg, VA.

Murphree, Anderson, SA - 24249, 23 Feb 1893, MS, srv Key's Co., 1st MS Vols.

Murphree, Leonard H., Emma G., WC - 15823, 5 Feb 1912 & SC - 18637, both MS, srv Taylor's Co., 1st MS Inf as a Pvt.

Murray, David, Malinda, WA - 9147, 12 Jul 1890 & SC - 2478, both MS, srv Cooper's Co., 1st MS Vols.

Myers, Henry alias **David Jobson, Catharine**, WC - 7294, 18 Jun 1889, MS, srv Kerr's Co., LA Mtd. Vols.

Nabers, Benjamin D., Elizabeth, WA - 10773, 5 Aug 1892, TX, srv in the 14th MS (?).

Nabers, Thomas Jackson, SA - 3787, 27 Jan 1887, TX, srv Golston's Co. in MS Vols.

Nail, Montgomery, Nancy, WA - 14842, 15 Dec 1898, MS, srv Co. I, 1st MS Vols.

Naron, George W., wid **P.**, WA - 20174, 5 Jan 1914, MS, srv as a Teamster in Qtr Mstr Dept. In 1848, BLW # 60788 - 160 - 55, sol. died 1 Mar 1911.

Neal, James R., Letitia, WA - 13717, 7 Jan 1897, MS, srv Capt. Cocke's Co., 2nd MS Vols. as a Pvt.

Neilson, Charles A., SC - 17142, 28 Sep 1888, MS, srv Blythe's Co., 2nd MS Vols.

Nelson, Thomas K., Delia E., WA - 5599, 22 Dec 1887, MS, srv Liddell's Co., 2nd MS Inf.

Neville, William, SC - 4145, 7 Mar 1887, MS, srv Co., I 1st TX Mtd. Vols.

Newman, Albert M., Minerva, WC - 1892, 28 Apr 1887, MS, srv Crump's Co., 1st MS Vols.

Newman, Alexander, SC - 5667, 12 May 1887, MS, srv Co. B, 1st MS Rifles.

Newman, Harry L., SC - 7327, 16 Apr 1887, TX, srv Co. D, 2nd MS Vols.

Newman, James, Penelope L., WC - 2567, 21 Jul 1887 & SA - 3846, both TX, srv Crowson's Co., 3rd (?) MS Vols.

Newman, Martin, SA - 24707, 19 Apr 1895, TX, srv as a Pvt under Capt. Wolf in a MS unit.

Newman, Solomon, Mary J., WA - 14945, 9 Feb 1899, MS, srv Co. B, 1st MS Inf, OW I - #16732 Rej.

Newsom, Joseph D., Lela, WA - 20561, 21 Oct. 1920 & SA - 24449, both MS, srv Co. F, 6th LA Vols as a Pvt., BLW #44581 - 120 - 55, also see WO - 1626211 for C.W. srv. sol. died 18 Dec 1919, Meridian, MS.

Neyland, Robert H., Sarah, WC - 4981, 7 Feb 1888, CA & SC - 11937 in MS, srv Co. B, 1st MS Vols as a Pvt in 1846-7, BLW #63670 - 160 - 47, sol. died 16 Nov 1920, note reads "dropped - not sol.'s widow."

Nichols, James R., Elizabeth Emeline, WC - 13120, 27 Oct 1902, MS & SC - 9547 in TN, srv Co. I, 13th U.S. Inf

Noland, Avery, Kate McW., WC - 2566, 9 Jun 1887, MS, srv Crump's Co., 1st MS Vols.

Norman, Benjamin F., Sarah A., WC - 8056, 3 Mar 1892 & SC - 10664, both TX, srv Co. D, 1st MS Vols.

Norris, Alexander S., SC - 10204, 14 Jun 1887, MS, srv Co. E, 4th LA Vols.

Norwood, Alexander T., SC - 6400, 4 Feb 1887, LA, srv Co. B, 3rd (?) MS Vols.

Nunaley, Moses E., SA - 24561, 9 Jun 1894, MS, srv Cox's AL Vols.

Nutter, William M., Julia A., WC - 658, 11 Feb 1887, CA, srv Co. C, 1st MS Vols.

O'Bannon, Dagobent B., SC - 19482, 3 Apr 1891, MS, srv Co. L, 1st VA Inf.

O'Bryan, Daniel, Sarah, WA - 13996, 7 Jun 1897, MS & SC - 14070 in LA, srv Co. C, 4th WS Arty.

O'Grady, John alias **John P. Ray, Mary E.,** WC - 15095, 20 Oct 1904 & SC - 2588, both MS, srv 5th U.S. Inf.

O'Neal, H. G., SA - 23361, 20 Feb 1891, TX, srv Manning's Co., MS Vols.

O'Neal, Henry F., Sally W., WC - 8746, 19 Jun 1893 & SC - 9416, both TX, srv Co. B, 1st MS Vols.

O'Rourke, Patrick O., Catherine, WA - 4947, 24 Sep 1887, OH, srv Co. G, 2nd MS Vols.

Oaks, James F., SC - 2942, 7 Mar 1887, LA, srv Co. D, 2nd MS Vols.

Oates, Henderson M., SA - 23200, 19 Nov 1890, MS, srv Sim's Co., AL Vols.

Odum, Jesse, Mary Ann, WC - 7972, 13 Nov 1891 & SC - 2678, both LA, srv Co. G, 1st MS Vols.

Onley, James W., Susan, WC - 15011, 13 Mar 1908 & SC - 17859, both LA, srv Co. H, 2nd MS Vols as a Pvt.

Orme, William James, Elizabeth D., WC - 10510, 2 Dec 1887, MS, srv Co. H, 4th TN Vol Inf as a Pvt.

Orr, John, SA - 13066, 17 May 1887, MS, srv on U.S.S. Transport *Whiteville.*

Orr, Valentine B., Mary J., WC - 11571, 1 Feb 1898 & SC - 9883, both TX, srv Co. I, 1st MS Vol Rifles.

Osborn, Samuel, SA - 25050, 28 Apr 1898, MS, srv Co. A in LA Cav.

Osbourn, Jeremiah, Margaret, WA - 4723, 3 Sep 1887, MS, srv Hufty's Co., 6th LA Vols.

Osterhout, Silas, SA - 13067, 20 May 1887, AR, srv LaLeur's Co., ? MS Vols.

Ott, Peter W. or **Peter William, Mary E. McC.,** WC - 6224, 27 Mar 1889 & SC -

6401, both MS, srv Kerr's Co., Briscoe's Bttn LA Mtd. Vols.

Oury, Charles, Hannah, WC - 8334, 29 Jun 1888, LA, srv Co. B, 1st MS Rifles.

Pannell, Simeon, SA - 5010, 24 Feb 1887, MS, srv Co. A, 2nd MS Vols, OW I - #22346 Rej.

Parish, Robert T., Julia, WC - 5401, 10 Feb 1887, LA, srv Daniel's Co., 2nd MS Vols.

Parker, William H., Mary E., WA - 13722, 13 Jan 1897, MS, srv Bank's Co., AL Vols.

Parkerson, William D., Sarah C., WC - 11367, 20 Nov 1897, MS, srv Co. I, 1st TN Inf as a Bugler.

Parr, Giles S., Matilda C., WC - 10859, 1 Feb 1893 & SC - 8849, both TX, srv Co. C, 2nd MS Vols as a Pvt.

Parrish, Joel T., Mary T., WC - 5743, 21 Nov 1887, AL, srv Roger's Co., 1st MS Rifles.

Patman, Hawkins B., SC - 3484, 12 Feb 1887, MS, srv Co. A, 1st Bttn AL Vols.

Patton, Alfred, Pricilla, WC - 2606, 19 Apr 1887, MO, srv Co. G, 1st MS Vols.

Patton, Thomas S., Sarah C., WA - 16160, 30 Apr 1901 & SC - 9423, both AR, srv Co. E, 2nd MS Vol Inf as a Pvt.

Paul, Frederick William, SC - 11090, 23 Jun 1887, MS, srv Co. F, 1st LA Inf.

Pearson, John M., Mary C., WC - 15291, 26 Jul 1909 & SC - 4007, both GA, srv Co. A, 2nd MS Vols as a Pvt.

Peebles, Jacob, Virginia R., WC - 12100, 6 Feb 1900, AL & SC - 4846 in MS, srv Co. E, 5th LA Inf as a Sgt.

Peery, James, Frances S., WC - 11432, 13 Jul 1898 & SC - 8299, both AR, srv Co. C, 2nd MS Vol Inf as a Pvt.

Peine, Charles, Mary P., WA - 19964, 23 May 1912, MS, no srv shown on card.

Pender, Lewis C., Alice A., WC - 2380, 13 Jun 1887, TX, srv Downing's Co., 1st MS Vols, see **Coorpender.**

Penny (Penry), Thomas, Catherine, WC - 13878, 3 Feb 1904 & SC - 3485, both MO, srv Co. A, 2nd MS Vols as a Pvt.

Perkins, William M., Louisa, WC - 10272, 24 Mar 1896 & SC - 11300, both TX, srv Co. A, 1st MS Vols (Rifle Bttn).

Perry, James A., SC - 4713, 18 Feb 1887, MS, srv Co. G, 16th U.S. Inf.

Perryman, Felix G., Angeline, WC - 5802, 6 Apr 1888, MS, srv Overton's Co., 2nd MS Vols.

Peterson, Charles alias **Charles Boster,** SC - 20625, 7 May 1887, MS, srv *U.S.S.s North Carolina, Pennsylvania & Cumberland* as a Seaman.

Peyton, Elijah A., Sarah F., WC - 14945, 25 Oct 1906 & SC - 12836, both MS, srv Co. H, 1st MS Vols.

Phillips, George, Elizabeth, WC - 10209, 25 Apr 1896, WI, SC - 4004, srv Co. E, 1st MS Rifles as a Pvt.

Phillips, Rufus E., Amanda J., WC - 9086, 12 Sep 1893, LA, srv Co. I, 1st MS Inf.

Phillips, Seborn Moses, Emily C., WC - 2384, 10 Jun 1887, CA, srv Sharp's Co., 1st MS Vols.

Phillips, George, SC - 4004, 4 Feb 1887, WI, WA - 13305, srv Co. E, 1st MS Rifles.

Phipps, David, Mary E., WA - 1686, 12 Mar 1887, MS, srv Cooper's Co., 1st MS

Rifle Vols, OW WF - #10894.

Pierce, Gardner W., Magdalena V., WC - 1593, 12 Apr 1887, TX, srv Lamar's Co., MS Vols & TX Vols.

Pierce, Hugh W., Amanda J., WC - 5327, 1 Aug 1887, MS, srv Co. E, 1st MS Vols, OW I - #7318.

Pierce, John T., Mary Jane, WC - 9413, 17 Oct 1890, MS, srv Co. G, 4th LA Vols.

Pierce, Simeon, SC - 7338, 16 Mar 1887, MS, srv Co. A, 2nd MS Vols.

Pigg, John, SC - 11092, 13 Aug 1887, LA, srv Co. B, 1st Bttn MS Rifle Vols.

Piper, Charles L. alias **Charles P. Hager**, SC - 9481, 5 May 1887, WI, srv Co. F, 1st MS Vols as a Sgt., CW Army I - #545891 & WO - 724497 for srv in Band & Co. D, 24th WI Inf.

Pisino, Antonio, SA - 9844, 17 Mar 1887, MS, srv Co. B, 1st NY Vols as a Pvt.

Pittman, William H., SC - 3592, 26 Feb 1887, MS, srv Co. D, 3rd (?) MS Inf.

Pleasants, Frank P., Mary E., WC - 6097, 26 Nov 1887, MS, srv Co. D, 1st MS Vols, OW W - #20043 Rej.

Plunket, James, SA - 25145, 5 Oct 1899, MS, srv Co. A, MS Vols as a Pvt (alleged).

Poag, Samuel G. W., Malissa, WC - 10833, 10 May 1897 & SC - 16142, both MS, srv Dorsey's Co., 1st Bttn MS Vols.

Poindexter, John J., Etha L., WC - 6320, 7 May 1889, TX, srv Co. H, 1st MS Rifles as a Lt.

Poindexter, William S. P., Mary J., WC - 8027, MS, srv Co. A, 3rd US Art.

Pollard, Samuel, SC - 13977, no filing date given, CA, srv Waldo's Co. (?), 1st MS Mtd Vols (?).

Ponder, Jesse B., SA - 23645, 12 Sep 1891, MS, srv Co. E, 2nd MS Inf.

Pope, William, Queen E., WC - 2603, 31 Aug 1887, TN, srv Gaines' Co., 2nd MS Vols.

Porey, Camile, SA - 21610, 4 May 1889, MS, srv Grivot's Co. LA Arty as a Drummer.

Porter, David Henry, Louisa, WC - 3233, 14 Feb 1887, IL, srv Co. D 3rd (?) MS Inf Vols.

Porter, Richard F., SA - 24531, 13 Apr 1894, MS, srv Powell's Co., 15th AL Vols.

Porter, William, SC - 10358, 9 Jun 1887, AR, srv Co. D in Bttn MS Rifles.

Posey, Benjamin L., Kate M., WC - 11341, 31 Dec 1897 & SC - 15393, both MS, srv Co. E, 1st SC Vols as a Pvt.

Posey, Carnot, Jane, WC - 4374, 26 Mar 1888, MS, srv Co. B, 1st MS Vols, OW Minor's File # 29989.

Posey, Richard W., SA - 25119, 22 Jun 1899, MS, srv Norman's Co., AL Vols as a Pvt.

Postell, Elijah C., Rebecca A., WC - 9073, 14 Mar 1894 & SC - 7335, both MS, srv Co. B, Palmetto SC Vols.

Postlewaite, Henry, Frances, WC - 5278, 18 Jun 1888, MS, srv Galbert's Co., 4th GA Vols.

Powel, Samuel, Mary E., WC - 13133, 11 Oct 1902 & SC - 3599, both MS, srv Co. E, 1st TN Vols as a Capt.

Powell, James L., SC - 13354, 22 Nov 1887, TX, srv Delay's Co., 1st MS Vols.

Powell, John A., Julia A., WC - 8222, 2 Oct 1890, AL & SC - 12689 in MS, srv Co.

C, 1st TN Vols.

Powell, Madison S., Sarah A., WA - 3284, 16 May 1887, MS, srv as a Teamster, no other srv data on the card.

Power, Stephen F., Rosina I., WC - 12140, 3 Jul 1900 & SC - 13705, both MS, srv Clark's Co., 2nd MS Vols.

Pratt, John W., or **W. J.**, SA - 24815, 1 May 1896, TX, srv Patterson's Co. E, MS Vols.

Prentiss, William H. alias **William H. Rice, Eliza J.**, WC - 7773, 10 Oct 1891, MS & SC - 10584 in SC, srv Co. A, GA Mtd. Vols (Golding's Co.).

Prestridge, William A., srv Co. A, 1st MS Vols, filed 12 Apr 1887, rest of the card was covered by another card when microcopy was made.

Prewitt, Wilson M., Mary H., WC - 5575, 4 Sep 1888, MS, srv Liddell's Co., 2nd MS Vols.

Priar, William J., Sarah Ann, WA - 3074, 16 May 1887, MS, srv Willis' Co., 1st MS Rifles.

Price, David B. alias **Henry D. B., Margia A. L.**, WC - 8605, 19 Aug 1892, CA & SC - 4150 in TX, srv Co. H, 2nd MS Vols Inf.

Price, D. B., see **David B.**

Prickett, William C., Maria, WC - 7812, 3 Nov 1890, OH, srv Co. B, 2nd MS Rifles.

Pruett, Emory, Mary J., WC - 5998, 9 Apr 1887, LA, srv Sharp's Co., 1st MS Vols OW I - #23586 Rej.

Pryor, Belfield, Elizabeth, WC - 15015, 20 May 1908 & SC - 19450, both TN, srv Co. C, 1st Bttn MS Rifles.

Pryor, Richard S., Lucy B., WC - 5328, 8 Mar 1887, MS, srv Co. A, 5th LA Vols.

Puckett, Anthony B. alias **Thomas B., Georgeanna H.**, WA - 13481, 28 Jul 1896, AL, SA - 24335, srv McManus' Co,. 1st MS Vols. OW IF - #5959.

Puckett, Thomas B., see **Anthony Puckett.**

Pugh, David R., Mary M. M., WC - 14656, 5 Jul 1904 & SC - 17651, TX, srv Co. F, 2nd MS Vol Inf as a Pvt.

Putt, Malinda J., WA - 15041, 14 Apr 1899 & SA - 23704, both MS, srv Chisholm's Co., 2nd AL Vols as a Pvt.

Pyles, Milton, Iphigenia, WC - 468, 21 Mar 1887, MS, srv Co. I, 1st MS Vols OW W - #20120 Rej.

Quigles, Frank, SC - 16737, 17 Jul 1888, MS, srv Co. E, 1st OH Inf.

Quin, William S., SC - 12323, 18 Feb 1887, MS, srv Co. D, GA Mtd. Vols.

Quinn, Peter, Barbara, WC - 9820, 13 Apr 1895 & SC - 6855, both MS, srv Co. D, 2nd MS Vols, OW I - #17259 Rej.

Quinnelly, Steven D., Martha H., WC - 15777, 19 May 1910 & SC - 14632, both MS, srv Ligon's Co., Raiford's Bttn AL Vols as a Pvt.

Rainwater, John P., Melinda, WA - 15755, 17 Aug 1900, TX & SC - 4464 in MS, srv Co. A in MS Vol Rifles.

Ramey, William F., SA - 24299, 5 Apr 1893, TX, srv Capt. Ives' Co., MS Vols.

Ramsey, Simon D., Mary E., WC - 10927, 23 Mar 1897 & SC - 4183, both MS, srv Co. B, Crowson's Bttn MS Vol Rifles.

Ramsey, Thomas J., Rebecca, WC - 11948, 24 Nov 1899 & SC - 4482, both MS, srv Co. B, 1st Bttn MS Rifle Vols.

Randolph, Thaddeus D., Mary A. Light, WA - 17343, 5 Nov 1903, MS, srv Taylor's Co., 1st MS Vols, OW IF - #5984.

Raspberry, James, Jane R., WA - 774 or 7741, 26 Feb 1889, MS, srv in the MS Vols.

Ratliff (Ralliff), William, Martha E., WC - 6988, 15 May 1889, MS, srv Co. H, 2nd MS Vols.

Ray, John P. alias **John O'Grady, Mary E.**, WC - 15095, 20 Oct 1904 & SC - 2588, both MS, srv Co. K, 5th U.S. Inf.

Ray, Richard W., SA - 21387, 18 Mar 1889, TN, srv as a Recruit unassigned in 2nd MS Vols.

Read, Jesse, Nancy J., WA - 12908, 3 Sep 1895 & SC - 10840, both MS, srv Co. A, 1st MS Rifles (Vols.).

Reading, Randolph G., Mary I. or **J.**, WA - 12342, 9 Oct 1894, TX & SC - 19721 in MS, srv Co. E, 4th LA Vols.

Redus, James W., Leah, WC - 1645, 7 Apr 1887 & SC - 5388, both TX, srv Key's Co., 3rd (?) MS Rifles.

Reedy, John W., Elentheria, WC - 6331, 23 Mar 1889, MS, srv Acker's Co., 2nd MS Vols.

Reid, David M. B., Louise, WA - 11221, 15 Mar 1893, MS, srv as a Teamster in Qtr Mstr Dept of U.S. Army 1847-8.

Reid, Hugh James, SC - 18743, 17 Dec 1889, MS, srv Comstock's Co., 3rd LA Inf.

Renner, Daniel G., Minnie A., WA - 7494, 17 Dec 1888, MS, srv Galbraith's Co., 3rd LA Vols.

Reno, John D., Martha A., WC - 2389, 16 Jun 1887, MS, srv Jackson's Co., 2nd MS Vols.

Reynolds, Hugh J., Eveline W., WC - 13589, 31 Oct 1903, TX & SC - 7348 in MS, srv Co. G, Palmetto Regt. of SC Vols as a Pvt. 1846-8, BLW #23955 - 160 - 47, sol. died 23 Sep 1903.

Reynolds, Sherod, SC - 2391, 8 Mar 1887, MS, srv Co. D, 1st MS Vols.

Rhodes, Eli H., SA - 24129, 29 Oct 1892, MS, srv Co. D under Col. Davis as a Pvt, IW SO - 4934.

Rhodes, John, Jane S., WA - 14686, 4 Aug 1898 & SC - 8811, both TX, srv Cos. H & I, 2nd MS Vols.

Rhymes, William L., Amarillas, WC - 6263, 20 Nov 1888, MS, srv Downing's Co., 1st MS Vols.

Rhyne, John, Elizabeth, WC - 9422, 1 Sep 1894 & SC - 2386, both AR, srv Co. H, 2nd MS Rifle Vols.

Rice, Harvey, SC - 6872, 9 Apr 1887, MS, srv Co. E, 1st GA Inf.

Rice, John F., SA - 21556, 20 Apr 1889, PA, srv under Col. Davis in 1st MS Rifles.

Rice, John W., Augusta H., WC - 9268, 20 Feb 1893, MS, srv as a Capt. in 13th U.S. Inf.

Rice, Spencer L., SC - 19555, 10 Aug 1889, MS, srv Co. F, 3rd TX Mtd Vols.

Rice, William H., alias **William H. Prentiss, Eliza J. Prentiss**, WC - 1773, 10 Oct 1891, MS & SC - 10584 in SC, srv Co. A in Bttn of GA Mtd. Vols.

Rich, Edward C., Frances C., WC - 10541, 15 Jul 1895 & SC - 7630, both TX, srv

Co. A, 2nd MS Vols, also see OW I - #17403 file #47836.

Richard, Theopold, SA - 22999, 30 Aug 1890, MS, srv Co. G, 5th U.S. Inf, OW I - #22380.

Richardson, Henry, Lydia A., WC - 6983, 12 Jun 1889, MS, srv Co. A, 3rd MO Vols.

Richardson, Samuel J., Susan Ann, WC - 16310, 20 Sep 1920 & SC - 6168, both LA, srv Co. B, 1st MS Vol Inf as a Pvt in 1846-7, BLW #9743 - 160 - 47, sol. died 17 Jul 1920 in LA.

Rickerson, James M., Anna C., WA - 8544, 30 Nov 1889, FL, srv Henry's Co., 1st MS Rifles.

Ricks, Edward, Annie, WC - 7541, 30 Oct 1890, MS, srv Johnson's Regt. TX Vols.

Riley, Hugh A., WC - 547, 9 Mar 1887, LA, srv Co. H, 1st MS Rifles, OW I - #20557 Rej.

Riley, John S., SC - 7344, 2 Apr 1887, TX, srv Co. E, 2nd MS Vols trans. to Mear's Co. AR Cav, died 12 Jun 1915.

Riley, William, Elizabeth, WC - 5020, 1 Jun 1888, MS, srv Gibbs' Co., 1st AL Vols.

Rimes, John, Ophelia C., WC - 5105, 12 Aug 1887, MS, MA - 13543, 21 Sep 1896, srv Downing's Co., 1st MS Vols.

Ripley, Hiram D., SC - 4184, 19 Feb 1887, MS, srv Co. G, 1st MS Vols.

Rivercomb, George, Mary J., WC - 1629, 1 Feb 1887, AR, srv Co. B, 1st MS Rifles.

Roberson, William, Lucinda C., WC - 13571, 5 Dec 1903 & SC - 13451, both TX, srv Co. F, 2nd MS Rifles as a Cpl.

Roberts, Joseph M., Catharine E., WC - 2610, 12 Jul 1887, AL, srv Downing's Co., 1st MS Vols.

Roberts, Simeon, Sarah W., WC - 3817, 2 Apr 1887, TX, srv Liddell's Co., 2nd MS Vols.

Robertson, Ira G., Mary A., SC - 16063, 4 Feb 1887, MS, srv Co. B, 1st OH Inf & Co. I 1st U.S. Arty as a Pvt 1846-8, BLW #4443 - 160 - 47 & BLW #42447 - 160 - 47, CW WO - 810086 for srv Co. D, 71st IN Inf (sub 6th IN Cav.), Co. M, 1st MI Light Arty., Co. A, 17th KS Inf, Cos. L & M, 16th KS Cav, also srv Co. G 11th U.S. Inf 1869-71.

Robertson, William M., Sarah C., WC - 2951, 18 Oct 1887, MS, srv Co. B, 2nd Bttn (?) MS, OW I - #20911 Rej.

Robertson, Young, Mary Jane, WC - 7384, 11 Feb 1891 & SC - 4180, both MS, srv Co. B in Bttn MS Riflemen.

Robinson, John B., Harriet, WC - 15555, 25 Jun 1910 & SC - 7633, both MS, srv Co. G, 6th LA Mtd. Vols as a Pvt.

Rodgers, Louis W., Espy P., WC - 8176, 5 Aug 1892 & SC - 6423, both MS, srv Co. B, Seibel's AL Vol. Inf.

Roe, John Henry, Mary A., WA - 10025, 5 Aug 1891, MS srv Co. E, SC Vols (Palmetto Regt.).

Rogers, Jefferson C., Martha, WC - 14967, 19 Mar 1907, TX, srv Co. E, 2nd MS Vols as a Pvt.

Rogers, Samuel, Louisa F., WA - 16236, 6 Jun 1901, MS, SA - 22088, srv

Holderige's Co., 2nd MS Vols as a Pvt.

Rogers, Samuel T., Lucy A., WC - 2346, 21 Jun 1887, MS, srv Comstock's Co. LA Vols.

Rogers, William E., Martha E., WC - 5975, 29 Dec 1888 & SC - 8851, both TX, srv Co. E, 2nd MS or MO Vols.

Rooney, Thomas A., Sallie A., WA - 18075, 13 Jun 1905, GA, srv as a Pvt in 1st MS Rifles.

Ross, Ravenna, Margaret, WC - 7640, 10 Jun 1890, TX, srv Co. H, 1st MS Rifles.

Rosseau (Rousseau), William James, SC - 19566, 15 Jun 1891, MS, srv Co. A, 1st Bttn AL Vols, see Rousseau.

Rosser, John Q. C., SA - 23020, 9 Sep 1890, MS, srv as a Teamster in Qtr Mstr Dept., OW I - #19478 Rej.

Rotramel, William S., Ellen D., WC - 9709, 22 Nov 1894, TX, srv Cooper's Co., 1st MS Rifles, also see contesting widow **Nancy,** WC - 5879, 29 Sep 1888, filed in MS.

Rousseau, William J., SC - 19566, 15 Jun 1891, MS, srv Co. A, 1st Bttn AL Vols, died 4 Jan 1916.

Routh, Jacob, SC - 11899, 5 Apr 1887, MS, srv Co. F, 3rd (?) MS Vol. Inf, sol. died 31 Aug 1914.

Rundberg, John I., SC - 11205, 22 Aug 1887, MS, srv Clark's Co., 2nd MS Inf.

Runnels, Ellis J., SC - 6867, 23 Mar 1887, MS, srv McManus' Co., 1st MS Rifles.

Russ, Luther F., SC - 12247, 23 Apr 1887, MS, srv Hunt's Co., 3rd LA Vols.

Russell, Alexander, Louisa, WA - 16988, 28 Feb 1903, no place of filing given, srv in MS Vols.

Russell, John G., Winnie J., WC - 3521, 15 Feb 1887, LA, srv Croson's Co., 1st Bttn MS Vols.

Russell, Oscar, SC - 18757, 26 Aug 1887, MS, srv Co. I, 2nd MS Vols., CW Army #1109998 for srv Co. A 2nd RI Cav.

Russell, Samuel D., Eliza J., WC - 7255, 18 Nov 1889, MS, srv Lawrence's Co., 5th LA Vols.

St. John, Arthur, Caroline E., WC - 14308, 7 Nov 1903, AR & SC - 6432 in MS, srv Co. F, 1st MS Vols as a Pvt.

Saliasbury, James M., SA - 21639, 15 May 1889, MS, srv Forne's Co,. Galley's Bttn LA Arty.

Sanders, Hiram, Epsa, WA - 8965, 17 Apr 1890, MS, srv Backento's Co., U.S. Mtd. Rifles.

Sanders, James, SC - 14887, 24 Feb 1888, LA, srv Estelle's Co., 2nd MS Vols.

Sanders, Robert H., SC - 11677, 20 Sep 1887, AR, srv Willis' Co., 2nd MS Vols.

Sandiford, Bill alias **Bill Ashby** or **Thomas S. Ashley,** SA - 25292, 11 Jun 1902, TX, srv Johnson's Co., MS Vol Inf as a Pvt. (alleged).

Saunders, Benjamin, Hannah C., WA - 8944, 21 Apr 1890, MS, srv Co. H, 1st MS Vols.

Sawyer, William C., SC - 3515, 21 Mar 1887, TN, srv Co. E, 2nd MS Vols.

Saxon, H. J., SA - 23893, 22 Aug 1872, TX, srv Co. H, 2nd MS Vols.

Sayre, Elias B., Sarah W., WC - 241, 12 Mar 1887, MS, srv Co. G, 4th OH Vols.

Schmaling, Joseph, Elizabeth, WC - 6721, 6 Dec 1889, MS, srv Crump's Co., 1st

MS Vols.

Scoggins, William J. J., Sarah E., WC - 10875, 17 Feb 1890 & SC - 9648, both TX, srv Key's Co., 1st Bttn MS Vols as a Pvt.

Scott, Joseph, Sarah, WC - 14896, 31 Jan 1908, OK & SC - 13157 in KS, srv Co. I, 2nd MS Vols as a Pvt.

Scott, Rankin L., Amanda, WC - 5216, 27 Aug 1887, MS, srv Mercer's Co., 6th LA Vols, OW W - #22335 Rej.

Scott, William R., Martha A. L., WC - 14757, 1 Jun 1904, TN & SC - 14528 in MS, srv Co. C, 2nd MS Vol Inf as a Pvt.

Seale, Andrew J., Addie M., WC - 1758, 5 Apr 1887 & SC - 2744, both MS, srv Co. A, 1st AL Vols as a 2nd Lt.,

Seale, Benajah B., Elmira E., WC - 11573, 1 Jun 1898 & SC - 12245, both FL, srv Co. A, 2nd MS Vols as a Sgt.

Seater, Robert, SC - 3739, 4 Feb 1887, MS, srv Co. K, 2nd MS Inf.

Sellers, Anderson E., Nancy, WA - 12330, 3 Oct 1894, MO, srv Liddell's Co., 1st MS Vols.

Sells, Thomas, SC - 3018, 28 Feb 1887, MS, srv Lloyd's Indpt. Co,. GA Mtd Vols.

Selman, Thomas B., WC - 12325, 3 Sep 1897 & SC - 20018, both AL, srv Co. G, 1st MS Vols (Downings Co.).

Setzler, George A., Mary A., WC - 9654, 14 Sep 1894 & SC - 4867, both MS, srv Co. D, 1st MS Rifle Bttn.

Shackelford, Josephus, SC - 19816, 29 Feb 1892, AL, srv Anderson's Bttn MS Vols Co. D,, sol. died 6 Jun 1915.

Shackelford, Wyley J., SA - 24278, 20 Mar 1893, TX, srv in the MS Vols.

Shaifer, George W., SC - 12777, 15 Nov 1887, MS, srv Co. H, 1st MS Rifles.

Sharman, James A. alias **James A. Sherman, Lucy J.**, WA - 8169, 3 Jul 1889, GA, srv Co. K, 1st MS Vol Inf.

Shaw, Edward L., Julia A., WC - 6254, 2 Apr 1889 & SC - 14298, both MS, srv Kerr's Co., LA Mtd Vols, 2nd Lt.

Shaw, Franklin, SC - 17822, 26 Dec 1888, AL, srv Co. A, 2nd MS Vols.

Shaw, Gustavus M., Julia F., WC - 11995, 19 Dec 1899, WI, SC - 14682, srv Co. D, 2nd MS Vols as Cpl., XC - 2664740.

Shaw, Robert J., Elizabeth A., WC - 7249, 26 May 1890 & SC - 2286, both MS, srv Co. F, 1st MS Vols (DeLay's Co.).

Shelton, Edward B., Maria L., WC - 2285, 27 Aug 1887, VA, srv Daniel's Co., 2nd MS Vols.

Shelton, John, Sarah Jane, WC - 11494, 2 Feb 1898 & SC - 4202, both AR, srv Co. D, MS Vol Rifles, OW I - #19900 Rej.

Shelton, Obediah N., Frances E., WC - 6135, 11 Feb 1889, TX, srv Acker's Co., 2nd MS Vols OW WF - #19746 Rej.

Sherard, Benjamin W., Ann, WC - 4891, 22 May 1888, MS, srv Co. B, 1st VA Vols, OW W - #19747 Rej.

Sherman, James A., alias **James A. Sharman, Lucy J.**, WA - 8169, Jul 1886, GA, srv Co. K, 1st MS Inf.

Shields, Richard, SC - 12325, 19 Feb 1887, MS, srv Co. H, 2nd MS Vols.

Shinpock, William H., Ann E. B., WC - 7482, 8 Apr 1891 & SC - 15197, both MS, srv Co. F, 13th U.S. Inf.

Short, Aaron B., SC - 12039, 21 Oct 1887, MS, srv Co. G, 2nd MS Inf.

Short, Edward M., Narciss Grace, WC - 12327, 24 Mar 1888, MS, srv Lenow's & Lacey's Co., Thomas Regt. TN Mtd. Vols as a Pvt, by Special Act of 1 Mar 1901.

Sibley, Edward alias **Edward Dougharty, Julia C.**, WC - 10676, 27 Jul 1896, MS & SC - 16403 in WI, srv on *U.S.S. Columbus* as a Landsman.

Siegrist, Martin, SA - 10209, 19 Mar 1887, MS, srv as a Teamster in the Qtr Mstr Dept.

Sifford, Henry, SA - 10210, 15 Mar 1887, IA, srv Capt Briggs' MS Vols as a Pvt (alleged).

Sillers, Joseph, Matilda B., WC - 5330, 12 Jul 1888, MS, srv Crump's Co., Davis' 1st MS Vols.

Simmons, George or **George S. Crane, Sarah Crane**, WA - 7140, 14 Sep 1888, IN, srv McClung's Co., 1st MS Vols.

Simons, Allard B., SA - 25106, 11 Apr 1899, MS, srv Co. B, 7th (?) MS Vols as a Pvt.

Simpson, James G., Catherine, WC - 13122, 28 Jul 1902 & SC - 18608, both LA, srv Co. H, 2nd MS Vols as a Cpl.

Sims, William C., Julia Ann, WC - 10011, 13 Nov 1895 & SC - 19419, both TX, srv Co. F, 2nd MS Vols.

Singleton, Perry H., Abigail, WC - 5803, 25 Oct 1888, TX, srv Jackson's Co. E, 2nd MS Vols.

Sitley, Edward alias **Edward Dougherty**, SC - 16403, 25 May 1887, MS, WC - 10676, srv on *U.S.S. Columbus*.

Skelton, William R., Juana Justice, WC - 328, 18 Mar 1887, LA, srv Co. C, 1st MS Rifles.

Skinner, Harrison J., Mary L., WC - 5531, 24 Aug 1888, MS, srv Echols' Co., 13th U.S. Inf.

Slade, Thomas Pugh, SC - 10586, 29 Jun 1887, CA, srv Co. A, 1st MS Vols.

Slavens, Charles L., Sarah Jane, WC - 1829, 11 Feb 1887, MS, srv Co. B, 2nd TX Mtd. Vols.

Sloan, Rankin, Sarah, WC - 3002, 26 Mar 1887, AR, srv Co. C, Anderson's Bttn. MS Rifles.

Sly, Louis, SA - 5940, 17 Feb 1887, MS, srv Cos. A & G, 8th U.S. Inf.

Smedes, Charles E., SC - 12456, 2 Nov 1887, MS, srv Co. H, 1st MS Rifles.

Smith, Abram R., Laura Ann, WC - 9909, 28 May 1895 & SC - 15274, both MS, srv Co. G, 1st GA Vol Inf.

Smith, Charles A., Lucy B., WA - 5386, 21 Nov 1887, TX, srv Co. D, 2nd MS Vols.

Smith, Charles W., Nancy V., WA - 4300, 25 Jul 1887, MS, no srv shown on the card.

Smith, Edward, Lucy E., WC - 15512, 27 Jun 1910, IN & SC - 12157 in MS, srv Co. C, 16th U.S. Inf as a Pvt.

Smith, George A., Emma L., WC - 14019, 10 Aug 1900, TX & SC - 5951 in LA, srv Co. B, 1st MS Vols as a Pvt.

Smith, Harvey N., Mary A., WC - 9294, 20 Feb 1894 & SC - 2718, both TX, srv

Co. E, 2nd MS Vol Inf.

Smith, James, SC - 2515, 12 Mar 1887, MS, srv Co. A, 3rd U.S. Dragoons.

Smith, James A., SC - 15324, 19 Feb 1887, MS, srv Co. B, 13th U.S. Inf.

Smith, Jasper N., SA - 25071, 11 Aug 1898, MS, srv Cox's MS Vols as a Pvt (alleged).

Smith, John A., SA - 21389, 16 Mar 1889, MS, srv Lornbratle's Co., AL Vols.

Smith, John H., Melissa S., WC - 1718, 4 Apr 1887, MS, srv Co. I, 1st MS Vols.

Smith, Spencer, SA - 24031, 15 Aug 1892, MS, srv Co. G, 4th LA Vols.

Smith, William, SC - 10468, 30 Jun 1887, MS, srv Co. I, 2nd U.S. Dragoons.

Smith, William, Margaret Ellen, WA - 4310, 12 May 1887, MS, srv as a Teamster in Qtr Mstr Dept. U.S. Army 1846-7.

Smithwick, Edward W., SC - 14232, 21 Sep 1887, MS, srv Co. F, 2nd MS Vols, OW IC - 8875 file #6116.

Snow, William A., SA - 12789, 16 May 1887, MS, srv Btty C, 3rd U.S. Arty (alleged).

Snow, William J., SA - 24353, 23 May 1893, MS, srv White's Indian Scouts in AL Vols.

Sojourner, Sylvester D., Elizabeth M., WC - 12183, 2 Apr 1900 & SC - 4757, both MS, srv Downing's Co., 1st MS Vol Rifles.

Somerville, James, Cornelia B., WC - 1183, 18 May 1887, VA, srv Co. D, 1st MS Vols.

Sowell, James C., SA - 23075, 27 Sep 1890, TX, srv Daniel's Co., 2nd MS Vols.

Sparks, James P., Lucy Bradley a sister, sister's A - 5587, 21 Dec 1887, KY, srv Clarke's Co., 2nd MS Vols.

Spear, John, SC - 8230, 4 Feb 1887, MS or MA, srv Co. K, 9th U.S. Inf.

Staggs, Thomas N., SA - 23870, 4 Apr 1892, TX, srv Co. A, Anderson's Bttn MS Vols.

Stanford, John F., SA - 16115, 27 Apr 1887, MS, srv Bradford's Co. Pontotoc Rovers in MS Vols.

Stanford, William C., SA - 12070, 29 Apr 1887, TX, srv Bradford's Co., 1st MS Rifles.

Staples, Solomon G., Adeline A., WC - 1246, 12 Mar 1887, MS, srv Co. G, 4th LA Vols as a Capt.

Starnes, John, Cassandew E., WA - 17344, 5 Nov 1903, AR & SC - 18281 in MS, srv Co. C, 2nd MS Vols.

Steadman, George, W., Mary S., WA - 19978, 6 Jul 1912, MS, no srv shown on the card.

Steele, Abner N., Ellen Caroline, WC - 3338, 18 Feb 1887, no place of filing given, srv Key's Co., 1st Bttn MS Rifles.

Steele, Daniel, SA - 22773, 31 May 1890, MS, srv Co. B, 9th U.S. Inf.

Steele, James I. V., Mary, WC - 4235, 5 Mar 1888, TX, srv Co. H, 1st MS Vols.

Steele, Jesse G., SC - 13646, 20 Sep 1887, MS, srv Co. F, 2nd MS Rifles.

Steele, Robert J., Rowena G., WC - 7071, 13 Mar 1890 & SC - 11423, both CA, srv Co. E, 1st MS Vols.

Stephens, James N., SC - 18392, 6 Jun 1889, AR, srv Key's Co. in Bttn MS Vols.

Stevens, Nelson L. alias **Abraham Moses**, SC - 16255, 7 May 1888, MS, srv Co.

C, 2nd LA Vols.

Stewart, James D., SC - 9521, 2 Mar 1887, MS, srv Co. B, 1st MS Vols.

Stewart, James I., Elizabeth M., WC - 13001, 2 Oct 1901 & SC - 9557, both TX, srv Co. C, 2nd MS Vol Inf as a Pvt.

Stockard, James P., Mary E., WC - 4556, 29 Apr 1887, CO, srv Diley's Co. F, 1st MS Vols.

Stockton, Joseph M., Ann, WA - 7046, 21 Aug 1888, MS, srv Clay's Co. in 1st MS Rifles.

Stockwell, Albert C., SC - 16568, 26 Jun 1887, MS, srv Co. A, 2nd IL Vols, see Army WO - #919092 for **Brazil Brown** who srv Co. I, 16th IL Cav, also see IO - 83811 for former husband **Drury Ezell** who srv Co. E, 116th IL Inf & 47th Co., 2nd Bttn V.R.C., also see LW #587117 for srv Cos. C & K, 10th IL Inf.

Stokes, Redden, Catharine, WA - 16115, 30 Mar 1901, CA & SC - 14238 in UT, srv Co. C, 2nd MS Vols, OW IF - #23324 Rej.

Stone, William M., SA - 24188, 30 Dec 1892, MS, srv Johnson's & Smith's TX Mtd Vols.

Stovall, William A., Catharine, WC - 15981, 26 Aug 1913, LA & SC - 16487 in TX, srv Co. C, 2nd MS Inf as a Pvt in 1847-8, sol. died 27 Aug 1912 Oakdale, LA.

Stratton, Jesse K., Endorah E., WA - 10076, 29 Aug 1891 & SC - 13598, both MS, srv Deason's Co. 2nd MS Rifles.

Strong, John, Emeline M., WC - 1406, 11 Feb 1887, MS, srv Co. F, 1st MS Vols.

Strong, William, Sarah E., WA - 2098, 8 Mar 1887, MS, srv Carson's MS Vols.

Strong, William M., Hannah G., WC - 1901, 25 Feb 1887, MS, srv Co. F, 1st MS Vols.

Stroud, Thomas J., Nancy L., WA - 17527, 16 Mar 1904, TN & SC - 1957 in TX, srv Co. F, 2nd MS Vols OW I - #20927 Rej.

Stubblefield, Stephen P., Sarah A., WC - 13398, 21 Apr 1903 & SC - 5945, both TX, srv Co. A, 1st MS Vols as a Pvt.

Stubblefield, Wlliam H., Laurena E., WC - 15365, 20 Sep 1909 & SC - 6179, both MS, srv Co. A, 1st MS Inf as a Pvt.

Summerford, Edward C., Sarah H., WA - 2646, 11 Apr 1887, MS, srv in the SC Vols.

Summerford, William M., Martha Ann, WA - 10908, 26 Sep 1892, MS, srv Dancley's Co., AL Vols as a Pvt (alleged).

Summers, Thomas J., Middy E., WC - 2888, 11 Oct 1887, AL, srv Anderson's Co., MS Vols.

Sutherland, William, Emily, WA - 19112, 10 Aug 1908 & SC - 13277, both KY, srv Co. K ,1st TX Foot Riflemen & MS Vols.

Swann, Thomas, Jane, WC - 951, 17 May 1887, MS, srv Co. F, 1st MS Vols.

Sweat, Robert W., SA - 23731, 19 Nov 1891, AL, srv Co. I, 1st or 2nd MS Vols, IW - S - #5046.

Sweeney, Oliver, SC - 13644, 7 Jun 1887, MS, srv Co. D, 3rd LA Vols.

Sweeten, Samuel M., SC - 15117, 31 Mar 1888, AR, srv Jackson's Co., 2nd MS Vols.

Tanner, James C., Margaret A., WC - 10586, 24 Nov 1896, MS, srv Co. K, 1st MS Rifles as a Pvt.

Tanner, William M., Mary H., WC - 16132, 17 May 1915, VA & SC - 12126 in NC, srv Co. D, 2nd MS Rifles as a Pvt in 1846-8, sol. died 14 Apr 1915.

Tate, Arthur, Margaret M., WA - 17548, 2 Apr 1904, MS, srv Crowson's Co., 1st MS Rifles as a Pvt.

Taylor, Benjamin F., Emaline, WC - 859, 26 Mar 1887, MS, srv Co. D, 1st MS Vols.

Taylor, Ferdinand, SA - 6351, 24 Feb 1887, MS, srv Co. A, 2nd MS Vols, OW I - #22733 Rej.

Taylor, John alias John T. Camp, SA - 25444, 14 Apr 1905, AR, srv Co. D, 2nd MS Vol Inf.

Taylor, John Z., SC - 9184, 17 May 1887, MS, srv Co. K, 1st TX Vols.

Teague, Abner W., Elizabeth, WC - 12469, 8 Mar 1901 & SC - 6683, both SC, srv Downing's Co., 1st MS Rifles.

Teague, Hardy J., Laura A., WC - 15465, 22 Jun 1909, OH, srv Co. A, 2nd MS Inf as a Pvt.

Terry, Lamkin S., Martha A., WC - 9125, 26 Sep 1893 & SC - 14471, both MS, srv Co. H, 2nd MS Inf.

Tharington, Andrew J. or Thorington, SC - 12256, 23 Mar 1887, MS, srv Picken's Co., Coffey's Regt. AL Vols.

Thomas, Edwin C., Charlotte, WA - 7011, 14 Aug 1888, KY, srv Davis' Co., 1st MS Vols.

Thomas, James, SC - 4219, 22 Mar 1887, MS, srv Co. B, 1st Bttn Vol Rifles.

Thomas, Samuel B., Eliza B., WC - 14960, 1 May 1908 & SC - 13649, both MS, srv Co. G, 1st MS Rifles as a 2nd Lt.

Thomas, Wesley H., Esther M., WC - 2891, 3 Oct 1887, MS, srv Deason's Co., 2nd MS Inf.

Thomas, William M., Catina A., WC - 12138, 16 Feb 1899, AL & SC - 13772 in MS, srv Cutter's Co., 2nd KY Vol. Inf.

Thompson, D. T., SA - 25184, 28 Apr 1900, MS, srv Brigg's Co., 1st MS Vols (alleged).

Thompson, Frank T., H. Jane, WA - 18008, 20 Apr 1905, AR, srv Co. I, 1st MS Vols as a Pvt.

Thompson, Henry B., SC - 10375, 15 Jun 1887, CA, srv Co. C, 1st MS Vol Inf.

Thompson, John, Laura, WC - 6948, 10 Mar 1890, MS, srv as an Asst Surgeon in 1st MS Vols.

Thompson, John K., Lucy C., WC - 5307, 12 Dec 1887, AR, srv Co. B, 2nd MS Vols.

Thompson, Joseph H., SC - 1780, 10 Mar or 19 Feb 1887, MS, srv Co. G, 1st MS Rifles.

Thompson, Walter Alvis, SC - 8867, 28 Feb 1887, NC, srv Co. I, 1st MS Rifles.

Thompson, William, SC - 1850, 7 Mar 1887, MS, srv Co. F, 1st MS Vols.

Thompson, William, Jane A., WC - 5720, 8 Jun 1888, MS, srv Co. D, 2nd MS Vols as a Pvt.

Thompson, William B., Josephine, WC - 9876, 19 Sep 1895 & SC - 10875, both TX, srv Co. D, 2nd MS Vols.

Thorn, Albert C., SC - 9274, 23 Aug 1887, MS, srv Fairchild's Co., in 3rd LA Vols.

Thornton, Thomas, SC - 2315, 14 Mar 1887, MS, srv Co. C, 3rd U.S. Inf.

Threat, Elbert G., SA - 12846, 21 Mar 1887, MS, srv Adams Co., 2nd MS Vols.

Thweatt, Elbert G., Mary, WA - 9555, 2 Jan 1891 & SC - 16327, both MS, srv Co. H, 2nd MS Vols (Adams' Co.).

Thweatt, James, Susan C., WC - 856, 5 Apr 1887, MS, srv Co. D, 2nd MS Vols.

Thweatt, Uriah W., Jennette, WC - 15326, 7 Jun 1909 & SC - 1864, both MS, srv Co. H, 2nd MS Vols as a Pvt.

Tierce, Tucker R., Sarah E., WC - 5732, 18 Oct 1888 & SC - 4224, both CA, srv Rogers' Co., 1st MS Vols.

Tilden, Joseph W., SA - 23058, 22 Sep 1890, MS, srv in the U.S.M.C.

Tilden, Thomas W., Helen, WC - 6079, 30 Jan 1889, CA, srv in the 1st MS Vols.

Tillman, John C., Amanda M., WC - 2062, 8 Oct 1887, MO, srv as a Recruit in MS Vols, OW I - #18497 Rej.

Tinnin, Hugh P., Fannie, WC - 10067, 27 Feb 1893 & SC - 14468, both MS, srv Co. E, 1st MS Vol Inf.

Tobe, Luther D. alias **Luther D. Green,** SA - 25039, 22 Mar 1898, MS, srv Blythe's Co., 2nd MS Vols.

Tolin, Richard, Sally A., WA - 10248, 3 Dec 1891, MS, srv Co. C, Sante Fe Bttn MO Mtd Vols.

Toomes, Benjamin F., Mary A., WC - 5731, 27 Feb 1888, MS, srv Crowson's Co., 1st Bttn MS Rifles.

Townsend, Littleton M., Martha E., WC - 936, 30 Mar 1887, MS, srv Co. B, MS Bttn Vols.

Travers, Robert J., Martha Ann, WC - 9677, 18 May 1894 & SC - 4794, both MS, srv Downman's Co., 1st Bttn AL Vols (Raiford's Bttn).

Traviss, Joshua H., Nancy, WA - 3549, 3 Jun 1887, IL, srv in the MS Vols.

Tredway, William, SC - 17160, 13 Aug 1888, MS, srv Co. D, 2nd MS Vols, sol died 16 Apr 1917, Cockrum, MS.

Trousdale, Leonidas, SC - 3251, 18 Feb 1887, TN, srv Co. D, 1st MS Inf.

Tucker, James H., SC - 8985, 16 Mar 1887, TX srv Co. F, 1st MS Vols.

Tucker, William D., Cynthia M., WC - 9768, 9 Jun 1894 & SC - 14503, both TN, srv Co. I. 1st MS Inf Vols.

Turnbo, Andrew J., Sarah A., WA - 13583, 12 Oct 1896, TX, srv Clay's Co.. MS Vols as a Pvt (alleged) BLW #79041 - 160 - 47, sol died 3 Sep 1889.

Turnbull, John E., SC - 1863, 3 Mar 1887, TX, srv Co. F. 1st MS Vols.

Turner, Asa L., Martha A., WC - 15200, 10 Apr 1906 & SC - 19348, both TX, srv Daniels' Co.. 2nd MS Vol Inf.

Turner, David J., wid S. A. E., WA - 6909, 24 Jul 1888, MS, srv in a FL Regt, OW W - #25071 Rej.

Turner, Eaton B., SC - 12740, 14 Feb 1887, MS, srv Co. D, Anderson's Bttn MS Vols.

Turner, Joshua, Mary E., WC - 13209, 19 Aug 1902 & SC - 8564, both in SC, srv Co. E, 1st MS Vols.

Tyler, Albert G., SC - 9903, 17 Mar 1887, MS, srv Co. E, 5th LA Vols.

Ueltschy, Albert, Julia A., WC - 12897, 30 Jun 1900, MS, srv Co. I, 11th U.S. Inf as a Pvt.

Umphlett, Job, SC - 17958, 2 Mar 1889, TN, srv Co. K, 1st MS Vols.

Underwood, Ripley C., SC - 4553, 17 Mar 1887, MS, srv Co. F, 2nd MS Rifles.

Vance, George W., Mary L., WC - 3047, 27 Dec 1887, MS, srv Howard's Co., 1st MS Vols.

Vance, John D., Elizabeth A., WC - 10978, 3 Sep 1897 & SC - 14845, both MS, srv Co. D, 1st MS Vols.

Vanderburg, Martin, SC - 6213, 24 Feb 1887, MS, srv Co. C, 1st NC Vols.

Vaughan, Henry, wid E. A., WA - 8050, 21 May 1889, MS, srv in the AL Vols.

Vaughn, Word G., Laura E., WC - 8667, 3 Feb 1890 & SC - 3896, both TX, srv Delay's Co. F, 1st MS Vol Inf (Rifles).

Volgher, Charles alias Charles Fongel or Charles P. Bird, SC - 9604, 4 Feb 1887, UT Terr., srv Co. B, 1st MS Vols.

Von Deering, Ferdinand, Catherine, WA - 1208, 1 Oct 1888, MS, srv in the 1st LA Vols.

Waddell, Anderson M., Alberta, WC - 12063, 10 Nov 1899 & SC - 20053, both TX, srv Co. G, 1st MS Vol Rifles.

Wadlington, David M., Martha A., WC - 7015, 20 Aug 1889, MS, srv Co. G, 4th KY Vols.

Wadsworth, Alexander, Barbara, WC - 9504, 4 Sep 1893 & SC - 1390, both NC, srv Co. E, 2nd Vols as a Pvt.

Wages, James G., Harriet, WA - 17803, 25 Nov 1904, MS, srv Co. D, 1st Bttn MS Rifles as a Pvt.

Wagner, Charles H., Margaret F., WC - 552, 22 Mar 1887, MS, srv as an Asst Surgeon in 1st TX Rifles.

Waldrop, John W., SC - 19989, 26 Feb 1887, TX, srv Co. A, Davis' MO Vols & Co. E, 1st MS Vols.

Walker, Benjamin F., Jane A., WC - 13074, 8 Jun 1901, MS, srv Coleman's Co., 1st AL Mil Inf as a Pvt.

Walker, William, Frances, WC - 8682, 8 Mar 1893 & SC - 1253, both MS, srv Co. G, 1st MS Vol Rifles.

Walters, John, SC - 8679, 16 Feb 1887, MS, srv Co. D, 2nd MS Vols.

Walton, George W., Amanda J., WA - 13561, 2 Oct 1896 & SC - 9996, both TX, srv Co. C, 2nd MS Vols.

Wample, Thomas J., SA - 25355, 18 Jul 1903, MS, srv as Pvt in Capt. Laster's Co., 8th Inf.

Ward, Edward Wesley, Mary E., WC - 16250, 27 Jul 1917 & SC - 15679, both MS, srv Co. E, 2nd TN Inf as a Pvt in 1846-7, BLW #312-100-47, sol. died 4 Jul 1917 Water Valley, MS.

Ward, Hiram, Margaret Ann, WC - 2228, 13 Aug 1887, MS, srv Co. C, 2nd MS Vols.

Ward, James G., Amanda C., WC - 5110, 9 Apr 1888, TX, srv Acker's Co., 2nd MS Vols.

Ward, John Warren, Mary E., WC - 14085, 16 May 1905 & SC - 3917, both MS, srv Desha's Indpt Co., AL Vols as Pvt.

Ware, John R., Louisa J., WC - 13127, 3 Dec 1900 & SC - 1401, both MS, srv Co. A, 1st MS Vol Rifles as a Pvt.

Ware, Robert, SA - 17810, 12 Dec 1887, LA, srv Elder's Co., 2nd MS Vols.

Warren, William E., Amanda L., WC - 3610, 6 Jun 1887, AL, srv Blythe's Co., 2nd MS Vols.

Washer, Thomas, Mary L. C., WC - 5650, 12 Sep 1888 & SC - 1493, both IL, srv Co. K, 1st MS Vols.

Watson, Marshall D., Nancy L., WC - 5485, 9 Aug 1888, MS, srv Co. M, TN Vols as a Pvt., OW I - #7835.

Watson, William B., Victoria A., WC - 1800, 24 Feb 1887, MS, srv Co. A in MS Rifle Bttn.

Way, William J. D., Annie E., WC - 10006, 14 May 1895 & SC - 19723, both TX, srv Co. B, 1st MS Rifles.

Weaver, John G., SC - 7871, 16 May 1887, TX, srv Co. D, 2nd MS Vols.

Webster, George Henry, Mary, WC - 10920, 12 Apr 1897 & SC - 6468, both IL, srv Co. B, 3rd MS Inf (Rifles) as a Sgt., OW - I - #22626 Rej.

Weems, Daniel, SC - 10797, 18 Jul 1887, AR, srv Co. F, 2nd MS Rifle Vols, sol. died 16 Sep 1916 Lebanon, AR.

Welden, Bennett M., SC - 8835, 4 Feb 1887, MS, srv Co. A, 2nd IL Vols.

Wellons, Marcus C., SC - 7855, 25 Mar 1887, MS, srv Co. D, 1st MS Rifles.

Wells, James B., Catharine R., WC - 11152, 21 Jul 1897, AR & SC - 10488 in MS, srv Co. E, Seymour's Bttn GA Vols as a 2nd Lt., OW I - #20502 Rej.

Wells, Joseph T. alias Joseph Bennett, SA - 25153, 14 Dec 1899, GA, srv Norwood's Co., MS Vols.

West, Douglass, SC - 15300, 15 Mar 1888, LA, srv Co. B, 1st MS Rifles.

West, Osborn F., Fannie A., WC - 3348, 30 Jan 1888, MS, srv Capt. Wilson's Co., 2nd MS Vols as a Cpl.

Westbrook, John W., SC - 4253, 23 Mar 1887, AL, srv Co. K, 1st MS Rifles.

Westrope, James M., SC - 1714, 7 Feb 1887, MS, srv Co. B, 1st MS Vols.

Whatley, Seborn J., Minerva, WA - 10145, 2 Oct 1891, TX, srv as a Pvt in 12th (?) MS.

Wheeler, James F., Bedy, WC - 15203, 20 Jul 1908 & SC - 8613, both MS, srv Co. K, 1st TX Vol Rifles as a Pvt.

Wheeler, Noah W. S., Margaret A., WC - 5116, 20 Jun 1887, MS, srv Shiver's Co., 1st TX Rifles.

Whitaker, John W., Martha W., WA - 14062, 14 Jul 1897, MS, srv under Col Campbell, no other srv on the card.

White, Devernia, SC - 8921, 10 Feb 1887, MS, srv Co. B, 1st AL Vols.

White, Elihu L, Narcissa, WC - 7328, 3 Oct 1890 & SC - 1488, both MS, srv Co. H, 14th U.S. Inf.

White, J. M., Lavissa C., WA - 20188, 12 Mar 1914 & SA - 25337, both MS, srv Buckley's Co., 2nd MS Vols 1847-8, sol died 20 Jun 1903.

White, John, Lucy E., WC - 4411, 11 Mar 1887, MS, srv Desha's Indpt Co., AL Vols.

White, Thomas C., SC - 11451, 6 Sep 1887, MS, srv Co. F, 2nd MS Vols.

Whitehead, Calvin, Georgia A., WC - 13523, 16 Sep 1901, AL & SC - 14952 in TX, srv Steele's Co., 2nd MS Vols as a Pvt.

Whitmore, Rolla M., SA - 25409, 2 Jun 1904, Indian Terr., srv Co. E, 1st MS

Riflemen as a Pvt.

Whitmarsh, Elliott J., SA - 18096, 4 Jan 1888, MS, srv Co. A, 2nd MS Vols.

Wilburn, John A., SC - 14045, 19 Mar 1887, MS, srv Crowson's Co., Anderson's Bttn MS Vols.

Wilcox, John A., Mary E., WC - 6652, 26 Oct 1889, DC, srv as Lt Col in 2nd MS Vols.

Wiles, John H. or **John Henry, Sarah H.**, WC - 10878, 6 Mar 1897 & SC - 6482, both MS, srv Co. I, 1st GA Vols.

Wiley, Benjamin T., Abigail, WC - 13602, 25 Feb 1903 & SC - 16594, both CA, srv Co. C, 2nd MS Vols as a Pvt.

Wilkerson, Elijah J., SC - 1687, 26 Feb 1887, OH, srv Co. B, 2nd MS Rifles.

Wilkerson, Nathaniel J., SA - 15927, 15 Aug 1887, MA, srv Capt. J. D. Bradford's Pontotoc Rovers in MS Vols as a Pvt 1846, BLW #77414 - 160 - 47.

Wilkerson, Stephen P., Jane E., WC - 10967, 9 Nov 1896 & SC - 14305, both TX, srv Co. A, 3rd MS Vols (Rifles).

Wilkerson, Thomas T., SC - 1623, 26 Feb 1887, MS, srv Co. I, 1st MS Vol Rifles.

Wilkins, Billy alias **William H. McClatchy**, SA - 24996, 10 Nov 1897, TX, srv in the 1st MS Vols (Rifles).

Wilkins, James L., SC - 6480, 18 Apr 1887, TX, srv Daniels' Co., 2nd MS Rifles.

Wilkinson, William J., SA - 19428, 21 May 1888, TX, srv Kyles' Co., 3rd MS Vols.

Williams, Charles H., Mary E., WC - 12308, 29 Jun 1900, MS & SC - 3899 in TX, srv Co. D, 1st Bttn MS Rifle Vols.

Williams, Eli, Martha A., WC - 5628, 4 Aug 1888, MS, srv Daniels' Co., 2nd MS Vols.

Williams, George, Ida L., WC - 1752, 11 Feb 1887, MS, srv Sharpe's Co., 1st MS Rifles, OW I - #19125 Rej.

Williams, George D., SA - 7151, 4 Feb 1887, MD, srv Co. C, 1st MS Rifles.

Williams, Gideon, Sarah S., WC - 2080, 13 May 1887, TX, srv in the MS Vols.

Williams, James N., SC - 9429, 4 Feb 1887, AL, srv Co. E, 3rd MS Rifles as a Musician.

Williams, James W., Ellen M., WC - 6835, 6 Nov 1889 & SC - 1608, both MS, srv Co. E, 1st MS Vols.

Williams, John N., SC - 7725, 4 Feb 1887, AR, srv Co. E, 1st MS Inf.

Williams, Presley S., SA - 19787, 30 Jun 1888, TX, srv Jackson's Co., 2nd MS Vols.

Williams, Robert Fitzgerald, SC - 14996, 23 Aug 1887, CA, srv Co. A, 1st MS Inf as a Sgt.

Williams, Stephen C. L., Susan, WA - 17308, 10 Oct 1903 & SC - 14202, both TX, srv Co. 2nd MS Vols as a Pvt 1846-7, BLW #46585 - 160 - 47, sol. died 8 Aug 1903.

Williams, Thomas alias **Henry Basey, Elizabeth Basey**, WC - 10688, 1 Mar 1897, MS, SC - 6910, srv on *U.S.S. Raritan*.

Williams, Velareous, Melissa E., WA - 5735, 13 Jan 1888, TX, srv in the 1st MS Vols.

Williamson, George D., Susan C., WC - 3158, 17 Nov 1887 & SC - #8, both MD, srv Co. C, 1st MS Riflemen, Willis' Co.

Williamson, James, Martha H., WA - 8535, 25 Nov 1889, TN, srv Downing's Co.,

1st MS Rifles, OW IF - #779.

Williford, John W., Elizabeth, WC - 4530, 11 Jan 1888, TX, srv Co. K, 1st MS Vols.

Willis, Alexander Charles, Louisa, WA - 1617467, 27 Jun 1928, MS, srv Co. B, 5th U.S. Inf 1846-8, sol died in 1878 in Delhi, LA.

Willis, Piatte A., Sarah E., WC - 5648, 7 Jul 1888, MS, srv Co. I, in MS Vols.

Wilson, David, SA - 24963, 23 Jul 1897, MS, srv Crowson's Co., in a MS Bttn.

Wilson, George A., Castila A., WC - 5235, 24 Mar 1888, AR, srv Co. B, Bttn MS Riflemen.

Wilson, Gyles Lyons, Sevelia A., WC - 11415, 8 Aug 1890, TX, srv Co. C, 2nd MS Rifles, OW I - #23541 Rej.

Wilson, James C., SA - 24691, 19 Mar 1895, MS, srv Co. G in Indpt OH Vols.

Wilson, James W., SA - 24376, 19 Jun 1893, LA, srv Daniels' Co., MS Vols.

Wilson, John G., Margaret A., WA - 11097, 28 Jan 1893, MS, srv in MS Vols.

Winkler, Jacob alias **Jacob S., Eliza J.**, WA - 15426, 26 Dec 1899, MS & SC - 19355 in WI, srv Co. K, 1st TX Rifles.

Winn, Wesley, Mary, WA - 12004, 7 Apr 1894, MS, srv Davis' Co., 2nd MS Vols.

Wise, John F., SA - 23448, 11 Apr 1891, MS, no srv shown on the card.

Wolbrecht, Frederick, Elizzabeth, WA - 18682, 22 Apr 1907, MS, srv as a Pvt no other srv on the card.

Wolfe, Charles W., SC - 7788, 11 Apr 1887, MS, srv Pike's Co., 1st AR Vols.

Wolff, Alexander D., SC - 6892, 18 Mar 1887, TX, srv Co. D, 1st Bttn MS Vols.

Wolff, Francis A., Mary S., WC - 13654, 23 Jul 1903, FL & SC - 2080 in MS, srv Co. I, 1st MS Vols., OW IF - #6441.

Wood, Augustus, Elizabeth J., WC - 9901, 1 Feb 1894 & SC - 19059, both CA, srv Crump's or Clendenin's Co., 1st MS Vols.

Wood, James B., SC - 7422, 28 Mar 1887, MS, srv Co. C, 2nd MS Rifles, dupl. # C - 1716.

Wood, William W. W., Euphemia, WC - 2101, 28 May 1887, MS, srv Galbraith's Co., 5th LA Vols.

Woodliff, William C., SC - 10440, 23 Mar 1887, MS, srv Co. K, 1st MS Vols.

Woodsum, Oliver, see **Oliver Wood**, WC - 7827, MS.

Wooldridge, Samuel D., Catharine E., WC - 10947, 28 Mar 1892 & SC - 7516, both TX, srv Co. G, 1st MS Vols as a Cpl.

Word, Charles S., Drusella E., WC - 15955, 12 Jun 1913, TN & SC - 1498 in MS, srv Co. F, 1st MS Inf as Pvt.

Word, William W. W., Euphemie, WC - 2101, 28 May 1887, MS, srv Galbraith's Co., 5th LA Vols., see **Wood**.

Wren, Robert alias **Robert E., Mary E.**, WA - 11804, 2 Jan 1894, AR, srv 1st MS Vols.

Wright, Michael, Mary J., WC - 15211, 5 Feb 1909 & SC - 11108, both MS, srv Co. I, 2nd MS Inf as a Pvt.

Wyatt, Wilford D., SC - 15517, 12 Apr 1888, IL, srv Co. B, Bttn MS Rifles 1847-8, BLW #26014 - 160 - 47, CW Army IC - 656058 & WO - 1132747 for srv as Capt in Co. E, 7th IL Inf & Lt Col 7th IL Inf, sol. died 1 Nov 1904 in Quincy, IL.

Wynn, Osborn S., Mary Ann, WC - 6839, 11 Feb 1890 & SC - 11994, both MS, srv Co. B, 2nd MS Rifles, Davis' Co.

Wynne, Richard, SC - 7399, 8 Apr 1887, CA, srv Co. H, 2nd MS Inf.

Wynne, Robert P., Artamisa, WC - 6268, 26 Feb 1889, MS, srv Co. D, 1st MS Rifles.

Yancey, Joseph, Anna J., WC - 14463, 17 Dec 1904, AZ & SC - 10049 in CA, srv Taylor's Co., 1st MS Rifles.

Yancey, Tryon M., Rosa Bailey, WC - 13979, 4 May 1898 & SC - 18719, both CA, srv Taylor's Co., 1st MS Vol. Rifles.

Young, Andrew J., Sarah, WC - 6855, 7 Feb 1890 & SC - 14408, both in SC, srv Co. I, 2nd MS Vols.

Young, Jacob T., Mollie, WC - 2897, WC - 2897, 13 Sep 1887, KY, srv Co. D, 1st MS Vols.

Young, Joseph T., SA - 12189, 29 Apr 1887, CA, srv Taylor's Co., 1st MS Rifles.

Young, Thomas P., SA - 7238, 4 Feb 1887, MS, srv in the 1st TN Cav.

Yow, Henry, Mary Elizabeth, WC - 5838, 17 Sep 1887, MS, srv Green's Co., AL Vols.

Source: Virgil D. White, trans.; *Index to Mexican War Pension Files*; Waynesboro, TN: The National Historical Publishing Co.; 1989.

How to Access Mexican War Pension Files
From the National Archives

To obtain **NATF Form 85 - Military Pension and Bounty Land Warrant Records** from the National Archives:

1. Provide your name and postal mailing address.
2. Specify the form Number **(NATF 85)**.
3. State the number of forms you will need (Limit of 5 per order).

Forms may be ordered by:

1. Email addressed to **inquire@nara.gov**
   or
2. Letter addressed to the **National Archives and Records Administration, Attn: NWCTB, 700 Pennsylvania Avenue, NW, Washington, D.C. 20408-0001**.

Return completed Forms to the same address.

Mexican War Grave Locations and Registrations Within the State of Mississippi

The following was drawn from the Official Grave Registration List (RG 58, MF 1) (M.D.A.H.); Mexican War Grave Registrations (RG 60, vols. 688/689, Series 465) (M.D.A.H.); and H. Grady Howell, Jr.; *Mississippi Rifles, A History of Mississippi's Role in the Mexican War, 1846-1848*; unpublished manuscript. Please note that those soldiers referenced as "Buried in MS?" are actually buried in Mexico.

Abert, Charles H.; Buried in MS?

Abston, Albert L.; born ca 1826/died September 13, 1846; Died in Marshall County, MS.

Acker, Joel M.; died December 5, 1892; Buried in Aberdeen Odd Fellows Cemetery, Monroe County, MS.

Ainsworth, W. B.; Buried in Claiborne or Hinds County.

Alexander, Henley; born July 1, 1812/died July 3, 1882; Buried in Mt. Pleasant Cemetery, Webster County, MS.

Alexander, J. M.; died February, 1847; Marker in MS.

Alexander, Norris S.; born ca 1823/died May 20, 1904; Buried in Natchez City Cemetery, Adams County, MS.

Anderson, Garland; born July 9, 1784/died February 22, 1847; Marker in Cockrum Cemetery, DeSoto County, MS.

Anderson, I. L.; Buried in Wilkinson County, MS.

Anderson, Jabez S.; born February 18, 1826/died June 10, 1859; Buried in Cockrum Cemetery, DeSoto County, MS.

Anderson, T. J.; Buried in Atkinson Cemetery (?), Claiborne County (?), MS.

Anderson, Thomas J.; died September 12, 1909; Buried in Goldenlink Cemetery, Sharkey County, MS.

Andrews, George W.; Buried in Auburn Cemetery, Hinds County, MS.

Applewhite, Rev. James; born November 24, 1792/died February 19, 1872; Buried in Applewhite Cemetery, Carroll County, MS.

Archer, C. H.; born October 5, 1818/died January 14, 1892; Buried in Ebenezer Cemetery, Webster County, MS.

Arnold, Solomon A.; born November 18, 1828/died January 17, 1904; Buried in Pickens Cemetery, Holmes County, MS.

Arnold, Stephen B.; born August 27, 1808/died August 24, 1868; Buried in Oak Grove Cemetery, Carroll County, MS.

Arthur, Rufus K.; born ca 1819 (1820)/died August 31, 1855 (1858?); Buried in Cedar Hill Cemetery, Warren County, MS.

Askew, Joseph Jackson; born 1817/died 1884; Buried in Evergreen Cemetery, Carroll County, MS.

Atchison, J. W. R.; born 1837/died December 6, 1859; Buried in Gadberry Cemetery, Carroll County, MS.

Atkinson, A. B.; Buried in Claiborne County (?), MS.

Atkinson, Edward A.; born September 15, 1813/died April 20, 1871; Buried in Old Cumberland Cemetery, Webster County, MS.

Austin, William K.; born 1826/died 1852; Buried in Scooba Cemetery, Kemper County, MS.

Ayers, John B.; Buried in Old Salem Cemetery, Benton County, MS.

Bailey, John B.; born January 25, 1821/died July 11, 1856; Buried Old Stewart Cemetery, Wilkinson County, MS.

Banks, Robert B.; Buried in MS?

Barefield, Erwin; born ca 1814/died May 17, 1856; Died in Marion, MS.

Barksdale, William; born August 21, 1821/died July 3, 1863; Buried in Greenwood Cemetery, Hinds County, MS.

Barnes, John M.; Buried in MS?

Barron, Ezekiel; born April 28, 1816/died August 30, 1863; Buried in Bethlehem Cemetery, Choctaw County, MS.

Baskett, L. T.; born February 9, 1830/died December 27, 1902; Buried in Greenwood Oddfellows Cemetery, Leflore County, MS.

Bass, John E.; Buried in MS?

Bates, Charles J.; born January 20, 1826/died December 22, 1860; Buried in R. Bates Family Cemetery, Amite County, MS.

Bates, M. P.; born July 15, 1828/died December 16, 1900; Buried in Liberty Cemetery; Amite County, MS.

Batton, Daniel H.; born ca 1820/died March 18, 1850; Died in Issaquena County, MS.

Batts, Theodore D.; born November 25, 1824 (March 16, 1828?)/died September 10, 1872 (May 9, 1906?); Buried in Blanchard Cemetery, Bolivar County, MS.

Bell, James H.; born ca 1826/died October 21, 1853; Died in Yazoo County, MS.

Bell, William H.; Buried in MS?

Best, Berry O.; born August 6, 1826/died May 30, 1901; Died in Tallahatchie County, MS.

Best, Francis; Buried in Old Woodville Cemetery, Wilkinson County, MS.

Bigby, James N.; Buried in MS?

Bird, G. J. W.; Buried in MS?

Blackman, Dobson Coleman; born March 14, 1828/died October 15, 1902; Buried in Ebenezer Cemetery, Tate County, MS.

Blackwell, Nicholas; born March 28 , 1801/died January 6, 1849; Buried in Ingomar Cemetery, Union County, MS.

Blakely, James W.; Buried in MS?

Bobb, John Jr.; born May 30, 1823/died October 7, 1889; Died in Warren County, MS.

Bond, George D.; born May 17, 1802/died April 8, 1850; Buried in Glenwood Cemetery, Yazoo County, MS.

Bond, J. S.; died February 22, 1847; Marker (body ?) in Palestine Cemetery, Hinds County, MS.

Boone, Jordan R.; born May 5, 1827/died May 11, 1849; Buried in Rienzi Cemetery, Alcorn County, MS.

Booth, Pinkney; Buried in Hinds Chapel, DeSoto County, MS.

Booth, William; born January 17, 1803/died May 8, 1875; Buried in Booth Cemetery, Carroll County, MS.

Borman, Frederick; born February 27, 1813/died September 14, 1881; Buried in Cedar Hill Cemetery, Warren County, MS.

Bowen, Robert; Buried in MS?

Bowling, James; born ca 1814/died November 12, 1867; Buried in Natchez, Adams County, MS.

Boyd, George B.; born May 17, 1802/died April 8, 1850; Buried in Glenwood Cemetery, Yazoo County, MS.

Boyd, James; Buried in MS?

Brabham, James; born September 14, 1815/died February 28, 1859; Buried in Brabham Cemetery, Amite County, MS.

Bradford, Charles T.; Buried in MS?

Bradford, G. S.; born May 10, 1801/died September 25, 1874; Buried in Black Hawk Cemetery, Carroll County MS.

Bradford, G. S.; born May 3, 1815/died March 26, 1892; Buried in Spring Hill Cemetery, Webster County, MS.

Bradley, Thomas; Buried in Old Raymond Cemetery, Hinds County, MS.

Bragg, Benjamin; born June 4, 1822/died October 31, 1910; Buried in Pleasnat Grove Cemetery, Alcorn County, MS.

Branch, John S.; died February, 1847; Buried in MS?

Brewer, W. F.; born March 10, 1801/died September 25, 1874; Buried in Black Hawk Cemetery, Carroll County, MS.

Bright, William H.; Buried in MS?

Brister, Albert W.; born September 7, 1813/died January 6, 1902; Buried in Antioch Cemetery, Lawrence County, MS.

Brister, William; born November 11, 1804/died December 9, 1877; Buried in Antioch Cemetery, Lawrence County, MS.

Britnee, A. R.; born February 1, 1807/died October 8, 1886; Buried in Gray Cemetery, Carroll County, MS.

Bronihan, A. P.; died September 24, 1846; Buried in MS.

Brook, George; Buried in MS?

Brooks, J. R.; born 1821/died 1898; Buried in Center Ridge Cemetery, Kemper County, MS.

Brown, Albert; born May 27, 1819/died February 24, 1896; Buried in Black Water Cemetery, Kemper County, MS.

Brown, J. S.; Buried in MS?

Brown, Leonidas B.; born ca 1827/died September 19, 1860; Died in Tunica County, MS.

Brownlee, Adam; born ca 1816/died February 13, 1853; Died in Warren County, MS.

Bruce, J. W.; Buried in MS (Source *Port Gibson Correspondent*, May 27, 1847, p. 2).

Bryant, William J.; Buried in McCraine Cemetery, Wilkinson County, MS.

Buckley, Benjamin C.; born ca 1813/died November 22, 1868; Buried in Lawrence County, MS.

Burland, C. M.; Buried in MS?

Burnett, Phillip; Buried in MS?

Burney, Elonzo Pleasant; born ca 1824 (25?)/May 24 (30?), 1880; Buried in Damascus Cemetery, Copiah County, MS.

Burney, Richard S.; born ca 1823/died ?; Buried in Stovall Cemetery, Hinds County, MS.

Burns, J. S.; born March 30, 1814/died May 12, 1892; Buried in Old Cumberland Cemetery, Webster County, MS.

Burns, William L.; born September, 1808/September, 1901; Buried in Vaiden Cemetery, Carroll County, MS.

Burrell, James H.; born ca 1828/died February 2, 18?8; Died in Leake County, MS.

Burrell, Rouse; born ca 1805/died ca 1882; Buried in Buzzard Roost Cemetery, George County, MS.

Burrus, Phillip Johnson; born ca 1807; Buried in Yazoo City Cemetery; Yazoo County, MS.

Burwell, William T.; born September 13, 1819/died September 8, 1847; Marker in Cedar Hill Cemetery, Warren County, MS.

Butler, D. L.; died February, 1847; Buried in MS?

Butler, George Jasper; born February 6, 1828/died July 17, 1855; Buried in Butler Family Cemetery, Amite County, MS.

Butler, George P.; born April 2, 1780/died January 6, 1865; Buried in Butler Family Cemetery, Amite County, MS.

Butler, J. W.; born February 6, 1822/died October 2, 1883; Buried in Talbert Cemetery, Amite County, MS.

Cagle, Henry; born August 13, 1807/died May 1, 1888; Buried in Old Salem Cemetery, Carroll County, MS.

Cain, William F.; born May 15, 1810/died May 29, 1876; Buried in Woodlawn Cemetery, Pike County, MS.

Calcoate, James L.; born ca 1817/died November 28, 1858; Buried in Natchez City Cemetery, Adams County, MS.

Caldwell, Samuel S.; born ca 1822/died February 20, 1850; Died in Yazoo County.

Caldwell, W. L.; born October 5, 1812/died December 13, 1892; Buried in Vaiden Cemetery, Carroll County, MS.

Callaway, William M.; born July 31, 1813/died November 15, 1882; Buried in Union Methodist Cemetery, Kemper County, MS.

Calvert, Adam; born December 6, 1822/died October 20, 1880; Buried in Zion Cemetery, Kemper County, MS.

Calvert, James; born February, 1810/died March 22, 1891; Buried in Zion Cemetery, Kemper County, MS.

Campbell, Robert Bond; born ca 1829/died May, 1863; Killed in Siege of Vicksburg, Warren County, MS.

Capshaw, A. C.; Buried in Yellow Academy School Cemetery, Yazoo County, MS.

Carnathan, J. C.; born June 20, 1811/died March 12, 1877; Buried in Scooba Cemetery, Kemper County, MS.

Carson, Stephen D. (G.?); Buried in MS?

Caulfield, James D. (M.D.); born January 12, 1823/died August 15, 1862; Buried in Liberty Cemetery, Amite County, MS.

Chamberlin, M. A.; born 1814/died May 17, 1882; Buried in Chamberlin Cemetery, Kemper County, MS.

Chambley, Riley Salem; born July 31, 1813/died February 14, 1885; Buried in Carroll County, MS.

Champion, Sidney Smith; born March 23, 1823/died September 17, 1868; Buried in Champion Family Cemetery, Hinds County, MS.

Chance, Reuben W.; died September 25, 1846; Buried in MS?

Chapman, J. A.; Buried in MS?

Chapman, T. C.; Buried in MS?

Charlton, E. F.; Buried in MS?

Charlton, E. S.; Buried in MS?

Charlton, Richard; born December 21, 1825/died July 30, 1880; Buried in Raymond Odd Fellows Cemetery, Hinds County, MS.

Chew, Walter S.; born August 13, 1811/died July 22, 1880; Buried in Black Hawk Cemetery, Carroll County, MS.

Clariday, Richard; born ca 1816/died October 27, 1871; Died in Hinds County, MS.

Clark, Charles; born May 24, 1811/died December 18, 1877; Buried in Clark Family Cemetery, "Doro Plantation," Bolivar County, MS.

Clark, Francis; Buried in MS?

Clark, Henry D.; Buried in Yazoo County, MS.

Clark, John Calvin; born February 8, 1828/died July 17, 1873; Buried in Greenwood Cemetery, Jackson County, MS.

Clark, W. E.; Buried in MS?

Clay, Stephen W.; born September 25, 1806/died April 25, 1887; Buried in Enondale Cemetery, Kemper County, MS.

Clay, T. J.; born February 11, 1814/died September 14, 1880; Buried in Mt Hebron Cemetery, Kemper County, MS.

Clay, Thomas Wynne; born April 10, 1816/died August 10, 1855; Buried in Natchez City Cemetery, Adams County, MS.

Clements, William H.; born ca 1827/died August 13, 1878; Buried in Warren County, MS.

Coakley, John; born ca 1813/died May 24, 1880; Died in Hinds County, MS.

Cobb, Alpheus; Buried in (Carroll County?) MS.

Cobb, P. B.; born September 20, 1798/died March 3, 1887; Buried in Love Cemetery, DeSoto County, MS.

Cochrum, William; Buried in Hickory Flat Cemetery, Benton County, MS.

Coffey, Chesley Sheldon; born June 30, 1816/died February 10, 1869; Buried in Fayette Cemetery, Jefferson County, MS.

Cohron, John B.; born September 4, 1818/died February 9, 1858; Buried in New Salem Cemetery, Carroll County, MS.

Colburn, John C.; born March 21, 1811/died 1867; Buried in Evergreen Cemetery, Carroll County, MS.

Colburn, Samuel G.; born June 6, 1814/died February 16, 1864; Buried in Evergreen Cemetery; Carroll County, MS.

Cole, Andrew J.; born December 7, 1821/died August 29, 1894; Died in Lafayette County, MS.
Cole, Samuel M.; born ca 1827/died October 24, 1846; Buried in Holly Springs Cemetery, Marshall County, MS.
Coleman, James S.; Buried in MS?
Collier, John; born March 21, 1809/died March 9, 1892; Buried in Enon Cemetery, Carroll County, MS.
Collier, Jonathan; born 1824; Buried in Washington County, MS.
Collins, Robert A.; born February 20, 1821/died March 9, 1878; Buried in Grenada City Cemetery, Grenada County, MS.
Collinsworth, Addison; Died February , 1847; Reported buried in MS.
Colly, C. C.; died November 25, 1876; Buried in Cedar Rest Cemetery, Hancock County, MS.
Conger, J.; Buried in MS?
Conn, James W.; Buried in MS?
Conner, Daniel; died April 24, 1882; Died in Rankin County, MS.
Cook, Henry Felix; born January 14, 1819/died August 29, 1887; Buried in Cedar Hill Cemetery, Warren County, MS.
Cooke, A. D.; born March 6, 1817/died August 29, 1897; Buried in Enon Cemetery, Carroll County, MS.
Cooper, L. A.; Buried in MS?
Cooper, W. G.; Buried in MS?
Coopwood, Capt.; Buried in MS?
Coorpender, Lewis; Buried in MS.
Coorpender, William F.; born ca 1824/died April 30, 1862; Died in Hinds County, MS.
Corwine, A. B.; Buried in Yazoo County, MS.
Cotton, Charles F.; Buried in MS?
Couch, William; died February, 1847; Buried in MS?
Coulter, S. M.; Buried in Old Canton Cemetery, Madison County, MS.
Courtney, Thomas; Buried in MS?
Cox, David; born March 10, 1779/died January 13, 1848; Buried in Cox Cemetery, Amite County, MS.
Cozart, B. H.; Buried in New Salem Cemetery, Benton County, MS.
Crane, Charles; born December 25, 1812/died November 11, 1895; Buried in Antioch Cemetery, Lawrence County, MS.
Creight, William; born ca 1802/died ?; Buried in Old City Cemetery (Aberdeen), Monroe County, MS.
Crittenden, Harvey S.; Buried in MS?
Crosby, Rev. G. L.; born 1808/died 1862; Buried in Rosehill Cemetery, Lincoln County, MS.
Crowley, James W.; born November 10, 1814/died May 10, 1888; Buried in Marvin Hill Cemetery, Webster County, MS.
Crump, George P.; Buried in MS?
Currie, L.; born October 18, 1811/died February 27, 1880; Buried in Enondale Cemetery, Kemper County, MS.

Daniel, E. M.; born July 6, 1808/died June 30, 1882; Buried in Bluff Springs Cemetery, Kemper County.

Dart, John; Buried in MS?

Daughdrill, W. S.; born October 18, 1808/died December 16, 1892; Buried in Shiloh Cemetery, Lawrence County, MS.

Daughtry, Enos; born December 6, 1806/died December 16, 1893; Buried in Bass Cemetery, Lawrence County, MS.

Daughtry, John M.; Buried in MS?

Davenport, Thomas; born September 5, 1820/died October 17, 1898; Buried in Fayette Cemetery, Jefferson County, MS.

Davis, Edward A. C.; born June 12, 1847/"Died while in the service of his country at Saltillo, Mexico;" Marker in Matthews Family Cemetery, Benton County, MS.

Davis, Reuben; born January 18, 1813/died October 14, 1890; Buried in Aberdeen Odd Fellows Rest Cemetery, Monroe County, MS.

Davis, Robert H.; born ca 1824/died 1865; Buried in Warren County, MS.

Delay, William; born May 3, 1814/died September 15, 1871; Buried in St. Peter's Cemetery, Lafayette County, MS.

Dennis, Joe G.; Buried in Mahoney Cemetery, Leflore County, MS.

Denson, John S.; Buried in MS?

Dodds, Stephen, Buried in MS?

Donly, Sam I.; born October 22, 1820/died June 2, 1888; Buried in Malmaison Cemetery, Carroll County, MS.

Donnelly, James W.; Buried in Wilkinson County, MS.

Doss, Washington L.; born ca 1826/died January 25, 1900; Died in West Point, Clay County, MS.

Dotson, W. M.; born June 16, 1830/died July, 1921; Buried in Greenwood Cemetery, Hinds County, MS.

Douglass, E. (Rev.); born June 9, 1814/died September 1, 1900; Buried in Shiloh Cemetery; Lawrence County, MS.

Downing, Jacob; born January 3, 1812/died July 30, 1890; Buried in Cedar Hill Cemetery, Warren County, MS.

Downing, Joseph A.; died September 22, 1846; Buried in MS?

Downing, Reuben Newman; born December 20, 1820/died September 9, 1853; Buried in Bolton Family Cemetery, Hinds County, MS.

Dubose, Daniel D.; died September 23, 1846; Buried in MS?

Dugan, John; Buried in MS?

Dunavant, P. J.; died February, 1847; Buried in MS?

Dunlap, E.; Buried in MS?

Dunleve, S.; born ca 1820/died May 30, 1858; Buried in Natchez City Cemetery, Adams County, MS.

Dupree, James H.; Buried in MS?

Durden, Jonathan; born ca 1813/died October 4, 1876; Died in Carroll County, MS.

Eakin, Robert T.; born March 8, 1806/died August 5, 1892; Buried in Carroll County, MS.

Edmondson, Charles M.; born July 11, 1822/died August 1, 1905; Buried in Williamsburg Methodist Church Cemetery, Covington County, MS.

Edwards, Benjamin F.; born ca 1818/died March 30, 1880; Died in Hinds County, MS.

Edwards, Benjamin Harrison; born May 9, 1825/died April 24, 1910; Buried in Old Florence Cemetery, Rankin County, MS.

Edwards, Samuel M.; Buried in MS?

Eggleston, Richard H.; born December 12, 1828/died February 23, 1847; Marker in Cedar Hill Cemetery, Warren County, MS.

Eiland, Bryant; born May 25, 1806/died November 23, 1878; Buried in Milligen Springs Cemetery, Webster County, MS.

Eilbott, Leon; Buried in MS?

Elliott, Joseph W.; Born March 26, 1803/died November 6, 1880; Buried in Arnold Family Cemetery, Bolivar County, MS.

Ellis, Charles H.; Buried in MS?

Ellis, Thomas B.; born 1823/died 1850 (?); Buried in Sivley Cemetery, DeSoto County, MS.

Erwin, John; died May 18, 1900; Buried in Bluff Springs Cemetery, Carroll County, MS.

Erwin, W. T.; Buried in Stone Cemetery, Claiborne County, MS.

Estelle, William M.; born ca 1825/died March 23 (28?), 1868; Buried in Greenwood Cemetery, Hinds County, MS.

Evans, Ezekiel W.; died August, 1882; Buried in Houston City Cemetery, Chickasaw County, MS.

Evans, James A.; born ca 1827/died September 16, 1872; Died in Clay County, MS.

Everett, George C.; born September 5, 1825/died November 28, 1888; Buried in Everett Cemetery, Carroll County, MS.

Everett, Turner G.; born December 17, 1821/died August 26, 1885; Buried in Everett Cemetery, Carroll County, MS.

Fairchild, Joseph B.; born ca 1826/died April 27, 1862; Buried in Old Fairchild Cemetery, Hinds County, MS.

Falkner, William C.; born ca 1825/died November 6, 1889; Buried in Old Ripley City Cemetery, Tippah County, MS.

Fancher, James H.; born 1821/died April 15, 1882; Buried in Black Hawk Cemetery, Carroll County, MS.

Farish, C.; died November 18, 1889; Buried in Rosemont Cemetery, Wilkinson County, MS.

Farrar, George Harding; died September 30, 1846; Died in Rankin County, MS.

Farthing, R. E.; born 1814/died 1894; Buried in Old Silver Creek Cemetery, Lawrence County, MS.

Felts, Kindred; born 1811/died 1901; Buried in Bluff Springs Cemetery, Carroll County, MS.

Felts, Robert; Buried in MS?

Ferguson, James A.; born 1819/died 1883; Buried in Old Plank Cemetery, Carroll County, MS.

Fisher, Robert; born February 5, 1810/died December 22, 1847; Died in Yazoo County, MS.

Flemming, William H.; Buried in MS?

Fletcher, Crawford; Buried in MS?

Fletcher, Lorenzo Dow; born April 10, 1828/died December 14, 1910; Buried in Kosciusko City Cemetery, Attala County, MS.

Floyd, Samuel H.; born January 19, 1823/died March 1, 1855; Buried in Raleigh Cemetery, Smith County, MS.

Folkes, Benjamin; born July 12, 1821/died October 13, 1908; Buried in Cedar Hill, Warren County, MS.

Fondren, S. R.; Buried in MS?

Forester, Alfred; born 1805/died November 21, 1872; Buried in Wake Forest Cemetery, Webster County, MS.

Foster, John; born 1826/died September 25(23?), 1903; Buried in Greenwood Cemetery, Hinds County, MS.

Fowler, William; born March 13, 1818/died August 19, 1874; Buried in Double Springs Cemetery, Webster County, MS.

Fox, Robert; Buried in Natchez City Cemetery, Adams County, MS.

Freidricks (Fredericks), Jacob; ca 1820/died October, 1853; Died in Hinds County, MS.

Friar, William J.; ca 1820/died November 6, 1886; Died at Greenville, Washington County, MS.

Fullilove, D. D.; born October 23, 1817/died February 17, 1887; Buried in Vaiden Cemetery, Carroll County, MS.

Fullilove, Thomas J.; born August 20, 1807/died October 21, 1888; Buried in Vaiden Cemetery, Carroll County, MS.

Furguson, Shadric B.; born May 15, 1807/died June 26, 1872; Buried in Union Methodist Cemetery, Kemper County, MS.

Gaffney, Edward; Buried in MS?

Galbraith, James D.; Capt., Co. E "Sparrow Volunteers," 4th LA Vols.; Buried in Washington Cemetery, Adams County, MS.

Gallman, W. B.; Believed buried in Palestine Cemetery, Hinds County, MS.

Gardner, Thomas S.; born September 22, 1807/died August 12, 1859; Buried in New Salem Cemetery, Carroll County, MS.

Garratt, Evans; died February, 1847; Buried in MS?

Garrett, William; born 1800/died 1865; Buried in Bass Cemetery, Lawrence County, MS.

Gartley, William; died October 3, 1856; Buried in the Mound Bluff Cemetery, Madison County, MS.

Geofray, Jean; born ca 1810/died December 15, 1852; Buried in Ratton Bayou Cemetery, Hancock County, MS.

Gibbs, Charles Hanson (Hansen); born September 22, 1822/died October 10, 1855 (8?); Buried in Old Raymond Cemetery, Hinds County, MS.

Gibson, Ralph J.; born December 12, 1825/died December 14, 1880; Buried in McComb Hollywood Cemetery, Pike County, MS.

Gill, Robert H.; born 1807/died December 18, 1849; Buried in Pleasant Hill Cemetery, Leake County, MS.

Gill, W. G.; born November 26, 1812/died October 24, 1872; Buried in Rush Cemetery, Kemper County, MS.

Gillespie, Samuel; born August 17, 1818/died August 12, 1868; Buried in Black Hawk Cemetery, Carroll County, MS.

Gilmore, William; born February 18, 1808/died April 29, 1890; Buried in Chapel Hill Cemetery, Kemper County, MS.

Girault, George R.; Obituary published in *Port Gibson Standard* December 13, 1857; Buried in Wintergreen Cemetery, Claiborne County, MS.

Gladden, Adhley H.; died April, 1862; Buried at Corinth, Alcorn County, MS.

Godwin, J. H.; born February 20, 1825/died March 16, 1860; Buried in Gower Cemetery, Warren County, MS.

Gordin, George Gains; born January 7, 1817/died April 1, 1883; Buried in Vaiden Cemetery, Carroll County, MS.

Gordon, James J.; born ca 1828/died ?; Died in Warren County, MS.

Gordon, John L.; born November 30, 1823/died May 2, 1883; Buried in Vaiden County Cemetery, Carroll County, MS.

Goubeneaux, Charles; born November 19, 1825/died July 22, 1854; Buried in Masonic Cemetery, Lawrence County, MS.

Graves, J. H.; Buried in MS?

Gray, Joe; Buried in Union Baptist Cemetery, Kemper County, MS.

Gray, William; born September 21, 1796/died September 5, 1857; Buried in White Family Cemetery; DeSoto County, MS.

Greaves, Stephen Arne Decatur; born January 30, 1817 (January 7, 1819?)/died November 17, 1880; Buried in Chapel of the Cross Cemetery, Madison County, MS.

Gregg, Robert; Buried in MS?

Griffin, Daniel B.; born October 10, 1816/died November 3, 1876; Buried in Black Jack Cemetery, Neshoba County, MS.

Griffith, Richard; born January 11, 1814/died June 29, 1862; Buried in Greenwood Cemetery, Hinds County, MS.

Grisham, William H.; died Sepetember, 1846; Buried in MS?

Grizzle, Wilson P.; born July 29, 1828/died September 9, 1872; Buried in Hatley Cemetery, Monroe County, MS.

Guion, Walter Burling; born July 16, 1806/died October, 1864; Buried in Natchez City Cemetery, Adams County, MS.

Gullett, Richard; born 1828/died August 9, 1918; Buried in Webster County, MS.

Halsey, Seymour; born October 8, 1802/died July 16, 1852 (72 ?); Buried in Cedar Hill Cemetery, Warren County, MS.

Hamilton, Charles B.; born December, 1818/died February 12, 1851; Buried in Lebanon Cemetery, DeSoto County, MS.

Hammond, Job; Buried in MS?

Hampton, William Henry; born ca 1822/died September 26, 1855; Died in Warren County, MS.

Hamson, W. D.; died February, 1847; Buried in MS?

Hancock, John A. G.; born ca 1823/died May 4, 1899; Died in Lauderdale County, MS.

Handley, Seborn J.; born November 13, 1813/died June 28, 1848; Buried in Blackjack Cemetery, Yazoo County, MS.

Hanks, Charlie; Buried in Goodwyn Cemetery, DeSoto County, MS.

Hanks, Talliaferro; born January 8, 1822/died December 28, 1905; Died in Carroll County, MS.

Hardy, Robert W.; born June, 1814/died August 18, 1885; Buried in the Old Field Cemetery, Webster County, MS.

Harlin, John; born May 24, 1802/died April 16, 1880; Buried in Carroll County, MS.

Harper, William B.; Buried in Sullivan Family Cemetery, Neshoba County, MS.

Harrell, Josiah J.; born 1832/died March 31, 1859; Buried in Vaiden Cemetery, Carroll County, MS.

Harrell, Wells C.; born December 5, 1813/died April 9, 1895; Died in Hinds County, MS.

Harrell, William; born September 13, 1813/died March 1, 1886; Buried in Mt. Olive Cemetery, Kemper County, MS.

Harris, Lewis Bingaman; born March 19, 1827/died May 10, 1891; Buried in Hazlehurst Cemetery (Old Section), Copiah County, MS.

Harris, Thomas G.; born August 26, 1810/died April 12, 1877; Buried in Hopewell Cemetery, Carroll County, MS.

Harris, W. H. (Rev.); born March 14, 1808/died June 29, 1855; Buried in Hopewell Cemetery, Carroll County, MS.

Harrison, G. W.; Buried in MS?

Harriss, William H.; born May 14, 1809/died July 16, 1852; Buried in Black Hawk Cemetery, Carroll County, MS.

Hartzog, Major A.; born December 1, 1811/died September 7, 1897; Buried in Silver Creek Methodist Cemetery, Lawrence County, MS.

Hasty, William H.; born ca 1825/died June 14, 1892; Died in Rankin County, MS.

Hays, A. J.; Buried in MS?

Hays, J. C.; Buried in MS?

Heaton, Joseph; died September 23, 1846; Buried in MS?

Henderson, John L.; born ca 1805/died July 1, 1846; Died in Warren County, MS.

Henry, R. C.; born August 22, 1827/died September 20, 1907; Buried in Camp Ground Cemetery, Lafayette County, MS.

Herring, Joshua A.; born January 5, 1819/died March 19, 1854; Buried in Vaiden Cemetery, Carroll County, MS.

Herrod, Andrew J.; born May 4, 1827/died June 6, 1911; Died in Warren County, MS.

Hickey, William V.; Buried in MS?

Hill, Albert; born September 11, 1815/died September 7, 1848; Buried in Hill Family Cemetery, Carroll County, MS.

Hill, Eli; born July 3, 1822/died March 28, 1852; Buried in Hill Cemetery, Carroll County, MS. (A tombstone in Greenwood Cemetery, LeFlore County, MS, reads **Elijah Bell Hill**, a Mexican War Veteran, born 1805).

Hill, Josiah; born January 2, 1808/died January 12, 1863; Buried in Hill Cemetery, Carroll County, MS.

Hill, M. C. (Z. ?); born 1818/died December 21, 1906; Buried in Deans Cemetery, Tishomingo County, MS.

Hindman, Robert Holt; born June 20, 1822/died May 8, 1849; Buried in Tippah

County, MS.

Hindman, Thomas C.; born October 10, 1792/died July 18, 1855; Buried in Booker Cemetery, Tippah County, MS.

Hines, Harrison H.; born 1811/died January 18, 1850; Buried in Black Hawk Cemetery, Carroll County, MS.

Hobbs, Calvin; died November 9, 1891; Died at Beauregard, Copiah County, MS.

Hodge, William I.; born 1821/died ?; Died in Wilkinson County, MS.

Hoffman, Warren; Buried in (Carroll County ?) MS.

Hoggany, B.; died February, 1847; Buried in MS?

Holland, Charles; born March 21, 1820/died December 6, 1884; Buried in Shady Grove Cemetery, George County.

Holland, George H.; born June 26, 1818/died February 16, 1865; Buried in New Hope Cemetery, Webster County, MS.

Holliday, John; born August 10, 1803/died March 16, 1881; Buried in Odd Fellows Rest Cemetery, Monroe County, MS.

Holliday, Shack; died January, 1901; Buried in pauper's section, New Albany Cemetery, Union County, MS.

Hollingsworth, David M.; Buried in Yazoo County, MS.

Hollingsworth, E.; Buried in (Carroll County ?) MS.

Holt, John Saunders; born December 5, 1826 (May 17, 1817?)/died February 27, 1886 (March 1, 1886?); Buried in Natchez City Cemetery, Adams County, MS.

Holt, John T.; ca 1818/died October 22, 1884; Buried in Crystal Springs Cemetery, Copiah County, MS.

Howard, B. D.; Buried in Carroll County, MS?

Howard, L. T.; Buried in Carroll County MS?

Howell, Joseph D.; Buried in MS?

Howell, W. W.; born February 1, 1822/died July 8, 1909; Buried in Odd Fellows Cemetery, Oktibbeha County, MS.

Hudspeth, John; Buried in MS?

Hutchinson, Irenius R. (Or Junius R.?); born ca 1820/died July 1, 1862; Died in Wilkinson County, MS.

Hutchison, W. F.; Buried in MS?

Ingraham, William W.; died February, 1847; Buried in MS?

Ingram, Amaziah; Obituary published in *Port Gibson Standard* April 9, 1867; Buried in Wintergreen Cemetery, Claiborne County, MS.

Ingram, N.; Buried in Raymond Cemetery, Hinds County, MS.

Irvin, Tilman J.; born March 18, 1830/died June 12, 1906; Buried in Center Hill Cemetery, Monroe County, MS.

Jackson, John H.; Buried in Wilkinson County, MS.

Jackson, Mathew; born 1797/died January 18, 1853; Buried in Scooba Cemetery, Kemper County, MS.

Jackson, Nedom; born 1805/died June 11, 1881; Buried in Mt. Pleasant Cemetery, Kemper County, MS.

Jackson, Obert; born 1802/died October, 1859; Buried in Scooba Cemetery, Kemper County, MS.

Jacobs, Solomon D.; born November 23, 1797/died May 22, 1858; Buried in

Cleremont (Plantation) Cemetery, Adams County, MS.

Jenkins, Caradine T.; born June, 1827/died October 17, 1905; Buried in Salem Cemetery, Choctaw County, MS.

Jeter, John; born ca 1823/died August 6, 1870; Died in Warren County, MS.

Johnson, Alfred; born February 8, 1809/died March 30, 1891; Buried in Mt. Zion Cemetery, Newton County, MS.

Johnson, D. B.; Buried in MS?

Johnson, James; born August 30, 1812/died May 15, 1884; Buried in Evergreen Cemetery, Carroll County, MS.

Johnson, Peter W.; born ca 1817/March 10, 1885; Died in Carrollton, Carroll County, MS.

Johnson, Robert; Buried in Trinity Cemetery, Smith County, MS.

Johnson, William K.; Buried in Attala County, MS.

Johnston, Jacobs; born May 10, 1764/died April 12, 1851; Buried in Pleasant Hill Cemetery, DeSoto County, MS.

Jones, D. A.; died February, 1847, Buried in MS?

Jones, George H.; Buried in Wilkinson County, MS.

Jones, O. W.; Buried in Carroll County, MS?

Jones, Seaborn D.; born 1809/died May 19, 1867; Buried in Wilkinson County, MS.

Jones, Stephen; Buried in MS?

Jones, Thomas L.; born February 18, 1821/died July 12, 1846; Buried in St. Peter's Cemetery, Lafayette County, MS.

Jones, William H.; born ca 1822/died April 6, 1874; Died in Lafayette County, MS.

Joyce, Robert A.; died February, 1847; Buried in MS?

Keep, Henry; ?.

Kelly, Samuel; Buried in New Salem Cemetery, Hinds County, MS.

Kelly, Zachariah; born September 15, 1818/died February 8, 1913; Buried in Evergreen Cemetery, Wilkinson County, MS.

Kennedy, John; Buried in MS?

Kenner, D. F.; Buried in MS?

Key, A. M.; Buried in Old Raymond Cemetery, Hinds County, MS.

Keyes, William McCord; born October 19, 1825/died August 17, 1850; Buried in Aberdeen Odd Fellows Cemetery, Monroe County, MS.

Kilgore, Josiah Greer; died June 3, 1848; Buried in Kilgore Cemetery, Clay County, MS.

Kilvey, James H.; Buried in MS?

Kincannon, James; born September 26, 1832/died June 30, 1905; Buried in Verona Cemetery, Lee County, MS.

Kinchloe, David Anderson; born October 18, 1823/died September 9, 1878; Buried in Sardis Rose Hill Cemetery, Panola County, MS.

King, George; Buried in Burnsville Cemetery, Tishomingo County, MS.

Kirk, J. H.; died 1891; Buried in Mt. Pleasant Cemetery, Kemper County, MS.

Kirk, J. W.; born ca 1827/died June 21, 1881; Died in Yazoo County, MS.

Knight, John E.; born July 16, 1816/died November 21, 1893; Buried in Bahala Chapel Cemetery, Lawrence County, MS.

Knowles, Steven D.; born 1813/died September 23, 1852; Buried in Knowles

Cemetery, Monroe County, MS.

Kopperl, Charles; born 1814/died January 1, 1865; Buried in Vaiden Cemetery, Carroll County, MS.

Laird, Eli; born 1828/died May 13, 1899; Buried in Greenwood Cemetery, Hinds County, MS.

Laird, Isham C.; Buried in MS?

Lamb, G. B.; born August 27, 1812/died December 15, 1891 (1901?); Buried in North Union Cemetery, Webster County, MS.

Lambert, James; born February 15, 1813/died June 17, 1889; Buried in Lambert Cemetery, Lawrence County, MS.

Lane (Lain), James H.; born ca 1804 (1825?)/died July 25, 1848; Buried in Rienzi Cemetery, Alcorn County, MS.

Lanehart, Adam; born ca 1822/died March 3, 1847; Died in Wilkinson County, MS.

Langford, Joseph H.; Buried in MS?

Langley, William H.; born ca 1829/died January 16, 1847; Died in Warren County, MS.

Larkin, Earl Willis; born May 16, 1812/died December 2, 1887; Buried in Silver Creek Methodist Cemetery, Lawrence County, MS.

Lawrence, William A.; Buried in Wilkinson County, MS.

Lawson, Charles; born ca 1820/died July 8, 1846; Died in Warren County, MS.

Leonard, Josah; born September 11, 1795/died January 23, 1859; Buried in Cantrell Cemetery, Scott County, MS.

Lewis, D. B.; Buried in MS?

Lewis, Edward P.; Buried in MS?

Lewis, G. P.; born July 20, 1815/died July 18, 1894; Buried in New Hope Cemetery, Webster County, MS.

Lindsey, Hugh Nelson; born December 6, 1823/died July 23, 1854; Buried in Draughn Family Cemetery, Wilkinson County, MS.

Lindsey, William; Probably buried in MS.

Locke, Jacob J.; Buried in MS?

Lockheart, John M. M. D.; born November 10, 1810/died March 2, 1849; Buried in Hopewell Cemetery, Carroll County, MS.

Long, Samuel B.; born July 2, 1817/died September 9, 1858; Buried in Long Cemetery, Carroll County, MS.

Lott, William; born ca 1828/died March 3, 1851; Died in Carroll County, MS.

Love, David E.; Buried in Carroll County, MS?

Love, Thomas Neely; born June 16, 1818/January 23, 1855; Buried in Friendship Cemetery, Lowndes County, MS.

Loving, Christopher B.; born March 26, 1826/died September 30, 1855; Buried in Carroll County, MS.

Lowe, William; died May 11, 1847; Died in Hinds County, MS.

Lowell, Henry H.; Buried in MS?

Lowery, Mark Perrin; born December 30, 1828/died February 27, 1885; Buried at Blue Mountain, MS.

Luckin, John J.; born July 4, 1823/died June 2, 1899; Died in Newman, Hinds County, MS.

Lyman, Charles; Buried in Shiloh Cemetery, Claiborne County, MS.

Lynch, Isaac; born ca 1822/died January 2, 1847; Died in Warren County, MS.

Lytle, Armstrong; born ca 1816/died August 2, 1849; Died in Yazoo County, MS.

Maben, William; Buried in MS?

Mabry, T. F.; Buried in MS?

McBride, James W.; born July 29, 1816/died January 18, 1892; Buried in Maben Cemetery, Webster County, MS.

McBride, John A.; born 1810/died January 15, 1884; Buried in Hopewell Cemetery, Carroll County, MS.

McCain, James; born May 22, 1802/died August 8, 1857; Buried in Old Corinth Cemetery, DeSoto County, MS.

McCaulla, William; born 1820/died 1857; Buried in Salem Cemetery, Carroll County, MS.

McClanahon, T. O.; Buried in MS?

McClung, Alexander Keith; born June 11, 1811/died March 25, 1855; Buried in Cedar Hill Cemetery, Warren County, MS.

McCorkle, Andrew H.; born May 27, 1814/died May 24, 1876; Buried in Hopewell Cemetery, Carroll County, MS.

McDaniel, Henry D.; born December 10, 1825/died March 31, 1888; Buried in Old Terry Creek Church Cemetery, Pike County, MS.

McDonald, James; born November 14, 1814/died August 21, 1906; Buired in Rose Hill Cemetery, Lauderdale County, MS.

McFarland, Alexander B.; born ca 1825/died June 24, 1846; Died in Warren County, MS.

McGary, Martin H.; born ca 1801/died July 6, 1870; Buried in Williams' Springs Cemetery, Choctaw County, MS.

McGinnis (Magonos); Joseph (alias) L.; born March 8, 1825/died April 15, 1899; Buried in Cedar Hill Cemetery, Warren County, MS.

McGowen, John; born October 3, 1799/died February 19, 1862; Buried in New Bethlehem Cemetery, DeSoto County, MS.

McGuin, John E. C.; born ca 1818/died April 15, 1858; Died in Tate County, MS.

McInnis, Malcolm; born ca 1818/died June 20, 1847; Buried in Old Raymond Cemetery, Hinds County, MS.

McKay, Daniel A.; born February 11, 1820/died February 16, 1904; Died in Wesson, MS.

McKinney, W. H.; Buried in MS?

McLaughlin, J. A.; Buried in MS?

McLeod, O. C.; born July 5, 1802/died May 31, 1859; Buried in Sharkey Cemetery, Carroll County, MS.

McManus, John L.; Buried in MS?

McNair, Evander; born April 15, 1820/died November 13, 1902; Buried in Pike County, MS. (Also recorded to have died July 30, 1917 and buried in the Old Asylum Cemetery, Hinds County, MS.)

McNorris (McNarris?), John; Buried in MS?

McNulty, F. J.; died February 22, 1847; Marker in Raymond Cemetery, Hinds County, MS.

McWillie, Capt.; Buried in MS?

Machan, Henry L.; Buried in Old Salem Cemetery, Benton County, MS.

Mahaffey, John T.; born December 28, 1803/died April 7, 1849; Buried in Shiloh Cemetery, Lawrence County, MS.

Mallett, J. H.; Buried in MS?

Malone, J. F. (T.?); Buried in MS?

Manning, Melie; born 1785/died 1879; Buried in Manning Cemetery, Walthall County, MS.

Manning, Reuben S.; born October 17, 1805/died February 21, 1859; Buried in Manning Private Cemetery, DeSoto County, MS.

Maples, John Wesley; born ca 1823/died ?; Died in Warren County, MS.

Maples, W. J.; Buried in Hollywood Cemetery, Pike County, MS.

Maples, Wesley I.; Buried in Yokena Cemetery, Warren County, MS.

Mapp, L. J.; Buried in MS?

Markham, Hugh Mercer; born ca 1815/died January 19, 1864; Died in Hinds County, MS.

Markham, John B.; Buried in MS?

Martin, Charles; born ca 1821/died September 22, 1876; Died in Union County, MS.

Martin, Francis Marion Sr.; born December 18, 1825/died July 3, 1896; Buried at Cato, Rankin County, MS.

Martin, G. W.; born 1826/died April 14, 1924; Buried in Slade Cemetery, Lamar County, MS.

Martin, John A.; Buried in MS?

Martin, Plummer M.; Buried in MS?

Martin, Russell M.; Buried in MS?

Massie, Nat; Buried in MS?

Mathews, Frederick; died September 23, 1846; Buried in MS?

Mattingly, John F.; born ca 1818/died April 25, 1857; Died in Rodney, Jefferson County, MS.

Maum, James W.; Buried in Oakdale Cemetery, Rankin County, MS.

Maxey, Thomas R.; born June, 1809/died March 25, 1888; Buried in Bethel Cemetery, Benton County, MS.

Maxwell, Thomas H.; born December 8, 1811/died February 27, 1893; Buried in Bethel Cemetery, Lawrence County, MS.

Mayfield, Isaac; born November 29, 1803/died June 18, 1893; Buried in Amory Masonic Cemetery, Monroe County, MS.

Meachem, Silas; died September 22, 1846; Buried in MS?

Mellon, Thomas Armour; born November 13 (18?), 1826/died May 15, 1873; Buried in Old Raymond Cemetery, Hinds County, MS.

Mercer, W. N. (M.D.); U.S.N.; Born ca 1808/died ca 1875; Buried in Laurel Hill Chapel Cemetery, Adams County, MS.

Miles, William R.; born March 25, 1817/died January 1, 1900; Buried in Glenwood Cemetery, Yazoo County, MS.

Miller, James Madison; December 15, 1815/died May 10, 1870; Buried in Evergreen Cemetery, Wilkinson County, MS.

Miller, John R.; born April 20, 1824/died October 1, 1864; Buried in Palestine Cemetery, Hinds County, MS.

Miller, Joseph; Buried in MS?

Miller, William H.; Buried in Wilkinson County, MS.

Mobley, Middleton Rufus; born September 21, 1821/died August 19, 1887; Died in Yazoo County, MS.

Money, Pierson; born August 8, 1809/died December 31, 1893; Buried in Evergreen Cemetery, Carroll County, MS.

Mooney, Egbert; born April 3, 1797/died April 3, 1882; Buried in Sandford & Bullock Cemetery, Covington County, MS.

Moore, C.; born ca 1822/died September 26, 1886; Died at Taylor, Lafayette County, MS.

Moore, James P.; born ca 1821/died November 13, 1886; Died in Tate County, MS.

Moore, Robert L.; born ca 1815/died February 23, 1847; Buried in Cedar Hill Cemetery, Warren County, MS.

Moreland, J. P.; born February 26, 1826/died March 29, 1899; Buried in Moreland Cemetery, Calhoun County, MS.

Morgan, Hiram; born ca 1816/died March 29, 1862; Died at Rolling Fork, MS.

Morris, Howard; Buried in MS?

Morris, Joseph W.; Buried in MS.?

Moseley, J. P.; Buried in MS?

Mott, Christopher Haynes; born June 22, 1826/died May 5, 1862; Buried in Hill Crest Cemetery, Marshall County, MS.

Munce, Thomas S.; born ca 1810/died August 14, 1858; Buried in Natchez City Cemetery, Adams County, MS.

Murdock, William M.; born December 28, 1805/died October 17, 1857; Buried in Murdock Cemetery, Carroll County, MS.

Murphree, Leonard H.; born 1827/died August 17, 1902; Buried in Okolona Odd Fellows Cemetery, Chickasaw County, MS.

Murphy, Daniel D.; born August 8, 1814/died July 24, 1859; Buried in Vaiden Cemetery, Carroll County, MS.

Nail, A. S.; born July 19, 1816/died August 12, 1889; Buried in Bethel Cemetery, Carroll County, MS.

Nairne, William; born June 24, 1816/died January 20, 1887; Buried in Bass Cemetery, Lawrence County, MS.

Naron, G. W.; born April 16, 1828/died March 1, 1911; Buried in Maben Cemetery, Webster County, MS.

Nathaniel, Wells (M.D.) (Nathaniel Wells?); born January 25, 1805/died December 20, 1864; Buried in New Salem Cemetery; Carroll County, MS.

Neal, Samuel; born September 22, 1811/died February 25, 1889; Buried in New Hope Cemetery, Lawrence County, MS.

Neely, A. J.; Buried in MS?

Neill, G. F.; born August 10, 1810/died April 27, 1877; Buried in Evergreen Cemetery, Carroll County, MS.

Nelms, W. B.; born 1811/died August 8, 1883; Buried in Bethany Cemetery, Webster County, MS.

Nelson, A. R.; born January 4, 1815/died October 23, 1903; Buried in Edgeworth Cemetery, Webster County, MS.

Newman, Albert M.; Buried in MS?

Newman, Solomon; ca 1824/died May 17, 1860; Died in Brookhaven, MS, Buried in Wilkinson County, MS.

Newson, Lewis; born June 19, 1824/died July 14, 1847; Buried in Smith Cemetery, Lawrence County, MS.

Neyland, Robert H.; born February 1, 1824/died November 17, 1920; Buried in McCraine Cemetery, Wilkinson County, MS.

Nicholson, John T.; born 1826/died February 16, 1857; Buried in Black Hawk Cemetery, Carroll County, MS.

Noland, Avery; born January 18, 1828/died September 1, 1883; Died at Kirkwood, Madison County, MS.

Norfleet, John R.; born 1805/died April 11, 1859; Buried in Norfleet Family Cemetery, Marshall County, MS.

Nutters, William M.: Buried in MS?

Odoms, Jesse; Buried in MS?

O'Keefee, John; born August 3, 1817/died June 9, 1863; Buried in Heggie Cemetery, Carroll County, MS.

Oliver, William D.; born 1811/died August 1, 1882; Buried in Evergreen Cemetery, Carroll County, MS.

O'Neal, Bardin; born March 14, 1806/died August 12, 1876; Buried in Jefferson Cemetery, Carroll County, MS.

Orr, William; Buried in Carroll County, MS?

Otto, John F.; born March 31, 1845/died June 19, 1925; Buried in Harmony Cemetery, Carroll County, MS.

Owens, Robert; Buried in MS?

Park, R. H.; born 1816/died August 19, 1854; Buried in Old Union Cemetery, Monroe County, MS.

Parker, James; died April 15, 1894; Buried in Woodlawn Cemetery, Pike County, MS.

Parkinson, Richard; Buried in MS?

Parr, R. E.; Buried in MS?

Patterson, Andrew B.; died June 18, 1852; Died in Warren County, MS.

Patterson, William H. H.; born ca 1819/died February 26, 1856; Died in Lowndes County, MS.

Patton, Alfred; born June 28, 1820/died April 12, 1885; Buried in Terry Cemetery, Hinds County, MS.

Payne, John; born December 8, 1807/died March 19, 1880; Buried in Payne Cemetery, Lee County, MS.

Peace, John; died February, 1847; Buried in MS?

Percell, George Dowell; born June, 1811/died March, 1886; Buried in Black Hawk Cemetery, Carroll County, MS.

Perryman, Felix G.; born March 4, 1812/died July 31, 1884; Buried in Gray's Creek Baptist Church Cemetery, DeSoto County, MS.

Peyton, Elijah A.; born May 9, 1823 (October 26, 1827?)/died February 25, 1906;

Buried in Greenfield Cemetery, Washington County, MS.

Phillips, Seaborne Moses; born ca 1823/died May 23, 1861; Buried in Greenwood Cemetery, Hinds County, MS.

Phillips, William M.; died February, 1847; Buried in MS?

Pierce, Hugh W.; died November 7, 1871; Died in Hinds County, MS.

Pierce, Simeon; born ca 1827/died February 2, 1910; Buried in Starkville, Oktibbeha County, MS.

Pinson, J. S.; born September 26, 1806/died June 29, 1885; Buried in Ebenezer Cemetery, Webster County, MS.

Pleasants, Frank P.; born ca 1823/died June 9, 1877; Died in Carroll County, MS.

Poindexter, John J.; Buried in MS?

Poor, F. J.; Buried in MS?

Porter, William C.; Buried in MS?

Postell, Elijah C.; born November 18, 1824/died February 14, 1894; Buried in Souls Chapel Cemetery, Madison County, MS.

Potts, Samuel; Buried in MS?

Power, Stephen Francis; born August 12, 1828/died January 21, 1900; Buried in Natchez City Cemetery, Adams County, MS.

Preston, John; Buried in MS?

Preston, Thomas; born March 28, 1790/died December 23, 1857; Buried in Ainsworth Cemetery, Rankin County, MS.

Price, Charles M.; born July 10, 1811(14?)/died December 20, 1850; Buried in Greenwood Cemetery, Hinds County, MS.

Puckett, Anthony S.; born February 20, 1827 (22?)/died October 19, 1853; Buried in Brandon Cemetery, Rankin County, MS.

Pyles, Milton; born ca 1802/died October 20, 1879; Died in Yazoo County, MS.

Quinnelly, Steve; Buried in Mt. Pisgah Cemetery, Clarke County, MS.

Quitman, John Anthony; born September 1, 1798 (9?)/died July 17, 1858; Buried in Natchez City Cemetery, Adams County, MS.

Raine, Henry T.; born ca 1825/died June 20, 1850; Died in Warren County, MS.

Rairdon, Patrick; Buried in MS?

Ramsey, George W. (M.D.); died September 25, 1846; Buried in Carroll County, MS?

Randle, Peyton; born August 31, 1813/died January 7, 1886; Buried in Vaiden Cemetery, Carroll County, MS.

Randolph, Thadeus D.; Buried in MS?

Raney, James; died 1852; Buried in Big Creek Cemetery, Hinds County, MS.

Ray, Chesley; born ca 1826/died January 16, 1847; Died in Warren County, MS.

Rayborn, Willis; born 1811/died August 13, 1906; Buried in Providence Cemetery, Lawrence County, MS.

Read, Jesse; born ca 1823/died August 18, 1895; Buried in Gerrinton, Carroll County, MS.

Redditt, P. E.; born June 16, 1815/died August 3, 1855; Buried Redditt Cemetery, Carroll County, MS.

Reed, T. W.; died February 13, 1853.

Reed, Thomas; born April 11, 1817/died August 14, 1891; Buried in Natchez City

Cemetery, Adams County.

Reid, Hugh James; born February 25, 1827/died November 16, 1905; Buried in Odd Fellows Cemetery, Lexington, Holmes County, MS.

Reid, W. I.; born October 13, 1818/died February 4, 1872; Buried in Black Hawk Cemetery, Carroll County, MS.

Reinharot (Reinhardt), Michael; born September 15, 1790/died October 24, 1852; Buried in Lanier Cemetery, Marshall County, MS.

Revill, Joseph C.; Buried in MS?

Rice, John; born ca 1823/died November 22, 1847; Died in Warren County, MS.

Riddle, John R.; born December, 1804/died January 31, 1865; Buried in Booth Cemetery, Carroll County, MS.

Riley, Jim; Buried in Ebenezer Cemetery, DeSoto County.

Rimes, John F.; born ca 1820/died January 21 (25?), 1885; Died in Terry Cemetery, Hinds County, MS.

Rimes, W. L.; Buried in Terry Cemetery, Hinds County, MS.

Ripley, H. D.; Buried in MS?

Ripley, W. E.; Buried in MS?

Roberts, Benjamin F.; Buried in MS?

Roberts, G. B.; born April 23, 1814 (1816?)/died September 6, 1885; Buried in North Union Cemetery, Webster County, MS.

Roberts, J. M.; Buried in MS?

Robertson, William B.; born March 30, 1808/died April 4, 1882; Buried in Black Hawk Cemetery, Carroll County, MS.

Robinson, Francis M.; died February, 1847; Believed buried in MS.

Robinson, William L.; Buried in Old Salem Cemetery, Benton County, MS.

Rogers, R. T.; born September 20, 1810/died May 16, 1890; Buried in New Salem Cemetery, Carroll County, MS.

Rogers, William P.; born December 17, 1819/died October 4, 1862; Buried in Corinth, Alcorn County, MS.

Ronderburge, J. I.; Buried in Itta Bena Cemetery, Leflore County, MS.

Rose, Terrell; born July 14, 1812/died November 29, 1898; Buried in Alva Cemetery, Webster County, MS.

Ross, W. R.; born September 16, 1814/died December 24, 1888; Buried in Midway Cemetery, Carroll County, MS.

Rousseau, William James; born June 1, 1829/died February 16, 1916; Buried in Starkville Odd Fellows Cemetery, Oktibbeha County, MS.

Royston, Thomas A.; Buried in New Salem Cemetery, Benton County, MS.

Russell, A.; born May 1, 1801/died December 26, 1893; Buried in New Hope Cemetery, Lawrence County, MS.

Russell, C. H.; Buried in MS?

Russell, Daniel R.; born July 20, 1821/died June 6, 1870; Buried in Evergreen Cemetery, Carroll County, MS.

Sanders, William H.; died August 17, 1868; Buried in Camp Ground Cemetery, Tishomingo County, MS.

Saunders, R. M.; Buried in MS?

Saunders, T. W.; Buried in MS?

Schad, William; Buried in MS?

Schmaling, Joseph; born February 13, 1815/died December 19, 1885; Buried in Cedar Hill Cemetery, Warren County, MS.

Scott, William Henry; Buried in MS?

Scovel, Joseph; born ca 1803/died ca 1904; Buried in Greenwood Cemetery, Jackson County, MS.

Seater, Robert; born July 2, 1816/died February 12, 1892; Buried in Canton Cemetery, Madison County, MS.

Seay, William; died February, 1847; Reportedly buried in MS?

Sellers, William; Buried in MS?

Sellman, Eli; Buried in MS?

Sellman, T.; Buried in MS?

Shackelford, Richard D.; born ca 1822/died November 23, 1854; Died in Hinds County, MS.

Shaifer, George Wilson Humphreys; born October 22, 1822 (January 3, 1822/died ?); Buried in Claiborne County, MS.

Sharman, James A.; born ca 1818/died August 15, 1863; Died in Quitman, MS.

Sharp, John McNitt; born November 22, 1795/died May 20, 1862/ Buried in family plot on *Cedar Grove Plantation*, Yazoo County, MS.

Shaw, Jesse T.; born August 22, 1810/died January 23, 1879; Buried in Bethany Cemetery, Webster County, MS.

Shaw, Robert J.; born ca 1817/died August 24, 1888; Died at Mashaulaville, MS (?).

Shields, R. W.; Buried in MS?

Shook, Robert L.; Buried in Yazoo County, MS.

Sillers, Joseph; born ca 1822/died May 6, 1865; Died in Warren County, MS.

Simpson, T. L.; Buried in MS?

Sinclair, P.; Buried in MS?

Skelton, William R.; Buried in MS?

Smith, Andrew; born December 9, 1793/died December 30, 1865; Buried in Black Hawk Cemetery, Carroll County, MS.

Smith, Douglas; born 1802/died 1888; Buried in Smith-Mathews Cemetery, Carroll County, MS.

Smith, E. W.; Buried in MS?

Smith, Marshall; Buried in MS?

Smith, T. C.; Buried in MS?

Snedicon, Platt; died September 24, 1846; Buried in MS?

Sojourner, Sylvester D.; born February 27, 1820/November 30, 1899; Died in Copiah County, MS.

Speight, Jesse; born September 22, 1798/died May 10, 1847; Buried in Aberdeen Odd Fellows Cemetery, Monroe County, MS.

Spencer, George W.; born June 26, 1810 (1816?)/died March 29, 1862 (1882?); Buried in Monte Vista Cemetery, Webster County, MS.

Spencer, James B.; Buried in Old Salem Cemetery, Benton County, MS.

Spencer, William P.; Buried in MS?

Spurlock, Walter; Buried in Wilkinson County, MS.

Stafford, S. B.; Buried in MS?

Stamps, Anthony; born 1806/died 1887; Buried in Lambert Cemetery, Lawrence County, MS.

Steele, James J. V.; born ca 1823/died May 11, 1868; Died in Hinds County, MS.

Stephens, J. Z.; born August 18, 1828/died July 3, 1908; Buried in Plank Cemetery, Carroll County, MS.

Stevens, Levi H.; Buried in MS?

Stevenson, J. M. Jr.; Buried in MS?

Stewart, J. H.; Buried in MS?

Stewart, James D.; died June 25, 1905; Buried in Greenwood Cemetery, Hinds County, MS.

Stewart, James E.; Buried in MS?

Stewart, John; Buried in MS?

Stockard, John P.; born ca 1820/died January 27, 1860; Buried in Lafayette County, MS.

Stone, Dudley; born February 29, 1805/died May 16, 1884; Buried in Midway Cemetery, Carroll County, MS.

Stone, J.; Buried in MS?

Stout, Henry; Buried in MS?

Streater, Frank R.; born April 10, 1822/died October 17, 1907; Buried in Black Hawk Cemetery, Carroll County, MS.

Stribeck, F. J.; Buried in MS?

Strong, Elisha; born 1792/died 1878; Buried in Aberdeen Odd Fellows Cemetery, Monroe County, MS.

Strong, William A.; born October 7, 1823/died July 5, 1865; Buried in Old Greenwood Cemetery, Leflore County, MS.

Strong, William Miller; born ca 1816/died June 27, 1878; Died in Tippah County, MS.

Stubblefield, Stephen P.; Buried in Yazoo County, MS.

Stubblefield, William Henry; born May 23, 1820/died May 8, 1907; Buried in Black Jack Baptist Church Cemetery, Yazoo County, MS.

Suit, Samuel C.; Buried in MS?

Sullivan, C. O.; Buried in MS?

Summerville (Somerville), James; born October 25, 1822/died March 28, 1877; Buried in Evergreen Cemetery, Carroll County, MS.

Sumrall, T. S.; Buried in MS?

Swann, Thomas; born ca 1811/died January 19, 1876; Died in Tippah County, MS.

Tanner, James C.; born ca 1820/died March 2, 1877; Died in Warren County, MS.

Tarver, Elisha L.; born December 15, 1813/died September 26, 1851; Buried in Tarver Cemetery, Amite County, MS.

Taylor, Benjamin F.; born ca 1827/died February 22, 1857; Died in Carroll County, MS.

Taylor, Green B.; Buried in MS?

Taylor, James H. R.; Buried in MS?

Teague, A. W.; Buried in MS?

Temmille, Joseph P.; died September 22, 1846; Buried in MS?

Terrill, W. H.; born September 13, 1813/died September 17, 1863; Buried in Black Hawk Cemetery, Carroll County, MS.

Terry, Lampkin Straughn; born January 23, 1828/died August 12, 1893; Buried in Coleman Cemetery, Attala County, MS.

Terry, T. C.; born May 1, 1816/died December 10, 1884; Buried in Bahala Chapel Cemetery, Lawrence County, MS.

Thomas, Samuel Beauchamp; born July 17 (18?), 1825/died June 13, 1907; Buried in Terry Cemetery, Hinds County, MS.

Thomas, Westley H.; Buried in Jesse Thomas Cemetery, Pike County, MS.

Thompson, Henry B.; Buried in Warren County, MS.

Thompson, J. H.; Buried in Hinds County, MS.

Thompson, James; Buried in MS?

Thompson, John; born ca 1820/died December 22, 1875; Died at Oxford, Lafayette County, MS.

Thornhill, Hillary B.; born August 4, 1824/died March 7, 1859; Buried in Owens' Cemetery, Walthall County, MS.

Thweatt, Uriah W.; born August 23, 1822/died May 3, 1909; Buried in Hurricane Baptist Church Cemetery, Attala County, MS.

Tigner, Clark H.; born 1820/died 1862; Buried in Tigner Cemetery, Wilkinson County, MS.

Tinnin, Hugh Perry; died January 4, 1893; Died in Rankin County, MS.

Title, Thomas H.; died February, 1847; Buried in MS?

Treadaway, William M.; born January 5, 1829/died April 16, 1917; Buried in Cockrum Cemetery, DeSoto County, MS.

Trotter, Henry G.; died Feburary, 1847; Buried in MS?

Tuberville, B. Lewis; Buried in Wilkinson County, MS.

Tucker, Marsden S.; born ca 1821/died January 14, 1847; Died in Warren County, MS.

Turner, L. M.; died September 21, 1846, Buried in MS?

Turner, S. T.; born November 3, 1809/died April 5, 1891; Buried in Eden (Edon ?) Cemetery, Carroll County, MS.

Tyler, Marvin; born February 13, 1807/died February 27, 1893; Buried in Shiloh Cemetery, Lawrence County, MS.

Tyree, John M.; Buried in MS?

Ultschey, Albert; born February 2, 1824/died February 15, 1884; Buried in Ultschey Family Cemetery, Scott County, MS.

Ussrey, T. J.; Buried in MS?

Van Dorn, Earl; born September 17, 1820/died May 7, 1863; Buried in Wintergreen Cemetery, Claiborne County, MS.

Van Hook, Marcus A.; born 1810/died 1896; Buried in Greenwood Cemetery, Hinds County, MS.

Vance, George W.; born June 29, 1826/died November 30, 1864; Buried in Liberty Baptist Church Cemetery, Carroll County, MS.

Vance, John D. Gray; born February 8, 1829/died August 6, 1897; Buried in Sparta Cemetery, Grenada County, MS.

Varnell, Francis W.; Co. E, 5th LA Vols.; Buried March 7, 1901, U.S. National

Cemetery, Natchez, Adams County, MS.

Vaughn, Thomas H.; born October 23, 1805/died September 19, 1896; Buried in Poplar Springs Cemetery, Carroll County, MS.

Ventress, Edward L.; Buried in MS?

Verrell, T. E.; born November 30, 1812/died March 5, 1882; Buried in Old Cumberland Cemetery, Webster County, MS.

Vinson, James W.; Buried in MS?

Waddill, A. M.; Buried in Raymond Odd Fellows Cemetery, Hinds County, MS. (Same as **M. A. Waddell**; died October 11, 1918)?

Wade, G. D. (Rev.); Buried in Pickens Cemetery, Holmes County, MS.

Wade, William Bartee; born ca October 9, 1823/died 1866; Buried in Friendship Cemetery, Lowndes County, MS.

Walker, Benjamin F.; died 1918; Buried in Tate County, MS.

Walker, William K.; born August 17, 1820/died February 12, 1893; Died in Warren County, MS.

Wall, James; born March 18, 1819/died September 8, 1862; Buried in McCormick Cemetery, Carroll County, MS.

Walters, John H.; born (January 12 ?) June 23, 1827/died March 7, 1912; Buried in New Hope Cemetery, Monroe County, MS.

Ward, Edward Wesley; died July 4, 1917; Buried in Oak Hill Cemetery, Yalobusha County, MS.

Ward (Word ?), John L.; born February 10, 1802/died November 23, 1883 (5 ?); Buried in Vaiden Cemetery, Carroll County, MS.

Ware, John R.; born October 13,1819/died April 15, 1900; Died in Carroll County, MS; Buried in Black Hawk Cemetery, Carroll County, MS.

Ware, Wilson; Buried in MS?

Watson, J. M.; Buried in MS?

Watson, Marshall D.; born May 20, 1816/died August 16, 1888; Buried in Cumberland Cemetery, Webster County, MS.

Watts, J. J.; Buried in MS?

Watts, N. G.; born ca 1816/died January, 1866; Buried in Warren County, MS.

Waugh, James; Buried in MS?

Weir, Hugh H. (M.D.); born 1807/died December 25, 1858; Buried in Vaiden Cemetery, Carroll County, MS.

Wells, Nathaniel; (See **Wells Nathaniel**).

West, Nathaniel; born January 21, 1802/died November 7, 1891; Buried in Harper (Nebo ?) Cemetery, Carroll County, MS.

White, Theodore; Buried in Sulphur Springs Cemetery, Wilkinson County, MS.

White, Thomas; Buried in MS?

White, Warren; Buried in family plot , Camden Highway, Madison County, MS.

Whitehead, W. W.; born October 9, 1799/died November 11, 1870; Buried in Whitehead Cemetery, Carroll County, MS.

Whitfield, Hatch; born May 5, 1794 (1798 ?)/died November 30, 1878; Buried in Whitfield (or Reynold's) Cemetery, Monroe County, MS.

Whitsett, James L.; born 1816/died May 11, 1857; Buried in Kemper County, MS.

Wilkinson, William H.; Buried in Wilkinson County, MS.

Williams, Charles S.; born 1823/died October 19, 1846; Buried in Old Raymond Cemetery, Hinds County, MS.

Williams, George; born ca 1820/died November 9, 1885; Died at Mickens, MS.

Williams, Gideon; Buried in MS?

Williams, J. W.; born October 17, 1816/died February 23, 1884; Buried in Silver Creek Methodist Cemetery, Lawrence County, MS.

Williams, James; Buried in MS?

Williams, James W.; born ca 1820/died October 14, 1889; Died in Rankin County, MS.

Williams, R. P.; born 1825/died November 28, 1856; Buried in Williams Cemetery, Carroll County, MS.

Williamson, Rufus R.; born ca 1817/died October 19, 1853; Died in Yazoo County, MS.

Willis, George; Buried in Carroll County, MS?

Willis, John C.; born June 30, 1819/died January 16 (17 ?), 1906; Buried in Cedar Hill Cemetery, Warren County, MS.

Wilson, G. M.; born December 22, 1812/died June 5, 1900; Buried in Wake Forest Cemetery, Webster County, MS.

Wilson, M. A.; born August 15, 1811/died September 11, 1886; Buried in Vaiden Cemetery, Carroll County, MS.

Winans, William; Buried in MS?

Winn, John C.; Buried in MS?

Withers, Lewis W.; born April 17, 1818/died November 9, 1871; Buried in Greenwood Cemetery, Hinds County, MS.

Wofford, James P.; born May 16, 1817/died April 3, 1901; Buried in Mt. Pleasant Cemetery, Webster County, MS.

Wofford, M.; Buried in Gulf Cemetery; Benton County, MS.

Wofford, W. M. (Col.); Buried in Gulf Cemetery, Benton County, MS.

Wolf, Francis A.; Buried in MS?

Wood, James B.; born December 23, 1822/died April 2, 1909; Buried in New Greensboro Cemetery, Webster County, MS.

Woodruff, J. O.; Buried in MS?

Wooldridge, S. D.; Buried in MS?

Wright, R. H.; Buried in MS?

Wynns, Robert P.; born ca 1823/died October 26, 1882; Died in Lauderdale County, MS.

Yates, L. D.; born April 11, 1817/died November 11, 1890; Buried in Clarkson Cemetery, Webster County, MS.

Young, J. A.; born September 24, 1812/died July 11, 1875; Buried in Edgeworth Cemetery, Webster County, MS.

Addendum

A RESOLUTION of the Legislature of the State of Mississippi, to the discharged soldiers of the first Mississippi Rifles.

Resolved by the Legislature of the State of Mississippi, That as a token of the high regard and approbation of the people of the State, each discharged soldier of the first Regiment of Mississippi Rifles, be, and he is hereby permitted to retain the Rifle and accoutrements used by him in the campaign against Mexico, in which he so gloriously distinguished himself, and which is hereby presented to him in the name of the State of Mississippi.

Approved March 4, 1848.

Source: *Laws of Mississippi, 1848.*

★

Meeting of the Mexican War Veterans

An adjourned meeting of the soldiers of the Mexican war, met in the Senate chamber in the city of Jackson, on Saturday, at 12 p.m. February 12, A.D. 1876. Colonel S. B. Thomas, chairman, and B. F. Edwards, Secretary. After reading the minutes of the preceding meeting the following names were enrolled, to-wit:

FIRST MISSISSIPPI REGIMENT.

Co. A--H. C. Stubblefield.

Co. B--J. D. Stewart, John T. Holt.

Co. C--J. M. Daughtry.

Co. D--James Summerville, John Cokely, F. M. Adair, I. G. Adair, John Vance, Tol. Hanks, T. J. Kyle, W. C. Harrell, J. Z. George,--Russell.

Co. E--E. McNair, J. E. McNair, J. M. Hooker, Dan. Conner, S. M. Coulter, Harry Hasty.

Co. G--F. M. Martin, H. D. Ripley, S. B. Thomas, B. F. Edwards, J. F. Rimes, Joshua Stone, J. S. Brown.

Co. H--E. A. Peyton, J. J. Larkin, Isaac Johnson, James Dupree.

SECOND MISSISSIPPI REGIMENT.

Co. A--A. B. Short.

Co. F--Sim. Easterling, Arch. Chaney.

Co. - --John A. G. Hancock.

Co. I--L. S. Terry, L. D. Fletcher, U. W. Threatt, T. B. Hight, C. Haws, J. G. Gilleland.

Co. K--J. B. Deason, J. L. Deason, L. B. Harris.

Co. - --J. M. Lidell, T. J. Lidell, A. Y. Long, W. G. Carson, E. B. Carson, H. D.

Leaverett.

FIRST MISSISSIPPI BATTALION.
Co. I--Calvin Hobbs, Thomas Courtney.
Co. - --Reuben Coleman, Wilis Merriman, Charles Harrison, W. H. Landers.

FIRST TENNESSEE REGIMENT.
Co. C--R. Charlton, A. J. Bettersworth, J. M. H. Martin.
Co. E--Samuel Powell.

FIRST LOUISIANA REGIMENT.
Co. - --John Conray.

FIRST TEXAS REGIMENT.
Co. E--F. E. Strippleman.

The following resolutions, offered by Gen. J. Z. George, were adopted:

Resolved, 1. That the services of the soldiers who served in the U.S. army in the Mexican war of 1846-'47, now residing in the State of Mississippi, be and they are hereby formed into an association to be called "The Association of Mexican War Veterans," and that each of the soldiers above named be and he is hereby made a member of said association upon his signifying his assent thereto to the secretary.

Resolved, 2. That the object of this association shall be for mutual help and assistance, and for the purpose of affording such aid as may be in our power to those of us who may be in needy and Indigent circumstances, and who may be unable to gain a living by labor, and also to assist the surviving widows and minor children of our deceased comrades.

Resolved, 3. That we believe that the time has now come when, according to the preceding of the history of the United States, the survivors of the Mexican war are entitled to pensions; and the same right exists on behalf of the widows and minor children of those who are dead.

Resolved, 4. That the officers of the association shall be a President, a 1st Vice-President, a 2d Vice-President, and Secretary and Treasurer, and they shall hold their offices for the term of one year, and until their successors are elected.

Resolved, 5. That there shall be an annual meeting of the members of this association, said meeting to be held in the city of Jackson, unless otherwise ordered for any particular meeting; at which meeting the officers of the Association shall be elected and such other business be transacted as may be deemed by the meeting necessary. Said meeting shall be held on the 22d of February in each year, unless the same occurs on Sunday, and in that event it shall be on the 23d of that month.

Resolved, 6. That there shall be an executive committee, composed of the officers of the Association, who shall have full power to act for the Association between the meetings of the same.

Resolved, 7. That it shall be the duty of the said executive committee to see that a memorial is prepared to Congress on the subject of pension for the Mexican war veterans.

Resolved, 8. That the Secretary of this meeting give notice through the public press of the State of the proceedings of this meeting, and request that all the survivors of the soldiers of said war, residing in the State, shall report their names and post offices to him, together with the company and regiment to which each belonged.

Resolved, 9. That is shall be the duty of said Executive Committee to take steps to ascertain the names and residences of all of said survivors and also the pecuniary condition of each, and also the names of the widows of such as are dead.

Resolved, 10. That the present meeting proceed to elect the officers of the Association for the ensuing year.

And thereupon the following officers were elected for the Association for the year 1876: Col. J. B. Deason, of Brookhaven, President; Col. S. B. Thomas, of Jackson, 1st Vice-President; Col. Sam. Powell, of Hernando, 2d Vice-President; Col. E. A. Peyton, of Jackson, Secretary, and Col. J. D. Stewart, of Jackson, Treasurer.

Col. Deason offered the following resolutions, which were adopted:

Resolved, 1. That the Executive Committee be requested to use their best efforts to obtain from the different railroads in the United States, approaching the city of Philadelphia, free passes for the veterans in the war with Mexico, to visit said city during the Centennial celebration of 1876, from Mississippi.

Resolved, 2. That the Executive Committee be authorized to confer with Gen Robert Patterson, with a view of making arrangements for all the Mexican war veterans who visit the city of Philadelphia from Mississippi, during the present Centennial, for their care and comfort during their stay at that place.

The following resolution, by Col. Stewart, was adopted.

Resolved, That the executive committee be directed to petition the Legislature of the State, in behalf of this association, to request our Senators and Representatives in Congress to urge the passage of a law by the national Legislature, granting pensions to the Mexican war veterans.

On motion, the President appointed Col. Sam. Powell, S. B. Thomas and J. D. Stewart, a committee to draft a Constitution and By-Laws for this association, and present the same at its next annual meeting.

On motion, the Secretary was directed to furnish the city papers with a copy of the proceedings of this meeting, with the request that the papers throughout the State notice the same.

On motion, the association adjourned to meet in Jackson, Feb. 22d. A.D., 1877.

J. B. DEASON, Pres't.

E. A. Peyton, Sec'y.

Source: *The Daily Clarion* (Jackson, MS); February 16, 1876.

★

The First Mississippi Rifles in Mexico.

We devote much of our space to-day to the publication of a complete and officially certified roll of the First Mississippi Rifles in Mexico--a regiment that was commanded by Col. Jefferson Davis, and that numbered nearly one thousand as brave and gallant men as ever fought for the flag. This record is not only of historic interest, but the publication just now will facilitate the making of proofs by the beneficiaries of the Mexican pension law, as it gives them the date of muster, etc. To the characteristic forethought of Hon. E. Barksdale, all who are interested are indebted for this publication. Source: *The Clarion* (Jackson, MS); Wednesday, March 2, 1887.

"Likenesses" of Mississippi Mexican War Veterans

Courtesy Library of Congress and Bobby Roberts

James Patton Anderson
Born: February 16, 1822
Died: September 20, 1872

Raised and commanded the 1st Battalion Mississippi Volunteers in the Mexican War. Colonel of the 1st Regiment Florida Infantry, C.S.A., in the Civil War, he rose to the rank of major-general in the Confederate army.

William Barksdale
Born: August 21, 1821
Died: July 3, 1863

Appointed Assistant Commissary with the rank of captain in the 2nd Regiment Mississippi Volunteer Infantry in the Mexican War. During the Civil War he entered the Confederate army as colonel of the 13th Regiment Mississippi Infantry. Rising to the rank of brigadier general, he was mortally wounded leading his brigade in its historic charge through the wheatfield at Gettysburg, PA, on July 2, 1863.

Courtesy Mississippi Department of Archives and History

Alexander Blackburn Bradford
Born: June 2, 1799
Died: July 9, 1873

Served in the Seminole War of 1836 and was elected major of the 1st Regiment
Mississippi Volunteer Infantry during the Mexican War. He was in the Provisional
Congress (House of Representatives) of the Confederate States of America and ended
the war serving in the Mississippi legislature.

Courtesy Mrs. Emmett E. McCool

Robert Bond Campbell
Born: ca 1829
Died: June 28, 1863

Served as a private in Company H, the "Union Grays," 2nd Regiment Mississippi Volunteer Infantry in the Mexican War. Elected Captain of Company C, 40th Regiment Mississippi Infantry, C.S.A., in the Civil War, he was promoted to Major of the regiment before being killed in action during the Siege of Vicksburg.

Courtesy Sidney S. Champion IV

Sidney Smith Champion
Born: March 23, 1823
Died: September 17, 1868

He served as a private in Company G, the "Raymond Fencibles," 1st Regiment Mississippi Volunteer Infantry in Mexico. Entering the Civil War as a sergeant in Co. I, 28th Regiment Mississippi Cavalry, he rose through the ranks as lieutenant and captain to the lieutenant-colonelcy of the regiment. One of the most significant battles of the Civil War was fought on his homeplace near Edwards, MS, the Battle of Champion Hill (May 16, 1863).

192

Charles Clark
Born: May 24, 1811
Died: December 18, 1877

Colonel of the 2nd Regiment Mississippi Volunteer Infantry during the Mexican War, he served as a brigadier-general and major-general of Mississippi State Troops. Wounded in the Battle of Baton Rouge (LA) on August 5, 1862, he was later elected a war-time governor of Mississippi (1863-1865).

Courtesy John D. and Mark Coffey

Chesley Sheldon Coffey
Born: July 1, 1816
Died: February 10, 1869

Elected as 2nd Lieutenant and promoted to Captain of Company G, the "Thomas Hinds Guards," 2nd Regiment Mississippi Volunteer Infantry in the Mexican War. Elected Captain Company D, the reactivated "Thomas Hinds Guards," 19th Regiment Mississippi Infantry, C.S.A., he was wounded and captured in the Battle of Williamsburg, VA, May 5, 1862.

Henry Mansfield Cook
Born: December 29, 1825
Died: 1902

Served as a private in Company K, the "Tombigbee Volunteers," 1st Regiment Mississippi Volunteer Infantry in Mexico. He was elected 2nd Lieutenant of Company E, "Carrington's Company," Baylor's Regiment Texas Cavalry, C.S.A., in the Civil War.

Jefferson Davis (and his wife Varina ca 1845)
Born: June 3, 1808
Died: December 6, 1889

Colonel of the 1st Regiment Mississippi Volunteer Infantry, he led his unit to glory
in Mexico in the Battles of Monterey (September, 1846) and Buena Vista (February,
1847,). Appointed Major-General of the Army of Mississippi in early 1861, not long
thereafter he was elected President of the Confederate States of America.

Courtesy Mississippi Department of Archives and History

Reuben Davis
Born: January 18, 1813
Died: October 14, 1890

Colonel of the 2nd Regiment Mississippi Volunteer Infantry in the Mexican War, during the Civil War he was appointed brigadier-general, and later major-general, of Mississippi State Troops.

Courtesy Sarah H. Parker and Virginia Hewitt Jones

Reuben Newman Downing (and friends ca early 1850's)

Born: December 20, 1820

Died: September 9, 1853

Captain of Company G, the "Raymond Fencibles," 1st Regiment Mississippi Volunteer Infantry, he was wounded in the Battle of Monterey, MX, on September 21, 1846. This image was taken shortly before the 1853 Yellow Fever Epidemic which swept the South and took his life. In the center of the picture is Col. H. W. Vick of Vicksburg and on the right is Murrey Smith.

198

Courtesy Linda Goff

Benjamin Harrison Edwards (and his wife Mariah)
Born: May 9, 1825
Died: April 24, 1910

He served as a private in Company E, the "State Fencibles," 1st Regiment Mississippi Volunteer Infantry in Mexico. He later served as a private in Company D, the "Rankin Farmers," 6th Battalion Mississippi Infantry (later Co. D, 46th Regiment Mississippi Infantry) C.S.A.

Courtesy Tommy Covington, Ripley Public Library

William Clark Falkner
Born: July 6, 1826
Died: November 6, 1889

Served as 1st Lieutenant, Company E "Tippah Guards," 2nd Regiment Mississippi Volunteer Infantry during the Mexican War. He began the Civil War as Captain of Company F, the "Magnolia Rifles," 2nd Regiment Mississippi Infantry, C.S.A.. He later became Colonel of the regiment and went on to command the 1st Regiment Mississippi Partisan Cavalry (aka 7th Regiment Mississippi Cavalry).

Courtesy Zaida Woodward Newell

Lorenzo Dow Fletcher
Born: April 10, 1828
Died: December 14, 1910

Private in Company H, the "Union Grays," 2nd Regiment Mississippi Volunteer Infantry in Mexico. During the Civil War he served as Captain of Company I, "Minute Men of Attala," 13th Regiment Mississippi Infantry, C.S.A.

Courtesy Mary G. Adams

Charles Hanson Gibbs
Born: ca 1823
Died: October 10, 1855

Private in Company G, 1st Regiment Mississippi Volunteer Infantry in Mexican War.
He died of Yellow Fever in Hinds County, MS.

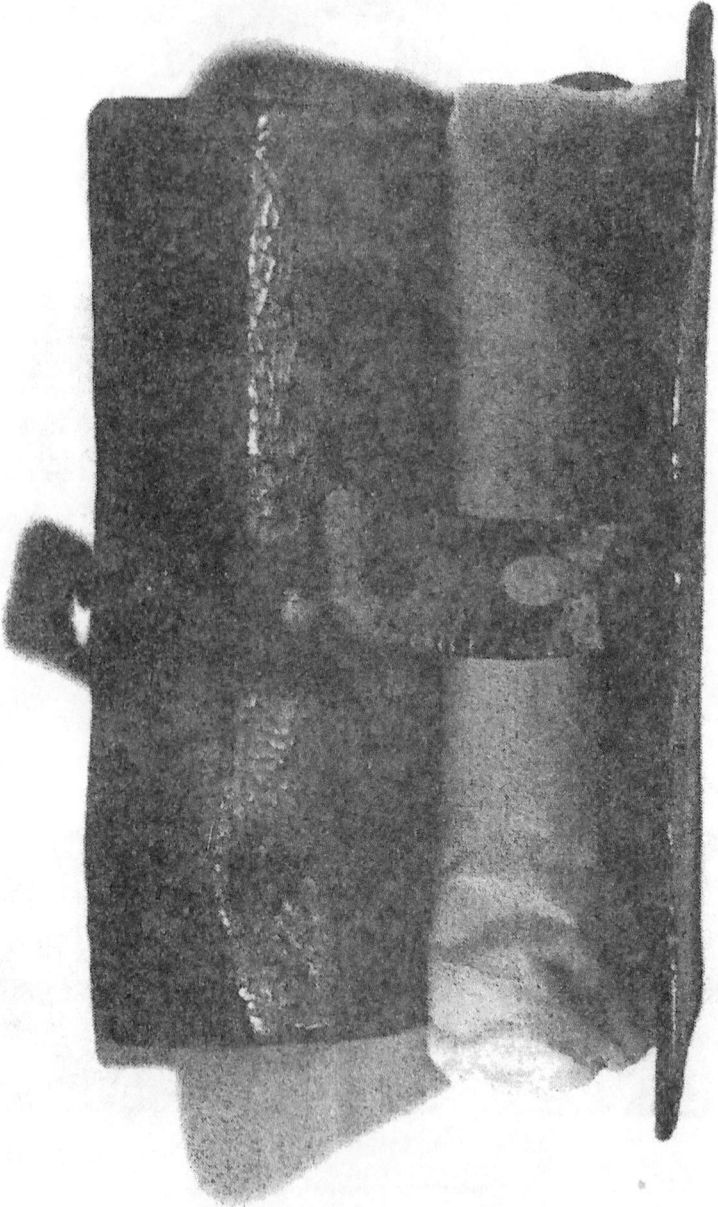

Cartridge pouch worn by Pvt. Charles Hanson Gibbs during the Mexican War. It was pierced by a Mexican musket ball during the Battle of Buena Vista, MX (February, 1847). The lead backing of the pouch deflected the ball and saved Gibbs' life.

Courtesy Tom Waggener

Thomas Arlander Graves
Born: November 15, 1830
Died: October 4, 1862

Served in the regular U.S. Army during the Mexican War. In the Civil War he formed a cavalry unit initially known as the "Copiah Horse Guards." He was killed in action in early October, 1862, while serving as a cavalryman under Gen. Sterling Price in the Battle of Corinth, MS.

Stephen Arne Decatur Greaves (and his two sons)
Born: January 1, 1819
Died: November 17, 1880

1st Lieutenant in Company G, 1st Regiment Mississippi Volunteers in Mexico. A "Unionist" in sentiment, living in Madison County, MS, he remained neutral and therefore a non-combatant during the Civil War.

Courtesy Mississippi Department of Archives and History

Richard Griffith
Born: January 11, 1814
Died: June 29, 1862

During the Mexican War he served as Adjutant of the 1st Regiment Mississippi Volunteers, with the rank of 1st lieutenant. He entered the Civil War as Colonel of the 12th Regiment Mississippi Infantry. Promoted to brigadier-general he was mortally wounded while leading his brigade in the Battle of Savage's Station, VA, and died the same day.

Thomas Carmichael Hindman (left) Robert Holt Hindman (right)
Born: January 28, 1828   **Born: June 20, 1822**
Died: September 28, 1868   **Died: May 8, 1849**

Thomas served as 2nd Lieutenant of Company E, the "Tippah Guards," 2nd Regiment Mississippi Volunteer Infantry. During the Civil War he rose in rank from colonel of the 2nd Regiment Arkansas Infantry, C.S.A., to brigadier- then major-general. He was assassinated in his home after the war for his opposition to the carpet-bag regime. His older brother, Robert Holt, served as a 2nd Sergeant in the same company in Mexico. He was slain by William C. Falkner when the two former comrades experienced a personal dispute after the Mexican War.

Andrew Melvorne Jackson
Born: November 7, 1823
Died: July 11, 1889

Captain of Company E, 2nd Regiment Mississippi Infantry during the Mexican War. In the Civil War he served as Adjutant of Gen. Henry Hopkins Sibley's Confederate Brigade in New Mexico, before being appointed Chief Justice of the New Mexico Territory by President Jefferson Davis.

208

Courtesy Bobby Mitchell and Martita Vaughn

Charles Marion LeSueur
Born: December 29, 1824
Died: September 17, 1889

He served as 1st Sergeant and 2nd Lieutenant of Company B, the "Marshall Relief Guards," 2nd Regiment Mississippi Volunteer Infantry in Mexico. In the Civil War he rose from Captain to Lieutenant-Colonel of the 4th Regiment Texas State Cavalry, C.S.A.

Courtesy *The Confederate Veteran*

Matthew F. Locke
Born: July 10, 1824
Died: June 4, 1911

A corporal in Company F, the "Lafayette Volunteers," 1st Regiment Mississippi Volunteer Infantry in the Mexican War. He assisted in bandaging the wound of Colonel Jefferson Davis, received on the Battlefield of Buena Vista, MX. Locke saw Confederate service as Colonel of the 10th Regiment Texas Cavalry.

Thomas Neely Love
Born: June 16, 1818
Died: January 23, 1855

Appointed Surgeon of the 2nd Regiment Mississippi Volunteers. He left behind a journal in which he recounted many poignant scenes of disease and death in this regiment. The author of this work has edited and published Love's journal under the title *A Southern Lacrimosa*.

Mark Perrin Lowrey
Born: December 30, 1828
Died: February 27, 1885

He enlisted as a private in Company E, 2nd Regiment Mississippi Volunteers in the Mexican War. During the Civil War he served as Colonel of the 4th Regiment Mississippi State Troops, then the 32nd Regiment Mississippi Infantry, C.S.A. He was promoted to brigadier-general and ably led his brigade for the balance of the war.

Courtesy Mississippi Department of Archives and History

Alexander Keith McClung
Born: ca 1811
Died: March 24, 1855

Lieutenant-Colonel of the 1st Regiment Mississippi Volunteers, he became a hero in the Battle of Monterey, MX. Seriously wounded in this battle he developed an addiction to pain-killing drugs. Combined with the addiction he already had for whiskey, and the fact that he was known as "The Black Knight of the South," for the large number of men he had killed in duels, he led a tormented, debt-ridden existence until he took his own life in the Eagle Hotel in Jackson, MS.

Courtesy *The Confederate Veteran*

Evander McNair
Born: April 15, 1820
Died: November 13, 1902

A 1st Sergeant in Company E, the "State Fencibles," 1st Regiment Mississippi Volunteer Infantry in Mexico, he commanded the 4th Regiment Arkansas Infantry, C.S.A., during the Civil War. He was elevated to brigadier-general. After recovering from wounds received in the Battle of Chickamauga, TN, his brigade was transferred to the Trans-Mississippi Department for the rest of the war.

Courtesy Richard Mellon

Thomas Armour Mellon
Born: November 13, 1826
Died: May 15, 1873

Served as 4th Sergeant in Company G, 1st Regiment Mississippi Volunteer Infantry in Mexico. He entered the Civil War as Captain of Company C, the "Downing Rifles," 3rd Regiment Mississippi Infantry, C.S.A. He was promoted steadily up the chain of command to Major, Lieutenant-Colonel and finally Colonel of the regiment.

Courtesy Billups-Garth Foundation, Columbus, MS.

Christopher Haynes Mott
Born: June 22, 1826
Died: May 5, 1862

Elected 1st Lieutenant of Company I, the "Marshall Guards," 1st Regiment Mississippi Volunteers in the Mexican War. Upon the secession of Mississippi in 1861, he was appointed brigadier-general in the Army of Mississippi. He resigned to become Colonel of the 19th Regiment Mississippi Infantry, C.S.A., and was mortally wounded during the Peninsula Campaign in the Battle of Williamsburg, VA.

Courtesy Albert Jacob Ott

Peter W. Ott
Born: ca 1825
Died: ca 1889

Shown here serving as a private in Briscoe's Louisiana Mounted Volunteers. He is holding an 1841 Whitney Rifle (aka "Mississippi Rifle"). He was one of many men living along the Gulf Coast of Mississippi who went directly to New Orleans to join the service during the Mexican War. Later, in the Civil War, he would join the Confederate States Marine Corps, and see service aboard the Confederate ironclad *C.S.S. Tennessee* in Mobile Bay.

Courtesy Connie McCaughan

Elijah A. Peyton (right) (and his brother Murray M. Peyton)
Born: October 26, 1827
Died: February 25, 1906

Elijah and a brother, John C. Peyton, both served in Company H, the "Vicksburg Volunteers," 1st Regiment Mississippi Volunteers. Elijah saw John die during that war. In 1861, Elijah and another brother Murray M., became officers in Company K, the "McWillie Blues" of the 3rd Regiment Mississippi Infantry, C.S.A. Elijah served as Captain of the company while his younger brother Murray was 1st Lieutenant. Elijah A. was promoted to Major and then Lieutenant-Colonel of the regiment by the end of the war.

Courtesy Mississippi Department of Archives and History

Carnot Posey
Born: August 5, 1818
Died: November 13, 1863

He served as 1st Lieutenant, Company B, the "Wilkinson Volunteers," 1st Regiment Mississippi Volunteer Infantry in Mexico. He was elected Colonel of the 16th Regiment Mississippi Infantry, C.S.A. in the Civil War and soon promoted to brigadier-general. Slightly wounded in battle at Bristoe Station, VA, on October 14, 1863, his wound became infected and he died in the home of a friend in Charlottesville, VA.

John Anthony Quitman
Born: September 1, 1798
Died: July 17, 1858

A former Governor of Mississippi, he would serve in that capacity twice before his death, he was appointed a brigadier-general of Volunteers by President James Knox Polk. Quitman led troops in successful campaigns under both Generals Zachary Taylor and Winfield Scott. At the close of the war with Mexico he served as the only civil and military governor of Mexico City.

William P. Rogers
Born: December 17, 1819

When to Mexico as 1st Lieutenant, then Captain of Company K, 1st Regiment Mississippi Volunteer Infantry, U.S.A.

Courtesy Mississippi Department of Archives and History

William P. Rogers
Died: October 4, 1862

He relocated to Texas after the Mexican War, but came back to Mississippi in 1862 as Colonel of the 2nd Regiment Texas Infantry, C.S.A. He was killed at the head of his troops during the bloody Battle of Second Corinth. The body of Colonel Rogers (foremost in the lower left corner of this image) lies propped against the bodies of his comrades who also died in the frontal assault against Battery Robinette.

222

Courtesy Amon Carter Museum, Fort Worth, TX

John McNitt Sharp
Born: November 22, 1795

Believed by the author to be pictured above as Captain of Company A, the "Yazoo Volunteers," 1st Regiment Mississippi Volunteer Infantry. He was wounded in the Battle of Buena Vista, MX.

Courtesy Polly Dawson

John McNitt Sharp
Died: May 20, 1862

Pictured above as the master of "Cedar Grove Plantation," in Yazoo County, Mississippi. He traveled to Tennessee in the wake of the Battle of Shiloh to accompany the body of his son-in-law, Col. Christopher Harrison, to "Cedar Grove" for burial. Soon after returning home with the corpse Col. Sharp died as a result of illness contracted from overexposure during his trip.

Courtesy Mississippi Department of Archives and History

William Henry Stubblefield
Born: May 23, 1820
Died: May 8, 1907

Served as a private in Company A, 1st Regiment Mississippi Volunteers in Mexico. During the Civil War he was elected 1st Lieutenant of Battery B, 1st Regiment Mississippi Light Artillery.

Courtesy Terry Family

Lampkin Straughn Terry
Born: January 23, 1828
Died: August 12, 1893

A private who rose to sergeant in Company H, the "Union Grays," 2nd Regiment Mississippi Volunteer Infantry in the Mexican War. In the Civil War he served as Captain of Company A, 15th Regiment Mississippi Infantry, C.S.A.

226

Courtesy Mississippi Department of Archives and History

Earl Van Dorn
Born: September 17, 1820
Died: May 7, 1863

A graduate of West Point Military Academy, Class of 1842, he saw service in the Indian Campaigns and the Mexican War. During the later he served as a Captain of United States Dragoons. At the outbreak of the Civil War he was serving as Major of the crack 2nd Regiment U.S. Cavalry. In Confederate service he was appointed a brigadier-general and was elevated to major-general. He was assassinated by a Tennessee medical doctor for violating "the sanctity of his home." Namely, the doctor's wife.

Courtesy *The Confederate Veteran*

William Bartee Wade
Born: October 9, 1823
Died: 1866

2nd Lieutenant of Company K, the "Tombigbee Volunteers," 1st Regiment Mississippi Volunteer Infantry during the Mexican War. He became Colonel of the 8th Regiment Confederate Cavalry in the Civil War. He was murdered by Union soldiers in Columbus, MS, after the end of the war.

Courtesy Emory A. Morgan

John H. Walters (with an unidentified niece)
Born: January 12 (or June 23), 1827
Died: March 7, 1912

Served as a private in Company D, the "Monroe Volunteers," 2nd Regiment Mississippi Volunteers in the Mexican War. On March 12, 1862, he enlisted as a Confederate soldier in Company H, 2nd Regiment Mississippi State Cavalry, and served once again as a true and faithful soldier.

Index

Cooper, William G. Jr. 22, 77, 111, 160
Coopewood, M. A. 111
Coopewood, Minerva 111
Coopewood, Thomas B. 111
Coopwood, Capt. 160
Coopwood, John 22, 101, 111
Coopwood, Thomas B. 22, 101, 111
Coor, Fleet M. 22, 83
Coorpender, Alice A. 112
Coorpender, Anna E. 112
Coorpender, Lewis C. 22, 77, 112, 160
Coorpender, William F. 22, 77, 112, 160
Copiah County, MS 10, 98, 158, 165,
      166, 175
"Copiah Horse Guards" 203
Corbell, John R. 22, 98
Corbin, Vincent 22, 92
Corbitt, John M. 112
Corinth, MS 5, 164, 174, 203, 217, 221
Cornelius, James A. 23, 100
Corwine, Amos Breckinridge 23, 69,
      112, 160
Corwine, Caroline A. 112
Cosby, James R. 23, 94
Cosby, Morris 23, 94
Cothran (Cothrum), William G. 23, 102,
      112
Cotten, Alathea A. 112
Cotton, Charles F. 23, 79, 160
Cotton, William A. 23, 71, 112
Couch, William 23, 72, 160
Coulter, Solomon M. 23, 74, 112, 160,
      181
Courtney, Eliza 112
Courtney, Thomas W. 23, 98, 112, 160,
      182
Covington County, MS 161, 171
Covington, James B. 23, 83
Covington, Joseph L. 23, 80
Cowan, J. C. 23, 72
Cowart, Andrew J. 23, 69
Cowger (Carger), Elizabeth 112
Cowger, Jacob H. (See Jacob H. Carger)
Cox, Allen 23, 86
Cox, Annie E. 112
Cox Cemetery 160
Cox, David 160
Cox, Edward 23, 78
Cox, Gilbert 112
Cox, John Q. A. 112
Cox, Reuben T. 23, 92
Cox, William R. 23, 99, 112

Cox's AL Volunteers 136
Coyle, Peter 23, 89
Cozart, B. H. 160
Cozart (Coyart?), George A. 23, 96
Craddock, William B. 23, 85
Craft, John 23, 72
Craft, John 23, 92
Craft, Mary 112
Craft, William H. 23, 79, 112
Craig, Robert A. 23, 96
Crane, Charles 160
Crane, George S. 112, 144
Crane, Sarah 112, 144
Cravens, John E. 23, 80
Crawford, A. G. H. 23, 95
Crawford, John H. 23, 79
Crawford, Thomas F. 23, 89, 112
Creamer, Henry 23, 73
Creed, Cornelius 112
Creed, Stephen 112
Creel, Burton 112
Creight, Martha 112
Creight, William 23, 80, 112, 160
Crenshaw, Cornelius M. 23, 86
Crenshaw, Nathaniel M. 23, 86, 112
Crimm, James F. 23, 97
Crittenden, Harvey S. 160
Cromer, Nancy S. 112
Cromer, Richard S. 23, 86, 112
Crook, Martin D. 23, 96
Crooks, Albert W. B. 115
Crosby, Rev. G. L. 160
Crosland, Alexander 23, 95, 112
Crosland, John A. 112
Crosland, Martha L. 112
Crosland, Nancy B. 112
Cross, Franklin A. 23, 90, 112
Cross, Isabell 112
Cross, Mary P. 112
Cross, William I. (J.?) 23, 90, 112
Crossin, John 23, 95
Crouch, Levi 23, 94
Crowder, James C. 23, 95
Crowley, James W. 160
Crowson, Elisha 10, 23, 98
"Crowson's (Capt.) Company" 10, 98,
      99
Crumby, Absalom L. 23, 100, 112
Crumby, Albert L. (See Walter K.
      Crumby) 112
Crumby, Mary Ann 112
Crumby, Walter K. 23, 100, 112

1st FL Infan. (C.S.A.) 187
1st GA Volunteers 131, 132, 140, 151
1st IL Volunteers 122, 126
1st KY Cav. 117
1st KY Volunteers 104
1st LA Mtd. Volunteers 126
1st LA Volunteers 117, 121, 132, 137, 149, 182
1st MA Volunteers 121
1st MI Light Art. 141
1st MI Volunteers 118
1st MS Volunteers (See 1st Regt. MS Volunteers)
1st MO Mtd. Infan. 114
1st MO Volunteers 106, 129
1st NY (U.S.?) Art. 130
1st NY Volunteers 138
1st NC Volunteers 108, 125, 126, 133, 149
1st OH Volunteers 124
1st PA Volunteers 110
1st Regt. MS Light Art. 224
1st Regt. MS Partisan Rangers (C.S.A.) 199
1st Regt. MS Volunteers vi, 3-8, 10, 12, 69-82, 181, 183, 189, 191, 194, 195, 197, 198, 201, 204, 205, 209, 212-215, 217, 218, 220, 222, 224, 227
1st SC Volunteers 138
1st TN Cav. 125, 131, 153
1st TN Volunteers 5, 106, 112, 116, 118, 127, 131, 133, 137, 182
1st TX Foot 10
1st TX Mtd. Volunteers 108, 135
1st TX Rangers 109
1st TX Rifles 149, 150, 152
1st TX Volunteers 103, 105, 116, 118, 126, 130, 132, 146, 147, 182
1st U.S. Artillery 104, 111
1st U.S. Dragoons 119
1st U.S. Infantry 106, 114
1st VA Volunteers 110, 136, 143
Fisher, George 28, 81
Fisher, George S. 28, 100
Fisher, John 28, 100
Fisher, Mary 117
Fisher, Robert 28, 69, 117, 162
Fisher's Indpt. Co. FL Volunteers 128
Fitzgerald, Edmund W. 117
Fitzgerald, Mary A. 117

Fitzsimmons, Melissa 117
Fitzsimmons, William T. 117
Flanagan, James 28, 81
Flanagan, William A. 28, 81
Flenoy's Volunteers 132
Fleming, William 28, 91
Fleming, William H. 28, 74, 162
Fletcher, Crawford 28, 74, 117, 163
Fletcher, Lorenzo Dow 28, 93, 117, 162, 181, 200
Fletcher, Sallie 117
Flippin, William 28, 95
FL Regt. 148
Flournoy, Jesse 28, 89
Flournoy, John G. 117
Flournoy, Sallie L. 117
Flowers, Ephraim A. 28, 91, 94, 117
Flowers, Graham H. 28, 91, 94, 117
Flowers, Julia 117
Flowers, Kate 117
Floyd, Elijah 28, 69, 117
Floyd, George W. 28, 79
Floyd, Henry 28, 69
Floyd, Mary Ann 117
Floyd, Samuel H. 163
"flying artillery" 2
Flyn, Zachariah K. 28, 87, 117
Flynn, Eliza C. 117
Flynn, Mary 117
Flynn, William P. 117
Fogg, William 29, 85
Foil, David 29, 95
Foil, John C. 29, 95, 117
Foil, Mary Ann 117
Folen, Edward 117
Folen, Jane 117
Folkes, Benjamin 117, 163
Folkes, James L. 117
Folkes, Lillie L. 117
Folly, Acy 29, 90
Fondran (Fondren), S. R. 29, 77, 163
Fongel, Charles 106, 117, 118, 149
Foot, Marcus L. 117
Forbes, Daniel 29, 69
Forbes, Joel 29, 73
Ford, Canaday 29, 91
Ford, Charles 117
Ford, Elizabeth C. 117
Ford, Emily 117
Ford, Henry F. 29, 72, 117
Ford, James F. 117
Ford, John J. 29, 83

Gore, Ashford 31, 102, 119
Gore, Margaret 119
Gore, Rufus 31, 87, 119
Gorman, John 31, 85
Goss, George H. 31, 98, 101
Gossett, Barnett 31, 90
Gotsel (Godsil ?), Patrick 31, 94
Goubeneaux, Charles 31, 95, 164
Gouldings's Co. GA Volunteers 110
Gourley, Hugh 31, 74
Gourley, Milton F. 31, 74
Gower Cemetery 164
Graham, Charles D. 119
Graham, James W. 31, 96
Graham, John 31, 85
Graham, Rebecca M. 119
Graham's Co. LA Volunteers 113
Grant, Alhaney 31, 95
Grant, James 31, 102
Grave Registrations 155-179
Graves, James H. 31, 77, 164
Graves, John C. 31, 96
Graves, Thomas Arlander 31, 203
Gray, Carrie A. 119
Gray Cemetery 157
Gray (Grey), Elizabeth 119, 120
Gray, George H. 31, 72, 119
Gray, James 31, 90
Gray, James W. 31, 89
Gray, Joe 164
Gray, John 31, 87
Gray, Peter 119
Gray, Robert 31, 83
Gray (Grey), William 119, 120
Gray, William 164
Gray, William P. 31, 73
Gray's Creek Baptist Church Cemetery 172
Greaves, Jennie B. 119
Greaves, Stephen Arne Decatur 31, 77, 119, 164, 204
Green, Belinda C. 120
Green, David L. 120
Green, F.G. 31, 74
Green, Girault 31, 74
Green, James E. 120
Green, John B. 120
Green, Luther D. 31, 96, 120, 148
Green, Martha A. 120
Green, Nancy E. 120
Green, Richard 31, 69, 120
Green, William B. 31, 83, 93, 120

Greenfield Cemetery 173
Greenlee, Francis M. 7, 31, 83
Green's Co. AL Volunteers 153
Greenville, MS 163
Greenwood Cemetery 156, 159, 161-165, 168, 172, 173, 175-177, 179
Greenwood Odd Fellows Cemetery 156
Greer, Anna E. 120
Greer, Elkanah Brackin 31, 79, 120
Gregg, Robert 31, 78, 120, 164
Gregory, Alston 31, 85
Gregory, Edward H. 31, 81
Grenada City Cemetery 160
Grenada County, MS 160, 177
Grey, J. W. 31, 72
Grey, William (See William Gray)
Griffin, Daniel B. 164
Griffin, James T. 32, 74, 100
Griffin, John W. 120
Griffin, Mack 32, 96
Griffin, Robert Henderson 32, 69, 120
Griffin, Thomas M. 120
Griffin, Thomas R. 32, 69, 120
Griffin, William N. 32, 89
Griffis, Pleasant A. 32, 95
Griffith, Peter O. D. 32, 79
Griffith, Richard 32, 69, 72, 164, 205
Grimes, Caleb 32, 69
Grimes, Richard 120
Grisham, Elizabeth C. 120
Grisham, Vincent S. 32, 77, 120
Grisham, William H. 32, 79, 164
Grissom, Charles 120
Grivot's LA Art. 138
Grizzle, Wilson P. 32, 87, 164
Grogan, George J. 32, 94
Grove, William 32, 102
Groves, Benjamin L. 32, 78
Groves, William A. 32, 92
Grugett, Benjamin F. 32, 81
Guess, Nancy 120
Guess, Walker 32, 102, 120
Guest, Isaac N. 32, 90, 120
Guest, Sallie 120
Guffee, Benjamin W. 32, 94
Guinn, Chesley 32, 90, 120
Guinn, Eliza Jane 120
Guion, Walter Burling 164
Gulf Cemetery 179
Gulf Coast of MS 216
Gulf of Mexico 6

Hicks, Moses 35, 97
Higdon, Alexander 35, 86
Higdon, James 35, 74, 122
Higdon, Mary Ann 122
Higdon, Russell Benjamin 35, 92
Higgason, John D. 35, 81, 122
Higginbotham, Thomas T. 35, 70
Higginbottom, Ransom C. 35, 76
Hight, Mary E. 123
Hight, Thomas B. 35, 93, 123, 181
Hill, Albert P. 35, 70, 165
Hill Crest Cemetery 171
Hill, Elijah Bell 123, 165
Hill Family Cemetery 165
Hill, George W. 123
Hill, James 35, 71
Hill, John H. 35, 96
Hill, John W. 35, 85
Hill, John W. 35, 86
Hill, Josiah 165
Hill, Larkin 123
Hill, M. C. (Z.?) 165
Hill, Margaret A. 123
Hill, Margaret L. 123
Hill, Nancy M. 123
Hill, Richard 35, 94, 123
Hill, Richard H. 35, 86, 123
Hill, Sanford H. 35, 78
Hilliard, John C. 35, 85
Hilliard, Thomas 35,96, 123
Hilton, Carl 35, 94
Hilyard, Thomas 123
Hindman, Robert Holt 35, 89, 165, 206
Hindman, Samuel 35, 72
Hindman, Thomas Carmichael 35, 89, 166, 206
Hinds Chapel 156
Hinds County, MS 3, 10, 74, 77, 91, 155-171, 173-179, 201
Hinds, Harrison H. 166
Hindsley, John J. 35, 81, 123
Hines, John 35, 89
Hinkley, Henry 35, 92
Hinsley, Mary 123
Hinson, James P. 123
Hinson, Mary A. 123
Hinton, William 35, 88
Hipple, Henry 35, 74
Hise, George W. 35, 78
Hoag's Co. IL Volunteers 124
Hobbs, Calvin 35, 74, 98, 123, 166, 182
Hobbs, J. P. 35, 76

Hobbs, John S. 35, 102
Hobbs, Mary E. 123
Hobbs, Thetus R. 123
Hobbs, William 35, 80, 123
Hoburg, Edward G. 35, 83
Hodge, Benjamin Louis 35, 73
Hodge, Francis 35, 93
Hodge, James 35, 100
Hodge, James L. 35, 71
Hodge, Margaret P. 123
Hodge, William I. (J.?) 35, 71, 123, 166
Hodnett, Thomas 35, 94
Hoffman, Warren 166
Hogan, Timothy 35, 95
Hoggany, Benjamin 35, 76, 166
Hoggatt, Jacob 123
Hoggatt, John 35, 97
Hoggatt, Mary E. 123
Holcomb, J. 36, 76
Holden, William E. 36, 85
Holdway, Howard DeCalb 36, 80, 123
Holland, Andrew J. 123
Holland, Celia A. 123
Holland, Charles 36, 86, 123, 166
Holland, Clarinda 123
Holland, Elizabeth 123
Holland, George H. 166
Holland, John M. M. 36, 80
Holland, Kemp S. 36, 69, 70
Holland, William H. 36, 86, 123
Holland, William Thomas 36, 96, 123
Holliday, John 166
Holliday, Shack 166
Hollingshead, Samuel B. 36, 84
Hollingsworth, David M. 36, 70, 123, 166
Hollingsworth, E. 36, 73, 166
Hollingsworth, Rosina 123
Holloway, Lewis M. 36, 100
Hollowell, Edwin (Edward?) O. 36, 85, 123
Hollowell, Maggie Eliza 123
Holly Springs, MS 160
Hollywood Cemetery 163
Holmead, John 36, 94, 123
Holmes County, MS 155, 174, 178
Holmes County Odd Fellows Cemetery 174
Holmes, Henry C. 123
Holmes, Nancy E. 123
Holt, Cassandra 123
Holt, John Saunders 36, 71, 123, 166

www.ingramcontent.com/pod-product-compliance
Lightning Source LLC
Chambersburg PA
CBHW021855020426
42334CB00013B/336